GIMP 2.8 Reference Manual 2/2

A catalogue record for this book is available from the Hong Kong Public Libraries.

This book contains seconf half of the GIMP Documentation Team manual. It has been splitted due to physical book size restrctions. Chapter 16 to 18 are included in this book. Chapter 1-15 are included in the first volume.

Published by Samurai Media Limited.

Email: info@samuraimedia.org

ISBN 978-988-14436-0-1

Contents

List of Examples

Chapter 16

Menus

16.1 Introduction to Menus

There are many places in GIMP where you can find menus. The aim of this chapter is to explain all the commands that are accessible from the image menu bar and the image menu you can get by right clicking in the canvas. All the context menus and the menu entries for the other dialogs are described elsewhere in the chapters that describe the dialogs themselves.

16.1.1 The Image Menu Bar

File   Edit   Select   View   Image   Layer   Colors   Tools   Filters   Windows   Help

This menu bar may contain other entries if you have added script-fus, python-fus or videos to your GIMP.

16.1.2 Context Menus

If you right-click on certain parts of the GIMP interface, a "context menu" opens, which leads to a variety of functions. Some places where you can access context menus are:

- Clicking on an image window displays the Image menu. This is useful when you are working in full-screen mode, without a menubar.

- Clicking on a layer in the Layers Dialog or on a channel in the Channels Dialog displays functions for the selected layer or channel.

- Right-clicking on the image menubar has the same effect as left-clicking.

- Right-clicking on the title bar displays functions which do not belong to GIMP, but to the window manager program on your computer.

16.1.3 Tear-off menus

There is an interesting property associated with some of the menus in GIMP. These are any of the menus from the Image context menu you get by right-clicking on the canvas and any of its submenus. (You can tell that a menu item leads to a submenu because there is an ▶ icon next to it.) When you bring up any of these menus, there is a dotted line at the top of it (tear-off line). By clicking on this dotted line, you detach the menu under it and it becomes a separate window.

Figure 16.1 The "windows" submenu and its tear-off submenu

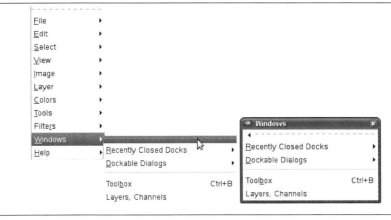

Tear-off menus are actually independent. They are always visible, their functions always apply to the current image, and they persist when all of the images are closed. You can close a tear-off submenu by clicking on the dotted line again or closing the window from the window manager on your computer (often by clicking on an X icon in the upper right corner of the window).

These tear-off submenus are also created in single-window mode, but are of less interest since they are masked by the window as soon as you click on it.

16.1.4 Tab menus

The following type of menus is not related to the image menu bar, but for the sake of completeness:

Every dockable dialog contains a Tab Menu button, as highlighted below. Pressing this Tab Menu button opens a special menu of tab-related operations, with an entry at the top that opens into the dialog's context menu.

Figure 16.2 A dockable dialog.

(a) *A dialog window with the Tab menu button highlighted.*   (b) *The Tab menu.*

See Section 3.2.3.2 to learn more about Tab menus.

16.2 The "File" Menu

16.2.1 Overview

Figure 16.3 The File menu

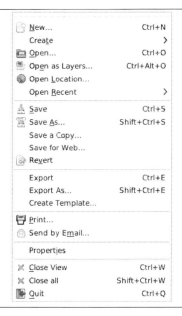

> ### Note
>
>
> Besides the commands described here, you may also find other entries in the menu.
> They are not part of GIMP itself, but have been added by extensions (plug-ins). You
> can find information about the functionality of a Plugin by referring to its documen-
> tation.

16.2.2 New

Using the New Image dialog, you can create a new empty image and set its properties. The image is
shown in a new image window. You may have more than one image on your screen at the same time.

16.2.2.1 Activate the command

- You can access the command in the Image menu through: File → New,

- or by using the keyboard shortcut Ctrl-N.

16.2.2.2 Basic Options

Figure 16.4 The "New Image" dialog

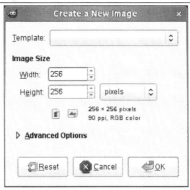

Template

Figure 16.5 The "Template" dialog

Rather than entering all the values by hand, you can select some predefined values for your image from a menu of templates, which represent image types that are somewhat commonly useful. The templates set values for the size, resolution, comments, etc. If there is a particular image shape that you use often and it does not appear on the list, you can create a new template, using the Templates dialog.

Image Size Here you set the Width and Height of the new image. The default units are pixels, but you can choose a different unit if you prefer, using the adjoining menu. If you do, note that the resulting pixel size is determined by the X and Y resolution (which you can change in the Advanced Options), and by setting "Dot for Dot" in the View menu.

If no image is open, the "New" image is opened in the empty image window, with the default size you have determined. If you open the "New"image when another is open (or has been), then it is opened in another window, with the same size as the first image.

> **Note**
>
> Keep in mind that every pixel of an image is stored in memory. If you create large files with a high pixel density, GIMP will need a lot of time and memory for every function you apply to the image.

Portrait/Landscape buttons There are two buttons which toggle between Portrait and Landscape mode. What they actually do is to exchange the values for Width and Height. (If the Width and Height are the same, these buttons are not activated.) If the X and Y resolutions are not the same (which you can set in Advanced Options), then these values are also exchanged. On the right of the dialog, image size, screen resolution and color space are displayed.

16.2.2.3 Advanced Options

Figure 16.6 New Image dialog (Advanced Options)

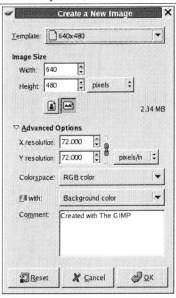

The Advanced Options are mostly of interest to more advanced GIMP users. You can display these options by clicking on the small triangle on the lower edge of the dialog window.

X and Y resolution The values in the X resolution and Y resolution fields relate mainly to printing: they do not affect the size of the image in pixels, but they may determine its physical size when it is printed. The X and Y resolution values can determine how pixels are translated into other measurement units, such as millimeters or inches.

> **Tip**
>
> If you want to display the image on the screen at the correct dimensions, select View → Dot for Dot Set the zoom factor to 100% to see the image at its true screen size. The calibration of the screen size is normally done when GIMP is installed, but if the image does not display at the correct size, you may have to adjust the screen parameters in the GIMP. You can do this in the Preferences dialog.

Colorspace You can create the new image in different color modes, as either an RGB image or a grayscale image.

> **RGB color** The image is created in the Red, Green, Blue color system, which is the one used by your monitor or your television screen.
>
> **Grayscale** The image is created in black and white, with various shades of gray. Aside from your artistic interests, this type of image may be necessary for some plug-ins. Nevertheless, the GIMP allows you to change an RGB image into grayscale, if you would like.

> You cannot create an indexed image directly with this menu, but of course you can always convert the image to indexed mode after it has been created. To do that, use the Image → Mode → Indexed command.

Fill Here, you specify the background color that is used for your new image. It is certainly possible to change the background of an image later, too. You can find more information about doing that in the Layer dialog.

> There are several choices:
>
> - Fill the image with the current Foreground color, shown in the Toolbox.
>   Note that you can change the foreground color while the "New Image" dialog window is open.
> - Fill the image with the current Background color, shown in the Toolbox. (You can change the background color too, while the dialog window is open.)
> - Fill the image with White.
> - Fill the image with Transparency. If you choose this option, the image is created with an alpha channel and the background is transparent. The transparent parts of the image are then displayed with a checkered pattern, to indicate the transparency.

> You can write a descriptive comment here. The text is attached to the image as a parasite, and is saved with the image by some file formats (PNG, JPEG, GIF).

> **Note**
>
> You can view and edit this comment in the Image Properties dialog.

16.2.3 Create

Figure 16.7 The "Create" submenu

Comment

This menu item replaces the "Acquire" menu which existed in GIMP previous versions in the Toolbox Menu and contains a lot of logos, buttons, patterns...

These commands vary somewhat, depending upon your system, since the GIMP makes calls to system functions.

16.2.3.1   Activate the Submenu

- You can access this submenu from the Image menu bar through File → Create

16.2.3.2   From Clipboard

When you copy a selection, it goes into the clipboard. Then you can create a new image with it.

This command has the same action as the Paste as new command.

The **Print Screen** keyboard key captures the screen and puts it in the clipboard. This command has the same action as "taking a screenshot of the entire screen" in the Screenshot dialog window. The Alt-Print Screen key combination grabs the active window in the screen with its decorations and puts it in the clipboard.

16.2.3.3   From Web page

This command opens a dialog where you can enter the URL of a Web page and get the image in GIMP.

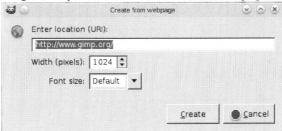

The command defaults to gimp.org. Please have a try to it.

16.2.3.4   Screenshot

Figure 16.8 The "Screenshot" window

The Screenshot command opens a dialog with two parts:

Area

Take a screenshot of a single window The mouse pointer becomes a cross. Click in the image window you want to capture. A new image is created. If the Include window decoration option is unchecked, the title bar and the blue frame around the image will be removed.

Take a screenshot of the entire screen This is useful if you want to capture a pop menu. A delay is then necessary, so that you have time to pull the pop menu down.

If the Include mouse pointer option is checked, then the mouse pointer and its coming with icon are also captured. The mouse pointer is captured in a separate layer. So you can move it to another place in the image.

Select a region to grab The mouse pointer becomes a cross. Click and drag to create a rectangular selection in the image window. This selection will be opened as a new image. Its size is adapted to the selection size.

Delay When taking a screenshot of the entire screen, the screen is captured after this delay. In the other cases, the mouse pointer turns to a cross after this delay.

16.2.3.5 Image capture devices

This item is present only if you have installed image capture devices.

Figure 16.9 Scanner and Camera

The kinds of devices used to take pictures are too varied to be described here. Fortunately, their use is fairly intuitive. In the example shown, you can start a scanner or take an image with a webcam.

16.2.3.6 Buttons, Logos, Patterns, Web Page Themes

An impressive list of script-fus. Have a look at it!

16.2.3.7 New brush from text...

TODO (this command fails on my system)

16.2.4 Open

The Open command activates a dialog that lets you load an existing image from your hard-drive or an external medium. For alternative, and sometimes more convenient, ways of opening files, see the following commands (Section 16.2.5 etc.).

16.2.4.1 Activate Dialog

- You can access the Open dialog from an image window through: File → Open.

- You can also open the Dialog by using the keyboard shortcut Ctrl-O.

16.2.4.2 File browsing

Figure 16.10 Open Dialog

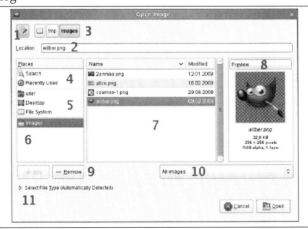

This browser looks like other browsers and it is mostly self-explanatory. It has some particuliar features nevertheless.

1. The button Type a file name toggles between add and remove the Location text box.

   The Ctrl-L key combination has the same action as this button.

2. In the Location text box you can type a path to an image file. If you don't type any path, the name of the selected file will be displayed. You can also type the first letters of the name: it will be auto-completed and a list of file names beginning with these letters will be displayed.

   When you search for a file or directory using the Search feature (see below, item 4), the label changes to Search and you can enter the name in this text box.

3. The path to the current folder is displayed. You can navigate along this path by clicking on an element.

4. With Search you can look for a file (or directory), even if you don't know the exact name of that file. Click on Search, type a file name or just a part of a file name in the text box above, and press **Enter**. Then the central frame (7) will list all files and directories of your home directory with names containing the text you typed in. Unfortunately you can't restrict the results to files of a specified type (10).

   Recently used is self-explanatory.

5. Here, you can access to your main folders and to your store devices.

6. Here, you can add bookmarks to folders, by using the Add or the Add to Bookmarks option you get by right-clicking a folder in the central panel, and also remove them.

7. The contents of the selected folder is displayed here. Change your current folder by double left clicking on a folder in this panel. Select a file with a single left click. You can then open the file you have selected by clicking on the Open button. A double left click opens the file directly. Please note that you can open image files only.

   Right-clicking a folder name opens a context menu:

The folder context menu

8. The selected image is displayed in the Preview window. If it is an image created by GIMP, file size, resolution and image composition are displayed below the preview window.

Tip

 If your image has been modified by another program, click on the Preview window to update it.

---

9. By clicking the Add button, you add the selected folder to bookmarks.

   By clicking the Remove, you remove the selected bookmark from the list.

10. You will generally prefer to display the names of All images. You can also select All files. You can also limit yourself to a particular type of image (GIF, JPG, PNG ...).

11. Select File Type: In most cases you don't need to pay any attention to this, because GIMP can determine the file type automatically. In a few rare situations, neither the file extension nor internal information in the file are enough to tell GIMP the file type. If this happens, you can set it by selecting it from the list.

16.2.5 Open as Layers

The Open Image as layers dialog is identical to the Open Image dialog. The layers of the selected file are added to the current image as the top layers in the stack.

16.2.5.1 Activate Command

- You can access this command from the image menubar through File → Open as layers,

- or by using the keyboard shortcut Ctrl-Alt-O.

16.2.6 Open Location

The Open Location dialog lets you load an image from a network location, specified by a URI, in any of the formats that GIMP supports.

16.2.6.1 Activate Command

- You can access this command from the Toolbox menubar or the image menubar through File → Open Location....

16.2.6.2 Description of the dialog window

Figure 16.11 The "Open Location" dialog window

The most typical schemes to open images with are:

file:// to open an image from a local drive

You can omit the "file://" prefix and open images simply by putting an absolute or relative path and filename in here.

The default base directory for relative paths depends on your operating system. It is typically `/home/<username>/` on Linux, `C:\\Documents and        Settings\\<username> \\My Documents\\My Images\\` on Windows and `/Users/<username>/` on Mac OS X.

ftp:// to open an image from a ftp server

http:// to load an image from a website

Tip

When you are visiting an Internet site, you can right-click on an image and choose "Copy link address" in the drop-down menu. Then paste it in the "Open Location" dialog to open it in GIMP.

Even if this command makes it very easy to grab images from web sites: *Please respect the copyright! Images, even if published on the Internet are not always free to be used for you.*

16.2.7 Open Recent

Selecting Open Recent displays a submenu with the names of the files that you have opened recently in GIMP. Simply click on a name to reopen it. See the Document History dialog at the bottom of the Open Recent submenu, if you cannot find your image.

16.2.7.1 Activate Command

- You can access this command from the image menubar through File → Open Recent,

16.2.8 Save

This command opens Section 15.5.5.

16.2.9 Save as

The Save as command displays the "Save Image" dialog. Since GIMP-2.8, the file is automatically saved in the XCF format and you can't *save* in another file format (for this, you have to *export* the file). The Save as dialog allows you to save with another name and/or to another folder.

16.2.9.1 Activating the Command

- You can access this command from the image menubar through File → Save as,

- or by using the keyboard shortcut Shift-Ctrl-S.

16.2.9.2   The "Save Image" dialog

Figure 16.12 The "Save Image" dialog

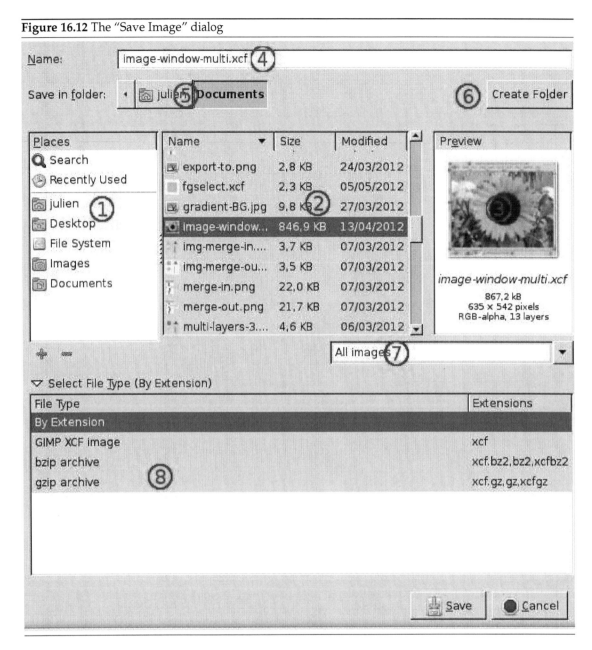

1. The left panel is divided into two parts. The upper part lists your main directories and your storage devices; you cannot modify this list. The lower part lists your bookmarks; you can add or remove *bookmarks*. To add a bookmark, select a directory or a file in the middle panel and click on the Add button at the bottom of the left panel. You can also use the Add to bookmarks command in the context menu, which you get by clicking the right mouse button. You can delete a bookmark by selecting it and clicking on the Remove button.

2. The middle panel displays a list of the files in the current directory. Change your current directory by double left-clicking on a directory in this panel. Select a file with a single left click. You can then save to the file you have selected by clicking on the Save button. Note that a double left click saves the file directly.

   You can right click on the middle panel to access the *Show Hidden Files* command.

3. The selected image is displayed in the Preview window. File size, resolution and image composition are displayed below the preview window.

If your image has been modified by another program, click on the preview to update it.

4. Enter the filename of the new image file here.

> **Note**
>
> If the image has already been saved, GIMP suggests the same filename to you. If you click on *Save*, the file is overwritten.

5. Above the middle panel, the path of the current directory is displayed. You can navigate along this path by clicking on one of the buttons.

6. If you want to save the image into a folder that doesn't yet exist, you can create it by clicking on Create Folder and following the instructions.

7. This button shows All Images by default. This means that all images will be displayed in the middle panel, whatever their file type. By developing this list, you can choose to show only one type of file.

8. At Select File Type, you can select a compressed format for your XCF file.

16.2.10   Save a Copy

The Save a Copy command does the same thing as the Save command, but with one important difference. It always asks for a file name and saves the image into the XCF file format, but it does not change the name of the active image or mark it as "clean". As a result, if you try to delete the image, or exit from GIMP, you are informed that the image is "dirty" and given an opportunity to save it.

This command is useful when you want to save a copy of your image in its current state, but continue to work with the original file without interruption.

16.2.10.1   Activate Command

- You can access this command from the image menubar through File → Save a Copy. There is no default keyboard shortcut.

16.2.11   Revert

The Revert command reloads the image from disk, so that it looks just like it did the last time it was saved — unless, that is, you or some application other than GIMP have modified the image file, in which case, the new contents are loaded.

> **Warning**
>
> When GIMP reverts a file, it actually closes the existing image and creates a new image. Because of this, reverting an image is not undoable, and causes the undo history of the image to be lost. GIMP tries to protect you from losing your work in this way by asking you to confirm that you really want to revert the image.

16.2.11.1   Activate Command

- You can access this command from the image menubar through File → Revert. There is no default keyboard shortcut.

16.2.12 Export

This command is called "Export" for a native XCF file. Then, it does the same thing as **Export As**. At early GIMP 2.8 releases, this menu label was "Export to". Since the version 2.8.10, "Export to" and "Export" have been renamed to "Export" and "Export As" after the manner of "Save" and "Save As".

The name becomes "Overwriting name.extension" for an imported image. So, you can export the imported image directly in its original file format, without going through the export dialog.

16.2.13 Export As...

Export As... allows you to save your image in a format other than XCF.

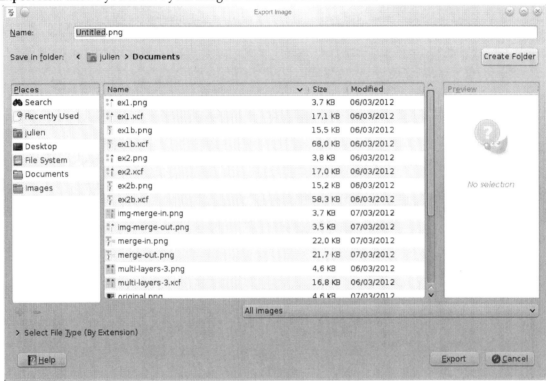

Note

 Please refer to Section 6.1 for information about exporting in different file formats.

16.2.13.1 Activating the Command

- You can access this command from the image menubar through File → Export As...,

- or by using the keyboard shortcut Shift-Ctrl-E.

16.2.14 Create Template

The Create Template command creates a template with the same dimensions and color space as the current image. A dialog pops up, which asks you to name the new template. Then the template is saved and becomes available in the New Image dialog. If you give a name that already exists, GIMP generates a unique name by appending a number to it. You can use the Templates dialog to modify or delete templates.

16.2.14.1   Activating the Command

- You can access this command from the image menu through File → Create Template. There is no default keyboard shortcut.

16.2.15   Print

Since the 2.4.0 release, GIMP has its own printing module. You can set page and image up. A preview button allows you to verify the result before printing.

Figure 16.13 The "Print" dialog

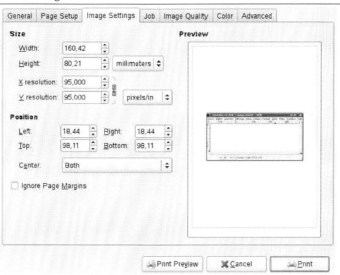

Note

See Printing your photos.

16.2.15.1   Activate Command

You can access this command from the image menubar through File → Print, or by using Ctrl-P.

16.2.16   Close

The Close command closes the active image.It is disabled if no image is open.

Closing an image is not undoable: once it is closed, everything is gone, including the undo history. If the image is not "clean" — that is, if you have changed it since the last time you saved it — you are asked to confirm that you really want to close it. Note that an image is marked as clean when it is saved to a file, even if the file format chosen does not preserve all the information in the image, so it is a good idea to think for a moment about what you are doing before closing an image. If there is the slightest possibility that you will regret it, save the file (automatically in the XCF file format since GIMP-2.8).

16.2.16.1   Activating the Command

- You can access this command from the image menu through File → Close,

- or by using the keyboard shortcut Ctrl-W.

- For most systems on which the GIMP runs, you can also execute it by clicking on a "Close" button somewhere on the image window titlebar. The location and appearance of this button are determined by the windowing system and the window manager. If no image is open, clicking on this button closes GIMP.

16.2.17 Close all

This command closes all images you have opened.

16.2.17.1 Activate the Command

- You can access this command from the image menubar through File → Close All,

- or by using the keyboard shortcut Shift-Ctrl-W.

16.2.18 Quit

The Quit command causes GIMP to close all images and exit. If there are any open images which contain unsaved changes (that is, they are not marked as "clean"), GIMP notifies you and displays a list of the unsaved images. You can then choose which images you would like to save, or you can cancel the command. Note that if you have a large number of images open, or are using a large part of the RAM on your system, it may take a little while for everything to shut down.

16.2.18.1 Activate Command

- You can access this command from the image menubar through File → Quit,

- or by using the keyboard shortcut Ctrl-Q.

- For most systems on which the GIMP runs, you can also execute it by clicking on a "Close" button somewhere on the main image window's titlebar. The location and appearance of this button are determined by the windowing system and the window manager. Clicking on this button closes GIMP when no image is open.

16.3   The "Edit" Menu

16.3.1   "Edit" Menu Entries

Figure 16.14 Contents of the Edit Menu

In this section, you will find help for commands in the Edit menu item.

Note

Besides the commands described here, you may also find other entries in the menu. They are not part of GIMP itself, but have been added by extensions (plug-ins). You can find information about the functionality of a Plugin by referring to its documentation.

16.3.2   Undo

If you have made drawing or editing changes to the image which you don't want to keep, the Undo command allows you to undo the last change and return the image to its previous state. Almost anything you do to an image can be undone in this way (with the exception of scripts, which deactivate this function). Further Undo operations may be performed, depending upon the number of Undo levels configured in the Environment page of the Preferences Dialog. See the section on Undoing for more information about GIMP's very sophisticated "Undo" functions.

The operation that has been "undone" is not lost immediately: you can get it back by using the Redo command right away. But if you perform another operation, the ability to "Redo" will be irretrievably lost.

16.3.2.1   Activate the Command

- You can access this command from the image menubar through Edit → Undo,

- by using the keyboard shortcut Ctrl-Z,

- or by simply clicking on the status you want in the Undo History dialog.

16.3.3   Redo

The Redo command reverses the effects of the Undo command. Each "Undo" action can be reversed by a single "Redo" action. You can alternate "Undo" and "Redo" as many times as you like. Note that you can only "Redo" an operation if the last action you did was an "Undo". If you perform any operation on the image after Undoing something, then the former Redo steps are lost, and there is no way to recover them. See the Undoing section for more information.

To see the operations which you have done and undone, use the Undo History dialog.

16.3.3.1   Activating the Command

- You can access this command from the image menubar through Edit → Redo,

- by using the keyboard shortcut Ctrl-Y,

- or by simply clicking on the status you want in the Undo History dialog.

16.3.4   Fade

This command is usually grayed out. It becomes active if you use the Fill function or the Blend tool, or if you apply some filters.

It allows you to modify the paint mode and opacity of the *last* drawable operation (Fill, Blend, Filter) by creating a blend between the current state of the layer and the previous state. It performs the following operations: copy the active drawable, undo the last action, paste the copy as a new layer, set its "Opacity", and merge both new layer and previously active drawable.

16.3.4.1   Activate the command

You can get to this command from the image Menu bar through: Edit → Fade...

16.3.4.2   Options

This command brings up a dialog window:

Figure 16.15 The "Fade" dialog

Mode This drop-down list allows you to choose a Layer merge mode.

Opacity This slider value is initially set to the opacity of the color you used with the Fill or Blend tool, which corresponds to the current state. Lowering the opacity to 0 changes the drawable to its previous state. Intermediate values produce a mixture of the two according to the mode you have chosen. The effect of this setting is visible in real time in the image, but you have to click on the Fade button to validate it.

16.3.5   Undo History

The Undo History command activates the Undo History dialog, which shows you thumbnails representing the operations you have done so far on the current image. This overview makes it easier for you to undo steps or to redo them.

Use the arrows for Undo and Redo, or simply click on the thumbnail, to bring the image back to a previous state. This is especially useful when you are working on a difficult task, where you often need to undo several steps at once. It is much easier to click on step 10 than to type Ctrl-Z ten times.

The "Clear undo History" command may be useful if you are working on a complex image and you want to free some memory.

16.3.5.1 Activating the Command

- You can access this command from the image menubar through Edit → Undo History. There is no default keyboard shortcut.

16.3.6 Cut

The Cut command deletes the contents of the image's selections, and saves them in a clipboard so that they can later be pasted using the "Paste", "Paste Into", or "Paste As New" commands. If there is no selection, the entire current layer is cut. The areas whose contents are cut are left transparent, if the layer has an alpha channel, or filled with the layer's background color, otherwise.

> Note
>
> The Cut command only works on the current active layer. Any layers above or below the active layer are ignored.

16.3.6.1 Activate the Command

- You can access this command from the image menubar through Edit → Cut,

- or by using the keyboard shortcut Ctrl-X.

16.3.7 Copy

The Copy command makes a copy of the current selection and stores it in the Clipboard. The information can be recalled using the Paste, Paste Into, or Paste As New commands. If there is no selection, the entire current layer is copied. "Copy" only works on the current active layer. Any layers above or below it are ignored.

16.3.7.1 Activate the Command

- You can access this command from the image menubar through Edit → Copy,

- or by using the keyboard shortcut Ctrl-C.

16.3.8 Copy Visible

The Copy Visible command is similar to the Copy command. However, it does not just copy the contents of the current layer; it copies the contents of the visible layers (or the selection of the visible layers), that is, the ones that are marked with an "eye".

> Note
>
> Please note that the information about the layers is lost when the image data is put in the clipboard. When you later paste the clipboard contents, there is only one layer, which is the fusion of all the marked layers.

16.3.8.1 Activating the Command

- You can access this command from the image menubar through Edit → Copy Visible.

16.3.9 Paste

The Paste command puts whatever is in the Clipboard from the last "Copy" or "Cut" command into the current image. The pasted section becomes a "floating selection" and is shown as a separate layer in the Layers Dialog.

If there is an existing selection on the canvas, it is used to align the pasted data. If there is already a selection, the data is pasted using the selection as a center point. If you want the selection to be used as a clipping region for the pasted data, you should use the "Paste Into" command.

Note

  You can have only *one* floating selection at any one time. You cannot work on any other layer while there is a floating selection; you have to either anchor it or remove it.

16.3.9.1 Activate the Command

- You can access this command from the image menubar through Edit → Paste.

- or by using the keyboard shortcut Ctrl-V.

16.3.10 Paste Into

The Paste Into command acts in a similar way to the Paste command. The primary difference becomes apparent if there is a selection within the canvas. Unlike the "Paste" command, which simply centers the pasted image data over the selection and replaces the selection with its own, "Paste Into" clips the pasted image data by the existing selection. The new selection can be moved as usual, but it is always clipped by the original selection area.

If no selection exists, the "Paste Into" command places the data from the Clipboard into the center of the canvas, as the "Paste" command does.

16.3.10.1 Activate the Command

- You can access this command from the image menubar through Edit → Paste Into.

16.3.11 Paste as

This command pastes the clipboard contents. Of course, you must use the "Copy" command before, so that you have something in the clipboard. Else you will be prompted a warning:

or, if there is something you have forgotten, it will be pasted! There is no way to empty the clipboard. This command leads to the sub-menu:

Figure 16.16 The "Paste as" sub-menu

New Image   Shift+Ctrl+V
New Layer
New Brush...
New Pattern...

- Section 16.3.11.1

- Section 16.3.11.2

- Section 16.3.11.3

- Section 16.3.11.4

16.3.11.1 Paste as New Image

The Paste As New Image command creates a new image and pastes the image data from the Clipboard into it. If the data is not rectangular or square in shape, any regions outside the selection are left transparent (an alpha channel is automatically created). Of course, you have to copy your selection before you use this command, so that you get an image with the same dimensions as the selection.

This command has the same action as the File → Create → From Clipboard command.

16.3.11.1.1 Activate the Command

- You can access this command from the image menubar through Edit → Paste as → New Image.

16.3.11.2 Paste as New Layer

The Paste As New Layer command creates a new layer in the active image and pastes the image data from the Clipboard into it. If the data are not rectangular or square in shape, any regions that do not extend to the edge of the canvas are left transparent (an Alpha channel is automatically created). Of course, you have to Copy your selection before you use this command.

16.3.11.2.1 Activate the Command

- You can access this command from the image menubar through Edit → Paste as → New Layer.

16.3.11.3 Paste as New Brush

This command opens a dialog window which lets you name the new brush. The brush appears in the Brushes dialog.

Figure 16.17 The "New Brush"dialog

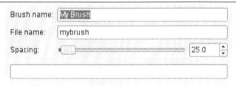

16.3.11.3.1 Options

Brush name Brush name is the name as it will be in the "Brushes" Dialog.

File name The new brush is saved as File name (with extension .gbr) in your personal brushes folder.

Spacing Spacing: When the brush draws a line, it actually stamps the brush icon repeatedly. If brush stamps are very close, you get the impression of a solid line.

16.3.11.3.2 Activate the Command

- You can access this command from the image menubar through Edit → Paste as → New Brush.

16.3.11.4 Paste as New Pattern

This command opens a dialog window which allows you to name your new pattern. The pattern appears in the Patterns dialog.

Figure 16.18 The "New Pattern"dialog

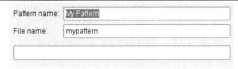

16.3.11.4.1 Options

Pattern name Pattern name is the name as it will be in the Pattern Dialog.

File name The new pattern is saved as File name (with extension `.pat`) in your personal `patterns` folder.

16.3.11.4.2 Activate the Command

- You can access this command from the image menubar through Edit → Paste as → New Pattern.

16.3.12 Buffer

Figure 16.19 The "Buffer" submenu of the "Edit" menu

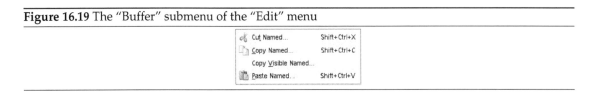

The commands in this submenu operate on *named buffers*. You can use the Buffers dialog to view and manage any named buffers you have created.

16.3.12.1 Activate the Submenu

- You can access this submenu from the image menubar through Edit → Buffer.

16.3.12.2 Sub-menu entries

Cut Named The Cut Named command cuts the content of the selection from the active layer in the usual way, but instead of storing the contents in the global clipboard, it stores it in a special buffer that you name using a pop-up dialog.

Copy Named The Copy Named command copies the contents of the selection from the active layer in the usual way, but instead of storing the content in the global clipboard, it stores it in a special buffer that you name using a pop-up dialog.

Copy Visible Named The Copy Visible Named command copies the content of the selection from all the visible layers in the usual way, but instead of storing the content in the global clipboard, it stores it in a special buffer that you name using a pop-up dialog.

Paste Named The Paste Named command simply brings up the Buffers dialog. By selecting one of the listed buffers, and pressing one of the buttons at the bottom, you can either Paste Buffer, Paste Buffer Into, or Paste Buffer as New.

16.3.13 Clear

The Clear command deletes everything in the current selection. If there is no current selection, the contents of the active layer are removed. If the active layer has an alpha channel, the deleted selection is made transparent. You can restore the original color to the transparent area using the Eraser tool, by setting it to Anti-Erase. If the layer does not have an alpha channel, the deleted area is filled using the current background color.

    Clearing a selection does not delete the selection itself. Unlike "Cut", "Clear" does not place the deleted contents in the Clipboard and the contents of the clipboard are unaffected.

16.3.13.1 Activate the Command

- You can access this command from the image menubar through Edit → Clear,

- or by using the keyboard shortcut **Delete**.

16.3.14 Fill with FG Color

The Fill with FG Color command fills the image's selection with the solid color shown in the foreground part of the Color Area of the Toolbox. (The color is also shown to the left of the menu entry.) If some areas of the image are only partially selected (for example, as a result of feathering the selection), they are filled in proportion to how much they are selected.

Note

 Please note that if the image has no selection, the whole active layer is filled.

16.3.14.1 Activate the Command

- You can access this command from the image menubar through Edit → Fill with FG Color,

- or by using the keyboard shortcut Ctrl-,.

Note

 You can also fill a selection by click-and-dragging from the Toolbox foreground color.

16.3.15 Fill with BG Color

The Fill with BG Color command fills the active layer selection with the solid color shown in the Background part of the Color Area of the Toolbox. (The color is also shown to the left of the menu entry.) If some areas of the image are only partially selected (for example, as a result of feathering the selection), they are filled in proportion to how much they are selected.

Note

 Please note that if the image has no selection, the whole active layer is filled.

16.3.15.1 Activate the Command

- You can access this command from the image menubar through Edit → Fill with BG Color,

- or by using the keyboard shortcut Ctrl-..

> **Note**
>
> You can also fill a selection by click-and-dragging from the Toolbox background color.

16.3.16 Fill with Pattern

The Fill with Pattern command fills the image's selection with the pattern shown in the Brush/Pattern/Gradient area of the Toolbox. (The pattern is also shown to the left of the menu entry.) If some areas of the image are only partially selected (for example, as a result of feathering the selection), they are filled in proportion to how much they are selected.

You can select another pattern by using the Pattern Dialog.

> **Note**
>
> Please note that if the image has no selection, the whole active layer is filled.

16.3.16.1 Activate the Command

- You can access this command from the image menubar through Edit → Fill with Pattern,

- or by using the keyboard shortcut Ctrl-;.

16.3.17 Stroke Selection

The Stroke Selection command strokes a selection in the image. There are two ways you can stroke the selection, either by using a paint tool or without using one. This means that the selection border, which is emphasized in the image with a dotted line, can be drawn with a stroke. There are various options which you can use to specify how this stroke should look.

> **Note**
>
> This command is only active if the image has an active selection.

16.3.17.1 Activate the Command

- You can access this command from the image menubar through Edit → Stroke Selection.

- You can also access it through the Selection Editor.

16.3.17.2 The "Stroke Selection" dialog

Note

 The options for stroking selections and for stroking paths are the same. You can find the documentation about the options in the dialog box in the Stroke Path section.

16.3.18   Stroke Path

The Stroke Path command strokes a path in the image. There are two ways you can stroke the path, either by using a paint tool, or without using one. There are various options which you can use to specify how this stroke should look.

Note

 This command is active only if there is a path in your image.

16.3.18.1   Activating the Command

- You can access this command from the image menubar through Edit → Stroke Path.

- You can also access it by clicking on the button with the same name in the Path dialog.

16.3.18.2   Description of the Dialog Window

Figure 16.20 The "Choose Stroke Style" dialog window

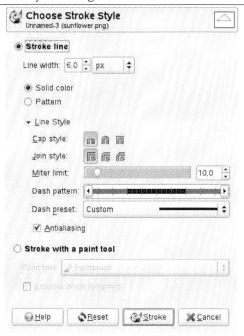

The Choose Stroke Style dialog box allows you to choose between stroking the path with the options you specify or stroking it with a paint tool. If you stroke the path with a paint tool, the current paint tool options are used to draw the stroke.

Stroke line

The stroke is drawn with the current foreground color, set in the Toolbox. By clicking on the triangle next to Line Style however, the dialog expands and you can set several additional options:

Line Width You can set the width of the stroke using the text box. The default unit is pixels, but you can choose another unit with the drop-down list button.

Solid color / Pattern You can choose whether the line is drawn in the *Solid* or the *Pattern* style. Here, Solid and Pattern are distinct from the dash pattern. If you select a Solid line with no dash pattern, an unbroken line is drawn in the foreground color set in the Toolbox. If you select a Patterned line with no dash pattern, an unbroken line is drawn with the pattern set in the Toolbox. If you select a line with a dash pattern, the color or pattern is still determined by the foreground color or pattern set in the Toolbox. That is, if you select a marbled pattern and Patterned, dashed lines, the dashes are drawn in the marbled pattern

Line Style This drop-list brings some detailed options :

- Cap Style : You can choose the shape of the ends of an unclosed path, which can be *Butt*, *Round* or *Square*.

- Join Style : You can choose the shape of the path corners by clicking on *Miter*, *Round* or *Bevel*.

- Miter limit : When two segments of a path come together, the mitering of the corner is determined by the Miter Limit. If the strokes were wide, and no mitering were done, there would be pointed ends sticking out at the corner. The Miter Limit setting determines how the gap, formed when the outer edges of the two lines are extended, will be filled. You can set it to a value between 0.0 and 100.0, by using the slider or the associated text box and its arrows.

Figure 16.21 Example of miter limit

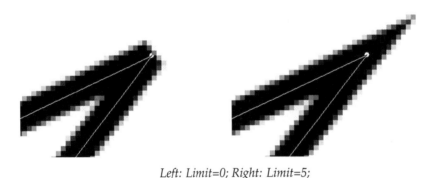

Left: Limit=0; Right: Limit=5;

- Dash Pattern : On the pixel level, a dashed line is drawn as a series of tiny boxes. You can modify the pattern of these boxes. The black area with thin vertical lines represents the pixels of the dash. If you click on a black pixel, you remove it from the dash. If you click on a white pixel, you add it to the dash. The gray areas indicate how the pattern will be repeated when a dashed line is drawn.

- Dash Preset : Instead of making your own dash pattern, you can choose one from the drop-down box. This pattern will then be displayed in the Dash pattern area, so you can get an idea of how it will look.

- Anti-aliasing : Curved strokes or strokes drawn at an angle may look jagged or stair-stepped. The anti-aliasing option smooths them out.

Stroking with a Paint Tool

Paint Tool You can select a paint tool to use to draw the stroke from the drop-down box. If you do that, the currently-selected options of the paint tool are used, rather than the settings in the dialog.

Emulate Brush Dynamics See Brush Dynamics.

16.3.19   The "Preferences" Command

This command displays the Preferences dialog, which lets you alter a variety of settings that affect the look, feel, and performance of the GIMP.

16.3.19.1   Activate Command

- You can access this command in the image menu bar through Edit → Preferences

16.3.20   Keyboard Shortcuts

How to use this command is described in Section 12.5.

16.3.20.1   Activate the Command

- You can access this command from the image menubar through Edit → Keyboard Shortcuts....

16.3.21   Modules

With the Modules command, you can show the various extension modules which are available and control which of them should be loaded. Modules perform functions such as choosing colors and display filtering. Any changes you make to the settings with the Module Manager command will take effect the next time you start GIMP. These changes affect GIMP's functional capabilities, its size in memory and its start-up time.

16.3.21.1   Activating the Command

- You can access this command from the image menubar through Edit → Modules

16.3.21.2   Description of the "Module Manager" Dialog

Figure 16.22 The "Module Manager" dialog window

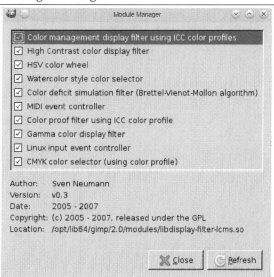

The window of the Module Manager shows the loadable modules.

Clicking on the boxes in the first column of the modules list will check or uncheck the modules. The next time you start GIMP, any checked module will be loaded.

You will notice the difference only when you try to use the modules. For example, there are several color selectors to select the foreground or background color. Some of these selectors are modules and will only be available when you check the respective option in the module manager:

Figure 16.23 Loaded modules example: Color selector modules

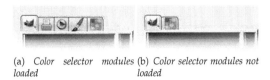

(a) Color selector modules (b) Color selector modules not
loaded   loaded

For loaded modules, information about the selected module is displayed at the bottom of the dialog.
In the second column, for each loaded module the purpose of the module is shown. For any module,
that is not loaded, the directory path of this module is shown.

When you click on the Refresh button, the list of modules will be updated: modules no longer on
disk will be removed, and new modules found will be added.

16.3.22 Units

The Units command displays a dialog which shows information about the units of measurement that
are currently being used by GIMP. It also allows you to create new units which can be used by GIMP in
a variety of situations.

16.3.22.1 Activate the Command

- You can access this command from the image menubar through Edit → Units.

16.3.22.2 Description of the "Unit Editor" dialog window

Figure 16.24 The "Unit Editor" dialog window

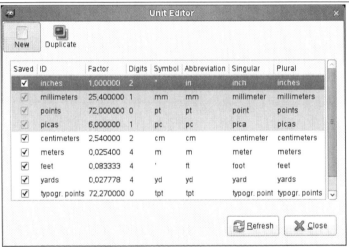

The figure above shows the "Unit Editor" dialog window. The list shows the units of measurement
which are currently defined. You can click on the New button or the Duplicate button to create a new
measurement unit, as described below.

Description of the list elements

- *Saved*: If this column is checked, a unit definition will be saved when GIMP exits. Some units are
  always kept, even if they are not marked with a check. These are highlighted in the list.

- *ID*: The string GIMP uses to identify the unit in its configuration files.

- *Factor*: How many units make up an inch.

- *Digits*: This field is a hint for numerical input fields. It specifies how many decimal digits the input
  field should provide to get approximately the same accuracy as an "inch" input field with two
  decimal digits.

- *Symbol*: The unit's symbol if it has one (e.g. " for inches). The unit's abbreviation is used if doesn't have a symbol.

- *Abbreviation*: The unit's abbreviation (e.g. "cm" for centimeters).

- *Singular*: The unit's singular form, which GIMP can use to display messages about the unit.

- *Plural*: The unit's plural form, which GIMP can use to display messages about the unit.

16.3.22.3 Defining New Units

Figure 16.25 The "New Unit" dialog

Adding the new unit "wilbers"

You can display the dialog shown above by clicking on either the New button or the Duplicate button on the Unit Editor dialog. The input fields on the dialog are described above.

If you click on the New button, most input fields are empty. If you click on the Duplicate button, the values initially displayed in the input fields of the dialog are the values of the unit you have currently selected in the Unit Editor dialog. You can then edit the values to create your new unit.

16.4 The "Select" Menu

16.4.1 Introduction to the "Select" Menu

Figure 16.26 The Contents of the "Select" menu

All	Ctrl+A
None	Shift+Ctrl+A
Invert	Ctrl+I
Float	Shift+Ctrl+L
By Color	Shift+O
From Path	Shift+V
Selection Editor	
Feather...	
Sharpen	
Shrink...	
Grow...	
Border...	
Distort...	
Rounded Rectangle...	
Toggle Quick Mask	Shift+Q
Save to Channel	
To Path	

This section explains the commands on the Select menu of the image menubar.

> **Note**
>
> Besides the commands described here, you may also find other entries in the menu. They are not part of GIMP itself, but have been added by extensions (plug-ins). You can find information about the functionality of a Plugin by referring to its documentation.

16.4.2 Select All

The Select All command creates a new selection which contains everything on the current layer.

16.4.2.1 Activate the Command

- You can access this command from the image menubar through Select → All,

- or by using the keyboard shortcut Ctrl-A.

- In addition, at the Selection Editor, you can access it through the Tab menu: Selection Editor Menu → All, or by clicking on the ⌐_⌐ icon button on the bottom of this dialog.

16.4.3 None

The None command cancels all selections in the image. If there are no selections, the command doesn't do anything. Floating selections are not affected.

16.4.3.1 Activating the Command

- You can access this command from the image menubar through Select → None.

- You can also use the keyboard shortcut Shift-Ctrl-A.

- In addition, at the Selection Editor, you can access it through the Tab menu: Selection Editor Menu → None, or by clicking on the ✖ icon button on the bottom of this dialog.

16.4.4 Invert

The Invert command inverts the selection in the current layer. That means that all of the layer contents which were previously outside of the selection are now inside it, and vice versa. If there was no selection before, the command selects the entire layer.

> **Warning**
>
> Do not confuse this command with the Invert colors command.

16.4.4.1 Activate the Command

- You can access this command from the image menubar through Select → Invert.

- You can also use the keyboard shortcut Ctrl-I,

- or click on the corresponding icon in the Selection Editor

16.4.5 Float

The Float command converts a normal selection into a "floating selection".

A floating selection (sometimes called a "floating layer") is a type of temporary layer which is similar in function to a normal layer, except that before you can resume working on any other layers in the image, a floating selection must be *anchored*. That is, you have to attach it to a normal (non-floating) layer, usually the original layer (the one which was active previously), for instance, by clicking on the image outside of the floating selection (see below).

Important

 You cannot perform any operations on other layers while the image has a floating selection!

You can use various operations to change the image data on the floating selection. There can only be one floating selection in an image at a time.

Tip

 If you display the layer boundary by using the Show Layer Boundary command, you may have difficulty selecting a precise area of the image which you want in a layer. To avoid this problem, you can make a rectangular selection, transform it into a floating selection and anchor it to a new layer. Then simply remove the original layer.

In early versions of GIMP, floating selections were used for performing operations on a limited part of an image. You can do that more easily now with layers, but you can still use this way of working with images.

16.4.5.1 Activate the Command

- You can access this command from the image menubar through Select → Float,

- or by using the keyboard shortcut Shift-Ctrl-L.

16.4.5.2 Creating a Floating Selection Automatically

Some image operations create a floating selection automatically:

- The "paste" operations, Paste Named Buffer, Paste or Paste Into, also create a floating selection.

- In addition, the Transform tools, Flip, Shear, Scale, Rotate and Perspective, create a floating selection when they are used on a selection, rather than a layer. When the Affect mode is *Transform Layer* and a selection already exists, these tools transform the selection and create a floating selection with the result. If a selection does not exist, they transform the current layer and do not create a floating selection. (If the Affect mode is *Transform Selection*, they also do not create a floating selection.)

- By click-and-dragging a selection while pressing the Ctrl-Alt keys (see Section 7.2.1) you also automatically create a floating selection.

16.4.5.3 Anchor a Floating Selection

You can anchor a floating selection in various ways:

- You can anchor the floating selection to the current layer the selection is originating from. To do this, click anywhere on the image except on the floating selection. This merges the floating selection with the current layer.

- Or you can use the Anchor layer command (Ctrl-H).

- You can also anchor the floating selection to the current layer by clicking on the anchor button of the Layers dialog.

- If you create a New Layer while there is a floating selection, the floating selection is anchored to this newly created layer.

16.4.6   By Color

The Select By Color command is an alternate way of accessing the "Select By Color" tool, one of the basic selection tools. You can find more information about using this tool in Select By Color.

16.4.6.1   Activating the Command

- You can access this command from the image menubar through Select → By Color,

- or by using the keyboard shortcut Shift-O.

16.4.7   From Path

The From Path command transforms the current path into a selection. If the path is not closed, the command connects the two end points with a straight line. The original path is unchanged.

16.4.7.1   Activating the Command

- You can access this command from the image menubar through Select → From Path.

- In addition, you can click on the Path to Selection button ▓ in the Path dialog to access the command.

- You can also use the keyboard shortcut Shift-V.

16.4.8   Selection Editor

The Selection Editor command displays the "Selection Editor" dialog window. This dialog window displays the active selection in the current image and gives you easy access to the selection-related commands. It is not really intended for editing selections directly, but if you are working on a selection, it is handy to have the selection commands all together, since it is easier to click on a button than to search for commands in the command tree of the menubar. The "Selection Editor" also offers some advanced options for the "Select to Path" command.

16.4.8.1   Activating the Command

- You can access this command from the image menubar through Select → Selection Editor.

16.4.8.2   Description of the "Selection Editor" dialog window

Figure 16.27 The "Selection Editor" dialog window

The Buttons The "Selection Editor" dialog window has several buttons which you can use to easily access selection commands:

- ⬚ The Select All button.

- ✕ The Select None button.

- ▨ The Select Invert button.

- ⬇ The Save to Channel button.

- ⬡ The To Path button. If you hold the **Shift** key while clicking on this button, the "Advanced Settings" dialog is displayed. Please see the next section for details about these options.

- ✎ The Stroke Selection button.

The display window In the display window, selected areas of the image are white, non-selected areas are black, and partially selected areas are in shades of gray. Clicking in this window acts like Select by Color. See the example below.

Figure 16.28 Example of clicking in the "Selection Editor" display window

Clicking in the "Selection Editor" display window to "Select By Color". Note that this figure could just as well show the appearance of the "Selection Editor" display window when "Select By Color" is used in the image window.

CHAPTER 16. MENUS   16.4. THE "SELECT" MENU

16.4.8.3 The "Selection to Path Advanced Settings" dialog

Figure 16.29 The "Advanced Settings" dialog window

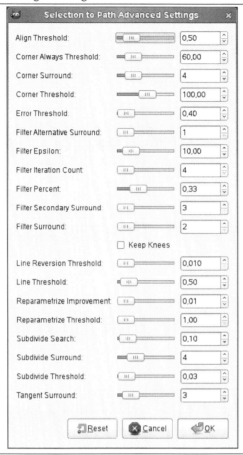

The "Selection to Path Advanced Settings" dialog, that you get by **Shift** clicking on the Selection to Path button, contains a number of options, most of which you can set with either a slider bar or a text box. There is also one check box. These options are mostly used by advanced users. They are:

- *Align Threshold*: If two endpoints are closer than this value, they are made to be equal.

- *Corner Always Threshold*: If the angle defined by a point and its predecessors and successors is smaller than this, it is a corner, even if it is within *Corner Surround* pixels of a point with a smaller angle.

- *Corner Surround*: Number of points to consider when determining if a point is a corner or not.

- *Corner Threshold*: If a point, its predecessors, and its successors define an angle smaller than this, it is a corner.

- *Error Threshold*: Amount of error at which a fitted spline[1] is unacceptable. If any pixel is further away than this from the fitted curve, the algorithm tries again.

---

[1] "Spline" is a mathematical term for a function which defines a curve by using a series of control points, such as a Bézier curve.

See Wikipedia for more information.

456

- *Filter Alternative Surround*: A second number of adjacent points to consider when filtering.

- *Filter Epsilon*: If the angles between the vectors produced by *Filter Surround* and *Filter Alternative Surround* points differ by more than this, use the one from *Filter Alternative Surround*.

- *Filter Iteration Count*: The number of times to smooth the original data points. Increasing this number dramatically, to 50 or so, can produce vastly better results. But if any points that "should" be corners aren't found, the curve goes wild around that point.

- *Filter Percent*: To produce the new point, use the old point plus this times the neighbors.

- *Filter Secondary Surround*: Number of adjacent points to consider if *Filter Surround* points defines a straight line.

- *Filter Surround*: Number of adjacent points to consider when filtering.

- *Keep Knees*: This check box says whether or not to remove "knee" points after finding the outline.

- *Line Reversion Threshold*: If a spline is closer to a straight line than this value, it remains a straight line, even if it would otherwise be changed back to a curve. This is weighted by the square of the curve length, to make shorter curves more likely to be reverted.

- *Line Threshold*: How many pixels (on the average) a spline can diverge from the line determined by its endpoints before it is changed to a straight line.

- *Reparametrize Improvement*: If reparameterization doesn't improve the fit by this much percent, the algorithm stops doing it.

- *Reparametrize Threshold*: Amount of error at which it is pointless to reparameterize. This happens, for example, when the algorithm is trying to fit the outline of the outside of an "O" with a single spline. The initial fit is not good enough for the Newton-Raphson iteration to improve it. It may be that it would be better to detect the cases where the algorithm didn't find any corners.

- *Subdivide Search*: Percentage of the curve away from the worst point to look for a better place to subdivide.

- *Subdivide Surround*: Number of points to consider when deciding whether a given point is a better place to subdivide.

- *Subdivide Threshold*: How many pixels a point can diverge from a straight line and still be considered a better place to subdivide.

- *Tangent Surround*: Number of points to look at on either side of a point when computing the approximation to the tangent at that point.

16.4.9   Feather

The Feather command feathers the edges of the selection. This creates a smooth transition between the selection and its surroundings. You normally feather selection borders with the "Feather Edges" option of the selection tools, but you may feather them again with this command.

16.4.9.1   Activating the Command

- You can access this command from the image menubar through Select → Feather.

16.4.9.2   Description of the "Feather Selection" dialog window

Figure 16.30 The "Feather Selection" dialog

Feather selection by Enter the width of the selection border feathering. The default units are pixels, but you can also choose other units with the drop-down menu.

16.4.10   Sharpen

The Sharpen command reduces the amount of blur or fuzziness around the edge of a selection. It reverses the effect of the Feather Selection command. The new edge of the selection follows the dotted line of the edge of the old selection. Anti-aliasing is also removed.

Note

    Please do not confuse this command with the Sharpen filter.

16.4.10.1   Activating the Command

- You can access this command from the image menubar through Select → Sharpen.

16.4.11   Shrink

The Shrink command reduces the size of the selected area by moving each point on the edge of the selection a certain distance further away from the nearest edge of the image (toward the center of the selection). Feathering is preserved, but the shape of the feathering may be altered at the corners or at points of sharp curvature.

16.4.11.1   Activating the Command

- You can access this command from the image menubar through Select → Shrink....

16.4.11.2   Description of the "Shrink" dialog

Figure 16.31 The "Shrink Selection" dialog

Shrink selection by Enter the amount by which to reduce the selection in the text box. The default unit is pixels, but you can choose a different unit of measurement from the drop-down menu.

Shrink from image border This option is only of interest if the selection runs along the edge of the image. If it does and this option is checked, then the selection shrinks away from the edge of the image. If this option is not checked, the selection continues to extend to the image border.

16.4.12   Grow

The Grow command increases the size of a selection in the current image. It works in a similar way to the Shrink command, which reduces the size of a selection.

16.4.12.1   Activating the Command

- You can access this command from the image menubar through Select → Grow.

16.4.12.2   Description of the "Grow Selection" dialog

Figure 16.32 The "Grow Selection" dialog window

Grow selection by You can enter the amount by which to increase the selection in the text box. The default unit of measurement is pixels, but you can choose a different unit by using the drop-down menu.

16.4.12.3   A Peculiarity of Rectangular Selections

When you grow a rectangular selection, the resulting selection has rounded corners. The reason for this is shown in the image below:

Figure 16.33 Why growing a rectangular selection results in rounded corners

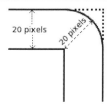

If you do not want rounded corners, you can use the Rounded Rectangle command with a 0% radius.

16.4.13   Border

Figure 16.34 Example of creating a border from a selection

(a) *An image with a selection*   (b) *After "Select Border"*

The Select Border command creates a new selection along the edge of an existing selection in the current image. The edge of the current selection is used as a form and the new selection is then created around it. You enter the width of the border, in pixels or some other unit, in the dialog window. Half of the new border lies inside of the selected area and half outside of it.

16.4.13.1   Activating the Command

- You can access this command from the image menubar through Select → Border.

16.4.13.2   Description of the "Border" dialog window

Figure 16.35 The "Border" dialog window

Border selection by Enter the width of the border selection in the box. The default units are pixels, but you can also choose the units with the drop-down menu.

Feather border If this option is checked, the edges of the selection will be feathered. This creates a smooth transition between the selection and its surroundings. Note than you can't use the Feather Edges option of the selection tools for this purpose.

Lock selection to image edges With this option enabled, an edge of an (usually rectangle) selection remains unchanged if it is aligned with an edge of the image; no new selection will be created around it.

Figure 16.36 Select border with and without "Lock to image edges"

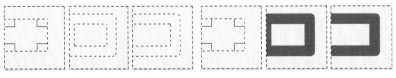

(a) *Select border without (middle) and with (right)*   (b) *Same selections filled with red.*
locked selection.

16.4.14   Distort

Figure 16.37 Example of using Distort on a selection

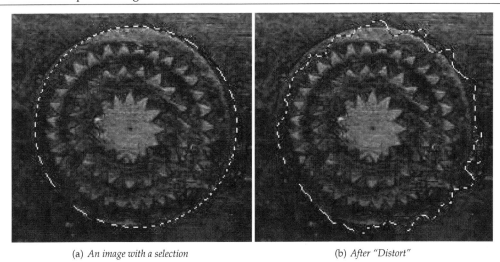

(a) *An image with a selection*   (b) *After "Distort"*

The "Distort" command deforms the selection contour.

16.4.14.1   Activating the Command

- You can access this command from the image menu bar through Select → Distort....

16.4.14.2   Description of the "Distort" Dialog Window

Figure 16.38 The "Distort" dialog

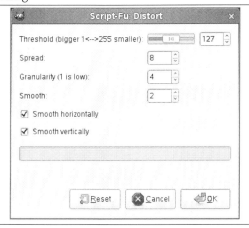

This command has several options which allow to increase or reduce the deformation. It is not possible to foresee the result and you have to experiment.

Threshold A higher threshold shrinks the distorted selection. A lower threshold makes the selection bigger.

If the active selection has a regular shape (e.g. rectangle or ellipse selection), this option controls if the new outline is more inside the original selection or more outside the original selection.

Spread A higher "Spread" increases the deformation.

Granularity A higher "Granularity" increases the deformation.

Smooth A higher "Smooth" decreases the deformation.

Deactivating Smooth horizontally or Smooth vertically increases the deformation.

16.4.15   Rounded Rectangle

Figure 16.39 Example of using Rounded rectangle on a selection

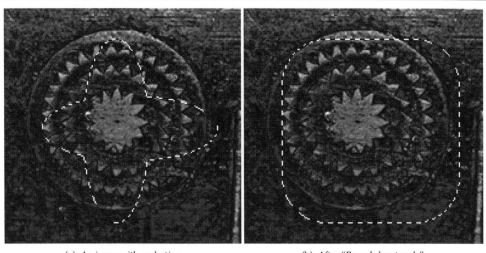

(a) *An image with a selection*   (b) *After "Rounded rectangle"*

The "Rounded Rectangle" Script-Fu command converts an existing selection (rectangular, elliptical or other shape) into a rectangular selection with rounded corners. The corners can be curved toward the inside (concave) or toward the outside (convex). To do this, the command adds or removes circles at the corners of the selection.

16.4.15.1   Activating the Command

- You can access this command from the image menu bar through Select → Rounded Rectangle.

16.4.15.2   Description of the "Rounded Rectangle" Dialog Window

Figure 16.40 The "Rounded Rectangle" dialog

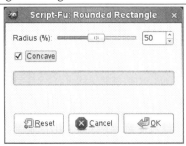

Radius (%) You can enter the radius of the rounded corner in percent by using a slider or a text field. This value is a percentage of the height or the width, whichever is less.

Concave If you check this box, the corners will be concave (curving toward the inside), rather than convex (curving toward the outside).

16.4.16   Toggle QuickMask

This command has the same action as clicking on the small button in the bottom left corner of the image. See Quick Mask

16.4.16.1   Activate Dialog

- You can access this command through Select → Toggle QuickMask.

- Default shortcut is Shift-Q

16.4.17   Save to Channel

The Save to Channel command saves the selection as a channel. The channel can then be used as a channel selection mask. You can find more information about them in the Channel Dialog section.

You will find a simple example how to use this command in the introduction of Section 17.16. It shows how to convert a selection to an alpha channel so that you can apply an alpha to logo filter to this selection.

16.4.17.1   Activate the Command

- You can access this command from the image menubar through Select → Save to Channel.

- You can also access it from the Selection Editor.

16.4.18   To Path

The To Path command converts a selection into a path. The image does not seem to change, but you can see the new path in the Paths Dialog. By using the Path tool in the Toolbox, you can precisely adapt the outline of the selection. You can find further information regarding paths in the Paths dialog section.

16.4.18.1   Activating the Command

- You can access this command from the image menu bar through Select → To Path.

- You can also access it from the Selection Editor or from the Paths Dialog which offers you a lot of Advanced Options.

16.5   The "View" Menu

16.5.1   Introduction to the "View" Menu

Figure 16.41 Contents of the View menu

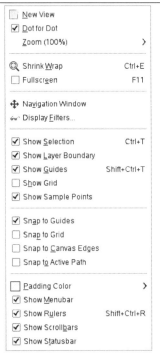

This section describes the View menu, which contains commands that affect the visibility or appearance of the image and various elements of the interface.

Note

Besides the commands described here, you may also find other entries in the menu. They are not part of GIMP itself, but have been added by extensions (plug-ins). You can find information about the functionality of a Plugin by referring to its documentation.

16.5.2   New View

The New View command creates a new image window for the current image, which you can set up differently from the existing display. You can create multiple views of any image, which are numbered .1, .2, etc., but only the zoom factor and other viewing options may be different. Any changes, other than viewing changes, which you make in one window also appear in the other displays which show the same image. The new views are not separate image files; they are simply different aspects of the same image. You might use multiple views, for example, if you were working on individual pixels at a high zoom factor. You could then see the effects your changes would have on the image at a normal size.

16.5.2.1   Activating the Command

- You can access this command from the image menubar through View → New View.

16.5.3   Dot for Dot

The Dot for Dot command enables and disables "Dot for Dot" mode. If it is enabled (checked) and the zoom factor is 100%, every pixel in the image is displayed as one pixel on the screen. If it is disabled, the image is displayed at its "real" size, the size it will have when it is printed.

The example below will illustrate this. Imagine the following image properties:

- Image size: 100x100 pixels

- Image resolution: 300 ppi (pixels per inch)

- Image displayed with Zoom=100%, "Dot for Dot" *enabled*:

   100x100 pixels

- Image displayed with Zoom=100%, "Dot for Dot" *disabled*:

   100 pixels ÷ 300 ppi = 1/3 inch   0.85 cm

For Dot for Dot mode to work properly, the resolution of the image must be the same as the screen resolution in the Preferences menu.

Enabling this mode is recommended if you are working on icons and web graphics. If you are working on images intended to be printed, you should disable Dot-for-Dot mode.

16.5.3.1   Activating the Command

- You can access this command from the image menubar through View → Dot for Dot.

16.5.4   Zoom

Figure 16.42 The "Zoom" submenu of the "View" menu

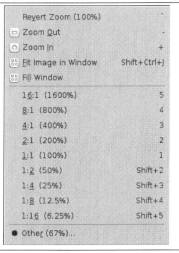

The Zoom submenu contains various commands which affect the magnification of the image in the image window (zooming). Enlarging an image (zooming in) is useful if you need to work with high precision, making pixel-level image modifications or precise selections. On the other hand, reducing an image (zooming out) is handy for getting an overall impression of the image and seeing the results of changes which affect the entire image. Please note that zooming is not undoable, since it does not affect the image data, only the way it is displayed.

Tip

Besides the entries in this submenu, there is also a zoom pull-down menu at the bottom edge of the image window (if the status bar is displayed), where several preset zoom levels are available.

You can also make settings regarding zooming in the Navigation dialog. You can also use the Zoom tool which lets you zoom a particular area of the image.

16.5.4.1 Activate the Submenu

- You can access this submenu from the image menubar through View → Zoom. Note that the "Zoom" label on the "View" menu shows the current zoom factor, for example, Zoom (100%).

16.5.4.2 Contents of the "Zoom" submenu

The various "Zoom" submenu commands are described below, along with their default keyboard shortcuts, if any.

Revert Zoom (Shortcut: Ä[grave accent,"backtick"]) This command will reset the zoom factor to the previous value, which is also shown by this label, for example Revert Zoom (100%). If you never changed the zoom factor of the active image, this entry is insensitive and grayed out.

Zoom Out (Shortcut: -) Each time "Zoom Out" is used, the zoom factor is decreased by about 30%. There is a minimum zoom level of 0.39%.

Zoom In (Shortcut: +) Each time "Zoom In" is used, the zoom factor is increased by about 30%. The maximum possible zoom level is 25600%.

Note

The keyboard shortcut for "Zoom In" has been somewhat controversial because this is a very common operation and on English keyboards, the **Shift** key must be pressed to use it. (This is not the case for European keyboards.) If you would like to have a different keyboard shortcut, you can create a dynamic shortcut for it; see the help section for User Interface Preferences for instructions.

Fit Image in Window (Shortcut: Shift-Ctrl-J). This command zooms the image to be as large as possible, while still keeping it completely within the window. There will usually be padding on two sides of the image, but not on all four sides.

Fit Image to Window This command zooms the image as large as possible without requiring any padding to be shown. This means that the image fits the window perfectly in one dimension, but usually extends beyond the window borders in the other dimension.

A:B (X%) With these commands, you can select one of the pre-set zoom levels. Each of the menu labels gives a ratio, as well as a percentage value. Please note that each zoom pre-set has its own keyboard shortcut. The current zoom is marked with a large dot.

Other This command brings up a dialog which allows you to choose any zoom level you would like, within the range of 1:256 (0.39%) to 256:1 (25600%).

Tip

 When you are working at the pixel level, you can use the New view command. This allows you to see what is happening to the image at its normal size at the same time.

16.5.5 Shrink Wrap

The Shrink Wrap command resizes the window so that it is exactly the same size as the image at the current zoom factor. If the image doesn't completely fit on the screen, the image window is enlarged so that the largest possible part of the image is shown. Please note that GIMP will do this automatically if you set the "Resize window on zoom" and "Resize window on image size change" options in the Image Window page of the Preferences dialog.

Note

 Please note also that the behavior described here is not performed by GIMP itself, but by the "window manager", a part of the operating system of your computer. For that reason, the functionality described may be different on your computer, or in the worst case, might not be available at all.

16.5.5.1 Activating the Command

- You can access this command from the image menubar through View → Shrink Wrap,

- or by using the keyboard shortcut Ctrl-J.

16.5.6 Full Screen

The Fullscreen command enables and disables displaying the image window on the entire screen. When it is enabled, the image window takes up the whole screen, but the image stays the same size. When you enable full-screen mode, the menubar may not be displayed, but if this happens, you can right-click on the image to access the image menu. You can set the default appearance for full-screen mode in the Preferences menu.

Pressing **TAB** key toggles the visibility of all present docks.

Note

 If you use GIMP on an Apple computer, full-screen mode may not work, since Apple doesn't provide the necessary functionality. Instead, you can maximize the image window by clicking on the *Green Button*, so the image occupies most of the screen.

16.5.6.1 Activating the Command

- You can access this command from the image menubar through View → Full Screen,

- or by using the keyboard shortcut **F11**.

- In multi-window mode, you can also get it by double-clicking on the title bar of the image window.

16.5.7   Navigation Window

The Navigation Window command opens the navigation window. This allows you to easily navigate through the image, to set zoom levels and to move the visible parts of the image. You can find more information about using it in the Navigation dialog chapter.

16.5.7.1   Activating the Command

- You can access this command from the image menubar through View → Navigation Window,

- You can also access it more rapidly by clicking on the ✥ icon in the lower right corner of the image window.

16.5.8   Display Filters

This command shows a dialog window when executed. This window can be used to manage the display filters and their options. Display filters are not to be confused with the filters in the filters-menu. Display filters do not alter the image data, but only one display of it. You can imagine display filters like big panes before your screen. They change your perception of the image. This can be useful for things like soft proofing prints, controlling the color management but also simulation of color deficient vision.

16.5.8.1   Activating the Command

You can access this command from the image menubar through View → Display Filters....

16.5.8.2   Description of the "Display Filters" Dialog

Figure 16.43 The "Configure Color Display Filters" dialog

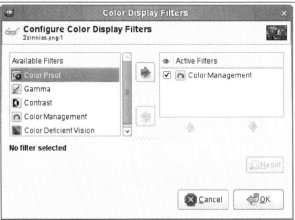

This dialog has two small selectboxes. The left selectbox displays the Available Filters. You can move a filter to the right selectbox by selecting it and clicking on the right arrow button. The Active Filters window on the right displays filters you have chosen and which will be applied if the adjacent box is checked. You can move filters from the right selectbox to the left selectbox by using the left arrow button. If you select a filter by clicking on its name, its options are displayed below the two selectboxes, in the Configure Selected Filter area.

- Simulation of deficient vision (Section 16.5.8.3; Section 16.5.8.5)

- Color Management (Section 16.5.8.6; Section 16.5.8.7)

- Others (Section 16.5.8.4)

16.5.8.3 Color Deficient Vision

The images you create, we hope, will be seen by many people on many different systems. The image which looks so wonderful on your screen may look somewhat different to people with sight deficiencies or on a screen with different settings from yours. Some information might not even be visible.

Figure 16.44 Description of the "Color Deficient Vision" dialog

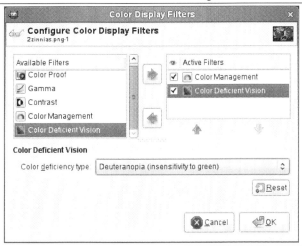

16.5.8.3.1 Options

Color Deficiency Type In this drop-down menu you can select from among:

Protanopia[2] **(insensitivity to red)** Protanopia is a visual deficiency of the color red. It's the well-known daltonism (red-green color blindness). Daltonism occurs fairly frequently in the population.

Protanopia is actually more complex than this; a person with this problem cannot see either red or green, although he is still sensitive to yellow and blue. In addition, he has a loss of luminance perception and the hues shift toward the short wavelengths.

Deuteranopia (insensivity to green) With deuteranopia, the person has a deficiency in green vision. Deuteranopia is actually like protanopia, because the person has a loss of red and green perception, but he has no luminance loss or hue shift.

Tritanopia (insensitivity to blue) With tritanopia, the person is deficient in blue and yellow perception, although he is still sensitive to red and green. He lacks some perception of luminance, and the hues shift toward the long wavelengths.

Figure 16.45 Example of protanopia

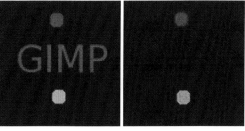

(a) *Original image*   (b) *A red-blind person cannot see the red (255,0,0) text on a black (0,0,0) background.*

---

[2] Greek: *proto*: first (color in the RGB Color System): *an*: negation; *op*: eye, vision.

Figure 16.46 Examples of the three types of vision deficiencies in one image

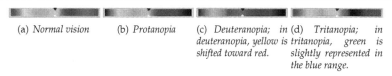

(a) *Normal vision*   (b) *Protanopia*   (c) *Deuteranopia; in deuteranopia, yellow is shifted toward red.*   (d) *Tritanopia; in tritanopia, green is slightly represented in the blue range.*

16.5.8.3.2 Examples

16.5.8.4 Gamma

Figure 16.47 The "Gamma" dialog

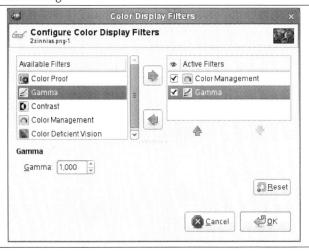

The correspondence between electrical intensity and color brightness is not exact and it depends upon the device (the camera, the scanner, the monitor, etc.). "Gamma" is a coefficient used to correct this correspondence. Your image must be visible in both dark and bright areas, even if it is displayed on a monitor with too much luminence or not enough. The "Gamma" Display Filter allows you to get an idea of the appearance of your image under these conditions.

Tip

 In case you want not only to change the gamma of the current display, but the change the gamma within the image itself, you can find a description in Section 14.5.7.

16.5.8.5   Contrast

Figure 16.48 The "Contrast" dialog

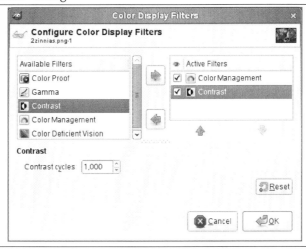

Here, we are back in the medical domain. "Contrast Sensitivity" is the capacity of the visual system to distinguish slight differences in contrast. Some people with cataracts (which means that the lens has opaque crystals that scatter light over the retina) or retinal disease (for instance, due to diabetes, which destroys the rods and cones) have a deficiency in sensitivity to contrast: for example, they would have difficulties distinguishing spots on a dress.

If you are interested in this subject, you can browse the Web for "contrast sensitivity".

16.5.8.5.1   Options

Contrast Cycles   With the "Contrast" Filter, you can see the image as if you were suffering from cataracts. You may have to increase the contrast of the image so that your grandmother can see it well. In most cases, only very low values of the Contrast Cycles parameter are of interest. Higher values create a side-effect which doesn't interest us here: if you increase the luminosity value above 255, the complementary color appears.

16.5.8.6   Color Management

Figure 16.49 The "Color Management" dialog

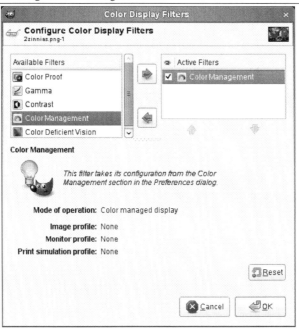

This filter allows to enable the GIMP color management for each image window. To learn more about the color management in GIMP, please read Section 11.1.

16.5.8.6.1   Options   All the customizing for the color management in GIMP has to be done in the GIMP preferences. You can find detailed information about this in Section 12.1.14.

16.5.8.7   Color Proof

The various systems for reproducing colors cannot represent the infinity of colors available. Even if there are many colors in common between the various systems and nature, some of the colors will not be the same. The "gamut" is the color range of a system. *Color Profiles* allow you to compensate for these differences.

Before you print an image, it may be useful for you to see if you will get the result you want by applying a profile. The "Color Proof" filter shows you how your image will look after a color profile has been applied.

Figure 16.50 The "Color Proof" dialog

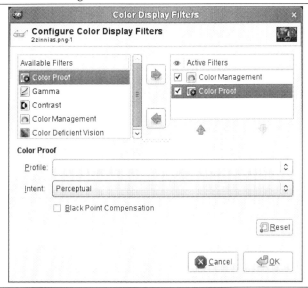

16.5.8.7.1 The "Color Proof" options

Profile This option allows to select a color profile that is used to simulate the color abilities of the printer. If the desired profile is not shown in the list you might want to add it by selecting a file. This can be done by selecting the last entry of the list.

Intent With this option you can select the rendering intent, which is the method used to determine how colors that can't be reproduced by a device ("are out of gamut") should be handled. The different rendering intents are described in detail in the glossary *Rendering Intent* .

Black Point Compensation Black point compensation allows a better representaion of dark colors of your image when printing.

16.5.9 Show Selection

The Show Selection command enables and disables displaying the dotted line surrounding the selection in the image window. Please note that the selection still exists, even if displaying this line is disabled.
    You can set the default for displaying the selection in the Image Window Appearance dialog.

16.5.9.1 Activating the Command

- You can access this command from the image menubar through View → Show Selection,

- or by using the keyboard shortcut Ctrl-T.

16.5.10 Show Layer Boundary

The Show Layer Boundary command enables and disables displaying the yellow dotted line that surrounds a layer in the image window. The dotted line is actually only visible when the layer is smaller than the image window. When the layer is the same size as the image window, the layer boundary is obscured by the image border.
    You can set the default for the layer boundary in the Image Window Appearance dialog.

16.5.10.1 Activating the Command

- You can access this command from the image menubar through View → Show Layer Boundary.

16.5.11   Show Guides

The Show Guides command enables and disables displaying of Guides in the image window.
    You can set the default for the guides in the Image Window Appearance dialog.

16.5.11.1   Activating the Command

- You can access this command from the image menubar through View → Show Guides,

- or by using the keyboard shortcut Shift-Ctrl-T.

16.5.12   Show Grid

By using the Show Grid command, you can enable and disable displaying the grid. When you enable it,
the grid overlays the image and makes it easier for you to line up selected image elements.
    You can set the default for the grid in the Image Window Appearance dialog.

Tip

   See also the Configure Grid command and the Snap to Grid command.

16.5.12.1   Activating the Command

- You can access this command from the image menubar through View → Show Grid.

16.5.13   Show Sample Points

This command enables and disables showing the sample points in the image window. Sample points
are used to display color informations of up to four pixels in the sample points dialog.

16.5.13.1   Activating the Command

- You can access this command from the image menubar through View → Show Sample Points.

16.5.14   Snap to Guides

The Snap to Guides command enables and disables snap to guides. When snap to guides is enabled,
the guides you set (see Show Guides) almost seems magnetic; when you move a layer or selection, the
guides appear to pull on it when it approaches. This is enormously useful for accurate placement of
image elements.

16.5.14.1   Activating the Command

- You can access this command from the image menubar through View → Snap to Guides.

16.5.15   Snap to Grid

The Snap to Grid command enables and disables snap to grid. When snap to grid is enabled, the grid you
set (see Show Grid) almost seems magnetic; when you move a layer or selection, the grid points appear
to pull on it when it approaches. This is enormously useful for accurate placement of image elements.

16.5.15.1   Activating the Command

- You can access this command from the image menubar through View → Snap to Grid.

16.5.16   Snap to Canvas

If this option is enabled, when you move a selection or a layer, they appear to pull on the canvas edges when it approaches. This is useful for accurate placement of image elements.

> **Note**
>
> Canvas edges are usually mingled with image edges: the canvas has, then, the same size as the image. But you can change canvas size in Image → Canvas Size.

16.5.16.1   Activating the Command

- You can access this command from the image menubar through View → Snap to Canvas.

16.5.17   Snap to Active Path

If this option is enabled, when you move a selection or a layer, they appear to pull on the next anchor point of the active path when it approaches. This is useful for accurate placement of image elements.

16.5.17.1   Activating the Command

- You can access this command from the image menubar through View → Snap to Path.

16.5.18   Padding Color

Figure 16.51 Contents of the "Padding Color" submenu

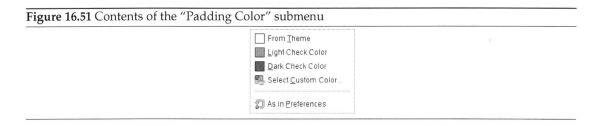

You can change the color of the canvas which surrounds the image by using the Padding Color command. The canvas is the surface the image lies on. It looks like a frame around the image in the image window. This is just a matter of personal preference, since the padding color does not have any effect on the image itself. Please note that this color is not the same as the color used by the Fill tool.

16.5.18.1   Activating the submenu

- You can access this submenu from the image menubar through View → Padding Color.

16.5.18.2   "Padding Color" Options

From Theme The color of the theme defined in Preferences Theme is used.

Light/Dark Check Color The check representing transparency, which is defined in Preferences Display is used.

Select Custom Color Opens the Color Selector window to let you choose a color to use.

As in Preferences The color selected in the Image Window Appearance is used.

16.5.19   Show Menubar

The Show Menubar command enables and disables displaying the menubar. It may be useful to disable it if you are working in full-screen mode. If the menubar is not displayed, you can right-click on the image to access the menubar entries.

You can set the default for the menubar in the Image Window Appearance dialog.

16.5.19.1   Activating the Command

- You can access this command from the image menubar through View → Show Menubar.

16.5.20   Show Rulers

The Show Rulers command enables and disables displaying the rulers. It may be useful to disable them if you are working in full-screen mode.

You can set the default for the rulers in the Image Window Appearance dialog.

16.5.20.1   Activating the Command

- You can access this command from the image menubar through View → Show Rulers,

- or by using the keyboard shortcut Shift-Ctrl-R.

16.5.21   Show Scrollbars

The Show Scrollbars command enables and disables displaying the scrollbars. It may be useful to disable them if you are working in full-screen mode.

You can set the default for the scrollbars in the Image Window Appearance dialog.

16.5.21.1   Activating the Command

- You can access this command from the image menubar through View → Show Scrollbars.

16.5.22   Show Statusbar

The Show Statusbar command enables and disables displaying the status bar. It may be useful to disable it when you are working in full-screen mode.

You can set the default for the status bar in the Image Window Appearance dialog.

16.5.22.1   Activating the Command

- You can access this command from the image menubar through View → Show Statusbar.

16.6   The "Image" Menu

16.6.1   Overview

Figure 16.52 The Contents of the "Image" Menu

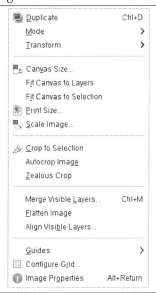

The Image menu contains commands which use or affect the entire image in some way, not just the active layer or some other specific part of the image.

> **Note**
>
> Besides the commands described here, you may also find other entries in the menu. They are not part of GIMP itself, but have been added by extensions (plug-ins). You can find information about the functionality of a Plugin by referring to its documentation.

16.6.2   Duplicate

The Duplicate command creates a new image which is an exact copy of the current one, with all of its layers, channels and paths. The GIMP Clipboard and the History are not affected.

> **Note**
>
> Don't mistake a duplicated image for a new view of this image. In a View → New View, all changes are passed on the original image.

16.6.2.1   Activating the Command

- You can access this command from the image menubar through Image → Duplicate,

- or by using the keyboard shortcut Ctrl-D.

16.6.3 Mode

Figure 16.53 The "Mode" submenu of the "Image" menu

The Mode submenu contains commands which let you change the color mode of the image. There are three modes.

16.6.3.1 Activating the Submenu

- You can access this submenu from the image menubar through Image → Mode.

16.6.3.2 The Contents of the "Mode" Submenu

- RGB

- Grayscale

- Indexed

- Assign Color Profile (see Color management)

- Convert to Color Profile (see Color management)

16.6.4 RGB mode

The RGB command converts your image to RGB mode. See the RGB description in the Glossary for more information. Normally, you work in this mode, which is well-adapted to the screen. It is possible to convert an RGB image to Grayscale or Indexed mode, but be careful: once you have saved the image, you can no longer retrieve the RGB colors, so you should work on a copy of your image.

16.6.4.1 Activating the command

- You can access this command from the image menu bar through Image → Mode → RGB.

16.6.5 Grayscale mode

You can use the Grayscale command to convert your image to grayscale with 256 levels of gray, from 0 (black) to 255 (white).

16.6.5.1 Activating the Command

- You can access this command from the image menubar through Image → Mode → Grayscale.

16.6.6 Indexed mode

The Indexed command converts your image to indexed mode. See indexed colors in the Glossary for more information about Indexed Color Mode.

16.6.6.1 Activating the Command

- You can access this command from the image menubar through Image → Mode → Indexed.

16.6.6.2   The "Convert Image to Indexed Colors" dialog

The Indexed command opens the Convert Image to Indexed Colors dialog.

Figure 16.54 The "Convert Image to Indexed Colors" dialog

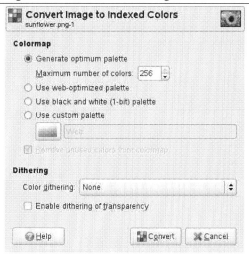

Colormap Options

- Generate optimum palette: This option generates the best possible palette with a default maximum number of 256 colors (classic GIF format). You can reduce this *Maximum Number of Colors*, although this may create unwanted effects (color banding) on smooth transitions. You may be able to lessen the unwanted effects by using dithering, however.

- Use web-optimized palette: use a palette that is optimized for the web.

- Use black and white (1-bit) palette: This option generates an image which uses only two colors, black and white.

- Use custom palette: This button lets you select a custom palette from a list. The number of colors is indicated for each palette. The "Web" palette, with 216 colors, is the "web-safe" palette. It was originally created by Netscape to provide colors that would look the same on both Macs and PCs, and Internet Explorer 3 could manage it. Since version 4, MSIE handles a 212 color palette. The problem of color similarity between all platforms has not been solved yet and it probably never will be. When designing a web page, you should keep two principles in mind: use light text on a dark background or dark text on a light background, and never rely on color to convey information.

  Some colors in the palette may not be used if your image does not have many colors. They will be removed from the palette if the Remove unused colors from final palette option is checked.

Dithering Options Since an indexed image contains 256 colors or less, some colors in the original image may not be available in the palette. This may result in some blotchy or solid patches in areas which should have subtle color changes. The dithering options let you correct the unwanted effects created by the Palette Options.

A dithering filter tries to approximate a color which is missing from the palette by instead using clusters of pixels of similar colors which are in the palette. When seen from a distance, these pixels give the impression of a new color. See the Glossary for more information on dithering.

Three filters (plus "None") are available. It is not possible to predict what the result of a particular filter will be on your image, so you will have to try all of them and see which works best. The "Positioned Color Dithering" filter is well adapted to animations.

Figure 16.55 Example: full color, with no dithering

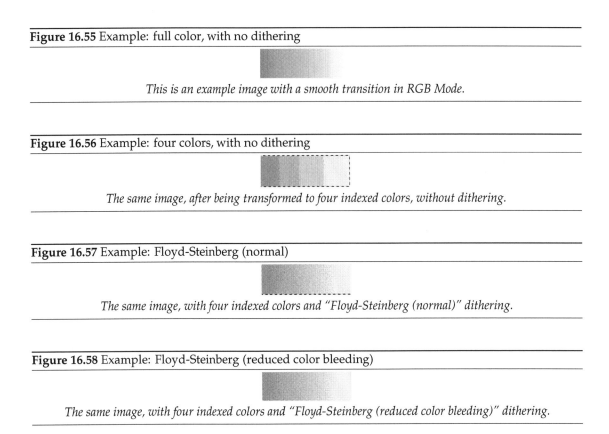

This is an example image with a smooth transition in RGB Mode.

Figure 16.56 Example: four colors, with no dithering

The same image, after being transformed to four indexed colors, without dithering.

Figure 16.57 Example: Floyd-Steinberg (normal)

The same image, with four indexed colors and "Floyd-Steinberg (normal)" dithering.

Figure 16.58 Example: Floyd-Steinberg (reduced color bleeding)

The same image, with four indexed colors and "Floyd-Steinberg (reduced color bleeding)" dithering.

In a GIF image, transparency is encoded in 1 bit: transparent or not transparent. To give the illusion of partial transparency, you can use the Enable dithering of transparency option. However, the Semi-flatten plug-in may give you better results.

Note

 You can edit the color palette of an indexed image by using the Colormap Dialog.

16.6.7 Transform

Figure 16.59 The "Transform" submenu of the "Image" menu

⇠ Flip <u>H</u>orizontally
❖ Flip <u>V</u>ertically

✣ Rotate 90° <u>c</u>lockwise
✤ Rotate 90° counter-cloc<u>k</u>wise
✥ Rotate <u>1</u>80°

<u>G</u>uillotine

The items on the Transform submenu transform the image by flipping it, rotating it or cropping it.

16.6.7.1 Activating the Submenu

- You can access this submenu from the image menubar through Image → Transform.

16.6.7.2   The Contents of the "Transform" Submenu

The Transform submenu has the following commands:

- Flip Horizontally; Flip Vertically

- Rotate 90° clockwise / counter-clockwise; Rotate 180°

- Guillotine

16.6.8   Flip Horizontally; Flip Vertically

You can flip the image, or turn it over like a card, by using the Flip Horizontally or Flip Vertically commands. These commands work on the whole image. To flip a selection, use the Flip Tool. To flip a layer, use the functions of the Layer → Transform menu or the Flip Tool.

16.6.8.1   Activate the Commands

- You can access the horizontal flip command from the image menubar through Image → Transform → Flip Horizontally.

- You can access the vertical flip command from the image menubar through Image → Transform → Flip Vertically.

16.6.9   Rotation

You can rotate the image 90° clockwise or counter-clockwise, or rotate it 180°, by using the rotation commands on the Transform submenu of the Image menu. These commands can be used to change between Portrait and Landscape orientation. They work on the whole image. If you want to rotate the image at a different angle, rotate a selection or rotate a layer, use the Rotate Tool. You can also rotate a layer by using the Layer Transform menu.

16.6.9.1   Activate the Commands

You can access these three commands from the image menubar through

- Image → Transform → Rotate 90 degrees CW,

- Image → Transform → Rotate 90 degrees CCW and

- Image → Transform → Rotate 180°.

16.6.10   Guillotine

The Guillotine command slices up the current image, based on the image's guides. It cuts the image along each guide, similar to slicing documents in an office with a guillotine (paper cutter) and creates new images out of the pieces. For further information on guides, see Section 12.2.2.

16.6.10.1   Activate the Command

- You can access this command from the image menubar through Image → Transform → Guillotine.

16.6.11   Canvas Size

The "canvas" is the visible area of the image. By default the size of the canvas coincides with the size of the layers. The Canvas Size command lets you enlarge or reduce the canvas size. You can, if you want, modify the size of the layers. When you enlarge the canvas, you create free space around the contents of the image. When you reduce it, the visible area is cropped, however the layers still extend beyond the canvas border.

When you reduce the canvas size, the new canvas appears surrounded with a thin negative border in the preview. The mouse pointer is a moving cross: click and drag to move the image against this frame.

16.6.11.1   Activating the Command

- You can access this command from the image menubar through Image → Canvas Size.

16.6.11.2   Description of the "Canvas Size" dialog

Figure 16.60 The "Canvas Size" dialog

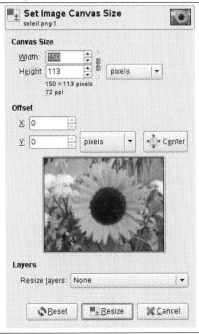

Canvas Size

Width; Height You can set the Width and the Height of the canvas. The default units are pixels but you can choose different units, e.g. percent, if you want to set the new dimensions relative to the current dimensions. If the Chain to the right of the Width and Height is not broken, both Width and Height keep the same relative size to each other. That is, if you change one of the values, the other one also changes a corresponding amount. If you break the Chain by clicking on it, you can set Width and Height separately.

Whatever units you use, information about the size in pixels and the current resolution are always displayed below the *Width* and *Height* fields. You cannot change the resolution in the Canvas Size dialog; if you want to do that, use the Print Size dialog.

Offset

The Offset values are used to place the image (the image, not the active layer) on the canvas. You can see the size and the content of the canvas in the preview of the dialog window. When the canvas is smaller than the image, the preview window shows it in a frame with a thin negative border.

X ; Y The X and Y specify the coordinates of the upper left corner of the image relative to the upper left corner of the canvas. They are negative when the canvas is smaller than the image. You can place the image in different ways (of course, the coordinates can't exceed the canvas borders):

- by click-and-dragging the image,
- by entering values in the X and Y text boxes,
- by clicking on the small arrow-heads. This increments the value by one pixel (unit).
- And when the focus is on a text box, you can use the keyboard arrow keys, **Up** and **Down** to change by one pixel (unit), or **PageUp** and **PageDown** to change the value by 10 pixels (units).

Layers Before the GIMP-2.4 version, "Canvas Size" had no influence on layer size. To change it, you had to use the Layer Boundary Size command. The "Layers" option now allows you to specify how, possibly, layers will be resized. The drop-down list offers you several possibilities:

Figure 16.61 The Resize layers list

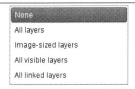

- None: default option. No layer is resized, only the canvas is.

- All Layers: all layers are resized to canvas size.

- Image-sized layers: only layers with the same size as the image are sized to canvas size.

- All visible layers: only visible layers, marked with a  icon, in the Layer Dialog, are sized to canvas size.

- All linked layers: only linked layers, marked with a in the Layer Dialog, are sized to canvas size.

Center The Center button allows you to center the image on the canvas. When you click on the Center button, the offset values are automatically calculated and displayed in the text boxes.

Note

When you click on the Resize button, the canvas is resized, but the pixel information and the drawing scale of the image are unchanged.

If the layers of the image did not extend beyond the borders of the canvas before you changed its size, there are no layers on the part of the canvas that was added by resizing it. Therefore, this part of the canvas is transparent and displayed with a checkered pattern, and it is not immediately available for painting. You can either flatten the image, in which case you will get an image with a single layer that fits the canvas exactly, or you can use the Layer to Image Size command to resize only the active layer, without changing any other layers. You can also create a new layer and fill it with the background you want. By doing this, you create a digital "passe-partout" (a kind of glass mount with a removable back for slipping in a photograph).

16.6.11.3 Example

Figure 16.62 Original image

We started with a green background layer 100x100 pixels, which defines a default canvas with the same size. Then we added a new red layer 80x80 pixels. The active layer limits are marked with a black and yellow dotted line. The red layer does not fill the canvas completely: the unoccupied part is transparent. The background color in the Toolbox is yellow.

Figure 16.63 Canvas enlarged (layers unchanged)

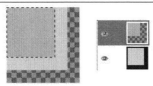

The canvas has been enlarged to 120x120 pixels. The layers size remained unchanged. The unoccupied part of the canvas is transparent.

Figure 16.64 Canvas enlarged (all layers changed)

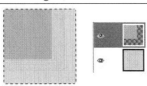

The canvas has been enlarged to 120x120 pixels. All layers have been enlarged to the canvas size. The undrawn part is transparent in the red layer and yellow (background color in Toolbox) in the green background layer.

16.6.11.4   What's Canvas Size useful for?

You may want to add some stuff around your image: enlarge canvas size, add a new layer that will have the same size as the new canvas and then paint this new layer. That's the converse of cropping.

You can also use this command to crop an image:

Figure 16.65 Resizing canvas

Click on the chain next to Width and Height entries to unlink dimensions. By modifying these dimensions and moving image against canvas, by trial and error, you can crop the part of the image you want. Click on the Center button and then on the Resize button.

Figure 16.66 Cropped image

Note

 The Crop tool is easier to use.

16.6.12   Fit Canvas to Layers

The Fit Canvas to Layers command adapts the canvas size to the size of the largest layer in the image, in both width and height.

When you create or open an image, the canvas size is defined as the image size and remains unchanged if you add new layers. If you add a layer larger than the canvas, only the area limited by the canvas will be visible. To show the whole layer, use this command.

16.6.12.1   Activate the command

- You can access this command from the image menubar through Image → Fit Canvas to Layers.

16.6.13   Fit Canvas to Selection

The Fit Canvas to Selection command adapts the canvas size to the size of the selection, in both width and height.

16.6.13.1   Activate the command

- You can access this command from the image menubar through Image → Fit Canvas to Selection.

16.6.14   Print Size

You can use the Print Size dialog to change the *dimensions of a printed image* and its *resolution*. This command does not change the number of pixels in the image and it does not resample the image. (If you want to change the size of an image by resampling it, use the Scale Image command.)

16.6.14.1   Activating the Dialog

- You can access this dialog from the image menubar through Image → Print Size.

16.6.14.2   Options in the "Print Size" Dialog

Figure 16.67 The "Print Size" dialog

The output resolution determines the number of pixels used per unit length for the printed image. Do not confuse the output resolution with the printer's resolution, which is a printer feature and expressed in dpi (dots per inch); several dots are used to print a pixel.

When the dialog is displayed, the resolution shown in the boxes is the resolution of the original image. If you increase the output resolution, the printed page will be smaller, since more pixels are used per unit of length. Conversely, and for the same reason, resizing the image modifies the resolution.

Increasing the resolution results in increasing the sharpness of the printed page. This is quite different from simply reducing the image size by scaling it, since no pixels (and no image information) are removed.

Width; Height You can set the printing Width and Height by using the text boxes. You can also choose the units for these values from the dropdown list.

As soon as you change the Width or the Height, the X and/or Y resolution values automatically change accordingly. If the two resolution values remain linked, the relationship of the width to the height of the image is also automatically maintained. If you would like to set these values independently of each other, simply click on the chain symbol to break the link.

X resolution; Y resolution You can set the resolution used to calculate the printed width and height from the physical size of the image, that is, the number of pixels in it.

Use the text boxes to change these resolution values. They can be linked to keep their relationship constant. The closed chain symbol between the two boxes indicates that the values are linked together. If you break the link by clicking on the chain symbol, you will be able to set the values independently of each other.

16.6.15 Scale Image

The Scale Image command enlarges or reduces the physical size of the image by changing the number of pixels it contains. It changes the size of the contents of the image and resizes the canvas accordingly.

It operates on the entire image. If your image has layers of different sizes, making the image smaller could shrink some of them down to nothing, since a layer cannot be less than one pixel wide or high. If this happens, you will be warned before the operation is performed.

If you only want to scale a particular layer, use the Scale Layer command.

Note

If scaling would produce an image larger than the "Maximum new image size" set in the Environment page of the Preferences dialog (which has a default of 128 Mb), you are warned and asked to confirm the operation before it is performed. You may not experience any problems if you confirm the operation, but you should be aware that very large images consume a lot of resources and extremely large images may take more resources than you have, causing GIMP to crash or not perform well.

16.6.15.1 Activate the Command

- You can access this command from the image menubar through Image → Scale Image.

16.6.15.2 The "Scale Image" Dialog

Figure 16.68 The "Scale Image" dialog

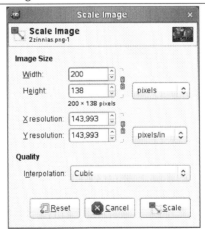

Image Size You should keep in mind that an image can be located in one of four places: in the image file, in RAM after it has been loaded, on your screen when it is displayed, or on paper after it has been printed. Scaling the image changes the number of pixels (the amount of information) the image contains, so it directly affects the amount of memory the image needs (in RAM or in a file).

However printing size also depends upon the resolution of the image, which essentially determines how many pixels there will be on each inch of paper. If you want to change the printing size without scaling the image and changing the number of pixels in it, you should use the Print Size dialog. The screen size depends not only on the number of pixels, but also on the screen resolution, the zoom factor and the setting of the Dot for Dot option.

If you enlarge an image beyond its original size, GIMP calculates the missing pixels by interpolation, but it does not add any new detail. The more you enlarge an image, the more blurred it becomes. The appearance of an enlarged image depends upon the interpolation method you choose. You may improve the appearance by using the Sharpen filter after you have scaled an image, but it is best to use high resolution when you scan, take digital photographs or produce digital images by other means. Raster images inherently do not scale up well.

You may need to reduce your image if you intend to use it on a web page. You have to consider that most internet users have relatively small screens which cannot completely display a large image. Many screens have a resolution of 1024x768 or even less.

Adding or removing pixels is called "Resampling".

Width; Height When you click on the Scale command, the dialog displays the dimensions of the original image in pixels. You can set the Width and the Height you want to give to your image by adding or removing pixels. If the chain icon next to the Width and Height boxes is unbroken, the Width and Height will stay in the same proportion to each other. If you break the chain by clicking on it, you can set them independently, but this will distort the image.

However, you do not have to set the dimensions in pixels. You can choose different units from the drop-down menu. If you choose percent as the units, you can set the image size relative to its original size. You can also use physical units, such as inches or millimeters. If you do that, you should set the X resolution and Y resolution fields to appropriate values, because they are used to convert between physical units and image dimensions in pixels.

X resolution; Y resolution You can set the printing resolution for the image in the X resolution and Y resolution fields. You can also change the units of measurement by using the drop-down menu.

Quality To change the image size, either some pixels have to be removed or new pixels must be added. The process you use determines the quality of the result. The Interpolation drop down list provides a selection of available methods of interpolating the color of pixels in a scaled image:

Interpolation

- None: No interpolation is used. Pixels are simply enlarged or removed, as they are when zooming. This method is low quality, but very fast.
- Linear: This method is relatively fast, but still provides fairly good results.
- Cubic: The method that produces the best results, but also the slowest method.
- Sinc (Lanczos 3): New with GIMP-2.4, this method gives less blur in important resizings.

Note

 See also the Scale tool, which lets you scale a layer, a selection or a path.

16.6.16 Crop to Selection

The Crop to Selection command crops the image to the boundary of the selection by removing any strips at the edges whose contents are all completely unselected. Areas which are partially selected (for example, by feathering) are not cropped. If the selection has been feathered, cropping is performed on the external limit of the feathered area. If there is no selection for the image, the menu entry is disabled and grayed out.

Note

 This command crops all of the image layers. To crop just the active layer, use the Crop Layer command.

16.6.16.1 Activate the command

- You can access this command on the image menu bar through Image → Crop to Selection.

16.6.17 Autocrop Image

The Autocrop Image command removes the borders from an image. It searches the active layer for the largest possible border area that is all the same color, and then crops this area from the image, as if you had used the Crop tool.

Caution

 Note carefully that this command only uses the *active layer* of the image to find borders. Other layers are cropped according to the same limits as limits in the active layer.

16.6.17.1 Activate the Command

- You can access this command from the image menubar through Image → Autocrop Image.

16.6.17.2 Example

Figure 16.69 "Autocrop" example

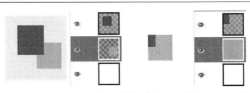

(a) *This image is made of three layers. One with a red square, another with a green square; both on a yellow semi-transparent background. Only green layer is active.*
(b) *"Autocrop" has cropped the green square and made a layer from it. The other layers have been cropped to the same size as the green one. Only a small part of the red square has been kept.*

16.6.18 Zealous Crop

The Zealous Crop command crops an image using a single solid color as a guide. It crops the edges, as with the Autocrop command, but it also crops the areas in the middle of the image which have the same color (at least, in principle).

Caution

 Please note that Zealous Crop crops all of the layers, although it only analyzes the active layer. This may lead to a loss of information from the other layers.

16.6.18.1 Example

Figure 16.70 "Zealous Crop" Example

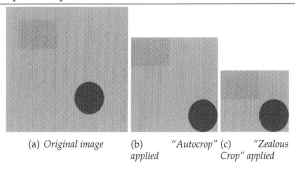

(a) *Original image*   (b)   *"Autocrop"* (c)   *"Zealous*
                       applied   *Crop" applied*

16.6.18.2 Activate the Command

- You can access this command from the image menu bar through Image → Zealous Crop.

16.6.19 Merge Visible Layers

The Merge Visible Layers command merges the layers which are visible into a single layer. Visible layers are those which are indicated on the Layers dialog with an "eye" icon.

Note

 With this command, the original visible layers disappear. With the New From Visible command, a new layer is created at top of the stack and original visible layers persist.

16.6.19.1 Activate the Command

- You can access this command from the image menubar through Image → Merge Visible Layers,

- or by using the keyboard shortcut Ctrl-M.

16.6.19.2   Description of the "Layers merge Options" Dialog

Figure 16.71 The "Layers Merge Options" Dialog

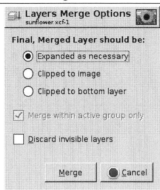

Final, Merged Layer should be: Visible layers are the layers which are marked with an "eye" icon in the Layers dialog.

- *Expanded as necessary*: The final layer is large enough to contain all of the merged layers. Please note that a layer in GIMP can be larger than the image.

- *Clipped to image*: The final layer is the same size as the image. Remember that layers in GIMP can be larger than the image itself. Any layers in the image that are larger than the image are clipped by this option.

- *Clipped to bottom layer*: The final layer is the same size as the bottom layer. If the bottom layer is smaller than some of the visible layers, the final layer is clipped and trimmed to the size and position of the bottom layer.

Merge within active group only This self-explanatory option is enabled when a layer group exists.

Discard invisible layers When this option is checked, non visible layers are removed from the layer stack.

Figure 16.72 "Merge visible layers" example

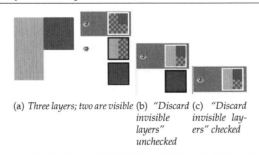

(a) *Three layers; two are visible* (b) *"Discard invisible layers" unchecked* (c) *"Discard invisible layers" checked*

16.6.20   Flatten Image

The Flatten Image command merges all of the layers of the image into a single layer with no alpha channel. After the image is flattened, it has the same appearance it had before. The difference is that all of the image contents are in a single layer without transparency. If there are any areas which are transparent through all of the layers of the original image, the background color is visible.

This operation makes significant changes to the structure of the image. It is normally only necessary when you would like to save an image in a format which does not support levels or transparency (an alpha channel).

16.6.20.1 Activate the Command

- You can access this command from the image menubar through Image → Flatten Image.

16.6.21 Align Visible Layers

With the Align Visible Layers command, you can very precisely position the visible layers (those marked with the "eye" icon). This degree of precision is especially useful when you are working on animations, which typically have many small layers. Clicking on Align Visible Layers displays a dialog which allows you to choose how the layers should be aligned.

Note

In GIMP 1.2, the default base for the alignment was the top visible layer in the stack. In GIMP 2, the default alignment base is the edge of the canvas. You can still align the image on the bottom layer of the stack, even if it is invisible, by checking Use the (invisible) bottom layer as the base in the dialog.

Figure 16.73 Example image for layer alignment

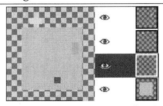

The example image contains four layers on a large (150x150 pixel) canvas. The red square is 10x10 pixels, the green rectangle is 10x20 pixels and the yellow rectangle is 20x10 pixels. The background layer (blue, 100x100 pixels) will not be affected by the command, since the Ignore lower layer option has been checked on the dialog. Note that the layers in the image seem to have a different order than their actual order in the stack because of their positions on the canvas. The yellow layer is the top layer in the image and the second one in the stack.

16.6.21.1 Activate the Command

- You can access this command from the image menubar through Image → Align Visible layers. There is no default keyboard shortcut. If the image holds a single layer only, you get a message from GIMP telling that there must be more than one layer in the image to execute the command.

Figure 16.74 The "Not enough layers" message

16.6.21.2   Description of the "Align Visible Layers" dialog

Figure 16.75 The "Align Visible Layers" dialog

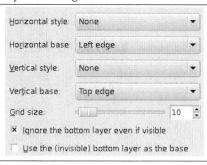

Horizontal Style; Vertical Style These options control how the layers should be moved in relationship to each other. You can choose:

- None: There will be no change in the horizontal or the vertical position, respectively.

- Collect: The visible layers will be aligned on the canvas, in the way that is determined by the Horizontal base and Vertical base options. If you select a Horizontal base of Right edge, layers may disappear from the canvas. You can recover them by enlarging the canvas. If you check the Use the (invisible) bottom layer as the base option, the layers will be aligned on the top left corner of the bottom layer.

Figure 16.76 Horizontal "Collect" alignment (on the edge of the canvas)

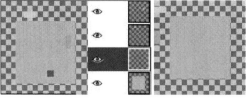

(a) *Original image with the layer stack* (b) *The layers have been moved horizontally so that their left edges are aligned with the left edge of the canvas.*

Figure 16.77 Horizontal "Collect" alignment (on the bottom layer)

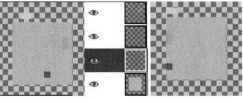

(a) *Original image with the layer stack* (b) *The layers have been moved horizontally so that their left edges align with the left edge of the bottom layer.*

• Fill (left to right); Fill (top to bottom): The visible layers will be aligned with the canvas according to the edge you selected with Horizontal base or Vertical base, respectively. The layers are arranged regularly, so that they do not overlap each other. The top layer in the stack is placed on the leftmost (or uppermost) position in the image. The bottom layer in the stack is placed on the rightmost (or bottommost) position of the image. The other layers are placed regularly between these two positions. If the Use the (invisible) bottom layer as the base option is checked, the layers are aligned with the corresponding edge of the bottom layer.

Figure 16.78 Horizontal "Fill" alignment (canvas)

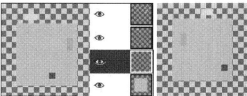

(a) *Original image with the layer stack* (b) *Horizontal filling alignment, Left to Right, with Use the (invisible) bottom layer as the base option not checked. The top layer in the stack, the green one, is placed all the way on the left. The bottom layer in the stack, the red one, is placed is on the right and the yellow layer is between the other two.*

Figure 16.79 Horizontal "Fill" alignment (bottom layer)

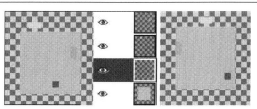

(a) *Original image with the layer stack* (b) *The same parameters as in the previous example, but with the lowest (blue) level as the base.*

• Fill (right to left); Fill (bottom to top): These settings work similarly to the ones described above, but the filling occurs in the opposite direction.

Figure 16.80 Vertical "Fill" alignment (bottom layer)

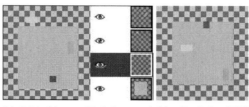

(a) *Original image with the layer stack* (b) *Vertical "Fill" alignment, bottom to top, bottom layer as base*

There must be at least three visible layers in the image to use the "Fill" options.

16.6.22   Guides

Figure 16.81 The "Guides" options of the "Image" submenu

> New Guide (by Percent)...
> New Guide...
> New Guides from Selection
> Remove all Guides

The Guides submenu contains various commands for the creation and removal of guides.

16.6.22.1   Activating the Submenu

- You can access this submenu from the image menubar through Image → Guides.

16.6.22.2   The Contents of the "Guides" Submenu

The Guides submenu contains the following commands:

- Section 16.6.23
- Section 16.6.24
- Section 16.6.25
- Section 16.6.26

16.6.23   New Guide

The New Guide command adds a guide to the image.

Tip

 You can add guides to the image more quickly, but less accurately, by simply clicking and dragging guides from the image rulers and positioning them where you would like.

16.6.23.1   Activate the Command

You can access this command from the image menubar through Image → Guides → New Guide

16.6.23.2 "New Guide" Options

When you select New Guide, a dialog opens, which allows you to set the Direction and Position, in pixels, of the new guide more precisely than by using click-and-drag.

Figure 16.82 The "New Guide" Dialog

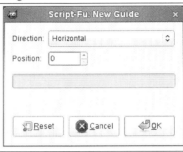

Direction You can choose the Direction of the guide, either Horizontal or Vertical, by using the drop-down list.

Position The coordinate origin for the Position is the upper left corner of the canvas.

16.6.24 New Guide (by Percent)

The New Guide (by Percent) command adds a guide to the image. The position of the guide is specified as a percentage of the canvas Height and Width.

> Tip
>
>
>
> You can add guides to the image more quickly by simply clicking and dragging guides from the image rulers and positioning them where you would like. Guides you draw with click-and-drag are not as precisely positioned as those you draw with this command, however.

16.6.24.1 Activate the Command

You can access this command from the image menubar through Image → Guides → New Guide (by Percent).

16.6.24.2 "New Guide (by Percent)" Options

When you select this menu item, a dialog opens, which allows you to set the Direction and Position, by percent, of the new guide.

Figure 16.83 The "New Guide (by Percent)" Dialog

Direction You can choose the Direction of the guide, either Horizontal or Vertical, by using the drop-down list.

Position You can also choose the Position of the new guide. The coordinate origin is in the upper left corner of the canvas.

16.6.25   New Guides from Selection

The New Guides from Selection command adds four guide lines, one for each of the upper, lower, left and right edges of the current selection. If there is no selection in the current image, no guides are drawn.

16.6.25.1   Activating the Command

You can access this command from the image menubar through Image → Guides → New Guides from Selection.

16.6.26   Remove all guides

The Remove all Guides command removes all guides from the image. Clicking-and-dragging one or two guides onto a ruler is a quicker way to remove them. This command is useful if you have positioned several guides.

16.6.26.1   Activate the Command

You can access this command from the image menubar through Image → Guides → Remove all guides.

16.6.27   Configure Grid

The Configure Grid command lets you set the properties of the grid which you can display over your image while you are working on it. The GIMP provides only Cartesian grids. You can choose the color of the grid lines, and the spacing and offsets from the origin of the image, independently for the horizontal and vertical grid lines. You can choose one of five different grid styles.

16.6.27.1   Activating the Command

- You can access this command from the image menubar through Image → Configure Grid.

16.6.27.2 Description of the "Configure Grid" dialog

Figure 16.84 The "Configure grid" dialog

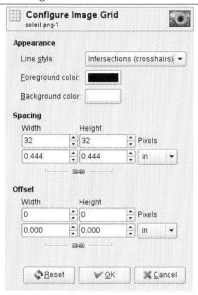

Appearance

In the Configure Image Grid dialog, you can set the properties of the grid which is shown when you turn on the image grid.

Line style

> **Intersections (dots)** This style, the least conspicuous, shows a simple dot at each intersection of the grid lines.
>
> **Intersections (crosshairs)** This style, the default, shows a plus-shaped crosshair at each intersection of the grid lines.
>
> **Dashed** This style shows dashed lines in the foreground color of the grid. If the lines are too close together, the grid won't look good.
>
> **Double dashed** This style shows dashed lines, where the foreground and background colors of the grid alternate.
>
> **Solid** This style shows solid grid lines in the foreground color of the grid.

Foreground and Background colors Click on the color dwell to select a new color for the grid.

> Spacing

Width and Height You can select the cell size of the grid and the unit of measurement.

> Offset

Width and Height You can set the offset of the first cell. The coordinate origin is the upper left corner of the image. By default, the grid begins at the coordinate origin, (0,0).

16.6.28 Image Properties

The "Image Properties" command opens a window that shows lots of different information for the image.

16.6.28.1 Activate the Command

- You can access this command from the image menubar through Image → Image Properties,

- or by using the keyboard shortcut Alt-Return.

16.6.28.2 Options

The properties window is divided into three tabs.

Figure 16.85 "Properties" tab

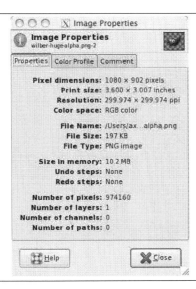

16.6.28.2.1 "Properties" tab

Pixel dimensions Shows the image height and width in pixels, that is, the *physical* size of the image.

Print size Shows the size the image will have when it is printed, in the current units. This is the *logical* size of the image. It depends upon the physical size of the image and the screen resolution.

Resolution Shows the print resolution of the image in pixel per inch.

Color space Shows the images color space.

File name Path and name of the file that contains the image.

File size Size of the file that contains the image.

File type Format of the file that contains the image.

Size in memory RAM consumption of the loaded image including the images journal. This information is also displayed in the image window. The size is quite different from the size of the file on disk. That is because the displayed image is decompressed and because GIMP keeps a copy of the image in memory for Redo operations.

Undo steps Number of actions you have performed on the image, that you can undo. You can see them in the Undo History dialog.

Redo steps Number of actions you have undone, that you can redo.

Number of pixels; Number of layers; Number of channels; Number of paths Well counted!

Figure 16.86 "Color profile" tab

16.6.28.2.2 **"Color profile" tab**   This tab contains the name of the color profile the image is loaded into GIMP with. Default is the built-in "sRGB" profile.

Figure 16.87 "Comments" tab

16.6.28.2.3 **"Comments" tab**   This tab allows you to view and edit a comment for the image.

16.7   The "Layer" Menu

16.7.1   Introduction to the "Layer" Menu

Figure 16.88 The Contents of the "Layer" Menu

The items on the Layer menu allow you to work on layers.

In addition to accessing the Layer menu from the Image menubar and by right-clicking on the image window, you can get to it by right-clicking on the thumbnail of a layer in the Layers dialog. You can also perform several of the operations on this menu by clicking on buttons in the Layers dialog, for example, resizing a layer, managing layer transparency and merging layers.

Figure 16.89 The Contents of the "Layer" local pop-menu

> Note
>
> Besides the commands described here, you may also find other entries in the menu. They are not part of GIMP itself, but have been added by extensions (plug-ins). You can find information about the functionality of a Plugin by referring to its documentation.

16.7.2 New Layer

The New Layer command adds a new, empty layer to the layer stack of the image, just above the active layer. The command displays a dialog in which you can specify the size of the new layer.

16.7.2.1 Activating the Command

- You can access this command from the image menubar through Layer → New Layer.

16.7.2.2 Description of the "New Layer" Dialog

Figure 16.90 The "New Layer" dialog

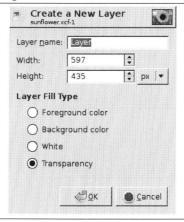

Under the title "Create a new layer" you can see the name of the image for that you create this new layer and next to the title a thumbnail of it. That is interesting to see if you have selected the good image when there is more than one image open.

Layer Name The name of the new layer. It does not have any functional significance; it is simply a convenient way for you to remember the purpose of the layer. The default name is "New Layer". If a layer with the name you choose already exists, a number is automatically appended to it to make it unique (e.g., "New Layer#1") when you click on the OK button.

Width; Height The dimensions of the new layer. When the dialog appears, the values are initialized to the dimensions of the image. You can change them by using the two text boxes. You can also change the units in the pull-down menu to the right.

Layer Fill Type There are four options for the solid color that fills the layer: the current Foreground color, the current Background color, White and Transparency.

16.7.3 New Layer Group

This command creates a new layer group directly. Please refer to Section 8.4.

16.7.3.1 Activating the Command

- You can access this command from an image menu through Layer → New Layer Group, or from the layer context menu you get by right clicking on the layer dialog.

16.7.4 New From Visible

This command merges the visible layers into a new layer at the top of the layer stack.

The aim is to further manipulate the result, but keep the steps that created this situation. Example: You want to selectively blur some areas of your multilayer image. You create a new layer from what you see, blur it and then apply a layer mask to erase the parts you want your original work to show.

16.7.4.1 Activating the Command

- You can access this command from the image menubar through Layer → New From Visible.

16.7.5 Duplicate layer

The Duplicate Layer command adds a new layer to the image which is a nearly identical copy of the active layer. The name of the new layer is the same as the name of the original layer, but with " copy" appended to it.

If you duplicate a background layer which does not have an alpha channel, the new layer is provided with one. In addition, if there are any "parasites" attached to the active layer, they are not duplicated. (If your understanding of the word "parasites" is limited to small, unpleasant creatures, please ignore the last sentence.)

16.7.5.1 Activate the Command

- You can access this command from the image menubar through Layer → Duplicate Layer, or from the local pop-up menu that you get by right-clicking on the Layer Dialog.

- In addition, at the Layer Dialog, you can access it through Duplicate of its context pop-up menu, or clicking on the icon button on the bottom of this dialog.

16.7.6 Anchor layer

If you have created a floating selection, a temporary layer, called a "floating layer" or "floating selection", is added to the layer stack. As long as the floating layer persists, you can work only on it. To work on the rest of the image, you must "anchor" the floating layer to the former active layer with the Anchor layer command. If the image does not contain a floating selection, this menu entry is insensitive and grayed out.

Note

If there is an active selection tool, the mouse pointer is displayed with an anchor icon when it is outside of the selection.

16.7.6.1 Activate the Command

- You can access this command from the image menubar through Layer → Anchor layer,

- or by using the keyboard shortcut Ctrl-H.

16.7.6.2 Alternative Ways of Anchoring a Floating Selection

There are more ways to anchor a floating selection:

- You can anchor the floating selection to the current layer the selection is originating by clicking anywhere on the image except on the floating selection.

- You can also anchor the floating selection to the current layer by clicking on the anchor button 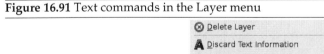 of the Layers dialog.

- If you create a New Layer while there is a floating selection, the floating selection is anchored to this newly created layer.

16.7.7 Merge Down

The Merge Down command merges the active layer with the layer just below it in the stack, taking into account the various properties of the active layer, such as its opacity and layer mode. The resulting merged layer will be in Normal mode, and will inherit the opacity of the layer below. If the layer below is not opaque, or if it is in some mode other than Normal, then this command will generally change the appearance of the image.

The most common use of Merge Down is to construct a layer, by starting with a "base layer" (usually opaque and in Normal mode, so that you can see what you are doing), and adding a "modification layer" on top of it, with whatever shape, opacity, and layer mode you need. In this case, merging down the modification layer will combine the two layers into one, without changing the way the image looks.

16.7.7.1 Activating the Command

- You can access this command from the image menubar through Layer → Merge Down.

16.7.8 Delete Layer

The Delete Layer command deletes the current layer from the image.

16.7.8.1 Activate the Command

- You can access this command from the image menubar through Layer → Delete Layer.

- In addition, at the Layer Dialog, you can access it through Delete Layer of its context pop-up menu, or clicking on the 🗑 icon button on the bottom of this dialog.

16.7.9 The Text Commands of the Layer Menu

These commands are displayed only if a text layer is present.

Figure 16.91 Text commands in the Layer menu

⊗ Delete Layer
A Discard Text Information
A Text to Path
A Text along Path
Stack ▶

16.7.9.1 The Text Commands

- Section 16.7.10

- [?para] [159]

- [?para] [159]

• In the Text to Selection drop-down list, the commands are identical to those of the Transparency sub-menu (in fact, the text is formed of areas of different transparency):

– **Text to Selection:** Section 16.7.38

– **Add to Selection:** Section 16.7.39

– **Subtract from Selection:** Section 16.7.40

– **Intersect with Selection:** Section 16.7.41

16.7.10   Discard Text Information

This command belongs to a group of Text commands displayed only if a text layer is present.

Figure 16.92 The Discard Text command among text commands in the Layer menu

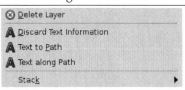

When you add text to an image, GIMP adds specific informations. This command lets you discard these informations, transforming the current text layer into a normal bitmap layer. The reason to do that is not evident.

Note that this transformation of text into bitmap is automatically performed when you apply a graphic operation to the text layer. You can get text information back by undoing the operation which modified the text.

16.7.10.1   Activating the Command

• You can access this command from the image menubar through Layer → Discard Text Information.

16.7.11   "Stack" Submenu

Figure 16.93 The "Stack" submenu

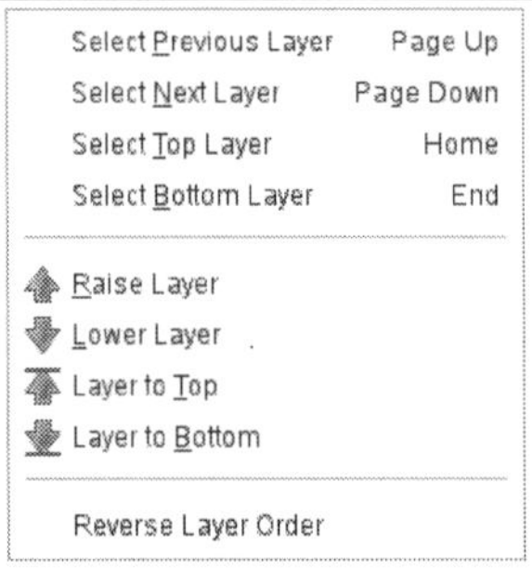

Select Previous Layer	Page Up
Select Next Layer	Page Down
Select Top Layer	Home
Select Bottom Layer	End
Raise Layer	
Lower Layer	
Layer to Top	
Layer to Bottom	
Reverse Layer Order	

The layer stack is simply the list of layers in the Layers dialog. The Stack submenu contains operations which either select a new layer as the active layer, or change the position of the active layer in the layer stack. If your image has only one layer, these commands are grayed out.

16.7.11.1   Activating the Submenu

• You can access this submenu from the image menubar through Layer → Stack.

16.7.11.2   The Contents of the "Stack" Submenu

The Stack submenu contains the following commands:

- Section 16.7.12

- Section 16.7.13

- Section 16.7.14

- Section 16.7.15

- Section 16.7.16

- Section 16.7.17

- Section 16.7.18

- Section 16.7.19

- Section 16.7.20

16.7.12   Select Previous Layer

The Select Previous Layer command selects the layer just above the active layer in the layer stack. The command highlights the layer in the Layers Dialog and makes it the new active layer. If the active layer is already at the top of the stack, this menu entry is insensitive and grayed out.

Note

 Note that on a standard Windows-style English keyboard, the default shortcut **Page_Up** does not refer to the key on the numeric keypad, but to the other **Page_Up** key in the group of six keys to the left of the numeric keypad.

Tip

 The keyboard shortcuts for Select Previous Layer and Select Next Layer may be very useful if you frequently pick colors from one layer to use for painting on another layer, especially when you use them with the color-picker tool, which you get by holding down the **Ctrl** key with most of the painting tools.

16.7.12.1   Activating the Command

- You can access this command from the image menubar through Layer → Stack → Select Previous Layer,

- or by using the keyboard shortcut **Up**.

Or you simply click on the layer name in the Layers Dialog.

16.7.13   Select Next Layer

The Select Next Layer command selects the layer just underneath the active layer in the layer stack. The command highlights the layer in the Layers Dialog and makes it the new active layer. If the active layer is already at the bottom of the stack, this menu entry is insensitive and grayed out.

> **Note**
>
> Note that on a standard Windows-style English keyboard, the default shortcut **Page_Down** does not refer to the key on the numeric keypad, but to the other **Page_Down** key in the group of six keys to the left of the numeric keypad.

16.7.13.1 Activating the Command

- You can access this command from the image menubar through Layer → Stack → Select Next Layer,

- or by using the keyboard shortcut **Down**.

Or you simply click on the layer name in the Layers Dialog.

16.7.14 Select Top Layer

The Select Top Layer command makes the top layer in the stack the active layer for the image and highlights it in the Layers dialog. If the active layer is already the top layer in the stack, this menu entry is insensitive and grayed out.

> **Note**
>
> Note that on a standard Windows-style English keyboard, the default keyboard shortcut **Home** does not refer to the key on the numeric keypad, but to the other **Home** key in the group of six keys to the left of the numeric keypad.

16.7.14.1 Activating the Command

- You can access this command from the image menubar through Layer → Stack → Select Top Layer,

- or by using the keyboard shortcut **Home**.

Or you simply click on the layer name in the Layers Dialog.

16.7.15 Select Bottom Layer

With the Select Bottom Layer command, you can make the bottom layer in the stack become the active layer for the image. It is then highlighted in the Layers dialog. If the bottom layer of the stack is already the active layer, this menu entry is insensitive and grayed out.

16.7.15.1 Activate the Command

- You can access this command from the image menubar through Layer → Stack → Select Bottom Layer,

- by using the keyboard shortcut **End**.

Or you simply click on the layer name in the Layers Dialog.

16.7.16   Raise Layer

The Raise Layer command raises the active layer one position in the layer stack. If the active layer is already at the top or if there is only one layer, this menu entry is insensitive and grayed out. If the active layer is at the bottom of the stack and it does not have an alpha channel, it cannot be raised until you add an alpha channel to it.

16.7.16.1   Activating the Command

- You can access this command from the image menubar through Layer → Stack → Raise Layer,

- or by clicking on the up-arrow icon at the bottom of the Layers dialog.

16.7.17   Lower Layer

The Lower layer command lowers the active layer one position in the layer stack. If the active layer is already at the bottom of the stack or if there is only one layer, this menu entry is insensitive and grayed out.

16.7.17.1   Activating the Command

- You can access this command from the image menubar through Layer → Stack → Lower Layer,

- or by clicking on the down-arrow icon at the bottom of the Layers dialog.

16.7.18   Layer to Top

The Layer to Top command raises the active layer to the top of the layer stack. If the active layer is already at the top or if there is only one layer, this menu entry is insensitive and grayed out. If the active layer is at the bottom of the stack and it does not have an alpha channel, you cannot raise it until you add an alpha channel to it.

16.7.18.1   Activating the Command

- You can access this command from the image menubar through Layer → Stack → Layer to Top,

- or by pressing the **Shift** key and clicking on the up-arrow icon at the bottom of the Layers dialog.

16.7.19   Layer to Bottom

The Layer to bottom command lowers the active layer to the bottom of the layer stack. If the active layer is already at the bottom of the stack or if there is only one layer, this menu entry is insensitive and grayed out.

16.7.19.1   Activating the Command

- You can access this command from the image menubar through Layer → Stack → Layer to Bottom,

- or by pressing the **Shift** key and clicking on the down-arrow icon at the bottom of the Layers dialog.

16.7.20   The "Reverse Layer Order" command

This command is self-explanatory.

16.7.20.1   Activating the command

- From the image Menu through: Layers → Stack → Reverse Layer Order.

16.7.21   The "Mask" Submenu

Figure 16.94 The "Mask" submenu of the "Layer" menu

The Mask submenu of the Layer menu contains commands which work with masks: creating a mask, applying a mask, deleting a mask or converting a mask into a selection. See the Layer Masks section for more information on layer masks and how to use them.

16.7.21.1   Activating the Submenu

- You can access this submenu from the image menubar through Layer → Mask

16.7.21.2   The Contents of the "Mask" Submenu

The Mask submenu contains the following commands:

- Section 16.7.22

- Section 16.7.23

- Section 16.7.24

- Section 16.7.25

- Section 16.7.26

- Section 16.7.27

- Section 16.7.28

- Section 16.7.29

- Section 16.7.30

- Section 16.7.31

16.7.22   Add Layer Mask

The Add Layer Mask command adds a layer mask to the active layer. It displays a dialog in which you can set the initial properties of the mask. If the layer already has a layer mask, the menu entry is insensitive and grayed out.

A layer mask lets you define which parts of the layer are opaque, semi-transparent or transparent. See the Layer Mask section for more information.

16.7.22.1   Activating the Command

- You can access this command from the image menubar through Layer → Mask → Add Layer Mask

- or from the pop-up menu you get by right-clicking on the active layer in the Layers Dialog.

16.7.22.2   Description of the "Add Layer Mask" Dialog

Figure 16.95 The "Add Layer Mask" dialog

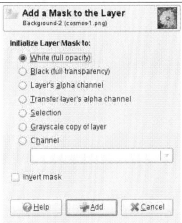

Initialize Layer Mask to   This dialog allows you several choices for the initial contents of the layer mask:

  White (full opacity)   With this option, the layer mask will make all of the layer fully opaque. That means that you will not notice any difference in the appearance of the layer until you paint on the layer mask.

  Black (full transparency)   With this option, the layer mask will make all of the layer fully transparent. This is represented in the image by a checkered pattern on which you will need to paint to make any part of the layer visible.

  Layer's alpha channel   With this option, the contents of the alpha channel are used to fill the layer mask. The alpha channel itself is not altered, so the transparency of partially visible areas is increased, leading to a more transparent layer.

  Transfer layer's alpha channel   This option sets the layer mask as the previous option, but resets the layer's alpha channel to full opacity afterwards. The effect is to transfer the transparency information from the alpha channel to the layer mask, leaving the layer with the same appearance as before. The visibility of the layer is now determined by the layer mask alone and not by the alpha channel. If in doubt, select this option instead of "Layer's alpha channel", because it will leave the appearance unaltered.

  Selection   This option converts the current selection into a layer mask, so that selected areas are opaque, and unselected areas are transparent. If any areas are partially selected, you can click on the QuickMask button to help you predict what the effects will be.

  Grayscale copy of layer   This option converts the layer itself into a layer mask. It is particularly useful when you plan to add new contents to the layer afterwards.

  Channel   With this option the layer mask is initialized with a selection mask you have created before, stored in the Channel dialog.

Invert Mask   If you check the Invert Mask box at the bottom of the dialog, the resulting mask is inverted, so that transparent areas become opaque and vice versa.

When you click on the OK button, a thumbnail of the layer mask appears to the right of the thumbnail of the layer in the Layers Dialog.

16.7.23   Apply Layer Mask

The Apply Layer Mask command merges the layer mask with the current layer. The transparency information in the layer mask is transferred to the alpha channel, that is created if it doesn't exist, and the layer mask is removed. If the active layer does not have a layer mask, the menu entry is insensitive and grayed out. See the Layer Masks section for more information.

16.7.23.1 Activating the Command

- You can access this command from the image menubar through Layer → Mask → Apply Layer Mask,

- or from the pop-up menu you get by right-clicking on the active layer in the Layers Dialog.

16.7.24 Delete Layer Mask

The Delete Layer Mask command deletes the active layer's layer mask, without modifying the active layer itself. If the active layer does not have a layer mask, the menu entry is insensitive and grayed out.

16.7.24.1 Activating the Command

- You can access this command from the image menubar through Layer → Mask → Delete Layer Mask,

- or from the pop-up menu you get by right-clicking on the active layer in the Layers Dialog.

16.7.25 Show Layer Mask

The Show Layer Mask command lets you see the layer mask better by turning the image invisible. When you click on the menu entry, a check is displayed next to it and the layer mask's thumbnail in the Layers Dialog is shown with a green border. The layer itself is not modified; you can turn it visible again later.

16.7.25.1 Activating the Command

- You can access this command from the image menubar through Layer → Mask → Show Layer Mask,

- or by holding down the **Alt** key (Ctrl-Alt on some systems) and single-clicking on the layer mask's thumbnail in the Layers Dialog.

- You can undo this action by unchecking the menu entry in the Layer → Mask submenu or by **Alt**-clicking (or Ctrl-Alt-clicking) again on the layer mask's thumbnail.

16.7.26 Edit Layer Mask

When you click on the Edit Layer Mask item on the Layer Mask submenu, a check is displayed next to it, the layer mask becomes the active component of the current layer and the layer mask is displayed in the Layers Dialog with a white border. When you uncheck it, the layer itself becomes the active component and it is displayed with a white border. You can also activate the component you want more simply by clicking on it in the Layers Dialog.

16.7.26.1 Activating the Command

- You can access this command from the image menubar through Layer → Mask → Edit Layer Mask.

- You can undo this action by unchecking the menu entry in the Layer → Mask menu or by clicking on the layer component in the Layers Dialog.

16.7.27 Disable Layer Mask

As soon as you create a layer mask, it acts on the image. The Disable Layer Mask command allows you to suspend this action. When you click on the menu entry, a check is displayed next to it and the border of the layer mask's thumbnail in the Layers Dialog turns red.

16.7.27.1 Activating the Command

- You can access this command from the image menubar through Layer → Mask → Disable Layer Mask,

- or by holding down the **Ctrl** key (Ctrl-Alt on some systems) and single-clicking on the layer mask's thumbnail in the Layers Dialog.

- You can undo this action by unchecking the menu entry in the Layer → Mask menu or by **Ctrl**-clicking (or Ctrl-Alt -clicking) again on the layer mask's thumbnail.

16.7.28 Mask to Selection

The Mask to Selection command converts the layer mask of the active layer into a selection, which replaces the selection that is already active in the image. White areas of the layer mask are selected, black areas are not selected, and gray areas are converted into feathered selections. The layer mask itself is not modified by this command.

16.7.28.1 Activating the Command

- You can access this command from the image menubar through Layer → Mask → Mask to Selection,

- or from the pop-up menu you get by right-clicking on the active layer in the Layers Dialog.

16.7.28.2 Illustration of "Layer Mask to Selection"

Figure 16.96 Illustration of "Layer Mask to Selection"

On the left, the original image with a selection. In the middle, the Layers Dialog with a layer mask created with the "Layer's alpha channel" option. On the right, the result after applying "Mask to Selection": the selection of the non-transparent pixels of the active layer replaces the initial selection.

16.7.29 Add Layer Mask to Selection

The Add to Selection command converts the layer mask of the active layer into a selection, which is added to the selection that is already active in the image. White areas of the layer mask are selected, black areas are not selected, and gray areas are converted into feathered selections. The layer mask itself is not modified by this command.

16.7.29.1 Activating the Command

- You can access this command from the image menubar through Layer → Mask → Add to Selection,

16.7.29.2 Illustration of Add Layer Mask to Selection

Figure 16.97 Illustration of Add Layer Mask to Selection

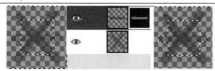

On the left, the original image with a selection. In the middle, the Layers Dialog with a layer mask created with the "Layer's alpha channel" option. On the right, the result after applying "Mask to Selection": the selection of the non-transparent pixels of the active layer is added to the initial selection.

16.7.30 Subtract Layer Mask from Selection

The Subtract from Selection command converts the layer mask of the active layer into a selection, which is subtracted from the selection that is already active in the image. White areas of the layer mask are selected, black areas are not selected, and gray areas are converted into feathered selections. The layer mask itself is not modified by this command.

16.7.30.1 Activating the Command

- You can access this command from the image menubar through Layer → Mask → Subtract from Selection,

16.7.30.2 Illustration of Subtract Layer Mask from Selection

Figure 16.98 Illustration of Subtract Layer Mask from Selection

On the left, the original image with a selection. In the middle, the Layers Dialog with a layer mask created with the "Layer's alpha channel" option. On the right, the result after applying "Mask to Selection": the selection of the non-transparent pixels of the active layer is subtracted from the initial selection.

16.7.31 Intersect Layer Mask with Selection

The Intersect with Selection command converts the layer mask of the active layer into a selection. The intersection of this selection and the selection that is already active form the new selection for the image. White areas of the layer mask are selected, black areas are not selected, and gray areas are converted into feathered selections. The layer mask itself is not modified by this command.

16.7.31.1 Activating the Command

- You can access this command from the image menubar through Layer → Mask → Intersect with Selection,

16.7.31.2 Illustration of Intersecting the Layer Mask with the Selection

Figure 16.99 Illustration of Intersecting the Layer Mask with the Selection

On the left, the original image with a selection. In the middle, the Layers Dialog with a layer mask created with the "Layer's alpha channel" option. On the right, the result after applying "Intersect Mask with Selection": the selection of the non-transparent pixels of the active layer is the common part between the initial selection and the mask.

16.7.32   The "Transparency" Submenu of the "Layer" menu

Figure 16.100 The "Transparency" submenu of the "Layer" menu

The Transparency submenu contains commands which use or affect the alpha channel of the active layer.

16.7.32.1   Activating the Submenu

- You can access this submenu from the image menu bar through Layer → Transparency.

16.7.32.2   The Contents of the "Transparency" Submenu

The Transparency submenu contains the following commands:

- Section 16.7.33
- Section 16.7.34
- Section 16.7.35
- Section 16.7.36
- Section 16.7.37
- Section 16.7.38
- Section 16.7.39
- Section 16.7.40
- Section 16.7.41

16.7.33   Add Alpha Channel

Add Alpha Channel: An alpha channel is automatically added into the Channel Dialog as soon as you add a second layer to your image. It represents the transparency of the image. If your image has only one layer, this background layer has no Alpha channel. In this case, you can Add an Alpha channel with this command.

16.7.33.1   Activate the Command

- You can access this command from the image menubar through Layer → Transparency → Add alpha Channel.

- In addition, at the Layer Dialog, you can access it through Add Alpha Channel of its context pop-up menu.

16.7.34   Remove Alpha Channel

This command removes the Alpha channel of the active layer, keeping the Apha channels of the other layers.

If the active layer is the background layer and if you have not added an Alpha channel before (then the layer name is in bold letters in the Layer Dialog), the command is grayed out, inactive.

If the active layer is not the background layer, transparency is replaced with the background color of the Toolbox.

16.7.34.1   Activate the Command

- You can access this command from the image menubar through Layer → Transparency → Remove Alpha Channel.

- In addition, at the Layer Dialog, you can access it through Remove Alpha Channel of its context pop-up menu.

16.7.35   Color to Alpha

This command is the same as Layer → Transparency: Section 16.8.34.

16.7.36   Semi-flatten

The Semi-Flatten command is described in the Semi-flatten filter chapter. The command is useful when you need an anti-aliased image with indexed colors and transparency.

16.7.36.1   Activate the Command

- You can access this command from the image menubar through Layer → Transparency → Semi-flatten.

16.7.37   Threshold Alpha

The Threshold Alpha command converts semi-transparent areas of the active layer into completely transparent or completely opaque areas, based on a threshold you set, between 0 and 255. It only works on layers of RGB images which have an alpha channel. If the image is Grayscale or Indexed, or if the layer does not have an alpha channel, the menu entry is insensitive and grayed out. If the Keep transparency option is checked in the Layers dialog, the command displays an error message.

16.7.37.1   Activating the Command

- You can access this command from the image menubar through Layer → Transparency → Threshold Alpha.

16.7.37.2   Description of the Dialog Window

Figure 16.101 The only one option of the "Threshold Alpha" dialog

Threshold You can set the transparency value to be used as a threshold by using the slider or by entering a value between 0 and 255 in the input box. All transparency values above this threshold will become opaque and all transparency values below or equal to this threshold will become completely transparent. The transition is abrupt.

> **Note**
>
> This command will never make completely transparent pixels (alpha value = 0) opaque.

Figure 16.102 Threshold Alpha example

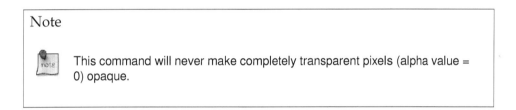

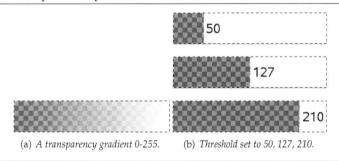

(a) *A transparency gradient 0-255.*   (b) *Threshold set to 50, 127, 210.*

16.7.38   Alpha to Selection

The Alpha to Selection command creates a selection in the current layer from the alpha channel, which encodes transparency. Opaque areas are fully selected, transparent areas are unselected, and translucent areas are partially selected. This selection *replaces* the existing selection. The alpha channel itself is not changed.

   The other commands in this group of operations are similar, except that instead of completely replacing the existing selection with the selection produced from the alpha channel, they either add the two selections, subtract the alpha selection from the existing selection, or create a selection that is the intersection of the two.

16.7.38.1 Activate the Command

- You can access this command from the image menubar through Layer → Transparency → Alpha to Selection

- or from the pop-up menu which appears when you right-click on the active layer in the Layer Dialog.

16.7.38.2 Example

Figure 16.103 Applying "Alpha to Selection"

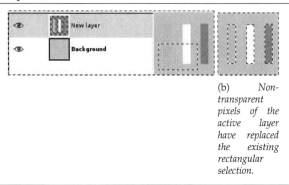

(b)   Non-transparent pixels of the active layer have replaced the existing rectangular selection.

16.7.39   Add Alpha channel to Selection

The Add to Selection command creates a selection in the current layer from the Alpha Channel. Opaque pixels are fully selected, transparent pixels are unselected, and translucent pixels are partially selected. This selection is *added* to the existing selection. The alpha channel itself is not changed.

The other commands in this group of operations are similar, except that instead of adding to the existing selection with the selection produced from the active layer, they either completely replace the selection with a selection produced from the alpha selection, subtract the alpha selection from the existing selection, or create a selection that is the intersection of the two.

16.7.39.1 Activate the Command

- You can access this command from the image menubar through Layer → Transparency → Add to Selection.

16.7.39.2 Example

Figure 16.104 Applying "Add to Selection"

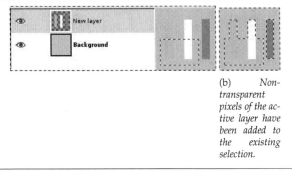

(b)   Non-transparent pixels of the active layer have been added to the existing selection.

16.7.40   Subtract from Selection

The Subtract from Selection command creates a selection in the current layer from the Alpha Channel. Opaque pixels are fully selected, transparent pixels are unselected, and translucent pixels are partially selected.This selection is *subtracted* from the existing selection. The Alpha channel itself is not changed.

16.7.40.1   Activate the Command

- You can access this command from the image menubar through Layer → Transparency → Subtract from Selection.

16.7.40.2   Example

Figure 16.105 Applying "Subtract from Selection"

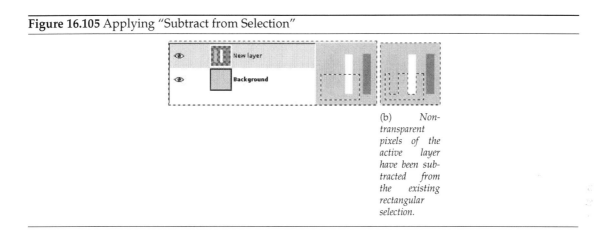

(b)   Non-transparent pixels of the active   layer have been subtracted   from the   existing rectangular selection.

16.7.41   Intersect Alpha channel with Selection

The Intersect with Selection command creates a selection in the current layer from the Alpha Channel. Opaque pixels are fully selected, transparent pixels are unselected, and translucent pixels are partially selected. This selection is *intersected* with the existing selection: only common parts of both selections are kept. The alpha channel itself is not changed.

16.7.41.1   Activate the Command

- You can access this command from the image menubar through Layer → Transparency → Intersect with Selection,

- or from the pop-up menu which appears when you right-click on the active layer in the Layers Dialog.

16.7.41.2 Example

Figure 16.106 Applying "Intersect with Selection"

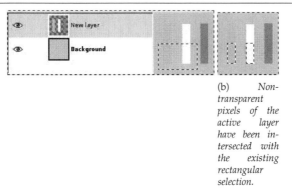

(b) Non-transparent pixels of the active layer have been intersected with the existing rectangular selection.

16.7.42 The "Transform" Submenu

Figure 16.107 The "Transform" Submenu of the "Layer" menu

The Transform submenu of the Layer menu contains commands which flip or rotate the active layer of the image.

16.7.42.1 Activating the Submenu

- You can access this submenu from the image menubar through Layer → Transform.

16.7.42.2 The Contents of the "Transform" Submenu

The Transform submenu contains the following commands:

- Section 16.7.43
- Section 16.7.44
- Section 16.7.45
- Section 16.7.46
- Section 16.7.47
- Section 16.7.48
- Section 16.7.49

16.7.43 Flip Horizontally

The Flip Horizontally command reverses the active layer horizontally, that is, from left to right. It leaves the dimensions of the layer and the pixel information unchanged.

16.7.43.1 Activating the Command

- You can access this command from the image menubar through Layer → Transform → Flip Horizontally.

16.7.43.2 Example

Figure 16.108 Applying "Flip Layer Horizontally"

(a) *Before applying the command* (b) *The layer after it has been flipped. It looks as if the image has been reflected along the central* vertical *axis of the layer.*

16.7.44 Flip Vertically

The Flip Vertically command reverses the active layer vertically, that is, from top to bottom. It leaves the dimensions of the layer and the pixel information unchanged.

16.7.44.1 Activating the Command

- You can access this command from the image menubar through Layer → Transform → Flip Vertically.

16.7.44.2 Example

Figure 16.109 Applying "Flip Layer Vertically"

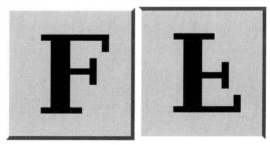

(a) *Before applying the command* (b) *The layer after it has been flipped. It looks as if the image has been reflected along the central* horizontal *axis of the layer.*

16.7.45 Rotate 90° clockwise

The Rotate 90° clockwise command rotates the active layer by 90° around the center of the layer, with no loss of pixel data. The shape of the layer is not altered, but the rotation may cause the layer to extend beyond the bounds of the image. This is allowed in GIMP and it does not mean that the layer is cropped. However, you will not be able to see the parts which extend beyond the boundary of the image unless you resize the image canvas or move the layer.

16.7.45.1   Activating the Command

- You can access this command from the image menubar through Layer → Transform → Rotate 90° clockwise.

16.7.45.2   Example

Figure 16.110 Applying "Rotate 90° clockwise"

(a) *Before applying the command* (b) *The layer after it has been rotated*

16.7.46   Rotate 90° counter-clockwise

The Rotate 90° counter-clockwise command rotates the active layer by 90° counter-clockwise around the center of the layer, with no loss of pixel data. The shape of the layer is not altered, but the rotation may cause the layer to extend beyond the bounds of the image. This is allowed in GIMP and it does not mean that the layer is cropped. However, you will not be able to see the parts which extend beyond the boundary of the image unless you resize the image canvas or move the layer.

16.7.46.1   Activating the Command

- You can access this command from the image menubar through Layer → Transform → Rotate 90° counter-clockwise.

16.7.46.2   Example

Figure 16.111 Applying "Rotate 90° counter-clockwise"

(a) *Before applying the command* (b) *The layer after it has been rotated*

16.7.47   Rotate 180°

The Rotate 180° command rotates the active layer by 180° around the center of the layer, with no loss of pixel data. The shape of the layer is not altered. Since the layers have a rectangular shape, a 180° rotation only invert them and they can't extend beyond the image limits.

16.7.47.1   Activating the Command

- You can access this command from the image menubar through Layer → Transform → Rotate 180°.

16.7.47.2   Example

Figure 16.112 Applying "Rotate 180°"

(a) *Before applying the command* (b) *The layer after it has been rotated. It is turned upside down.*

16.7.48   Arbitrary Rotation

The Arbitrary Rotation command rotates a layer by a specified angle. It is an alternate way of accessing the Rotate tool. See the section about that tool for more information.

16.7.48.1   Activating the Command

- You can access this command from the image menubar through Layer → Transform → Arbitrary Rotation,

- or by using the keyboard shortcut Shift-R.

16.7.48.2   Example

Figure 16.113 Applying "Rotate Arbitrary"

(a) *Before applying the command* (b) *The layer after it has been rotated 30° clockwise*

16.7.49   Offset

The Offset command shifts the *content* of the active layer. Anything shifted outside the layer boundary is cropped. This command displays a dialog which allows you to specify how much to shift the layer and how to fill the space that is left empty by shifting it.

16.7.49.1   Activating the Command

- You can access this command from the image menubar through Layer → Transform → Offset,

- or by using the keyboard shortcut Shift-Ctrl-O.

16.7.49.2   Using the "Offset" Command

Figure 16.114 The "Offset" dialog

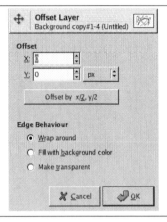

Offset

> **X; Y** With these two values, you specify how far the contents of the layer should be shifted in the horizontal (X) and vertical (Y) directions. You can enter the offsets in the text boxes. Positive values move the layer to the right and downward. The default unit is pixels, but you can choose a different unit of measurement with the drop-down menu. A unit of "%" is sometimes useful.

> **Offset by x/2, y/2** With this button, you can automatically set the X and Y offsets so that the contents are shifted by exactly half the width and half the height of the image.

Edge Behavior You can specify one of three ways to treat the areas left empty when the contents of the layer are shifted:

- *Wrap around*: The empty space on one side of the layer is filled with the part of the layer which is shifted out of the other side, so none of the content is lost.

- *Fill with background color*: The empty space is filled with the background color, which is shown in the Color Area of the Toolbox.

- *Make transparent*: The empty space is made transparent. If the layer does not have an alpha channel, this choice is not available (grayed out).

16.7.49.3   Example

Figure 16.115 Using "Offset" together with "Edge Behaviors"

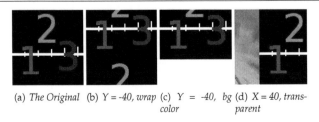

(a) *The Original* (b) *Y = -40, wrap* (c) *Y = -40, bg* (d) *X = 40, trans-*
color   *parent*

16.7.50   Layer Boundary Size

In GIMP, a layer is not always the same size as the image it belongs to. It might be smaller or it might be larger, in which case some parts of it are hidden. The Layer Boundary Size command displays a dialog in which you can set the dimensions for the active layer. This command changes the dimensions of the layer, but it does not scale its contents.

16.7.50.1   Activating the Command

- You can access this command from the image menubar through Layer → Layer Boundary Size.

16.7.50.2   Description of the "Layer Boundary Size" dialog

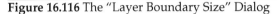

Figure 16.116 The "Layer Boundary Size" Dialog

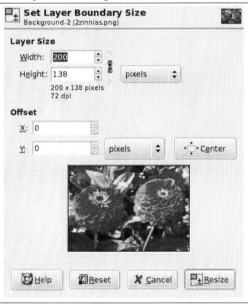

Layer Size

    Width; Height When the dialog is displayed, the original dimensions of the active layer are shown. You can change them by using the two text boxes. If these boxes are linked together with a chain, the width-to-height ratio is automatically maintained. If you break the chain by clicking on it, you can set the dimensions independently of each other.

    The default unit of measurement is pixels. You can change this by using the drop-down menu. For instance, you might use a "%" of the current size.

    X Offset; Y Offset By default, the resized layer is placed in the upper left corner of the image. Here, you can set the offset of the upper left corner of the layer relative to the same corner of the image. The default unit of measurement is pixels, but you can change it by using the drop-down menu. You can also place the layer in the center of the image by clicking on the Center button.

16.7.51   Layer to Image Size

The Layer to Image Size command resizes the layer boundaries to match the image boundaries, without moving the contents of the layer with respect to the image.

16.7.51.1   Activating the Command

- You can access this command from the image menubar through Layer → Layer to Image Size.

16.7.52   Scale Layer

The Scale Layer command resizes the layer and its contents. The image loses some of its quality by being scaled. The command displays a dialog where you can set parameters concerning the size of the layer and the image quality.

16.7.52.1   Activating the Command

• You can access this command from the image menubar through Layer → Scale Layer.

16.7.52.2   Description of the "Scale Layer" Dialog

Figure 16.117 The "Scale Layer" dialog

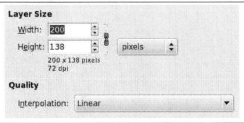

Layer Size   When you enlarge a layer, GIMP has to calculate new pixels from the existing ones. This procedure is called "interpolation". Please note that no matter which interpolation algorithm is used, no new information is added to the image by interpolation. If there are places in the layer which have no details, you will not get any new ones by scaling it. It is much more likely that the layer will look somewhat blurred after scaling. Similarly, when you reduce a layer, the image loses some of its quality when pixels are removed.

    Width; Height   The command displays a dialog which shows the dimensions of the original layer in pixels. You can set the new Width and Height for the layer in the two text boxes. If the adjacent chain icon is unbroken, the width and height are automatically adjusted to hold their ratio constant. If you break the chain by clicking on it, you can set them separately, but this will result in distorting the layer.

    However, you do not have to set the dimensions in pixels. You can choose different units from the drop-down menu. If you choose percent as units, you can set the layer size relative to its original size. You can also use physical units, like inches or millimeters. However if you do that, you should pay attention to the X/Y resolution of the image.

    If you enlarge a layer, the missing pixels are calculated by interpolation, but no new details are added. The more the layer is enlarged, and the more times it is enlarged, the more blurred it becomes. The exact result of the enlargement depends upon the interpolation method you choose. After scaling, you can improve the result by using the Sharpen filter, but it is much better for you to use a high resolution when scanning, taking digital photographs or producing digital images by other means. It is an inherent characteristic of raster images that they do not scale up well.

Quality   To change the size of the layer, GIMP either has to add or remove pixels. The method it uses to do this has a considerable impact on the quality of the result. You can choose the method of interpolating the colors of the pixels from the Interpolation drop-down menu.

    Interpolation

        None   No interpolation is used. Pixels are simply enlarged or removed, as they are when zooming. This method is low in quality, but very fast.

        Linear   This method is a good compromise between speed and quality.

        Cubic   This method takes a lot of time, but it produces the best results.

        Sinc (Lanczos3)   The Lanczos (pronounce "lanzosh") method uses the Sinc[3] mathematical function to perform a high quality interpolation.

---

[3] Sinus cardinalis

16.7.53 Crop to Selection

The Crop to Selection command crops only the active layer to the boundary of the selection by removing any strips at the edge whose contents are all completely unselected. Areas which are partially selected (for example, by feathering) are not cropped. If there is no selection for the image, the menu entry is insensitive and grayed out.

16.7.53.1 Activating the Command

- You can access this command from the image menubar through Layer → Crop to Selection.

16.7.53.2 Example

Figure 16.118 Applying "Crop to Selection"

On the left: before applying the command, the layer has a selection that has feathered edges.
On the right: after applying the command, the non-transparent pixels are not cropped, even if they are only
semi-transparent.

16.7.54 Autocrop Layer

The Autocrop Layer command automatically crops the active layer, unlike the Crop Tool, or the Crop Layer command which let you manually define the area to be cropped.

This command removes the largest possible area around the outside edge which all has the same color. It does this by scanning the layer along a horizontal line and a vertical line and cropping the layer as soon as it encounters a different color, whatever its transparency.

You can use this command to crop the layer to the dimensions of a subject that is lost in a solid background which is too large.

16.7.54.1 Activating the Command

- You can access this command from the image menubar through Layer → Autocrop Layer.

16.7.54.2 Example

Figure 16.119 Example

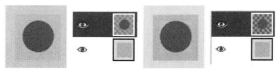

(a) *Before applying "Autocrop Layer"*   (b) *After applying "Autocrop Layer": the active layer, up, has been cropped to the size of the circle it contains. Its size is reduced, and the unoccupied part in the canvas is transparent, revealing the yellow and green colors of the underlying layer.*

16.8   The "Colors" Menu

16.8.1   Introduction to the "Colors" Menu

Figure 16.120 Contents of the "Colors" Menu

This section describes the Colors menu, which contains commands that affect the color of the image.

Note

Besides the commands described here, you may also find other entries in the menu. They are not part of GIMP itself, but have been added by extensions (plug-ins). You can find information about the functionality of a Plugin by referring to its documentation.

16.8.2   Colors Tools

All of the Colors tools are extensively described in the toolbox chapter, Section 14.5:

- Section 14.5.2
- Section 14.5.3
- Section 14.5.4
- Section 14.5.5
- Section 14.5.6
- Section 14.5.7
- Section 14.5.8
- Section 14.5.9
- Section 14.5.10

16.8.3 Invert

The Invert command inverts all the pixel colors and brightness values in the current layer, as if the image were converted into a negative. Dark areas become bright and bright areas become dark. Hues are replaced by their complementary colors. For more information about colors, see the Glossary entry about Color Model.

Note

 This command only works on layers of RGB and Grayscale images. If the current image is Indexed, the menu entry is insensitive and grayed out.

Warning

 Do not confuse this command with the Invert Selection command.

16.8.3.1 Activate the Command

You can access this command from the image menubar through Colors → Invert.

16.8.3.2 Example

Figure 16.121 Applying "Invert colors"

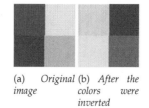

(a)   Original (b) After   the
image   colors   were
                inverted

16.8.4   Value Invert

16.8.4.1   Overview

Figure 16.122 Example for the "Value invert" filter

(a) *Original image*   (b) *"Value Invert" applied*

This filter inverts Value (luminosity) of the active layer or selection. Hue and Saturation will not be affected, although the color will sometimes be slightly different because of round-off error. If you want to invert Hue and Saturation also, use Colors → Invert.

Note that hue and saturation can be distorted quite a bit when applying twice this filter for colors with a high luminosity (for instance, HSV 102°,100%, 98%, a bright green, gives HSV 96°, 100%, 2% after a first application of the filter , and 96°, 100%, 98% after a second application). Thus, you should not expect to be able to apply this filter twice in a row and get back the image you started with.

Figure 16.123 Example of using this filter twice

(a) *Original image*   (b) *First application of* (c) *Second application:*
                         the filter   *the image is not exactly*
                                                       the same as the original
                                                       one.

16.8.4.2   Activate the filter

You can access this command from the image menu bar through Colors → Value Invert.

16.8.5   Use GEGL

GEGL (Generic Graphics Library) is a graph based image processing framework that will be used in all GIMP-3.0. With GEGL, the internal processing is being done in 32bit floating point linear light RGBA. By default the legacy 8bit code paths are still used, but a curious user can turn on the use of GEGL for the color operations with this option.

In addition to porting color operations to GEGL, an experimental GEGL Operation tool has been added, found in the Tools menu. It enables applying GEGL operations to an image and it gives on-canvas previews of the results.

> **Warning**
>
> Please note that GIMP remains 8-bits until GEGL covers the whole application.

16.8.5.1 Activating the option

You can access this option from the image menubar through Colors → Use GEGL. Clicking on this item toggles the use of GEGL.

16.8.6 The "Auto" Submenu

Figure 16.124 The "Colors/Auto" submenu

The Auto submenu contains operations which automatically adjust the distribution of colors in the active layer, without requiring any input from the user. Several of these operations are actually implemented as plugins.

16.8.6.1 Activate submenu

• You can access this submenu from the image window through Colors → Auto.

16.8.6.2 Automatic Color-Stretching

GIMP has several automatic commands for stretching the columns of the histogram for the color channels of the active layer. By pushing bright pixels to the right and dark pixels to the left, they make bright pixels brighter and dark pixels darker, which enhances the contrast in the layer.

Some of the commands stretch the three color channels equally, so that the hues are not changed. Other commands stretch each of the color channels separately, which changes the hues.

The way the stretching is done varies with the different commands and the results look different. It is not easy to predict exactly what each command will do. If you know exactly what you are doing, you can get the same results, and even more, with the Levels tool.

Here are examples of the results of these commands, all together on one page, so you can compare them more easily. The most appropriate command depends upon your image, so you should try each of them to see which command works best on it.

Figure 16.125 The original layer and its histograms

This layer doesn't have any very bright or very dark pixels, so it works well with these commands.

Figure 16.126 The Equalize command

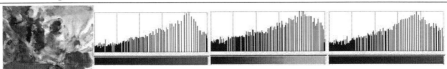

"Equalize" example

Figure 16.127 The White Balance command

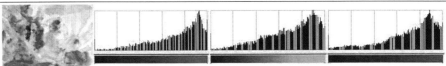

"White Balance" example

Figure 16.128 The Color Enhance command

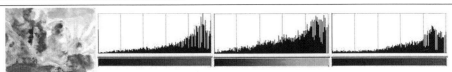

"Color Enhance" example

Figure 16.129 The Normalize command

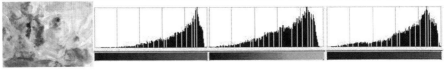

"Normalize" example

Figure 16.130 The Stretch Contrast command

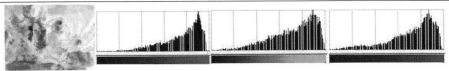

"Stretch Contrast" example

Figure 16.131 The Stretch HSV command

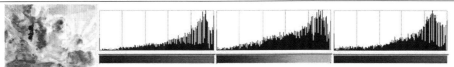

"Stretch HSV" example

16.8.7 Equalize

The Equalize command automatically adjusts the brightness of colors across the active layer so that the histogram for the Value channel is as nearly flat as possible, that is, so that each possible brightness value appears at about the same number of pixels as every other value. You can see this in the histograms in the example below, in that pixel colors which occur frequently in the image are stretched further apart than pixel colors which occur only rarely. The results of this command can vary quite a bit. Sometimes "Equalize" works very well to enhance the contrast in an image, bringing out details which were hard to see before. Other times, the results look very bad. It is a very powerful operation and it is worth trying to see if it will improve your image. It works on layers from RGB and Grayscale images. If the image is Indexed, the menu entry is insensitive and grayed out.

16.8.7.1 Activate the Command

- You can access this command from the image menubar through Colors → Auto → Equalize

- or by using the keyboard shortcut Shift-Page_Down.

16.8.7.2 "Equalize" example

Figure 16.132 Original image

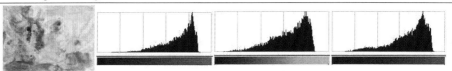

The active layer and its Red, Green, Blue histograms before "Equalize".

Figure 16.133 Image after the command

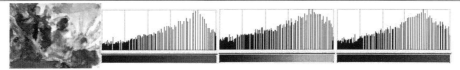

The active layer and its Red, Green, Blue histograms after treatment.
Histogram stretching creates gaps between pixel columns giving it a striped look.

16.8.8 White Balance

The White Balance command automatically adjusts the colors of the active layer by stretching the Red, Green and Blue channels separately. To do this, it discards pixel colors at each end of the Red, Green and Blue histograms which are used by only 0.05% of the pixels in the image and stretches the remaining range as much as possible. The result is that pixel colors which occur very infrequently at the outer edges of the histograms (perhaps bits of dust, etc.) do not negatively influence the minimum and maximum values used for stretching the histograms, in comparison with Stretch Contrast. Like "Stretch Contrast", however, there may be hue shifts in the resulting image.

This command suits images with poor white or black. Since it tends to create pure white (and black), it may be useful e.g. to enhance photographs.

White Balance operates on layers from RGB images. If the image is Indexed or Grayscale, the menu item is insensitive and grayed out.

16.8.8.1 Activate the Command

- You can access this command from the image menubar through Colors → Auto → White Balance.

16.8.8.2 "White Balance" example

Figure 16.134 Original image

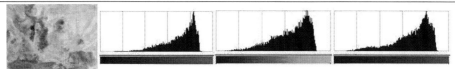

The active layer and its Red, Green and Blue histograms before "White Balance".

Figure 16.135 Image after the command

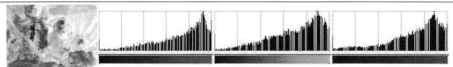

The active layer and its Red, Green and Blue histograms after "White Balance". Poor white areas in the image became pure white.
Histogram stretching creates gaps between the pixel columns, giving it a striped look.

16.8.9 Color Enhance

The Color Enhance command increases the saturation range of the colors in the layer, without altering brightness or hue. It does this by converting the colors to HSV space, measuring the range of saturation values across the image, then stretching this range to be as large as possible, and finally converting the colors back to RGB. It is similar to Stretch Contrast, except that it works in the HSV color space, so it preserves the hue. It works on layers from RGB and Indexed images. If the image is Grayscale, the menu entry is insensitive and grayed out.

16.8.9.1 Activate the command

- You can access this command from the image menubar through Colors → Auto → Color Enhance.

16.8.9.2 "Color Enhance" example

Figure 16.136 "Color Enhance" example (Original image)

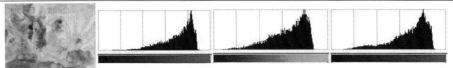

The active layer and its Red, Green and Blue histograms before "Color Enhance".

Figure 16.137 "Color Enhance" example (Image after the command)

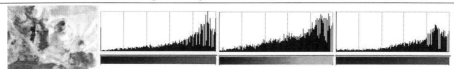

The active layer and its Red, Green and Blue histograms after "Color Enhance". The result may not always be what you expect.

16.8.10 Normalize

The Normalize command scales the brightness values of the active layer so that the darkest point becomes black and the brightest point becomes as bright as possible, without altering its hue. This is often a "magic fix" for images that are dim or washed out. "Normalize" works on layers from RGB, Grayscale, and Indexed images.

16.8.10.1 Activate the Command

- You can access this command from the image menu bar through Colors → Auto → Normalize.

16.8.10.2 "Normalize" Example

Figure 16.138 Original image

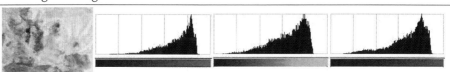

The active layer and its Red, Green and Blue histograms before "Normalize".

Figure 16.139 Image after the command

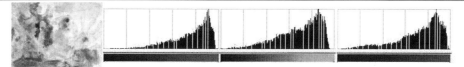

The active layer and its Red, Green and Blue histograms after "Normalize". The contrast is enhanced. Histogram stretching creates gaps between the pixel columns, giving it a striped look.

16.8.11 Stretch Contrast

The Stretch Contrast command automatically stretches the histogram values in the active layer. For each channel of the active layer, it finds the minimum and maximum values and uses them to stretch the Red, Green and Blue histograms to the full contrast range. The bright colors become brighter and the dark colors become darker, which increases the contrast. This command produces a somewhat similar effect to the Normalize command, except that it works on each color channel of the layer individually. This usually leads to color shifts in the image, so it may not produce the desired result. "Stretch Contrast" works on layers of RGB, Grayscale and Indexed images. Use "Stretch Contrast" only if you want to remove an undesirable color tint from an image which should contain pure white and pure black.

This command is also similar to the Color Balance command, but it does not reject any of the very dark or very bright pixels, so the white might be impure.

16.8.11.1 Activate the Command

- This command can be accessed from an image menubar as Colors → Auto → Stretch Contrast.

16.8.11.2   "Stretch Contrast" Example

Figure 16.140 Original image

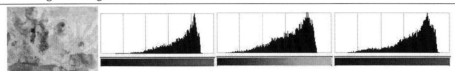

The layer and its Red, Green and Blue histograms before "Stretch Contrast".

Figure 16.141 Image after the command

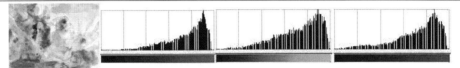

The layer and its Red and Green and Blue histograms after "Stretch Contrast". The pixel columns do not reach the right end of the histogram (255) because of a few very bright pixels, unlike "White Balance". Histogram stretching creates gaps between the pixel columns, giving it a stripped look.

16.8.12   Stretch HSV

The Stretch HSV command does the same thing as the Stretch Contrast command, except that it works in HSV color space, rather than RGB color space, and it preserves the Hue. Thus, it independently stretches the ranges of the Hue, Saturation and Value components of the colors. Occasionally the results are good, often they are a bit odd. "Stretch HSV" operates on layers from RGB and Indexed images. If the image is Grayscale, the menu entry is insensitive and grayed out.

16.8.12.1   Activate the Command

- You can access this command from the image menubar through Colors → Auto → Stretch HSV.

16.8.12.2   "Stretch HSV" example

Figure 16.142 Original image

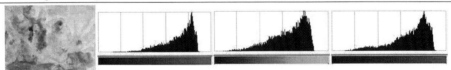

The active layer and its Red, Green and Blue histograms before "Stretch HSV".

Figure 16.143 Image after the command

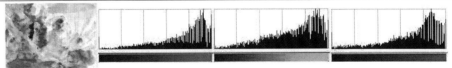

The active layer and its Red, Green and Blue histograms after "Stretch HSV". Contrast, luminosity and hues are enhanced.

16.8.13   The "Components" Submenu

This command leads to the following submenu

Figure 16.144 The "Components" submenu

- Section 16.8.14

- Section 16.8.15

- Section 16.8.16

- Section 16.8.17

16.8.13.1 Activating the command

This command is found in the image window menu under Colors → Components.

16.8.14 Channel Mixer

16.8.14.1 Overview

Figure 16.145 Example for the "Channel Mixer" filter

(a) *Original image*   (b) *"Channel Mixer" applied*

This command combines values of the RGB channels. It works with images with or without an alpha channel. It has monochrome mode and a preview.

16.8.14.2 Activate the command

You can find this command through Colors → Components → Channel Mixer.

16.8.14.3 Options

Figure 16.146 "Channel Mixer" command options

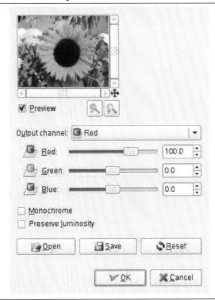

Output Channel From this menu you select the channel to mix to. Choices are Red, Green, or Blue. It is insensitive when Monochrome option is checked.

Red, Green, Blue These three sliders set the contribution of red, green or blue channel to output. Can be negative. These sliders are graduated from -200 to 200. They represent the percentage which will be attributed to the output channel. 100% corresponds to the value of the channel of the studied pixel in the image.

Monochrome This option converts the RGB image into a gray-scale RGB image. The Channel Mixer command is often used with this aim in view, because it often provides a better result than the other ways (see Grayscale in Glossary). Makes the Output Channel menu insensitive.

> Note
>
> The 21%, 72%, 7% settings give you the same gray luminosity (Value) as the Grayscale command in Image/Mode. (They were 30%, 59%, 11% in v2.2).

Preserve Luminosity Calculations may result in too high values and an image too much clear. This option lessens luminosities of the color channels while keeping a good visual ratio between them. So, you can change the relative weight of the colors without changing the overall luminosity.

16.8.14.4 Buttons

Open Load settings from a file.

Save Save settings to a file.

Reset Set default settings.

16.8.14.5 How does Channel Mixer work?

In RGB mode In this mode, you have to select an Output Channel . This channel is the one which will be modified. In the dialog window, its default value is 100%, corresponding to the value of the channel in the original image. It can be increased or decreased. That's why slider ends are -200 and 200.

Three RGB sliders let you give a percentage to every channel. For every pixel in the image, the sum of the calculated values for every channel from these percentages will be given to the Output Channel. Here is an example:

Figure 16.147 The original image and its channels

RGB values of the pixels in red, green, blue, gray squares are displayed. The black rectangle is special, because black (0;0;0) is not concerned by the command (0 multiplied by any percentage always gives 0). The result can't exceed 255 nor be negative.

Figure 16.148 Output channel is red. Green Channel +50

In the red square, the pixel values are 230;10;10. Relative values are 1;0.5;0. The calculation result is 230*1 + 10*0,5 + 10*0 =235. The same reasoning is valid for the green and the blue squares.
In the gray square, which contains red color, the calculation result is above 255. It is reduced to 255. A negative value would be reduced to 0.

Figure 16.149 Output channel is red. Green Channel +50%. The Preserve Luminosity option is checked.

The values attributed to the Red Output channel are lower, preventing a too much clear image.

In Monochrome mode When this option is checked, the image preview turns to grayscale, but the image is still a RGB image with three channels, until the command action is validated.

Figure 16.150 Monochrome option checked. Red: 100% Green: 50% Blue: 0%. Preserve Luminosity unchecked.

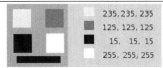

In every square, pixels have been converted into a gray level equal to the value of the Red channel in the original image (The background has been painted with pink afterwards to make all squares visible).

Here is how the Preserve Luminosity works in the monochrome mode: " For example, suppose the sliders were Red:75%, Green:75%, Blue:0%. With Monochrome on and the Preserve Luminosity option off, the resulting picture would be at 75%+75%+0% =150%, very bright indeed. A pixel with a value of, say, R,G,B=127,100,80 would map to 127*0.75+100*0.75+80*0=170 for each channel. With the Preserve Luminosity option on, the sliders will be scaled so they always add up to 100%. In this example, that scale value is 1/(75%+75%+0%) or 0.667. So the pixel values would be about 113. The Preserve Luminosity option just assures that the scale values from the sliders always adds up to 100%. Of course, strange things happen when any of the sliders have large negative values " (from the plug-in author himself).

> **Note**
>
> *Which channel will you modify?* This depends on what you want to do. In principle, the Red channel suits contrast modifications well. The Green channel is well adapted to details changes and the Blue channel to noise, grain changes. You can use the Decompose command.

16.8.15 Compose

16.8.15.1 Overview

Figure 16.151 Example for the "Compose" command

(a) *Decomposed image (RGB decomposition)*   (b) *"Compose" applied*

This command constructs an image from several grayscale images or layers, for instance from extracted RGB, HSV... components. You can also build an image from grayscale images or layers created independently.

16.8.15.2 Activate the command

- You can find this command in the image window menu under Colors → Components → Compose....
  It is enabled if your image is grayscale.

16.8.15.3 Options

Figure 16.152 "Compose" command options

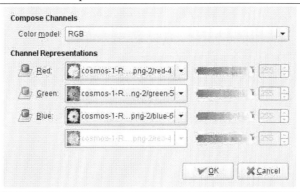

Compose Channels You can select there the color space to be used: RGB, HSV... The options are described in the following Decompose command.

Channel Representation Allows you to select which channel will be affected to each image channel. You may use this option, for example, to exchange color channels:

Figure 16.153 Channel Representation example: exchange two channels

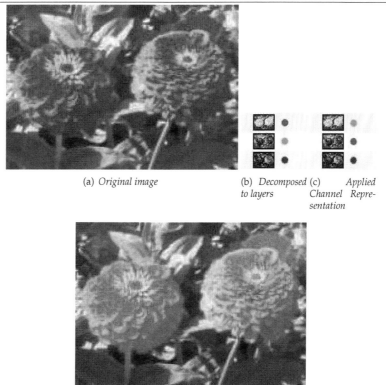

(a) *Original image*   (b) *Decomposed* (c)   *Applied*
                                            to layers   *Channel Repre-*
                                                              sentation

(d) *Composed image*

Mask Value: Instead of selecting a layer or an image to build the channel, you can give the channel a value from 0 to 255. But note that at least one channel must be formed from a layer or image.

Tip

If Compose options are different from Decompose ones, for instance an image de-composed to RGB then re-composed to LAB, you will get interesting color effects. Test it!

16.8.16 Decompose

16.8.16.1 Overview

Figure 16.154 Decomposition to images (RGB)

(a) *Original image*   (b) *Command "Decompose" applied (RGB decomposition) with Decompose to layers unchecked.*

Figure 16.155 Decomposition to layers (RGB)

(a) *Original image*   (b) *Command "Decompose" applied (RGB de-composition) with Decompose to layers checked.*

This command separates the channels (RGB, HSV, CMYK...) of an image into separated images or layers.

16.8.16.2 Activate the command

- You can find this command in the image window menu under Colors → Components → Decompose....

16.8.16.3   Options

Figure 16.156 "Decompose" command options

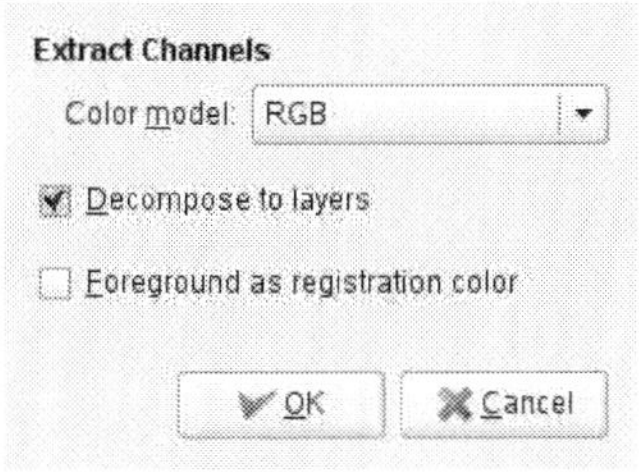

Extract Channels

Color model: RGB

☑ Decompose to layers

☐ Foreground as registration color

OK   Cancel

Extract Channels

Following options are described with Decompose to layers checked.

Color model

RGB If the RGB radio button is clicked, a grey level image is created with three layers (Red, Green and Blue), and two channels (Grey and Alpha).

This function is interesting when using Threshold tool. You can also perform operations like cutting, pasting or moving selections in a single RBG channel. You can use an extracted grayscale as a selection or mask by saving it in a channel (right-click>Select>Save to a channel).

RGBA If the RGBA radio button is clicked, a image is created similar at the RGB Decomposing with a additional Alpha layer filled with the transparencies values of the source image. Full transparent pixels are black and the full opaque pixels are white.

HSV This option decomposes image into three greyscaled layers, one for Hue, one for Saturation and another for Value.

Although Hue is greyscaled, it does represent hues. In color circle, white and black are starting and arrival points and are superimposed. They represent Red color at top of circle. Grey intermediate levels are corresponding to intermediate hues on circle: dark grey to orange, mid grey to green and light grey to magenta.

Saturation and Value: White is maximum Saturation (pure color) and maximum Value (very bright). Black is minimum Saturation (white) and minimum Value (black).

HSL This option is similar to HSV. Instead of the *Value*, the third layer contains the image's *L* component.

CMY This option decomposes image into three greyscaled layers, one for Yellow, one for Magenta and another for Cyan.

This option might be useful to transfer image into printing softwares with CMY capabilities.

CMYK This option is similar at the CMY Decomposing with an additional layer for Black.

This option might be useful to transfer image into printing softwares with CMYK capabilities.

Alpha This option extracts the image transparency stored in the Alpha channel in Channel dialog in a separate image. The full transparent pixels are Black the full opaque pixels are white. The graytones are smooth transitions of the transparency in the source image.

LAB This option decomposes image into three greyscaled layers, layer "L" for Luminance, layer "A" for colors between green and red, layer "B" for colors between blue and yellow.

The LAB Decomposing is a color model of the Luminance-Color family. A channel is used for the Luminosity while two other channels are used for the Colors. The LAB color model is used by Photoshop.

YCbCr In GIMP there is four YCbCr decompositions with different values. Each option decomposes image in three greyscaled layers, a layer for Luminance and two other for blueness and redness.

The YCbCr color model also called YUV is now used for digital video (initially for PAL analog video). It's based on the idea that the human eye is most sensitive to luminosity, next to colors. The YCbCr Decomposing use a transformation matrix and the different options are different

values recommended by ITU (International Telecommunication Union) applied to the matrix
.

Decompose to Layers If this option is checked, a new grey-scaled image is created, with each layer representing one of the channels of the selected mode. If this option is not checked, every channel is represented with a specific image automatically and clearly named in the name bar.

Example 16.1 Crop marks

Foreground as registration color
Source image

Cyan component

Black component

(Magenta and Yellow components omitted.)

This option is for specialists. It is related to CMYK printing. When checked, every pixel of the current foreground color will be black in each component of the decomposed images/layers. This allows you to make crop marks visible on all channels, providing a useful reference for alignment. A thin cross printed in registration black can also be used to check whether the printing plates are lined up.

16.8.17 Recompose

16.8.17.1 Overview

Figure 16.157 Example for the "Recompose" command

(a) *Original image (decomposed to RGB)*   (b) *Command "Recompose" applied*

This command reconstructs an image from its RGB, HSV... components directly, unlike the Compose command which uses a dialog.

16.8.17.2   Activate the command

• This command is found in the image window menu under Colors → Components → Recompose: This command is active after using Decompose.

16.8.18   The "Map" Submenu

This command leads to the following submenu

Figure 16.158 The "Map" submenu

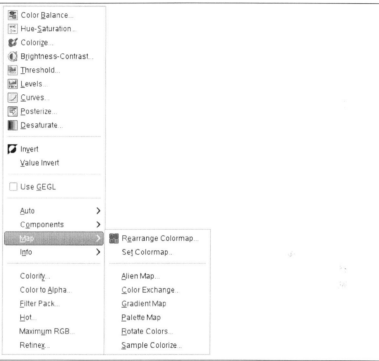

• Section 16.8.19

• Section 16.8.20

• Section 16.8.21

• Section 16.8.22

• Section 16.8.23

• Section 16.8.24

• Section 16.8.25

• Section 16.8.26

16.8.19   Rearrange Colormap

Figure 16.159 The "Rearrange Colormap" window

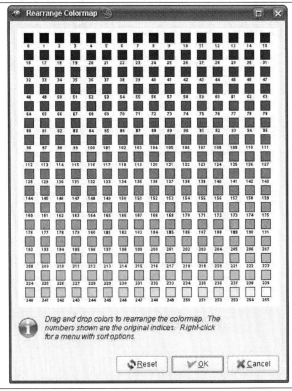

This command allows you to re-organize colors in the palette of *indexed* images. It doesn't modify the image. You can't add or remove colors; for that, see The Indexed Palette Dialog.

16.8.19.1   Activate Dialog

You can access this command from the image menu-bar through Colors → Map → Rearrange Colormap. If your image is not indexed, this command is grayed out and disabled.

16.8.19.2   Using the "Rearrange Colormap" dialog

Explanations supplied in the dialog window are enough: drag and drop colors to rearrange the colormap. You can sort colors in various ways by using the local pop-menu that you get by right-clicking:

Figure 16.160 The "Rearrange Colormap" pop-menu

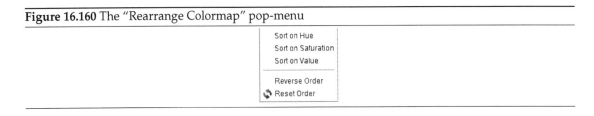

16.8.20   Set Colormap

Figure 16.161 The "Set Colormap" window

This command opens a dialog which allows you to select another palette to replace the color map of your indexed image. First click in the button with the name of the current palette (which is not the color map of your image yet) to open the Palette Selector:

Figure 16.162 The "Palette Selection" dialog

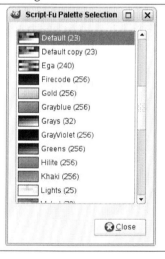

Once you have chosen the wanted palette, click the OK button in the "Set Palette" dialog to replace the image colormap.

16.8.20.1   Activate the command

This command is found in the image window menu under Colors → Map → Set Colormap.

16.8.21   Alien Map

16.8.21.1   Overview

Figure 16.163 Alien Map filter example

(a) *Original image*   (b) *Filter applied*

This filter renders very modified colors by applying trigonometric functions. Alien Map can work on images having RGB and HSV color models.

16.8.21.2   Activate the filter

You can find this filter in the image window menu under Colors → Map → Alien Map.

16.8.21.3   Options

Figure 16.164 Options for the "Alien Map" filter

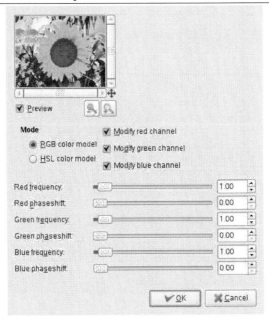

Preview This preview displays results of filter application interactively.

Mode Radio buttons RGB Color Channel and HSV Color Channel let you select the color space you want to use.

Check boxes Modify ... Channel let you select RGB/HSV Channel you want to work with.

Sliders For each channel, you can set Frequency (0-5) and Phaseshift (0-360) of sine-cosine functions, using either sliders or input boxes and their arrowheads.

Frequency around 0.3 to 0.7 provides a curve that is similar to the linear function (original image), only darker or with more contrast. As you raise the frequency level, you'll get an increasing variation in pixel transformation, meaning that the image will get more and more "alien".

Phase alters the value transformation. 0 and 360 degrees are the same as a sine function and 90 is the same as a cosine function. 180 inverts sine and 270 inverts cosine.

16.8.22 Color Exchange

16.8.22.1 Overview

Figure 16.165 "Color Exchange" filter example

(a) *Original image*   (b) *Filter applied*

This filter replaces a color with another one.

16.8.22.2 Activate the filter

This filter is found in the image window menu under Colors → Map → Color Exchange.

16.8.22.3   Options

Figure 16.166 Option of the "Two color exchange" filter

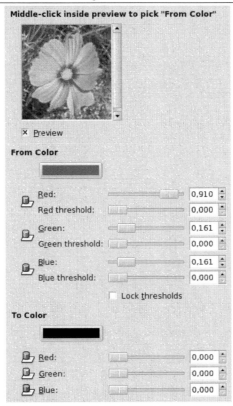

Preview In this preview, a part of the Image is displayed. A selection smaller than preview will be complete in preview. A bigger one will be cut out to be adapted to the preview.

If you middle-click inside preview , the clicked pixel color will be selected and will appear as From Color.

From color In this section, you can choose the color to be used to select pixels that will be concerned by color exchange.

Three sliders for RVB colors: If you have clicked on preview, they are automatically positioned. But you can change them. Each slider acts on color intensity. Input boxes and arrowheads work the same. Result is interactively displayed in the From swatch box.

Three sliders for thresholds, for each color. The higher the threshold, the more pixels will be concerned. Result is interactively displayed in Preview.

Lock Thresholds: This option locks threshold sliders which will act all the same.

To color Three cursors allow to select the color that pixels will have. Result is displayed in swatch box and in preview. You can also click on the color dwell to get a color selector.

16.8.23   Gradient Map

16.8.23.1   Overview

Figure 16.167 Example of gradient map

Example of Gradient Mapping. Top: Original image. Middle: a gradient. Bottom: result of applying the gradient to the original image with the Gradient Map filter.

This filter uses the current gradient, as shown in the Brush/Pattern/Gradient area of the Toolbox, to recolor the active layer or selection of the image to which the filter is applied. To use it, first choose a gradient from the Gradients Dialog. Then select the part of the image you want to alter, and activate the filter. The filter runs automatically, without showing any dialog or requiring any further input. It uses image color intensities (0 - 255), mapping the darkest pixels to the left end color from the gradient, and the lightest pixels to the right end color from the gradient. Intermediate values are set to the corresponding intermediate colors.

16.8.23.2   Activate the filter

You can find this filter in the image window menu under Colors → Map → Gradient Map.

16.8.24   Palette Map

16.8.24.1   Overview

This plug-in recolors the image using colors from the active palette that you choose in Dialogs → Palettes.

It maps the contents of the specified drawable (layer, selection...) with the active palette. It calculates luminosity of each pixel and replaces the pixel by the palette sample at the corresponding index. A complete black pixel becomes the lowest palette entry, and complete white becomes the highest. Works on both Grayscale and RGB image with/without alpha channel.

16.8.24.2   Activate the filter

You can access this filter in the image window menu under Colors → Map → Palette Map.

16.8.24.3 Example

Figure 16.168 The active palette is applied to a gradient image

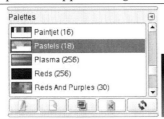 

(a) *The current palette, with 18 colors* (b) *The colors of the active palette are applied to a black to white gradient. The color with the lowest index in the palette (orange) replaces the black color in the gradient. The color with the highest index in the palette (red) replaces the white color in the gradient. The other colors spread out in the order of the palette.*

16.8.25 Rotate Colors

16.8.25.1 Overview

Figure 16.169 Example for the "Rotate Colors" filter

(a) *Original image*   (b) *Filter "Rotate Colors" applied*

Colormap Rotation lets you exchange one color range to another range.

16.8.25.2 Activating the filter

This filter is found in the image window menu under Colors → Map → Rotate Colors.

16.8.25.3   Main Options

Figure 16.170 Main Options of the "Color Map Rotation" filter

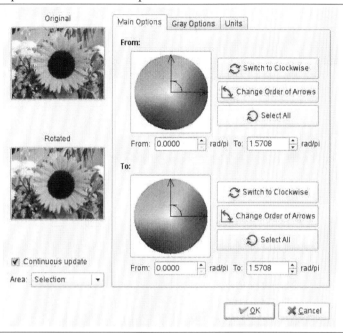

You have there two color circles, one for the "From" color range and the other for the "To" color range:

From The Color Circle: Two axis to define "From" range. The curved arrow in angle lets to recognise "From" axis and "To" axis of range. Click-drag these axis to change range.

Switch to Clockwise/Counterclockwise: Sets the direction the range is going.

Change Order of Arrows: Inverts From and To axis. This results in an important color change as colors in selection angle are different.

Select All selects the whole color circle.

From and To boxes display start axis and end axis positions (in rad/PI) which are limiting the selected color range. You can enter these positions manually or with help of arrow-heads.

To This section options are the same as "From" section ones.

16.8.25.4   Gray Options

Figure 16.171 Base image for Gray Options

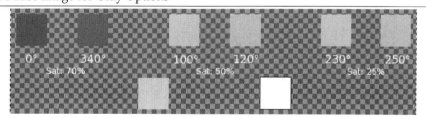

Three sectors are defined for Red, Green and Blue with different saturations. Gray and White colors are represented (0% Sat).

In this tab, you can specify how to treat gray. By default, gray is not considered as a color and is not taken in account by the rotation. Here, you can convert slightly saturated colors into gray and you can also convert gray into color.

Gray Color Circle At center of this color circle is a small "define circle". At center, it represents gray. If you increase gray threshold progressively, colors with saturation less than this threshold turn to gray.

Then, if you pan the define circle in the color circle, or if you use input boxes, you define *Hue* and *Saturation*. This color will replace all colors you have defined as gray. But result depends on Gray Mode too.

Gray Mode The radio buttons *Treat As This* and *Change As This* determine how your previous choices will be treated:

- With *Change to this*, gray will take the color defined by the define circle directly, without any rotation, whatever its position in the color circle.

- With *Treat as this*, gray will take the color defined by the define circle after rotation, according to "From" and "To" choices you made in the Main tab. With this option, you can select color only in the "From" sector, even if it is not visible in Gray tab.

Figure 16.172 Gray Mode

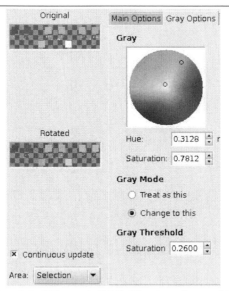

The small circle is on yellow and mode is "Change to this". Blue has changed to yellow. Note that Gray and White did so too.

Gray Threshold

Figure 16.173 Gray Threshold

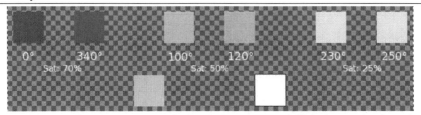

Gray-threshold is 0.25: the blue sector (sat 0.25) has turned to Gray (Note that Gray and White, that are 0% Sat., are not concerned).

You specify there how much saturation will be considered gray. By increasing progressively saturation, you will see an enlarging circle in color circle and enlarging selected areas in Preview if "Continuous update" is checked. In a black to white gradient, you can see enlarging color replacement as you increase threshold very slowly.

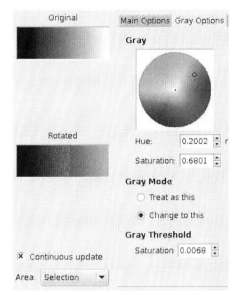

Black to White gradient, progressively filled with color, as threshold increases.

16.8.25.5 Previews

Original, Rotated The Original preview displays a thumbnail of the original image and the Rotated preview displays color changes interactively, before they are applied to the Image.

Continuous Update Continuous Update displays color changes continuously in the Rotated preview.

Area In this drop down list, you can select between

- Entire Layer: works on the whole layer (The image if there is no selection).
- Selection: displays selection only.
- Context: displays selection in image context.

16.8.25.6 Units

You can select here the angle unit used to locate colors in the Hue/Saturation circle. This choice is valid only for the current filter session: don't click on OK just after selecting unit, return to the wanted tab!

16.8.26 Sample Colorize

16.8.26.1 Overview

Figure 16.174 Example for the "Sample Colorize" filter

(a) *Original image*   (b) *Filter "Sample Colorize" applied*

This filter allows you to colorize old black-and-white images by mapping a color source image or a gradient against it.

Caution

 Your gray-tone image must be changed to RGB before using this filter (Image/Image>Mode>RGB).

16.8.26.2   Activate the filter

This filter is found in the image window menu under Colors → Map → Sample Colorize.

16.8.26.3   Options

Figure 16.175 Options of the "Sample Colorize" filter

The filter window is divided into two parts: Destination on the left, Sampling on the right.

Destination, Sample By default, displayed image previews reproduce the image you invoked the filter from.

   The sample can be the whole preview, or a selection of this preview. With the drop list, you can select another sample-image among the names of images present on your screen when you called the filter. If you choose From Gradient (or From Inverse Gradient), the selected gradient in Gradient Dialog (or its inverse) will be the sample. It will be displayed into the gradient bar below the sample preview. The sampling preview is greyed out and two cursors allow you to select the gradient range that will be applied to the image or selection.

   Destination is, by default, the source image. The drop list displays the list of images present on your screen when you evoked the filter and allow you to select another destination image. If there is a selection in this image, it will be gray-scaled, else the whole preview will be gray-scaled.

Show Selection This option toggles between the whole image and the selection, if it exists.

Show Colors This option toggles between colors and gray-scale.

Get Sample Colors When you click on this button, the gradient bar below the sample preview displays colors of the sample. If your sample holds few colors, transitions may be abrupt. Check Smooth Sample Colors option to improve them.

Use Subcolors is more difficult to understand. Let's say first that in a greyscale image there is information only for Value (luminosity, more or less light). In a RGB image, each pixel has information for the three colors and Value. So, pixels with different color may have the same Value. If this option is checked, colors will be mixed and applied to Destination pixels having that Value. If it is unchecked, then the dominating color will be applied.

Out Levels Two input boxes and two sliders act the same: they limit the color range which will be applied to destination image. You can choose this range accurately. Result appears interactively in destination preview.

In Levels Three input boxes and three sliders allow to fix importance of dark tones, mid tones and light tones. Result appears interactively in destination preview.

Hold Intensity If this option is checked, the average light intensity of destination image will be the same as that of source image.

Original Intensity If this option is checked, the In levels intensity settings will not be taken in account: original intensity will be preserved.

16.8.27 The "Info" Submenu

This command leads to the following submenu

Figure 16.176 The "Info" submenu

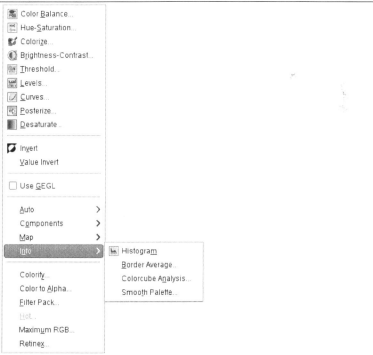

- Section 16.8.28

- Section 16.8.29

- Section 16.8.30

- Section 16.8.31

16.8.28 Histogram

The Histogram dialog is documented in Section 15.2.5.

16.8.29 Border Average

16.8.29.1 Overview

Figure 16.177 Example for the "Border Average" filter

(a) *Original image*   (b)
                             Filter
                             "Border
                             Aver-
                             age"
                             applied

This plug-in calculates the most often used color in a specified border of the active layer or selection. It can gather similar colors together so that they become predominant. The calculated color becomes the foreground color in the Toolbox. This filter is interesting when you have to find a Web page color background that differs as little as possible from your image border. The action of this filter is not registered in Undo History and can't be deleted with Ctrl-Z : it doesn't modify the image.

16.8.29.2 Activating the filter

This filter is found in the image window menu under Colors+Info → Border Average.

16.8.29.3 Options

Figure 16.178 Options of the "Border Average Filter"

Border Size You can set there the border Thickness in pixels.

Number of Colors The Bucket Size lets you control the number of colors considered as similar and counted with the same "bucket". A low bucket size value (i.e. a high bucket number) gives you better precision in the calculation of the average color. Note that better precision does not necessarily mean better results (see example below).

16.8.29.4   Examples illustrating the "Border Average" filter

Figure 16.179 Original image

Original image: colors are pure Red (255;0;0), pure Blue (0;0;255), and different but similar kinds of Green (0;255;0 , 63;240;63 , 48;224;47 , 0;192;38).

Figure 16.180 "Number of Colors" is set to 8:

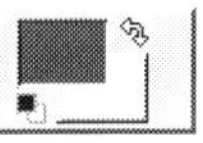

The resulting color is a Red (254,2,2).

The bucket size is low. So the bucket number is high. All color shades can be stored in different buckets. Here, the bucket containing red is the most filled. The resulting color is a nearly pure Red (254,2,2) and becomes the foreground color of the Toolbox.

Figure 16.181 "Number of Colors" is set to 64:

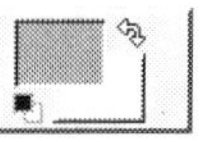

The resulting color is Green (32,224,32).

Here the bucket size is high, the number of buckets low. Similar colors (here green) are stored in a same bucket. This "green" bucket is now the most filled. All colors in this bucket have the same values for the two most significant bits: (00******;11******;00******). The remaining 6 bits may have any values from 0 to 63 for the respective channel. So in this bucket, color red channels range from 0 to 63, green channels from 192 to 255, blue channels from 0 to 63. The resulting color is Green (32,224,32), which, for every channel, is the average between the limits of the channel range (63 + 0)/2, (255+192)/2 , (63+0)/2.

16.8.30   Colorcube Analysis

16.8.30.1   Overview

Figure 16.182 Example for the "Colorcube" filter

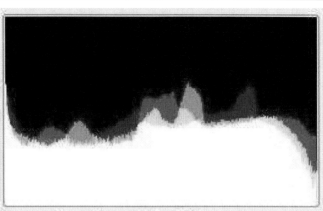

(a) *Original image*   (b) *Filter "Colorcube Analysis" applied*

Information is reduced since GIMP 2.4: size and color number of the active layer.

16.8.30.2   Activating the filter

You can find this filter in the image window menu under Colors → Info → Colorcube Analysis.

16.8.31   Smooth Palette

16.8.31.1   Overview

Figure 16.183 Example for the "Smooth Palette" filter

(a) *Original image*   (b) *Filter "Smooth Palette" applied*

It creates a striped palette from colors in active layer or selection. The main purpose of this filter is to create color-maps to be used with the Flame filter.

16.8.31.2   Activating the filter

This filter is found in the image window menu under Colors → Info → Smooth Palette.

16.8.31.3 Options

Figure 16.184 "Smooth Palette" options

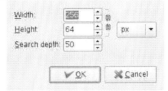

Parameter Settings You can set palette dimensions for Width and Height. Dimensions are linked when chain is not broken. You can also select unit.

Search Depth Increasing Search Depth (1 - 1024) will result in more shades in palette.

16.8.32 The Color Filters

The following color filters group contains miscellaneous filters to modify colors in an image, a layer or a selection. You can find some nice effects here.

- Section 16.8.33
- Section 16.8.34
- Section 16.8.35
- Section 16.8.36
- Section 16.8.37
- Section 16.8.38

16.8.33 Colorify

16.8.33.1 Overview

Figure 16.185 Example for the "Colorify" filter

(a) *Original image*   (b) *Filter "Colorify" applied*

This filter renders a greyscaled image like it is seen through a colored glass.

For every pixel, the filter computes a weighted average value of the RGB channels (this is equivalent to desaturating the image based on Luminosity). The resulted color is the product of this average value and the "colorify color".

Hence, this filter works only on images in RGB mode.

16.8.33.2   Activate the filter

This filter is found in the image window menu under Colors → Colorify.

16.8.33.3   Options

Figure 16.186 "Colorify" filter options

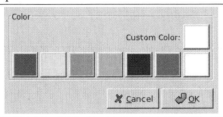

A color palette is available containing especially the RGB colors Red, Green, Blue and the CMY colors Cyan, Magenta, Yellow.

You can select your own color by clicking on the Custom Color swatch.

16.8.34   Color to Alpha

16.8.34.1   Overview

Figure 16.187 Example for "Color to Alpha"

(a) *Original image*   (b) *"Color to Alpha" applied on blue areas*

The Color to Alpha command makes transparent all pixels of the active layer that have a selected color. An Alpha channel is created. It will attempt to preserve anti-aliasing information by using a partially intelligent routine that replaces weak color information with weak alpha information. In this way, areas that contain an element of the selected color will maintain a blended appearance with their surrounding pixels.

16.8.34.2   Activate the filter

This filter is found in the image window menu under Colors → Color to Alpha.

16.8.34.3 Options

Figure 16.188 "Color to Alfa" command options

Color Clicking on the From color swatch provides a color selection dialog where you can select a color. If selection of a precise color is required, use the Color Picker then drag and drop the selected color from the color picker to the From color swatch. Right clicking on the color will display a menu where you can select Foreground or Background colors, White or Black.

16.8.35 Filter Pack

16.8.35.1 Overview

Figure 16.189 Example for the "Filter Pack" filter

(a) *Original image*   (b) *Filter "FilterPack" applied (more Blue, more Saturation)*

This tool offers you a collection of unified filters to treat the image. Of course, same functions can be performed by particular filters, but you have here an interesting, intuitive, overview.

16.8.35.2 Activate the filter

You can find this filter in the image window menu under Colors → Filter Pack.

16.8.35.3   Options

Figure 16.190 All the options for filter "Filter Pack"

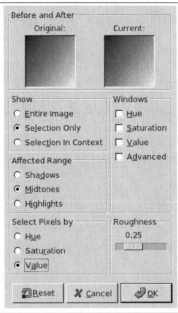

Original and Current previews Two previews display respectively before treatment and after treatment images.

Show Sets what you want to preview:

- Entire image

- Selection only: if a selection exists (default is the whole image).

- Selection in context: the selection within the image.

Windows You can choose between:

- Hue makes one preview for each of the three primary colors and the three complementary colors of the RGB color model. By clicking successively on a color, you add to this color into the affected range, according to Roughness. To subtract color, click on the opposite color, the complementary color.

Figure 16.191 Hue option of the "Filterpack" filter

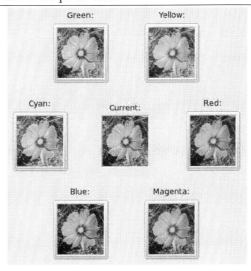

- Saturation: Three previews for more or less saturation.

Figure 16.192 The saturation option of the "Filterpack" filter

- Value: Three previews for more or less luminosity.

Figure 16.193 Value option of the "Filterpack" filter

- Advanced: developed later.

Affected range Allows you to set which brightness you want to work with.

- Shadows: dark tones.
- Midtones
- Highlights: bright tones

Select pixels by Determines what HSV channel the selected range will affect. You can choose between:

- Hue
- Saturation
- Value

Roughness This slider sets how image will change when you click on a window: taking a short step or a large one (0 - 1).

Advanced Options

Figure 16.194 Advanced options of the "Filterpack" filter

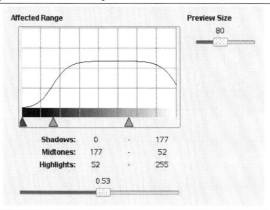

These advanced options let you work more precisely on the changes applied to the image and on the preview size.

Preview Size Something like a zoom on previews. Normal size is 80.

> Tip
>
>
>
> In spite of Preview Size option, this size is often too small. You can compensate this by working on an enlarged selection, for instance a face on a photo. Then, you invert selection to work on the other part of the image.

Affected range Here, you can set the tone range that the filter will affect.

The curve in this window represents the importance of the changes applied to the image. The aspect of this curve depends on the Affected range you have selected: Shadows, Midtons or Highlights. You can set the curve amplitude by using the Roughness slider in the main window of the filter.

By using the available controls (slider and triangles), you can precisely set the form of this action curve.

16.8.36 Hot

16.8.36.1 Overview

This command identifies and modifies pixels which might cause problem when displayed onto PAL or NTSC TV screen.

16.8.36.2 Activate the command

You can access the command from the image menu bar through Colors → Hot.

This command only works on images in RGB mode, and only if the active layer does not have an alpha channel. Otherwise the menu entry is insensitive and grayed out.

16.8.36.3   Options

Figure 16.195 "Hot" options

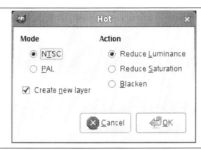

Mode You have to select the TV mode: PAL or NTSC.

Action You can select:

- Reduce Luminency
- Reduce Saturation
- Blacken: this will turn hot pixels to black.

Create a new layer With this option, work will be performed on a new layer instead of the image. This will give you peace of mind!

16.8.37   Max RGB

16.8.37.1   Overview

Figure 16.196 Example for the filter "Max RGB"

(a) *Original image*   (b) *Filter "Max RGB" applied*

For every pixel of the image, this filter holds the channel with the maximal/minimal intensity. The result is an image with only three colors, red, green and blue, and possibly pure gray.

16.8.37.2   Activate the filter

This filter is found in the image window menu under Colors → Max RGB.

16.8.37.3   Options

Figure 16.197 "Max RGB" options

Preview This preview displays, in real time, the resulting image after treatment by filter.

Parameter Settings Hold the maximal channels: For every pixel, the filter keeps intensity of the RGB color channel which has the maximal intensity and reduces other both to zero. For example: 220, 158, 175 max--> 220, 0, 0. If two channels have same intensity, both are held: 210, 54, 210 max--> 210, 0, 210.

Hold the minimal channels: For every pixel, the filter keeps intensity of the RGB color channel which has the minimal intensity and reduce both others to zero. For example: 220, 158, 175 min--> 0, 158, 0. If two minimal channels have same intensity, both are held: 210, 54, 54 min--> 0, 54, 54.

Grey levels are not changed since light intensity is the same in all three channels.

16.8.38   Retinex

16.8.38.1   Overview

Figure 16.198 "Retinex" example

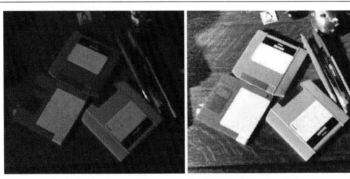

(a) *Original image*   (b) *"Retinex" filter applied. Note new details in the upper right corner.*

Retinex improves visual rendering of an image when lighting conditions are not good. While our eye can see colors correctly when light is low, cameras and video cams can't manage this well. The MSRCR (MultiScale Retinex with Color Restoration) algorithm, which is at the root of the Retinex filter, is inspired by the eye biological mechanisms to adapt itself to these conditions. Retinex stands for Retina + cortex.

Besides digital photography, Retinex algorithm is used to make the information in astronomical photos visible and detect, in medicine, poorly visible structures in X-rays or scanners.

16.8.38.2 Activate the filter

This filter is found in the image window menu under Colors → Retinex.

16.8.38.3 Options

Figure 16.199 "Retinex" filter options

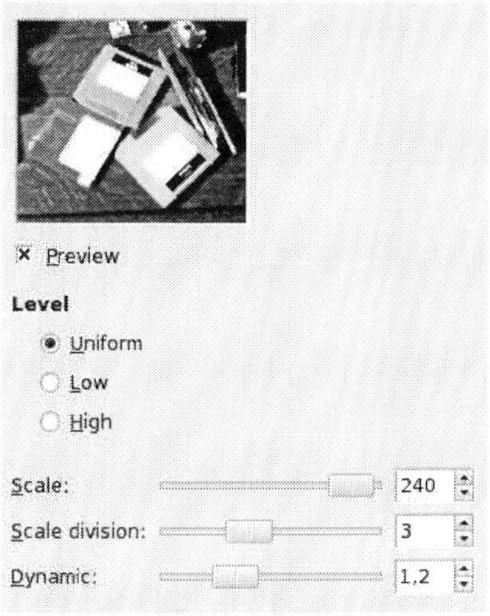

These options call for notions that only mathematicians and imagery engineers can understand. In actual practice, the user has to grope about for the best setting. However, the following explanations should help out the experimented GIMP user.

Level Here is what the plug-in author writes on his site [PLUGIN-RETINEX]: "To characterize color variations and the lightor, we make a difference between (gaussian) filters responses at different scales. These parameters allow to specify how to allocate scale values between min scale (sigma 2.0) and max (sigma equal to the image size)"...

    Uniform Uniform tends to treat both low and high intensity areas fairly.

    Low As a rule of thumb, low does "flare up" the lower intensity areas on the image.

    High High tends to "bury" the lower intensity areas in favor of a better rendering of the clearer areas of the image.

Scale Determines the depth of the Retinex scale. Minimum value is 16, a value providing gross, unrefined filtering. Maximum value is 250. Optimal and default value is 240.

Scale division Determines the number of iterations in the multiscale Retinex filter. The minimum required, and the recommended value is three. Only one or two scale divisions removes the multiscale aspect and falls back to a single scale Retinex filtering. A value that is too high tends to introduce noise in the picture.

Dynamic As the MSR algorithm tends to make the image lighter, this slider allows you to adjust color saturation contamination around the new average color. A higher value means less color saturation. This is definitely the parameter you want to tweak for optimal results, because its effect is extremely image-dependent.

16.9   The "Tools" Menu

16.9.1   Introduction to the "Tools" Menu

Figure 16.200 Contents of the "Tools" menu

The menu entries on the Tools menu access the GIMP tools. All of the tools available in GIMP are extensively described in the Tools section.

16.10   The "Filters" Menu

16.10.1   Introduction to the "Filters" Menu

Figure 16.201 The "Filters" menu

In GIMP terminology, a *filter* is a plug-in that modifies the appearance of an image, in most cases just the active layer of the image. Not all of the entries in this menu meet that definition, however; the word "filter" is often mis-used to mean any plug-in, regardless of what it does. Indeed, some of the entries in this menu do not modify images at all.

With the exception of the top three items of the Filters menu, all of the entries are provided by plugins. Each plug-in decides for itself where it would like its menu entry to be placed. Therefore, the appearance of this menu can be completely different for each user. In practice, though, the appearance does not vary very much, because most plug-ins come with GIMP when it is installed, and of course they are always in the same places in the menu.

Plug-ins are not restricted to just the Filters menu: a plug-in can place entries in any menu. Indeed, a number of GIMP's basic functions (for example, Semi-flatten in the Layer menu) are implemented by plug-ins. But the Filters menu is the default place for a plug-in to place its menu entries.

For general information on plug-ins and how to use them, see the section on Plug-ins. You can find information on the filters that are provided with GIMP in the Filters chapter. For filters you install yourself, please refer to the information which came with them.

16.10.2 Repeat Last

The Repeat Last command performs the action of the most recently executed plug-in again, using the same settings as the last time it was run. It does not show a dialog or request confirmation.

> **Note**
>
> Please note that this command repeats the most recently executed *plug-in*, regardless of whether it is in the Filters menu or not.

16.10.2.1 Activating the Command

- You can access this command from the image menubar through Filters → Repeat `filter`,

- or by using the keyboard shortcut Ctrl-F.

16.10.3 Re-show Last

The Re-show Last command shows the dialog of the most recently executed plug-in. Unlike the "Repeat Last" command, which does not display a dialog, the "Re-show Last" command displays a dialog window, if the plug-in has one. It is displayed with the settings you used the last time you ran the plug-in (assuming that the plug-in follows the GIMP programming conventions).

> **Note**
>
> Please note that this command repeats the most recently executed *plug-in*, regardless of whether it is in the Filters menu or not.

> **Tip**
>
> When you are using a plug-in, especially one that does not have a preview window, you may very well have to adjust the parameters several times before you are satisfied with the results. To do this most efficiently, you should memorize the shortcuts for Undo and Re-show Last: Ctrl-Z followed by Ctrl-Shift-F.

16.10.3.1 Activating the Command

- You can access this command from the image menubar through Filters → Re-show `filter`,

- or by using the keyboard shortcut Ctrl-Shift-F.

16.10.4 Reset All Filters

Normally, each time you run an interactive plug-in, its dialog is displayed with all of the settings initialized to the ones you used the last time you ran it. This may be a problem if you made a mistake setting the values and you can't remember what they were originally. One way to recover is to exit GIMP and start again, but the Reset all Filters command is a slightly less drastic solution: it resets the values for *all* plug-ins to their defaults. Because it is a dramatic step, it asks you to confirm that you really want to do it. Be careful: you cannot undo this command.

16.10.4.1 Activating the Command

- You can access this command from the image menubar through Filters → Reset all Filters.

16.10.5 The "Python-Fu" Submenu

Figure 16.202 The "Python-Fu" submenu

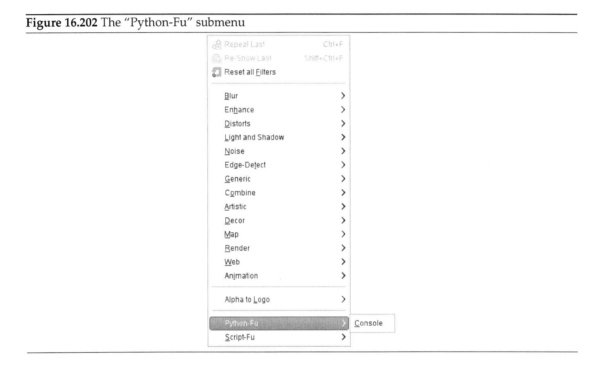

By default this submenu just contains the Python-Fu console.

Python-Fu is a set of Python modules that act as a wrapper to *libgimp* allowing the writing of plug-ins for GIMP.

16.10.5.1 Activating the submenu

- You can access this command from the image menu through Filters → Python-Fu

16.10.5.2 The Python-Fu Console

The Python-Fu console is a dialog window running a "Python shell" (a Python interpreter in interactive mode). This console is set up to make use of the internal GIMP library routines of *libgimp*.

You can use the Python-Fu console to interactively test Python commands.

The console consists of a large scrollable main window for input and output, where you can type Python commands. When you type in a Python command and then press the **Enter** key, the command is executed by the Python interpreter. The command's output as well as its return value (and its error message, if any) will be displayed in the main window.

Figure 16.203 The Python-Fu Console

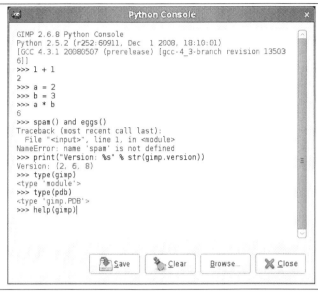

The Python-Fu Console Buttons

Save This command lets you save the content of the main window, that is the Python-Fu console input and output (including the ">>>" prompt).

Clear Wenn you click on this button, the content of the main window will be removed. Note that you can't get back the removed content using the Save command.

Browse When clicked, the procedure browser pops up, with an additional button Apply at the bottom of the window.

When you press this Apply button in the procedure browser, a call to the selected procedure will be pasted into the console window as a Python command:

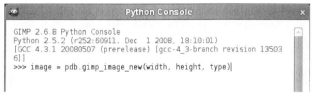

Applied PDB procedure

Now you just have to replace the parameter names (here: "width", "height", and "type") with actual values, e.g.

```
image = pdb.gimp_image_new(400, 300, RGB)
```

Then press **Enter** to execute the command.

You can (and should!) use the constants you find in the decription of the procedure's parameters, for example "RGB-IMAGE" or "OVERLAY-MODE". But note that you have to replace hyphens ("-") with underscores ("_"): RGB_IMAGE, OVERLAY_MODE.

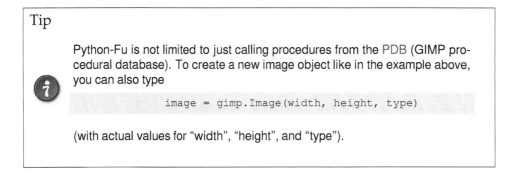

Tip

Python-Fu is not limited to just calling procedures from the PDB (GIMP procedural database). To create a new image object like in the example above, you can also type

```
image = gimp.Image(width, height, type)
```

(with actual values for "width", "height", and "type").

Close Pressing this button closes the console.

16.10.6 The "Script-Fu" Submenu

Figure 16.204 The "Script-Fu" submenu

This submenu contains some Script-Fu commands, especially the Script-Fu console. Script-Fu is a language for writing scripts, which allow you to run a series of GIMP commands automatically.

16.10.6.1 Activating the submenu

• You can access this command from the image menu through Filters → Script-Fu

16.10.6.2 Refresh Scripts

You will need this command every time you add, remove, or change a Script-Fu script. The command causes the Script-Fus to be reloaded and the menus containing Script-Fus to be rebuilt from scratch. If you don't use this command, GIMP won't notice your changes until you start it again.

Note that you won't get any feedback, unless saving, if one of your scripts fails.

16.10.6.3 Script-Fu Console

The Script-Fu console is a dialog window where you can interactively test Scheme commands.

The console consists of a large scrollable main window for output and a textbox used to type Scheme commands. When you type a Scheme statement and then press the **Enter** key, the command and its return value will be displayed in the main window.

Figure 16.205 The Script-Fu Console

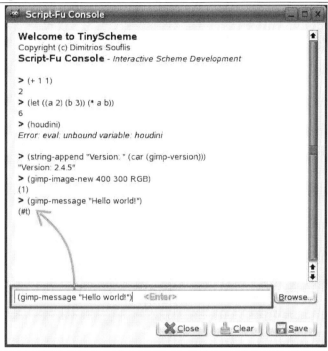

You will find more information about Scheme and examples how to use the Script-Fu console in Section 13.3.

The Script-Fu Console Buttons

Browse This button is next to the Scheme commands textbox. When clicked, the procedure browser pops up, with an additional button at the bottom of the window:

The additional button of the Procedure Browser

When you press this Apply button in the procedure browser, the selected procedure will be pasted into the text box:

Applied PDB procedure

Now you just have to replace the parameter names (here: "layer" and "mode") with actual values, and then you can call the procedure by pressing **Enter**.

Close Pressing this button closes the Script-Fu console.

Clear Wenn you click on this button, the content of the main window will be removed. Note that you can't get back the removed content using the Save command.

Save This command lets you save the content of the main window, that is the Script-Fu console output (including the ">"-characters).

16.10.6.4   Start Server

This command will start a server, which reads and executes Script-Fu (Scheme) statements you send him via a specified port.

Figure 16.206 The Script-Fu Server Options

Server Port   The port number where the Script-Fu server will listen. It is possible to start more than one server, specifying different port numbers, of course.

Server Logfile   Optionally you can specify the name of a file the server will use to log informal and error messages. If no file is specified, messages will be written to stdout.

The Script-Fu Server Protocol
The protocol used to communicate with the Script-Fu server is very simple:

- Every message (Script-Fu statement) of length L sent to the server has to be preceded with the following 3 bytes:

Table 16.1 Header format for commands

Byte #	Content	Description
0	0x47	Magic byte ('G')
1	L div 256	High byte of L
2	L mod 256	Low byte of L

- Every response from the server (return value or error message) of length L will be preceded with the following 4 bytes:

Table 16.2 Header format for responses

Byte #	Content	Description
0	0x47	Magic byte ('G')
1	error code	0 on success, 1 on error
2	L div 256	High byte of L
3	L mod 256	Low byte of L

Tip

If you don't want to get your hands dirty: there is a Python script named servertest.py shipped with the GIMP source code, which you can use as a simple command line shell for the Script-Fu server.

16.11   "Windows" Menu

This menu allows you to manage GIMP windows dialogs:

The "Windows" menu name is not well adapted to the new single-window mode. Nevertheless, its functions concern multi and single modes. Its display may vary according presence or absence of images and docks:

Figure 16.207 Contents of the "Windows" Menu

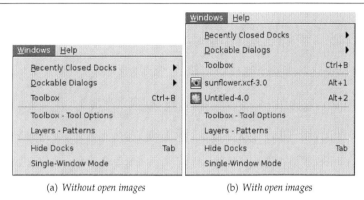

(a) *Without open images*   (b) *With open images*

1. **Recently Closed Docks**: this command opens the list of the docks you have closed recently. You can reopen them by clicking on their name. Please note that isolated windows are not concerned.

   For more information about docks, please see Dialogs and Docking.

2. **Dockable Dialogs**: this command opens the list of dockable dialogs. Please refer to Section 3.2.3.

3. **Toolbox**: clicking on this command or using the Ctrl-B shortcut, raises the toolbox usually together with the tool options dock.

4. The list of open image windows: clicking on an image name, or using the Alt-Number of the image shortcut, makes the image active.

5. The list of open docks: in this list, docks are named with the name of the active dialog in this dock. Clicking on a dock name raises this dock.

6. **Hide Docks (Tab)**: this command hides all docks (usually to the left and right of the image), leaving the image window alone. The command status is kept on quitting GIMP; then, GIMP starts with no dock in multi-window mode, but not in single-window mode, although the option is checked!

7. **Single Window Mode**: when enabled, GIMP is in a single window mode. Please see Single Window Mode.

16.12 The "Help" Menu

16.12.1 Introduction to the "Help" Menu

Figure 16.208 Contents of the "Help" menu

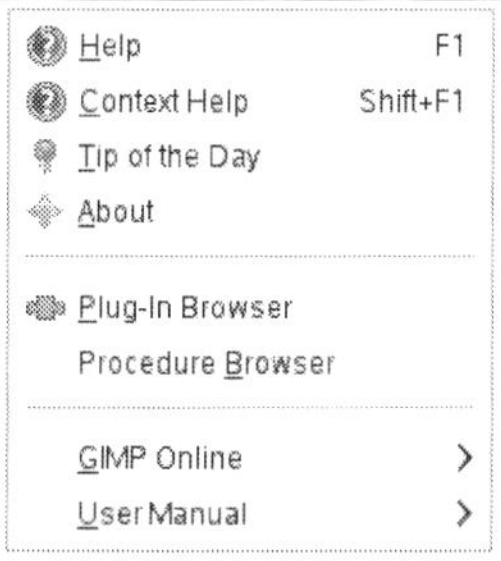

The Help menu contains commands that assist you while you are working with GIMP.

Note

Besides the commands described here, you may also find other entries in the menu. They are not part of GIMP itself, but have been added by extensions (plug-ins). You can find information about the functionality of a Plugin by referring to its documentation.

16.12.2   Help

The Help command displays the GIMP Users Manual in a browser. You can set the browser you would like to use in the Help System section of the Preferences dialog, as described in Section 12.1.5. The browser may be the built-in GIMP help browser, or it may be a web browser.

Tip

If the help does not seem to work, please verify that the "GIMP Users Manual" is installed on your system. You can find the most recent help online [GIMP-DOCS].

16.12.2.1   Activating the Command

- You can access this command from the image menubar through Help → Help (**F1**).

16.12.3   Context Help

The Context Help command makes the mouse pointer context-sensitive and changes its shape to a "?". You can then click on a window, dialog or menu entry and GIMP displays help about it, if it is available. You can also access context help at any time by pressing the **F1** key while the mouse pointer is over the object you would like help about.

16.12.3.1   Activating the Command

- You can access this command from the image menu through Help → Context Help

- or by using the keyboard shortcut Shift-F1.

16.12.4   Tip of the Day

The Tip of the Day command displays the Tip of the Day dialog. This dialog contains useful tips to help you gain a better understanding of some of the subtle points of using GIMP. New users will find it very valuable to pay attention to these, because they often suggest ways of doing something that are much easier or more efficient than more obvious approaches.

16.12.4.1   Activating the Command

- You can access this command in the image menu through Help → Tip of the Day.

16.12.4.2 Description of the dialog window

Figure 16.209 "Tip of the Day"Dialog window

Some tips contain a Learn more link to the corresponding GIMP manual page.

> ## New in GIMP 2.6
>
> The tip of the day is no longer displayed by default each time you start GIMP.

16.12.5 About

The About command shows the About window, which displays information about the version of The GIMP you are running and the many authors who wrote it.

16.12.5.1 Activating the "About" Command

- You can access this command in the image menu through Help → About

16.12.5.2 Description of the dialog window

Figure 16.210 The "About" dialog window

The Credits leads to the list of contributors to GIMP program, concerning programming, graphics and translation of the interface.

The Licence explains how to get the licence.

16.12.6   Plug-In Browser

The Plug-In Browser command displays a dialog window which shows all of the extensions (plug-ins) which are currently loaded in GIMP, both as a list and as a hierarchical tree structure. Since many of the filters are actually plug-ins, you will certainly see many familiar names here. Please note that you do not run the extensions from this dialog window. Use the appropriate menu entry to do that instead. For example, you can run filter plug-ins by using the Filter command on the image menubar.

16.12.6.1   Activating the Command

- You can access this command from the image menubar through Help → Plug-in Browser

16.12.6.2   Description of the "Plug-In Browser" dialog window

Figure 16.211 The list view of the "Plug-In Browser" dialog window

The figure above shows the list view of the Plug-In Browser. You can click on the name of a plug-in in the scrolled window to display more information about it. Select the List View by clicking on the tab at the top of the dialog.

You can search for a plug-in by name by entering part or all of the name in the Search: text box. The left part of the dialog then displays the matches found.

Figure 16.212 The tree view of the "Plug-In Browser" dialog window

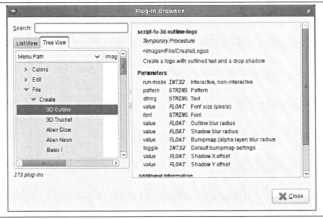

The figure above shows the tree view of the Plug-In Browser. You can click on the name of a plug-in in the scrolled window to display more information about it. You can click on the arrowheads to expand or contract parts of the tree. Select the Tree View by clicking on the tab at the top of the dialog.

You can search for a plug-in by name by entering part or all of the name in the Search: text box. The left part of the dialog then displays the matches found.

> **Note**
>
> Not everything in these huge dialog windows is visible at the same time. Use the scroll bars to view their content.

16.12.7 The Procedure Browser

The Procedure Browser command displays the procedures in the PDB, the Procedure Database. These procedures are functions which are called by the scripts or plug-ins.

16.12.7.1 Activating the Command

- You can access this command from the image menubar through Help → Procedure Browser

16.12.7.2 Description of the "Procedure Browser" dialog window

Figure 16.213 The "Procedure Browser" dialog window

The figure above shows the Procedure Browser dialog window. If you click on an item in the scrolled list on the left, information about it is displayed on the right. You can also search for a specific procedure by querying the procedural database with a regular expression on Search: text box:

by name Shows a list of procedures which have code names that contain the part of name you entered.

by description Shows a list of procedures which have blurbs that contain the word you entered.

by help Shows a list of procedures which have additional information text that contain the word you entered.

by author Shows a list of procedures which created by the author which has the part of name you entered.

by copyright Shows a list of procedures which copyright are hold by someone that have the part of name you entered.

by date Shows a list of procedures which have date of year that match the year you entered.

Note

 This query is processed with text but not date value, so you cannot find some procedure entries even if their date contains the year you entered. For example, a procedure dated 2000-2005 does not match if you search procedures with 2001, but it matches with 2000 or 2005.

by type Shows a list of procedures which have a one of four types: "Internal GIMP procedure", "GIMP Plug-In ", "GIMP Extension", or "Temporary Procedure".

16.12.8 GIMP online

Figure 16.214 The "GIMP Online" submenu of the Help menu

The GIMP online command displays a submenu which lists several helpful web sites that have to do with various aspects of GIMP. You can click on one of the menu items and your web browser will try to connect to the URL.

Chapter 17

Filters

17.1 Introduction

A filter is a special kind of tool designed to take an input layer or image, apply a mathematical algorithm to it, and return the input layer or image in a modified format. GIMP uses filters to achieve a variety of effects and those effects are discussed here.

The filters are divided into several categories:

- Section 17.2

- Section 17.3

- Section 17.4

- Section 17.5

- Section 17.6

- Section 17.7

- Section 17.8

- Section 17.9

- Section 17.10

- Section 17.11

- Section 17.12

- Section 17.13

- Section 17.14

- Section 17.15

- Section 17.16

17.1.1 Preview

Most filters have a Preview where changes in the image are displayed, in real time (if the "Preview" option is checked), before being applied to the image.

Figure 17.1 Preview submenu

Right clicking on the Preview window opens a submenu which lets you set the Style and the Size of checks representing transparency.

17.2 Blur Filters

17.2.1 Introduction

Figure 17.2 Original for demo

This is a set of filters that blur images, or parts of them, in various ways. If there is a selection, only the selected parts of an image will be blurred. There may, however, be some leakage of colors from the unblurred area into the blurred area. To help you pick the one you want, we will illustrate what each does when applied to the image shown at right. These are, of course, only examples: most of the filters have parameter settings that allow you to vary the magnitude or type of blurring.

Figure 17.3 Gaussian blur (radius 10)

The most broadly useful of these is the Gaussian blur. (Don't let the word "Gaussian" throw you: this filter makes an image blurry in the most basic way.) It has an efficient implementation that allows it to create a very blurry blur in a relatively short time.

Figure 17.4 Simple blur

If you only want to blur the image a little bit — to soften it, as it were — you might use the simple "Blur" filter. This filter runs automatically, without creating a dialog. The effect is subtle enough that you might not even notice it, but you can get a stronger effect by repeating it. In GIMP 2.0 the filter shows a dialog that allows you to set a "repeat count". If you want a strong blurring effect, this filter is too slow to be a good choice: use a Gaussian blur instead.

Figure 17.5 Selective blur

The Selective Blur filter allows you to set a threshold so that only pixels that are similar to each other are blurred together. It is often useful as a tool for reducing graininess in photos without blurring sharp edges. (In the example, note that the graininess of the background has been reduced.) The implementation is much slower than a Gaussian blur, though, so you should not use it unless you really need the selectivity.

Figure 17.6 Pixelize

The Pixelize filter produces the well-known "Abraham Lincoln" effect by turning the image into a set of large square pixels. (The Oilify filter, in the Artistic Filters group, has a similar effect, but with irregular blobs instead of perfectly square pixels.)

> Note
>
> You can find a nice explanation of the Abraham Lincoln effect at [BACH04]. You will see the Salvador Dali's painting "Gala Contemplating the Mediterranean Sea" turning to an Abraham Lincoln's portrait when looking at it from a distance.

Figure 17.7 Motion blur

The Motion Blur filter blurs in a specific direction at each point, which allows you to create a sense of motion: either linear, radial, or rotational.

Finally, the Tileable Blur filter is really the same thing as a Gaussian blur, except that it wraps around the edges of an image to help you reduce edge effects when you create a pattern by tiling multiple copies of the image side by side.

> Note
>
> Tileable Blur is actually implemented by a Script-Fu script that invokes the Gaussian blur plug-in.

17.2.2 Blur

17.2.2.1 Overview

Figure 17.8 The Blur filter applied to a photograph

(a) *Original*   (b) *Blur applied*

The simple Blur filter produces an effect similar to that of an out of focus camera shot. To produce this blur effect, the filter takes the average of the present pixel value and the value of adjacent pixels and sets the present pixel to that average value.

Filter advantage is its calculation speed. It suits big images.

Filter disadvantage is that its action is hardly perceptible on big images, but very strong on small images.

17.2.2.2 Activate the filter

You can find this filter through: Filters → Blur → Blur

17.2.3 Gaussian Blur

17.2.3.1 Overview

Figure 17.9 Example for the "Gaussian Blur" filter

(a) *Original*   (b) *Blur applied*

The IIR Gaussian Blur plug-in acts on each pixel of the active layer or selection, setting its Value to the average of all pixel Values present in a radius defined in the dialog. A higher Value will produce a higher amount of blur. The blur can be set to act in one direction more than the other by clicking the Chain Button so that it is broken, and altering the radius. GIMP supports two implementations of

Gaussian Blur: IIR G.B. and RLE G.B. They both produce the same results, but each one can be faster in some cases.

17.2.3.2 Activate the filter

You can find this filter in the image menu under Filters → Blur → Gaussian Blur

17.2.3.3 Options

Figure 17.10 "Gaussian" filter parameters settings

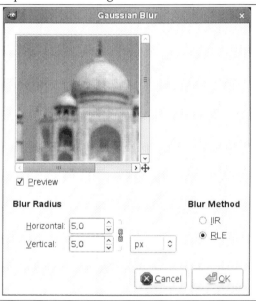

Blur Radius Here you can set the blur intensity. By altering the ratio of horizontal to vertical blur, you can give the effect of a motion blur. You can choose the unit with the drop list.

Blur Method

IIR IIR stands for "infinite impulse response". This blur works best for large radius values and for images which are not computer generated.

RLE RLE stands for "run-length encoding". RLE Gaussian Blur is best used on computer-generated images or those with large areas of constant intensity.

17.2.4 Selective Gaussian Blur

17.2.4.1 Overview

Figure 17.11 The Selective Gaussian Blur filter

(a) *Original*   (b) *Blur applied*

Contrary to the other blur plug-ins, the Selective Gaussian Blur plug-in doesn't act on all pixels: blur is applied only if the difference between its value and the value of the surrounding pixels is less than a defined Delta value. So, contrasts are preserved because difference is high on contrast limits. It is used to blur a background so that the foreground subject will stand out better. This add a sense of depth to the image with only a single operation.

17.2.4.2 Activate the filter

You can find this filter in the image menu under Filters → Blur → Selective Gaussian Blur

17.2.4.3 Options

Figure 17.12 "Selective Gaussian" filter parameters settings

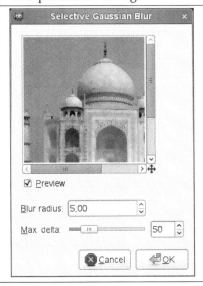

Blur radius Here you can set the blur intensity, in pixels.

Max. delta Here you can set the maximum difference (0-255) between the pixel value and the surrounding pixel values. Above this Delta, blur will not be applied to that pixel.

17.2.5   Motion Blur

17.2.5.1   Overview

Figure 17.13 Starting example for Motion Blur filter

(a) *Original image*   (b) *Linear blur*

Figure 17.14 Using example for Motion Blur filter

(a) *Radial blur*   (b) *Zoom blur*

The Motion Blur filter creates a movement blur. The filter is capable of Linear, Radial, and Zoom movements. Each of these movements can be further adjusted, with Length, or Angle settings available.

17.2.5.2   Activate the filter

You can find this filter in the image menu under Filters → Blur → Motion Blur

17.2.5.3 Options

Figure 17.15 "Motion Blur" filter options

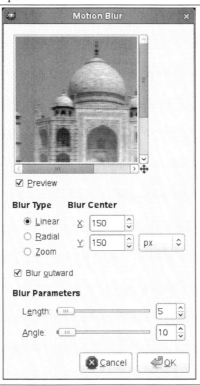

Blur Type

   Linear Is a blur that travels in a single direction, horizontally, for example. In this case, Length means as Radius in other filters:it represents the blur intensity. More Length will result in more blurring. Angle describes the actual angle of the movement. Thus, a setting of 90 will produce a vertical blur, and a setting of 0 will produce a horizontal blur.

   Radial motion blur that creates a circular blur. The Length slider is not important with this type of blur. Angle on the other hand, is the primary setting that will affect the blur. More Angle will result in more blurring in a circular direction. The Radial motion blur is similar to the effect of a spinning object. The center of the spin in this case, is the center of the image.

   Zoom Produces a blur that radiates out from the center of the image. The center of the image remains relatively calm, whilst the outer areas become blurred toward the center. This filter option produces a perceived forward movement, into the image. Length is the main setting here, and affects the amount of speed, as it were, toward the center of the image.

Blur Parameters

   Length This slider controls the distance pixels are moved (1 - 256)

   Angle As seen above, Angle slider effect depends on Blur type (0 - 360).

Blur Center With this option, you can set the starting point of movement. Effect is different according to the Blur Type you have selected. With Radial Type for instance, you set rotation center. With Zoom Type, vanishing point. This option is greyed out with Linear type.

Tip

You have to set the blur center coordinates. Unfortunately, you can't do that by clicking on the image. But, by moving mouse pointer on the image, you can see its coordinates in the lower left corner of the image window. Only copy them out into the input boxes.

17.2.6   Pixelise

17.2.6.1   Overview

Figure 17.16 Example for the "Pixelize" filter

(a) *Original*   (b) *"Pixelize" applied*

The Pixelize filter renders the image using large color blocks. It is very similar to the effect seen on television when obscuring a criminal during trial. It is used for the "Abraham Lincoln effect": see [BACH04].

17.2.6.2   Activate the filter

You can find this filter in the image menu through Filters → Blur → Pixelise

17.2.6.3 Options

Figure 17.17 "Pixelize" filter options

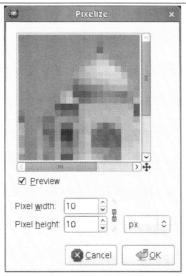

Pixel width, Pixel height Here you can set the desired width and height of the blocks.

By default, width and height are linked, indicated by the chain symbol next to the input boxes. If you want to set width and height separately, click on that chain symbol to unlink them.

Using the unit selection box you can select the unit of measure for height and width.

17.2.7 Tileable Blur

17.2.7.1 Overview

Figure 17.18 Example for the "Tileable" filter

(a) *Original*   (b) *Filter "Tileable Blur" applied*

This tool is used to soften tile seams in images used in tiled backgrounds. It does this by blending and blurring the boundary between images that will be next to each other after tiling.

Tip

If you want to treat only images borders, you can't apply filter to the whole image. The solution to get the wanted effect is as follows:

1. Duplicate layer (Layer → Duplicate Layer) and select it to work on it.

2. Apply "Tileable Blur" filter with a 20 pixels radius to this layer.

3. Select all (Ctrl-A) and reduce selection (Selection → Shrink) to create a border with the wanted width.

4. Give a feathered border to the selection by using Selection → Feather.

5. Delete selection with Ctrl-K.

6. Merge layers with Layer → Merge down.

17.2.7.2 Activate the filter

You can find this filter in the image menu under Filters → Blur → Tileable Blur.

17.2.7.3 Options

Figure 17.19 "Tileable Blur" filter options

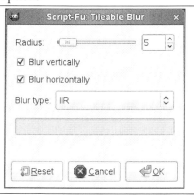

Radius The bigger the radius, the more marked is the blur. By selecting Horizontal and Vertical, you can make the horizontal and vertical borders tileable.

Blur vertically, Blur horizontally These options are self-explanatory.

Blur type Choose the algorithm to be applied:

IIR for photographic or scanned images.

RLE for computer-generated images.

17.3 Enhance Filters

Figure 17.20 The Enhance filters menu

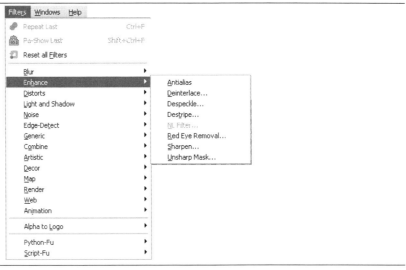

17.3.1 Introduction

Enhance filters are used to compensate for image imperfections. Such imperfections include dust particles, noise, interlaced frames (coming usually from a TV frame-grabber) and insufficient sharpness.

17.3.2 Antialias

17.3.2.1 Overview

This filter reduces alias effects (see Antialiasing) using the Scale3X edge-extrapolation algorithm.

Scale3X is derived from Scale2X, which is a graphics effect to increase the size of small bitmaps guessing the missing pixels without interpolating pixels and blurring the images.[1] Scale2X was originally developed to improve the quality of old Arcade and PC games with a low video resolution played with video hardware like TVs, Arcade monitors, PC monitors and LCD screens.[2]

The Antialias filter works as follows:

For every pixel,

1. the filter expands the original pixel in 9 (3x3) new pixels according to the Scale3X algorithm, using the colors of the pixel and its 8 adjacent pixels (extrapolation);

2. then the filter subsamples the new pixels to a weighted average pixel.

17.3.2.2 Activating the filter

You can find this filter through Filters → Enhance → Antialias.

17.3.2.3 Examples

The following examples illustrate the effect on some patterns. The small squares are one pixel in size (zoom 16:1).

---

[1] [SCALE2X].

[2] [AdvanceMAME].

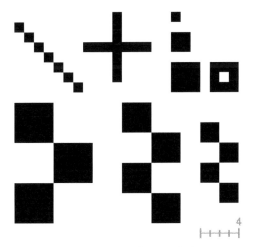

Original image (zoom 16:1)

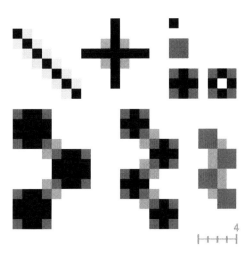

"Antialias" applied (zoom 16:1)

17.3.3   Deinterlace

17.3.3.1   Overview

Images captured by videocards, especially when fast movement is recorded, may look blurred and stripped, with split objects. This is due to how cameras work. They don't record 25 images per second, but 50, with half vertical resolution. There are two interlaced images in one frame. First line of first image is followed by first line of second image followed by second line of first image... etc. So, if there have been an important move between the two images, objects will appear split, shifted, stripped.

The Deinterlace filter keeps only one of both images and replaces missing lines by a gradient between previous and following lines. The resulting image, or selection, will be somewhat blurred, but can be improved by enhance filters

You can find interlaced images at [WKPD-DEINTERLACE].

17.3.3.2   Activating the filter

You can find this filter through Filters → Enhance → Deinterlace.

17.3.3.3 Options

Figure 17.21 Deinterlace filter options

Preview If checked, parameter setting results are interactively displayed in preview.

Keep odd fields, Keep even fields One of them may render a better result. You must try both.

17.3.3.4 Example

Figure 17.22 Simple applying example for the Deinterlace filter

(a) *Top: even lines pixels* (b) *"Keep even fields"* (c) *"Keep odd fields"*
are shifted by one pixel to the checked.   Top: odd lines checked.   Top: even lines
right. Bottom: one line is have been shifted to the have been shifted to the left,
missing. These images are right, to align themselves to align themselves with
zoomed to show pixels.   with the even lines. Bottom: the odd lines. Bottom: the
*   the empty line has been empty line persists, but*
*   filled with red.   joins up and down through*
*   a gradient.*

17.3.4 Despeckle

17.3.4.1 Overview

This filter is used to remove small defects due to dust, or scratches, on a scanned image, and also moiré effects on image scanned from a magazine. You should select isolated defects before applying this filter, in order to avoid unwanted changes in other areas of your image. The filter replaces each pixel with the median value of the pixels within the specified radius.

17.3.4.2 Activating the filter

You can find this filter through Filters → Enhance → Despeckle.

17.3.4.3   Options

Figure 17.23 "Despeckle" filter options

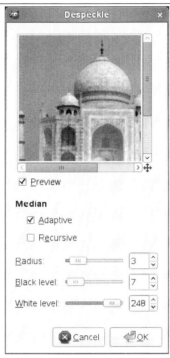

Preview If checked, parameter setting results are interactively displayed in preview.

Median

> **Adaptive** Adapts the radius to image or selection content by analyzing the histogram of the region around the target pixel. The adapted radius will always be equal to or smaller than the specified radius.
>
> **Recursive** Repeats filter action which gets stronger.

Radius Sets size of action window from 1 (3x3 pixels) to 20 (41x41). This window moves over the image, and the color in it is smoothed, so imperfections are removed.

Black level Only include pixels brighter than the set value in the histogram (-1-255).

White level Only include pixels darker than the set value in the histogram (0-256).

17.3.5   Destripe

17.3.5.1   Overview

It is used to remove vertical stripes caused by poor quality scanners. It works by adding a pattern that will interfere with the image, removing stripes if setting is good. This "negative" pattern is calculated from vertical elements of the image, so don't be surprised if you see stripes on the preview of an image that has none. And if pattern "strength"; is too high, your image will be striped.

If, after a first pass, a stripe persists, rectangular-select it and apply filter again (all other selection type may worsen the result).

17.3.5.2   Activating the filter

You can find this filter through Filters → Enhance → Destripe.

17.3.5.3   Options

Figure 17.24 "Destripe" filter options

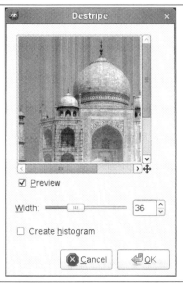

Preview If checked, parameter setting results are interactively displayed in preview. Scroll bars allow you to move around the image.

Create histogram This "histogram " is a black and white image showing the interference pattern more legibly.

Width Slider and input box allow to set "strength" of filter (2-100): more than 60 is rarely necessary and may create artifacts.

17.3.6   NL Filter

17.3.6.1   Overview

Figure 17.25 Example for the NL-Filter

(a) *Original image*   (b) *"NL Filter" applied*

NL means "Non Linear". Derived from the Unix **pnmnlfilt** program, it joins smoothing, despeckle and sharpen enhancement functions. It works on the whole layer, not on the selection.

This is something of a swiss army knife filter. It has 3 distinct operating modes. In all of the modes each pixel in the image is examined and processed according to it and its surrounding pixels values.

Rather than using 9 pixels in a 3x3 block, it uses an hexagonal block whose size can be set with the Radius option.

17.3.6.2 Activating the filter

You can find this filter through Filters $\rightarrow$ Enhance $\rightarrow$ NL Filter.

   The filter does not work if the active layer has an alpha channel. Then the menu entry is insensitive and grayed out.

17.3.6.3 Options

Figure 17.26 "NL Filter" options

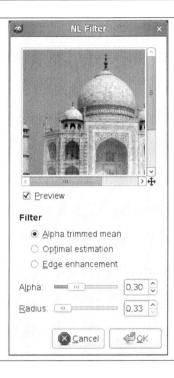

Preview When checked, parameter setting results are interactively displayed in preview.

Filter The Operating Mode is described below.

Alpha Controls the amount of the filter to apply. Valid range is 0.00-1.00. The exact meaning of this value depends on the selected operating mode. Note that this parameter is related to but not the same as the $alpha$ parameter used in the **pnmnlfilt** program.

Radius Controls the size of the effective sampling region around each pixel. The range of this value is 0.33-1.00, where 0.33 means just the pixel itself (and thus the filter will have no effect), and 1.00 means all pixels in the 3x3 grid are sampled.

17.3.6.4 Operating Modes

This filter can perform several distinct functions:

Alpha trimmed mean The value of the center pixel will be replaced by the mean of the 7 hexagon values, but the 7 values are sorted by size and the top and bottom $Alpha$ portion of the 7 are excluded from the mean. This implies that an $Alpha$ value of 0.0 gives the same sort of output as a normal convolution (i.e. averaging or smoothing filter), where $Radius$ will determine the "strength" of the filter. A good value to start from for subtle filtering is $Alpha = 0.0$, $Radius = 0.55$. For a more blatant effect, try $Alpha = 0.0$ and $Radius = 1.0$.

An `Alpha` value of 1.0 will cause the median value of the 7 hexagons to be used to replace the center pixel value. This sort of filter is good for eliminating "pop" or single pixel noise from an image without spreading the noise out or smudging features on the image. Judicious use of the `Radius` parameter will fine tune the filtering.

Intermediate values of `Alpha` give effects somewhere between smoothing and "pop" noise reduction. For subtle filtering try starting with values of `Alpha` = 0.8, `Radius` = 0.6. For a more blatant effect try `Alpha` = 1.0, `Radius` = 1.0 .

Optimal estimation This type of filter applies a smoothing filter adaptively over the image. For each pixel the variance of the surrounding hexagon values is calculated, and the amount of smoothing is made inversely proportional to it. The idea is that if the variance is small then it is due to noise in the image, while if the variance is large, it is because of "wanted" image features. As usual the `Radius` parameter controls the effective radius, but it probably advisable to leave the radius between 0.8 and 1.0 for the variance calculation to be meaningful. The `Alpha` parameter sets the noise threshold, over which less smoothing will be done. This means that small values of `Alpha` will give the most subtle filtering effect, while large values will tend to smooth all parts of the image. You could start with values like `Alpha` = 0.2, `Radius` = 1.0, and try increasing or decreasing the `Alpha` parameter to get the desired effect. This type of filter is best for filtering out dithering noise in both bitmap and color images.

Edge enhancement This is the opposite type of filter to the smoothing filter. It enhances edges. The `Alpha` parameter controls the amount of edge enhancement, from subtle (0.1) to blatant (0.9). The `Radius` parameter controls the effective radius as usual, but useful values are between 0.5 and 0.9. Try starting with values of `Alpha` = 0.3, `Radius` = 0.8.

17.3.6.4.1 Combination use The various operating modes can be used one after the other to get the desired result. For instance to turn a monochrome dithered image into grayscale image you could try one or two passes of the smoothing filter, followed by a pass of the optimal estimation filter, then some subtle edge enhancement. Note that using edge enhancement is only likely to be useful after one of the non-linear filters (alpha trimmed mean or optimal estimation filter), as edge enhancement is the direct opposite of smoothing.

For reducing color quantization noise in images (i.e. turning .gif files back into 24 bit files) you could try a pass of the optimal estimation filter (`Alpha` = 0.2, `Radius` = 1.0), a pass of the median filter (`Alpha` = 1.0, `Radius` = 0.55), and possibly a pass of the edge enhancement filter. Several passes of the optimal estimation filter with declining `Alpha` values are more effective than a single pass with a large `Alpha` value. As usual, there is a trade-off between filtering effectiveness and losing detail. Experimentation is encouraged.

17.3.7 Red Eye Removal

17.3.7.1 Overview

Figure 17.27 Example for the "Red Eye Removal" filter

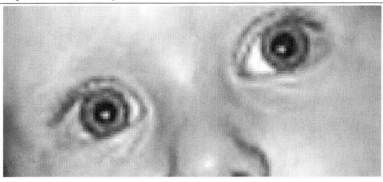

(a) *Original image*

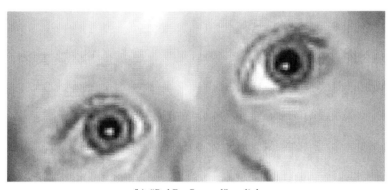

(b) *"Red Eye Removal" applied*

The aim of this filter is - guess what - to remove red eyes from an image. Before applying the "Red Eye Removal" you must do a selection (lasso or elliptical) of the boundary of the iris of the eye(s) having a red pupil. After only you can apply the filter on this selection. If you don't make this selection, the filter inform you that : "Manually selecting the eyes may improve the results".

17.3.7.2 Activating the filter

This filter is found in the image window menu under Filters → Enhance → Red Eye Removal.

17.3.7.3 Options

Figure 17.28 "Red Eye Removal" options

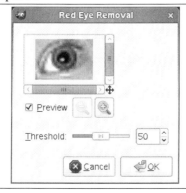

Preview If you check "Preview" you can see the modifications in real-time in the preview window. And you can choose the good value of threshold compared with what you see, and then validate it.

Threshold If you move the cursor of threshold the amount of red color to eliminate will vary.

17.3.8 Sharpen

17.3.8.1 Overview

Most of digitized images need correction of sharpness. This is due to digitizing process that must chop a color continuum up in points with slightly different colors: elements thinner than sampling frequency will be averaged into an uniform color. So sharp borders are rendered a little blurred. The same phenomenon appears when printing color dots on paper.

The Sharpen filter accentuates edges but also any noise or blemish and it may create noise in graduated color areas like the sky or a water surface. It competes with the Unsharp Mask filter, which is more sophisticated and renders more natural results.

Figure 17.29 Applying example for the Sharpen filter

(a) *Original image*   (b) *Filter "Sharpen" applied*

17.3.8.2 Activating the filter

You can find this filter through Filters → Enhance → Sharpen.

17.3.8.3 Options

Figure 17.30 "Sharpen" filter options

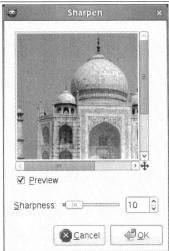

Preview If checked, parameter setting results are interactively displayed in preview. Scroll bars allow you to move around the image.

Sharpness The slider and input boxes allow you to set sharpness (1-99) and you can judge result in preview. By increasing sharpness, you may increase image blemishes and also create noise in graduated color areas.

17.3.9 Unsharp Mask

17.3.9.1 Overview

Figure 17.31 Applying example for the Unsharp Mask filter

(a) *Original image*   (b) *Filter "Unsharp mask" applied*

Out-of-focus photographs and most digitized images often need a sharpness correction. This is due to the digitizing process that must chop a color continuum up in points with slightly different colors: elements thinner than sampling frequency will be averaged into an uniform color. So sharp borders are rendered a little blurred. The same phenomenon appears when printing color dots on paper.

The Unsharp Mask filter (what an odd name!) sharpens edges of the elements without increasing noise or blemish. It is the king of the sharpen filters.

Tip

 Some imaging devices like digital cameras or scanners offer to sharpen the created images for you. We strongly recommend you disable the sharpening in this devices and use the GIMP filters instead. This way you regain the full control over the sharpening of your images.

To prevent color distortion while sharpening, Decompose your image to HSV and work only on Value. Then Compose the image to HSV. Go to Colors → Components → Decompose.... Make sure the Decompose to Layers box is checked. Choose HSV and click OK. You will get a new grey-level image with three layers, one for Hue, one for Saturation, and one for Value. (Close the original image so you won't get confused). Select the Value layer and apply your sharpening to it. When you are done, with that same layer selected, reverse the process. Go to Colors → Components → Compose.... Again choose HSV and click OK. You will get back your original image except that it will have been sharpened in the Value component.

17.3.9.2 Activating the filter

You can find this filter through Filters → Enhance → Unsharp Mask.

17.3.9.3 Options

Figure 17.32 "Unsharp Mask" filter options

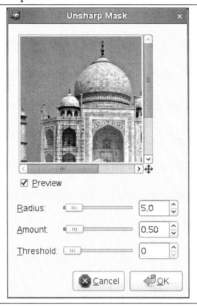

Preview If checked, parameter setting results are interactively displayed in preview. Scroll bars allow you to move around the image.

Radius The slider and input boxes (0.1-120) allow you to set how many pixels on either side of an edge will be affected by sharpening. High resolution images allow higher radius. It is better to always sharpen an image at its final resolution.

Amount This slider and input boxes (0.00-5.00) allow you to set strength of sharpening.

Threshold This slider and input boxes (0-255) allow you to set the minimum difference in pixel values that indicates an edge where sharpen must be applied. So you can protect areas of smooth tonal transition from sharpening, and avoid creation of blemishes in face, sky or water surface.

17.3.9.4 How does an unsharp mask work?

Using an unsharp mask to sharpen an image can seem rather weird. Here is the explanation:

Think of an image with a contrast in some place. The intensity curve of the pixels on a line going through this contrast will show an abrupt increase of intensity: like a stair if contrast is perfectly sharp, like an S if there is some blur.

Now, we have an image with some blur we want to sharpen (black curve). We apply some more blur: the intensity variation will be more gradual (green curve).

Let us subtract the blurredness intensity from the intensity of the image. We get the red curve, which is more abrupt : contrast and sharpness are increased. QED.

Unsharp mask has first been used in silver photography. The photograph first creates a copy of the original negative by contact, on a film, placing a thin glass plate between both; that will produce a blurred copy because of light diffusion. Then he places both films, exactly corresponding, in a photo enlarger, to reproduce them on paper. The dark areas of the positive blurred film, opposed to the clear areas of the original negative will prevent light to go through and so will be subtracted from the light going through the original film.

In digital photography, with GIMP, you will go through the following steps:

1. Open your image and duplicate it Image $\rightarrow$ Duplicate

2. In the copy, duplicate the layer Layer $\rightarrow$ Duplicate layer, then drop the Filters menu down and apply Blur $\rightarrow$ Gaussian Blur to the duplicated layer with the default IIR option and radius 5.

3. In the layer dialog of the duplicated image, change Mode to "Subtract", and in the right-clic menu, select "Merge down".

4. Click and drag the only layer you got into the original image, where it appears as a new layer.

5. Change the Mode in this layer dialog to "Addition".

Voilà. The "Unsharp Mask" plug-in does the same for you.

At the beginning of the curve, you can see a dip. If blurring is important, this dip is very deep; the result of the subtraction can be negative, and a complementary color stripe will appear along the contrast, or a black halo around a star on the light background of a nebula (black eye effect).

Figure 17.33 Black eye effect

17.4   Distort Filters

Figure 17.34 The Distort filters menu

17.4.1   Introduction

The distort filters transform your image in many different ways.

17.4.2 Blinds

17.4.2.1 Overview

Figure 17.35 Applying example for the Blinds filter

(a) *Original image*   (b) *Filter "Blinds" applied*

It generates a blind effect with horizontal or vertical battens. You can lift or close these battens, but not lift the whole blind up.

17.4.2.2 Activating the filter

You can find this filter through Filters → Distort → Blinds.

17.4.2.3 Options

Figure 17.36 "Blinds" filter options

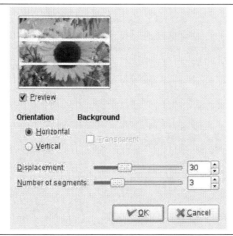

Preview All your setting changes will appear in the Preview without affecting the image until you click on OK.

Orientation Allows you to decide whether battens will be horizontal or vertical.

Background The batten color is that of the Toolbox Background. To be able to use the *Transparent* option, your image must have an Alpha channel.

Displacement Slider and input box allow to wide battens giving the impression they are closing, or to narrow them, giving the impression they are opening.

Number of segments It's the number of battens.

17.4.3 Curve Bend

17.4.3.1 Overview

Figure 17.37 Applying example for the Curve Bend filter

(a) Original image   (b) Filter "Curve Bend" applied

This filter allows you to create a curve that will be used to distort the active layer or selection. The distortion is applied gradually from an image or selection border to the other.

17.4.3.2 Activating the filter

You can find this filter through Filters → Distorts → Curve Bend.

17.4.3.3 Options

Figure 17.38 "Curve bend" filter options

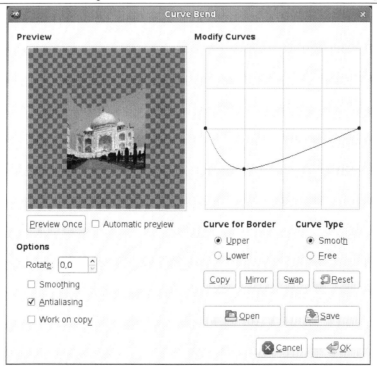

Preview The preview displays changes to image or selection without modifying the image until you press *OK*.

> **Preview once** This button allows you to update the preview each time you need it.
>
> **Automatic Preview** With this option, preview is changed in real time. This needs much calculation and may lengthen work. It is particularly evident when using "Rotation".

Options

> **Rotate** There, you can set the application angle of filter (0-360 counter-clockwise). 0 is default setting: The curve will be applied from the upper border and/or from the lower. Set to 90, it will be applied from left border and/or from the right one.
>
> **Smoothing, Antialiasing** The distort process may create hard and stepped borders. These two options improve this aspect.
>
> **Work on copy** This option creates a new layer called "Curve_bend_dummy_layer_b" which becomes the active layer, allowing you to see changes to your image in normal size without modifying the original image until you press the OK button.

Modify Curves In this grid, you have a marked horizontal line, with a node at both ends, which represents by default the upper border of image. If you click on this curve, a new node appears, that you can drag to modify the curve as you want. You can create several nodes on the curve.

You can have only two curves on the grid, one for the so named "upper" border and the other for the so named "lower" border. You can activate one of them by checking the Upper or Lower radio button.

If you use the Free *Curve Type* option, the curve you draw will replace the active curve.

Curve for Border There you can select whether the active curve must be applied to the Upper or the Lower border, according to the rotation.

Caution

 Remember that the curve border depends on the rotation. For example, with Rotate = 90° the upper curve will actually be applied to the left border.

Curve Type With the Smooth, you get automatically a well rounded curve when you drag a node.

The Free option allows you to draw a curve freely. It will replace the active curve.

Buttons

> **Copy** Copy the active curve to the other border.
>
> **Mirror** Mirror the active curve to the other border.
>
> **Swap** Swap the Upper and Lower curves.
>
> **Reset** Reset the active curve.
>
> **Open** Load the curve from a file.
>
> **Save** Save the curve to a file.

17.4.4   Emboss

17.4.4.1   Overview

Figure 17.39 Applying example for the Emboss filter

(a) *Original image*   (b) *Filter "Emboss" applied*

This filter stamps and carves the active layer or selection, giving it relief with bumps and hollows. Bright areas are raised and dark ones are carved. You can vary the lighting.

You can use the filter only with RGB images. If your image is grayscale, it will be grayed out in the menu.

17.4.4.2   Starting filter

You can find this filter through Filters → Distorts → Emboss.

17.4.4.3   Options

Figure 17.40 "Emboss" filter options

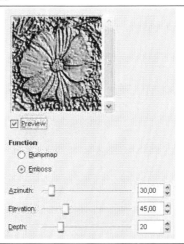

Preview   All your setting changes will appear in the Preview without affecting the image until you click on OK. Don't keep Preview checked if your computer is too slow.

Function

    Bumpmap   Relief is smooth and colors are preserved.

    Emboss   It turns your image to grayscale and relief is more marked, looking like metal.

Azimuth This is about lighting according to the points of the compass (0 - 360). If you suppose South is at the top of your image, then East (0°) is on the left. Increasing value goes counter-clockwise.

Elevation That's height from horizon (0°), in principle up to zenith (90°), but here up to the opposite horizon (180°).

Depth Seems to be the distance of the light source. Light decreases when value increases.

17.4.5 Engrave

17.4.5.1 Overview

Figure 17.41 Example for the "Engrave" filter

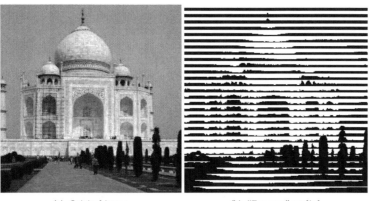

(a) *Original image*   (b) *"Engrave" applied*

This filter produces an engraving effect: the image is turned black and white and some horizontal lines of varying height are drawn depending on the value of underlying pixels. The resulting effect reminds of engravings found in coins and old book illustrations.

> Note
>
> The "Engrave" filter operates only on floating selections and layers with an alpha channel. If the active layer does not have an alpha channel please add it first.

17.4.5.2 Activating the filter

This filter is found in the image window menu under Filters → Distorts → Engrave.

17.4.5.3 Options

Figure 17.42 "Engrave" options

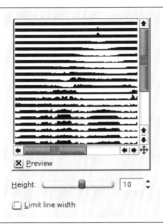

Preview The result of your settings will appear in the Preview without affecting the image until you click on OK.

Height This option specifies the height of the engraving lines. The value goes from 2 to 16.

Limit line width If this option is enabled thin lines are not drawn on contiguous color areas. See the figure below for an example of this option result.

Figure 17.43 Example result of Limit line width option

(a)   Original (b) Limit line (c) Limit line
image   width   option width   option
                enabled   disabled

17.4.6 Erase Every Other Row

17.4.6.1 Overview

Figure 17.44 Example for the "Erase Every Other row" filter

(a) *Original image*   (b) *"Erase Every Other row" applied*

This filter not only can erase each other row or column of the active layer but also can change them to the background color.

17.4.6.2 Activating the filter

This filter is found in the image window menu under Filters → Distorts → Erase Every Other Row.

17.4.6.3 Options

Figure 17.45 "Erase Every Other row" options

These options are self-explanatory. Only one remark: if the active layer has an Alpha channel, erased rows or columns will be transparent. If it doesn't have an Alpha channel (then its name is in bold letters in the Layer Dialog), the Background color of the toolbox will be used.

17.4.7 IWarp

17.4.7.1 Overview

Figure 17.46 Applying example for the IWarp filter

(a) *Original image*   (b) *Filter "IWarp" applied*

This filter allows you to deform interactively some parts of the image and, thanks to its Animate option, to create the elements of a fade in/fade out animation between the original image and the deformed one, that you can play and use in a Web page.

To use it, first select a deform type then click on the Preview and drag the mouse pointer.

17.4.7.2 Activating the filter

You can find this filter through Filters → Distort → Iwarp.

17.4.7.3 Options

The options of this filter are so numerous that they come in two tabs. The first tab contains general options. The second tab holds animation options.

Figure 17.47 "IWarp" filter options (Settings tab)

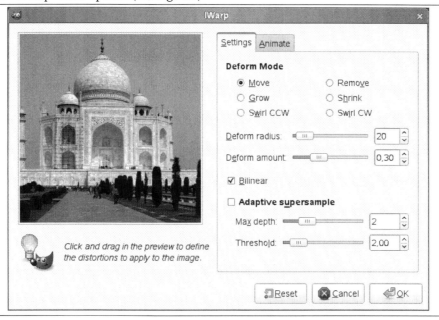

17.4.7.3.1   Settings   The Settings tab allows you to set parameters which will affect the preview you are working on. So, you can apply different deform modes to different parts of the preview.

Preview   Here, the Preview is your work space: You click on the Preview and drag mouse pointer. The underlying part of image will be deformed according to the settings you have chosen. If your work is not convenient, press the *Reset* button.

Deform Mode

    Move   Allows you to *stretch* parts of the image.

    Remove   This remove the distortion where you drag the mouse pointer, partially or completely. This allows you to avoid pressing Reset button, working on the whole image. Be careful when working on an animation: this option will affect one frame only.

    Grow   This option inflates the pointed pattern.

    Shrink   Self explanatory.

    Swirl CCW   Create a vortex counter clockwise.

    Swirl CW   Create a vortex clockwise.

Deform radius   Defines the radius, in pixels (5-100), of the filter action circle around the pixel pointed by the mouse.

Deform amount   Sets how much out of shape your image will be put (0.0-1.0).

Bilinear   This option smooths the IWarp effect.

Adaptive supersample   This option renders a better image at the cost of increased calculation.

    Max Depth   This value limits the maximum sampling iterations performed on each pixel.

    Threshold   When the value difference between a pixel and the adjacent ones exceeds this threshold a new sampling iteration is performed on the pixel.

Figure 17.48 "IWarp" filter options (Animation tab)

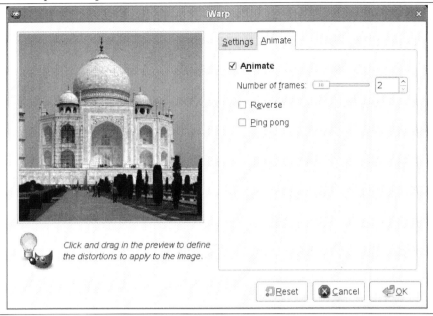

17.4.7.3.2 Animate   This tab allows to generate several intermediate images between the original image and the final deformation of this image. You can play this animation thanks to the Playback plug-in.

Number of frames That's the number of images in your animation (2-100). These frames are stored as layers attached to your image. Use the XCF format when saving it.

Reverse This option plays the animation backwards.

Ping pong When the animation ends one way, it goes backwards.

17.4.8 Lens Distortion

17.4.8.1 Overview

Figure 17.49 Example for the "Lens Distortion" filter

(a) *Original image*   (b) *"Lens Distortion" applied*

This filter lets you simulate but also correct the typical distortion effect introduced in photo images by the glasses contained in the camera lenses.

17.4.8.2 Activating the filter

This filter is found in the image window menu under Filters → Distorts → Lens Distortion.

17.4.8.3 Options

Figure 17.50 "Lens Distortion" options

The allowed range of all options is from -100.0 to 100.0.

Preview The result of your settings will appear in the Preview without affecting the image until you click on OK.

Main The amount of spherical correction to introduce. Positive values make the image convex while negative ones make it concave. The whole effect is similar to wrapping the image inside or outside a sphere.

Figure 17.51 Example result of Main option

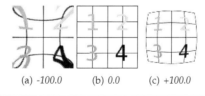

(a) -100.0   (b) 0.0   (c) +100.0

Edge Specifies the amount of additional spherical correction at image edges.

Figure 17.52 Example result of Edge option (Main set to 50.0)

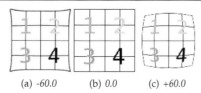

(a) -60.0   (b) 0.0   (c) +60.0

Zoom Specifies the amount of the image enlargement or reduction caused by the hypothetical lens.

Figure 17.53 Example result of Zoom option

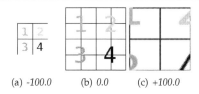

(a) -100.0   (b) 0.0   (c) +100.0

Brighten The amount of the "vignetting" effect: the brightness decrease/increase due to the lens curvature that produces a different light absorption.

The Main or Edge options must be non zero for this option to produce noticeable results.

Figure 17.54 Example result of Brigthen option (Main set to 75.0)

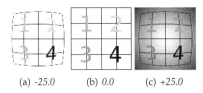

(a) -25.0   (b) 0.0   (c) +25.0

X shift, Y shift These two options specify the shift of the image produced by not perfectly centered pairs of lenses.

As above this option produces visible results only if the Main or Edge options are non zero.

Figure 17.55 Example result of X shift option (Main set to 70.0)

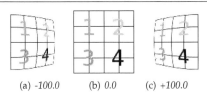

(a) -100.0   (b) 0.0   (c) +100.0

17.4.9 Mosaic

17.4.9.1 Overview

Figure 17.56 Applying example for the "Mosaic" filter

(a) *Original image*   (b) *Filter "Mosaic" applied*

It cuts the active layer or selection into many squares or polygons which are slightly raised and separated by joins, giving so an aspect of mosaic.

17.4.9.2 Activating the filter

You can find this filter through Filters → Distorts → Mosaic.

17.4.9.3 Options

Figure 17.57 "Mosaic" filter options

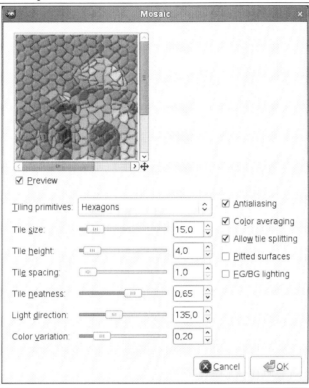

Preview All your setting changes will appear in the Preview without affecting the image until you click on OK. Note that the preview displays only a part of the whole image if the filter is applied to an selection. Don't keep Preview checked if your computer is too slow.

Tiling primitives This option is self-understanding:

Squares 4 edges

Hexagons 6 edges (hexa = 6)

Octagons & squares 8 or 4 edges (octa = 8)

Triangles 3 edges (tri = 3)

Tile size Slider and input box allow you to set the size of tile surface.

Tile height That's ledge, relief of tiles. Value is width of the lit border in pixels.

Tile spacing That's width of the join between tiles.

Tile neatness When set to 1, most of tiles have the same size. With 0 value, size is determined at random and this may lead to shape variation.

Light direction By default light comes from the upper left corner (135°). You can change this direction from 0 to 360 (counter clockwise).

Color variation Each tile has only one color. So the number of colors is reduced, compared to the original image. Here you can increase the number of colors a little.

Antialiasing This option reduces the stepped aspect that may have borders.

Color averaging When this option is unchecked, the image drawing can be recognized inside tiles. When checked, the colors inside tiles are averaged into a single color.

Allow tile splitting This option splits tiles in areas with many colors, and so allows a better color gradation and more details in these areas.

Pitted surfaces With this option tile surface looks pitted.

FG/BG lighting When this option is checked, tiles are lit by the foreground color of the toolbox, and shadow is colored by the background color. Joins have the background color.

17.4.10 Newsprint

17.4.10.1 Overview

Figure 17.58 Applying example for the Newsprint filter

(a) *Original image*   (b) *Filter "Newsprint" applied*

This filter halftones the image using a clustered-dot dither. Halftoning is the process of rendering an image with multiple levels of grey or color (i.e. a continuous tone image) on a device with fewer tones; often a bi-level device such as a printer or typesetter.

The basic premise is to trade off resolution for greater apparent tone depth (this is known as spatial dithering).

There are many approaches to this, the simplest of which is to throw away the low-order bits of tone information; this is what the posterize filter does. Unfortunately, the results don't look too good. However, no spatial resolution is lost.

This filter uses a clustered-dot ordered dither, which reduces the resolution of the image by converting cells into spots which grow or shrink according to the intensity that cell needs to represent.

Imagine a grid super-imposed on the original image. The image is divided into cells by the grid - each cell will ultimately hold a single spot made up of multiple output pixels in order to approximate the darkness of the original image in that cell.

Obviously, a large cell size results in a heavy loss in resolution! The spots in the cells typically start off as circles, and grow to be diamond shaped. This change in shape is controlled by a Spot function. By using different spot functions, the evolution in the shape of the spots as the cell goes from fully black to fully white may be controlled.

17.4.10.2 Starting filter

You can find this filter through Filters → Distorts → Newsprint.

17.4.10.3   Options

Figure 17.59 "Newsprint" filter options

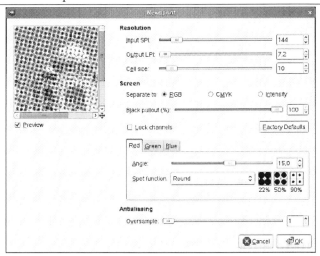

Preview   All your setting changes will appear in the Preview without affecting the image until you click
on OK. Note that the preview displays only a part of the whole image if the filter is applied to an
selection. Don't keep Preview checked if your computer is too slow.

Resolution   This group controls the cell size, either by setting the input and output resolutions, or directly.

> **Input SPI**   Resolution of the original input image, in Samples Per Inch (SPI). This is automatically
> initialised to the input image's resolution.
>
> **Output LPI**   Desired output resolution, in Lines Per Inch (LPI).
>
> **Cell size**   Resulting cell size, in pixels. Most often you will want to set this directly.

Screen

> **Separate To RGB, CMYK, Intensity**   Select which colorspace you wish to operate in. In *RGB* mode,
> no colorspace conversion is performed. In *CMYK*, the image is first internally converted to
> CMYK, then each color channel is separately halftoned, before finally being recombined back
> to an RGB image. In *Intensity* mode, the image is internally converted to grayscale, halftoned,
> then the result used as the alpha channel for the input image. This is good for special effects,
> but requires a little experimentation to achieve best results. Hint: try CMYK if you don't know
> which to go for initially.
>
> **Black pullout (%)**   When doing RGB->CMYK conversion, how much K (black) should be used?
>
> **Lock channels**   Make channel modifications apply to all channels.
>
> **Factory Defaults**   Restore the default settings which should give pleasing results.
>
> **Angle**   Cell grid angle for this channel.
>
> **Spot function**   Spot function to be used for this channel (see preview in blue cell-boxes).

Antialiasing   Proper halftoning does not need antialiasing: the aim is to reduce the color depth after all!
However, since this plugin is mainly for special effects, the results are displayed on screen rather
than by a black/white printer. So it is often useful to apply a little anti-aliasing to simulate ink
smearing on paper. If you do want to print the resulting image then set the antialising to 1 (ie, off).

> **Oversample**   Number of subpixels to sample to produce each output pixel. Set to 1 to disable this
> feature. Warning: large numbers here will lead to very long filter runtimes!

17.4.10.4   Example

Figure 17.60 Example for Newsprint

An example from plug-in author

17.4.11   Page Curl

17.4.11.1   Overview

Figure 17.61 Example for the Page Curl filter

(a) *Original image*   (b) *Filter "Page Curl" applied*

This filter curls a corner of the current layer or selection into a kind of cornet showing the underlying layer in the cleared area. A new "Curl Layer" and a new Alpha channel are created. The part of the initial layer corresponding to this cleared area is also transparent.

17.4.11.2   Activating the filter

This filter is found in the image window menu under Filters → Distorts → Page Curl.

17.4.11.3 Options

Figure 17.62 Options

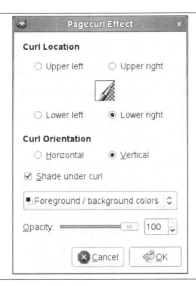

Curl Location You have there four radio buttons to select the corner you want raise. The Preview is redundant and doesn't respond to other options.

Curl Orientation *Horizontal* and *Vertical* refer to the border you want raise.

Shade under curl This is the shadow inside the cornet.

Foreground / background colors, Current gradient, Current gradient (reversed) This option refers to the outer face of the cornet.

Opacity Refers to the visibility of the layer part underlying the cornet. It may be set also in the Layer Dialog.

17.4.12 Polar Coords

17.4.12.1 Overview

Figure 17.63 Example for Polar Coords filter

(a) *Original image*   (b) *"Polar Coords" filter applied*

It gives a circular or a rectangular representation of your image with all the possible intermediates between both.

17.4.12.2 Activating the filter

You can find this filter through Filters → Distorts → Polar Coords.

17.4.12.3 Options

Figure 17.64 "Polar Coords" filter options

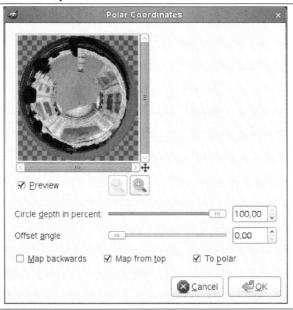

Preview The result of your settings will appear in the Preview without affecting the image until you click on OK.

Circle depth in percent Slider and input box allow you to set the "circularity" of the transformation, from rectangle (0%) to circle (100%).

Offset angle This option controls the angle the drawing will start from (0 - 359°), and so turns it around the circle center.

Map backwards When this option is checked, the drawing will start from the right instead of the left.

Map from top If unchecked, the mapping will put the bottom row in the middle and the top row on the outside. If checked, it will be the opposite.

To polar If unchecked, the image will be circularly mapped into a rectangle (odd effect). If checked, the image will be mapped into a circle.

17.4.12.4 Examples

Figure 17.65 With text

THE GIMP

If you have just written the text, you must Flatten the image before using the filter.

Figure 17.66 With two horizontal bars

17.4.13 Ripple

17.4.13.1 Overview

Figure 17.67 "Ripple" filter example

(a) *Original image*   (b) *Filter "Ripple" applied*

It displaces the pixels of the active layer or selection to waves or ripples reminding a reflection on disturbed water.

17.4.13.2 Activating the filter

You can find this filter through Filters → Distorts → Ripple.

17.4.13.3 Options

Figure 17.68 "Ripple" filter options

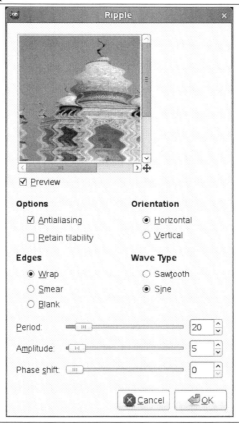

Preview The result of your settings will appear in the Preview without affecting the image until you click on OK.

Options

  Antialiasing This improves the scaled look the image borders may have.

  Retain tileability This preserves the seamless properties if your image is a tile pattern.

Orientation That's the Horizontal or Vertical direction of waves.

Edges Because ripples cause pixel displacement, some pixels may be missing on the image sides:

- With Wrap, pixels going out one side will come back on the other side, replacing so the missing pixels.
- With Smear, the adjacent pixels will spread out to replace the mixing pixels.
- With Blank, the missing pixels will be replaced by black pixels, if the layer does not have an Alpha channel. If an Alpha channel exists in the layer, transparent pixels replace the missing pixels after applying this option.

Wave Type Choose how the wave should look like:

- Sawtooth
- Sine

Period It is related to wavelength (0-200 pixels)

Amplitude It is related to wave height (0-200 pixels).

Phase shift It is angle to delay the wave (0-360 degree). Appling this filter again with the same setting but Phase shift differs by 180 brings the once processed image back to become almost similar to the first original image.

17.4.14 Shift

17.4.14.1 Overview

Figure 17.69 Example for the Shift filter

(a) *Original image*   (b) *Filter "Shift" applied*

It shifts all pixel rows, horizontally or vertically, in the current layer or selection, on a random distance and within determined limits.

17.4.14.2 Activating the filter

You can find this filter through Filters → Distorts → Shift.

17.4.14.3 Options

Figure 17.70 "Shift" filter options

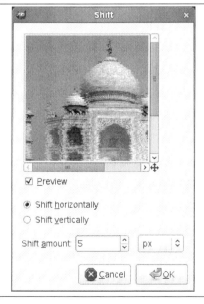

Preview The result of your settings will appear in the Preview without affecting the image until you click on OK.

Shift horizontally, Shift vertically This option sets the dimension where pixels are moved.

Pixels going out one side will come back on the other side.

Shift amount With this option, you can set the maximum shift, between 1 and 200 pixels, or in another unit of measurement.

17.4.15   Value Propagate

17.4.15.1   Overview

Figure 17.71 Example for the Value Propagate filter

(a) *Original image*   (b) *Filter "Value Propagate" applied*

This filter works on color borders. It spreads pixels that differ in a specified way from their neighbouring pixels.

17.4.15.2   Activating the filter

This filter is found in the image window menu under Filters → Distorts → Value Propagate.

17.4.15.3 Options

Figure 17.72 "Value propagate" filter options

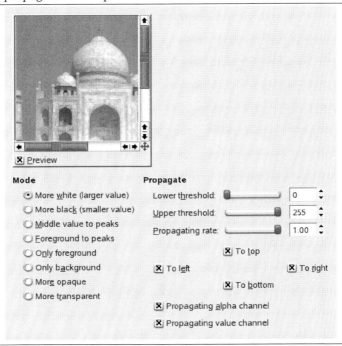

Preview The result of your settings will appear in the Preview without affecting the image until you click on OK.

Mode The examples will be about the following image:

More white (larger value) Pixels will be propagated from upper value pixels towards lower value pixels. So bright areas will enlarge.

Figure 17.73 More white

Bright pixels have been propagated to dark pixels in the four directions : top, bottom, right and left. Filter applied several times to increase effect.

More black (smaller value) Pixels will be propagated from lower value pixels towards upper value pixels. So dark areas will enlarge.

Figure 17.74 More black

Figure 17.75 To bottom only

The same as above with To bottom direction only checked.

Middle value to peaks On a border between the selected thresholds, the average of both values is propagated.

Figure 17.76 Middle value to peaks

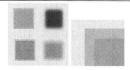

(a) A thin (b) Green
border with a area zoomed
transitional x800. A
color has thin border
been added (one pixel
to objects. It wide) has
is not visible been added.
around objects Its value is
with smoothed the average
borders. between grey
(90%) and
green (78%)
: (90 + 78) /
2 = 84.

Foreground to peaks The propagated areas will be filled with the foreground color of the toolbox.

Figure 17.77 Foreground to peaks

In this example, the foreground color in Toolbox is Red. A thin border, one pixel wide, red, is added around objects. With smoothed objects, this border is located at the furthest limit of smoothing. Here, another border appears inside. This is an artifact due to the small size of the object which makes the smoothing area of opposite sides to overlap.

Only foreground Only areas with the Toolbox Foreground color will propagate.

Figure 17.78 Only foreground

In this example, the foreground color in Toolbox is that of the green object. After applying filter several times, the green area is clearly enlarged.

Only background Only areas with the Background color will propagate.

More opaque, More transparent These commands work like "More white" and "More black". Opaque (transparent) areas will be propagated over less opaque (transparent) areas. These commands need an image with an alpha channel.

Figure 17.79 More opaque

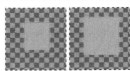

(a) Original (b) Filter layer, with a applied several transparent times: the background. green, opaque, area got increased.

Propagate

Lower threshold, Upper threshold A pixel will be propagated (spread) if the difference in value between the pixel and its neighbour is no smaller than the lower threshold and no larger than the upper threshold.

Propagating rate That's the propagating amount. The higher it will be the more colored the propagation will be.

To left, To top, To right, To bottom You can select one or more directions.

Propagating alpha channel If checked, the pixel alpha value will be propagated, otherwise the pixel will get the alpha of the neighbouring pixels. This checkbox is only visible when the active layer has an alpha channel.

Propagating value channel If checked, the pixel's color channels (gray channel on grayscaled images) will be propagated. The option is checked by default, of course. This checkbox too is only visible when the active layer has an alpha channel.

17.4.16 Video

17.4.16.1 Overview

Figure 17.80 Applying example for the "Video" filter

(a) Original image   (b) Filter "Video" applied

Apply low dot-pitch RGB simulation to the specified drawable.

17.4.16.2 Activating the filter

You can find this filter through Filters → Distorts → Video.

17.4.16.3 Options

Figure 17.81 "Video" filter options

Preview This preview is unusual: Changes appear always on the same image which is not yours.

Video Pattern It would be rather difficult to describe what each pattern will render. It's best to see what they render in the Preview.

Additive Set whether the function adds the result to the original image.

Rotated Rotate the result by 90°.

17.4.17 Waves

17.4.17.1 Overview

Figure 17.82 Example for the Waves filter

(a) *Original image*   (b) *Filter "Waves" applied*

With this filter you get the same effect as a stone thrown in a quiet pond, giving concentric waves.

17.4.17.2 Activating the filter

You can find this filter through Filters → Distorts → Waves.

17.4.17.3 Options

Figure 17.83 "Waves" filter options

Preview All your setting changes will appear in the Preview without affecting the image until you click on OK. Don't keep Preview checked if your computer is too slow.

Mode

> **Smear** Because of the waves, areas are rendered empty on sides. The adjacent pixels will spread to fill them.

> **Blacken** The empty areas will be filled by black color.

Reflective Waves bounce on sides and interfere with the arriving ones.

Amplitude Varies the height of waves.

Phase This command shifts the top of waves.

Wavelength Varies the distance between the top of waves.

17.4.18   Whirl and Pinch

17.4.18.1   Overview

Figure 17.84 Example for the Whirl and Pinch filter

(a) *Original image*   (b) *Filter applied*

"Whirl and Pinch" distorts your image in a concentric way.

"Whirl" (applying a non-zero Whirl angle) distorts the image much like the little whirlpool that appears when you empty your bath.

"Pinch", with a nil rotation, can be compared to applying your image to a soft rubber surface and squeezing the edges or corners. If the Pinch amount slider is set to a negative value, it will look as if someone tried to push a round object up toward you from behind the rubber skin. If the Pinch amount is set to a positive value, it looks like someone is dragging or sucking on the surface from behind, and away from you.

Tip

   The "pinch" effect can sometimes be used to compensate for image distortion produced by telephoto or fish-eye lenses ("barrel distortion").

Figure 17.85 Illustration

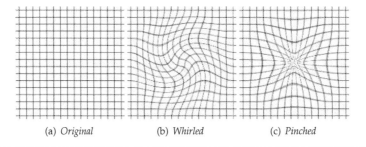

(a) *Original*   (b) *Whirled*   (c) *Pinched*

17.4.18.2   Activating the filter

You can find this filter through Filters → Distorts → Whirl and Pinch

---

17.4.18.3   Parameter Settings

Figure 17.86 "Whirl and Pinch" filter options

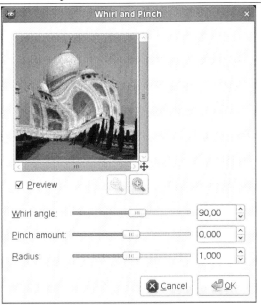

Preview Changes to parameters are immediately displayed into the *Preview*. The whirlpool is focused around the center of the current layer or selection.

Whirl angle Clockwise or counter clockwise (-360 to +360). Controls how many degrees the affected part of the image is rotated.

Pinch amount Whirlpool depth(-1 to +1). Determines how strongly the affected part of the image is pinched.

Radius Whirlpool width (0.0-2.0). Determines how much of the image is affected by the distortion. If you set *Radius* to 2, the entire image will be affected. If you set *Radius* to 1, half the image will be affected. If *Radius* is set to 0, nothing will be affected (think of it as the radius in a circle with 0 in the center and 1 halfway out).

17.4.19   Wind

17.4.19.1   Overview

Figure 17.87 "Wind" filter example

| (a) *Original image* | (b) *Filter "Wind" applied* |

The Wind filter can be used to create motion blur, but it can also be used as a general distort filter. What is characteristic about this filter is that it will render thin black or white lines. Wind will detect the edges in the image, and stretch out thin white or black lines from that edge. This is why you can create the illusion of motion, because the edges are what will be blurred in a photograph of a moving object.

17.4.19.2   Activating the filter

You can find this filter through Filters → Distorts → Wind.

17.4.19.3   Options

Figure 17.88 "Wind" filter options

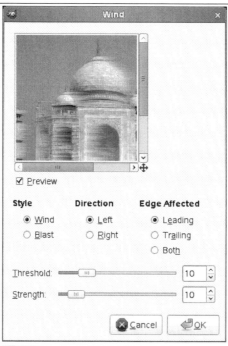

The interface is quite simple. You can set the *Strength* of the wind and a *Threshold* value. *Threshold* will restrict the effect to fewer areas of the image. *Strength* controls the amount of wind, so a high value will render a storm. You can also increase the effect by setting the *Style* to Blast, which will produce thicker lines than Wind.

You can only set the wind in two directions, either Left or Right. However, you can control which edge the wind will come from using the values Leading, Trailing or Both. Because Trailing will produce a black wind, it creates a less convincing motion blur than Leading, which will produce white wind.

The following illustrations are based on this image:

Preview All your setting changes will appear in the Preview without affecting the image until you click on OK. It reproduces a part of the image only, centred on the first modified area it encounters.

Style

   Wind This option is the most suggestive of a moving effect. Trails are thin.

Blast This option tries to suggest a blast due to an explosion. Trails are thick.

Direction You can select the direction, Left or Right, from which the wind comes.

Edge Affected

Leading Trails will start from the front border, falling on the object itself. It suggests that a violent wind is pulling color out.

Trailing Trails start from the back border of the object.

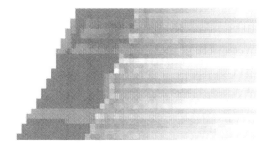

Both Combines both effects.

Threshold The threshold to detect borders. The higher it is, the fewer borders will be detected.

Strength Higher values increase the strength of the effect.

17.5   Light and Shadow Filters

Figure 17.89 The Light and Shadow filters menu

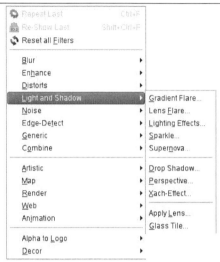

17.5.1   Introduction

Here you will find three groups of filters:

- The original *Light Effects* filters, which render several illumination effects of the image.

- Some *Script-Fu* and *Python-Fu* scripts, which create various kinds of shadows.

- *Glass Effects* filters result in an image as if it were seen through a lens or glass tiles.

17.5.2   Gradient Flare

17.5.2.1   Overview

Figure 17.90 Example for the Gradient Flare filter

(a) *Original image*   (b) *Filter "Gradient Flare" applied*

Gradient Flare effect reminds the effect you get when you take a photograph of a blinding light source, with a halo and radiations around the source. The Gradient Flare image has three components: *Glow* which is the big central fireball, *Rays* and *Second Flares*

17.5.2.2 Activating the filter

This filter is found in the image window menu under Filters → Light and Shadow → Gradient Flare

17.5.2.3 Options

The *Settings* tab allows you to set manually the parameters while the *Selector* tab let you choose presets in a list.

Preview When Auto update preview is checked, parameter setting results are interactively displayed in preview without modifying the image until you click on OK button.

Figure 17.91 "Gradient Flare" filter options (Settings)

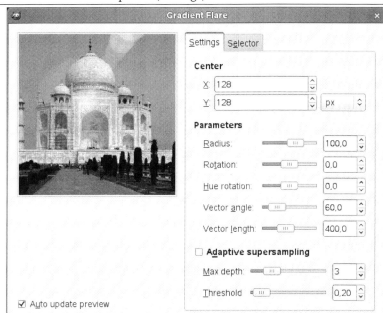

17.5.2.3.1 Settings

Center You can set X and Y (pixels) coordinates of glint using the input box or by clicking into the preview. The coordinate origin is at the upper left corner.

Parameters

> **Radius** The radius of the effect. The slider limits the range of possible values, but using the input box you can enter greater values.

> **Rotation** Turn the effect.

> **Hue rotation** Change the tint (color) of the effect.

> **Vector angle** Turn the Second flares.

> **Vector length** Vary the distance applied for the Second flares.

Adaptive supersampling Settings of the anti-aliasing following parameters like Depth and Threshold. (See also *Supersampling* .)

Figure 17.92 "Gradient Flare" filter options (Selector)

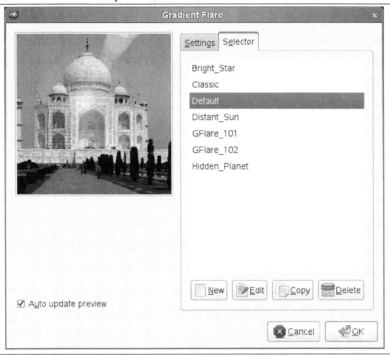

17.5.2.3.2 Selector   The Selector tab allows you to select a Gradient Flare pattern, to change it and save it.

New When you click on this button, you create a new Gradient Flare pattern. Give it a name of your choice.

Edit This button brings up the Gradient Flare Editor (see below).

Copy This button allows you to duplicate selected Gradient Flare pattern. You can edit the copy without altering the original.

Delete This button deletes the selected Gradient Flare pattern.

17.5.2.4   Gradient Flare Editor

The Gradient Flare Editor is also organized in tabs:

Figure 17.93 "Gradient Flare Editor" options (General)

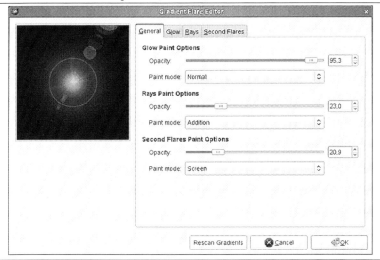

17.5.2.4.1   General

Glow Paint Options

    Opacity Slider and input box allows you to reduce glow opacity (0-100).

    Paint mode You can choose between four modes:

        Normal In this mode, the glow covers the image without taking into account what is beneath.

        Addition Pixel RGB values of glow are added to RGB values of the corresponding pixels in the image. Colors get lighter and white areas may appear.

        Overlay Light/Dark areas of glow enhance corresponding light/dark areas of image.

        Screen Dark areas of image are enlightened by corresponding light areas of glow. Imagine two slides projected onto the same screen.

Rays Paint Options Options are the same as for Glow Paint Options.

Second Flare Paint Options Options are the same as for Glow Paint Options.

Figure 17.94 "Gradient Flare Editor" options (Glow)

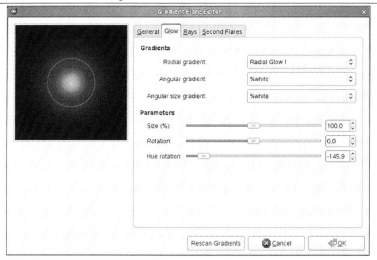

17.5.2.4.2   Glow

Gradients By clicking on the rectangular buttons, you can develop a long list of gradients. "%" gradients belong to the Editor.

> **Radial gradient** The selected gradient is drawn radially, from center to edge.
>
> **Angular gradient** The selected gradient develops around center, counter-clockwise, starting from three o'clock if the Rotation parameter is set to 0. Radial and angular gradients are combined according to the Multiply mode: light areas are enhanced and colors are mixed according to CMYK color system (that of your printer).
>
> **Angular size gradient** This is a gradient of radius size which develops angularly. Radius is controlled according to gradient Luminosity: if luminosity is zero (black), the radius is 0%. If luminosity is 100% (white), the radius is also 100%.

Parameters

> **Size (%)** Sets size of glow in percent (0-200).
>
> **Rotation** Sets the origin of the angular gradient (-180 +180).
>
> **Hue rotation** Sets glow color, according to the HSV color circle (-180 +180). (Cf. The triangle color selector.)

Figure 17.95 "Gradient Flare Editor" options (Rays)

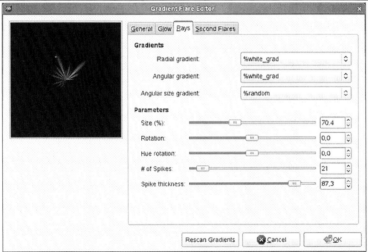

17.5.2.4.3 Rays

Gradients The options are the same as for Glow.

Parameters The first three options are the same as in Glow. Two are new:

> **# of Spikes** This option determines the number of spikes (1-300) but also their texture.
>
> **Spike thickness** When spikes get wider (1-100), they look like flower petals.

Figure 17.96 "Gradient Flare Editor" options (Second Flares)

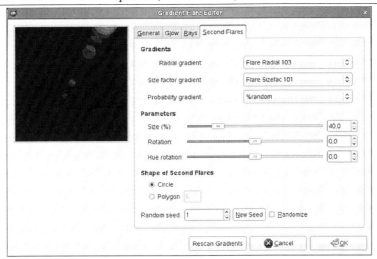

17.5.2.4.4   Second Flares

Gradients The options are the same as for Glow.

Parameters Options are the same as in Glow.

Shape of Second Flares Second flares, these satellites of the main flare, may have two shapes: Circle and Polygon. You can set the *Number* polygon sides. The option accepts 1 side (!), not 2.

Random seed The random generator will use this value as a seed to generate random numbers. You can use the same value to repeat the same "random" sequence several times.

Randomize When you click on this button, you produce a random seed that will be used by the random generator. It is each time different.

17.5.3   Lens Flare

17.5.3.1   Overview

Figure 17.97 Example for the Lens Flare filter

(a) *Original image*   (b) *Filter "Lens Flare" applied*

This filter gives the impression that sun hit the objective when taking a shot. You can locate the reflection with a reticule you can move, but you have not the possibilities that the Gradient Flare filter offers.

17.5.3.2   Activate the filter

You can find this filter in the image menu menu through Filters → Light and Shadow → Lens Flare.

17.5.3.3   Options

Figure 17.98 "Lens Flare" filter options

Preview If checked, parameter setting results are interactively displayed in preview. Scroll bars allow
you to move around the image.

Center of Flare Effect You can set X and Y (pixels) coordinates of glint using the input box or by clicking
into the preview. The coordinate origin is at the upper left corner.

Show position When this option is checked, a reticule appears in preview and you can move it with the
mouse pointer to locate the center of Lens Flare effect.

Tip

 The mouse cursor, which looks like a cross when it moves over the preview,
lets you locate the filter effect even without the reticule.

17.5.4 Lighting Effects

17.5.4.1 Overview

Figure 17.99 The same image, before and after applying Lighting filter

(a) *Original image*   (b) *Filter "Lighting Effects" applied*

This filter simulates the effect you get when you light up a wall with a spot. It doesn't produce any drop shadows and, of course, doesn't reveal any new details in dark zones.

17.5.4.2 Activate the filter

This filter is found in the image window menu under Filters → Light and Shadow → Lighting Effects.

17.5.4.3 Options

Figure 17.100 "Lighting" filter options

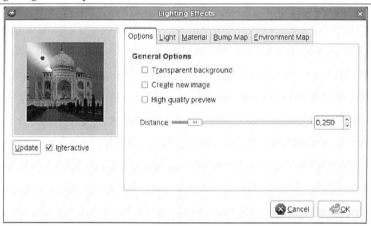

Preview When Interactive is checked, parameter setting results are interactively displayed in preview without modifying the image until you click on OK button.

    If Interactive is not checked, changes are displayed in preview only when you click on the Update button. This option is useful with a slow computer.

    Any other options are organized in tabs:

Figure 17.101 "Lighting" filter options (General Options)

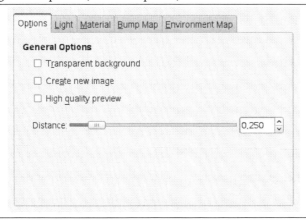

17.5.4.3.1 General Options

Transparent background Makes destination image transparent when bumpmap height is zero (height is zero in black areas of the bumpmapped image).

Create new image Creates a new image when applying filter.

High quality preview For quick CPU...

Distance You can specify the distance of the light source from the center of the image with this slider. The range of values is from 0.0 to 2.0.

Figure 17.102 "Lighting" filter options (Light Settings)

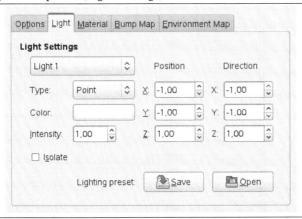

17.5.4.3.2 Light Settings In this tab, you can set light parameters. With Light 1 ... Light 6 you can create six light sources and work on each of them separately.

Type The filter provides several *light types* in a drop-down list:

  Point Displays a blue point at center of preview. You can click and drag it to move light all over the preview.

  Directional The blue point is linked to preview center by a line which indicates the direction of light.

  None This deletes the light source (light may persist...).

Color When you click on the color swatch, you bring a dialog up where you can select the light source color.

Intensity With this option, you can set light intensity.

Position Determines the light point position according to three coordinates: X coordinate for horizontal position, Y for vertical position, Z for source distance (the light darkens when distance increases). Values are from -1 to +1.

Direction This option should allow you to fix the light direction in its three X, Y and Z coordinates.

Isolate With this option, you can decide whether all light sources must appear in the Preview, or only the source you are working on.

Lighting preset You can save your settings with the Save and get them back later with the Open.

Figure 17.103 "Lighting" filter options (Material Properties)

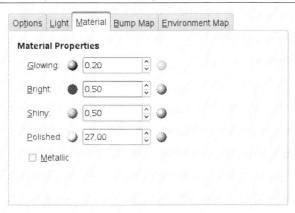

17.5.4.3.3 Material Properties These options don't concern light itself, but light reflected by objects. Small spheres, on both ends of the input boxes, represent the action of every option, from its minimum (on the left) to its maximum (on the right). Help pop ups are more useful.

Glowing With these option, you can set the amount of original color to show where no direct light falls.

Bright With this option, you can set the intensity of original color when hit directly by a light source.

Shiny This option controls how intense the highlight will be.

Polished With this option, higher values make the highlight more focused.

Metallic When this option is checked, surfaces look metallic.

Figure 17.104 "Lighting" filter options (Bump Map)

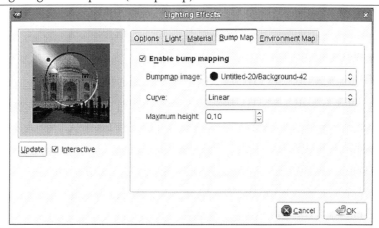

17.5.4.3.4 Bump Map In this tab, you can set filter options that give relief to the image. See *Bump mapping* .

Enable bump mapping With this option, bright parts of the image will appear raised and dark parts will appear depressed. The aspect depends on the light source position.

Bumpmap image You have to select there the grey-scale image that will act as a bump map. See Bump Map plug-in for additional explanations.

Curve This option defines the method that will be used when applying the bump map; that is, the bump height is a function of the specified curve. Four curve types are available: *Linear*, *Logarithmic*, *Sinusoidal* and *Spherical*.

Maximum height This is the maximum height of bumps.

Figure 17.105 "Lighting" filter options (Environment Map)

17.5.4.3.5 Environment Map

Enable environment mapping When you check this box, the following option is enabled:

Environment image You have to select there a RGB image, present on your screen. Please note that for this option to work you should load another image with GIMP *before* using it.

An example can be found at [BUDIG01].

17.5.5 Sparkle

17.5.5.1 Overview

Figure 17.106 Applying example for the Sparkle filter

(a) *Original image*   (b) *Filter "Sparkle" applied*

This filter adds sparkles to your image. It uses the lightest points according to a threshold you have determined. It is difficult to foresee where sparkles will appear. But you can put white points on your image where you want sparkles to be.

17.5.5.2 Activate the filter

This filter is found in the image window menu under Filters → Light and Shadow → Sparkle.

17.5.5.3   Parameter Settings

Figure 17.107 "Sparkle" filter options

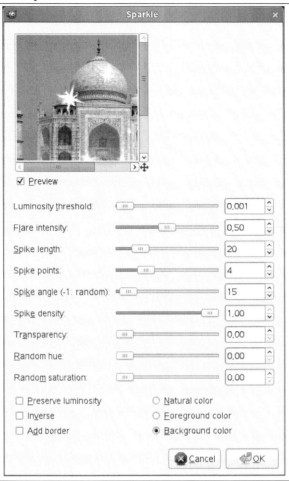

Sliders and input boxes allow you to set values.

Preview If checked, parameter setting results are interactively displayed in preview. Scroll bars allow
you to move around the image.

Luminosity threshold The higher the threshold, the more areas are concerned by sparkling (0.0-0.1).

Flare intensity When this value increases, the central spot and rays widen (0.0-1.0).

Spike length This is ray length (1-100). When you reduce it, small spikes decrease first.

Spike points Number of starting points for spikes (0-16). It's the number of big spikes. There is the
same number of small spikes. When number is odd, small spikes are opposite the big ones. When
number is even, big spikes are opposite another big spike.

Spike angle This is angle of first big spike with horizontal (-1 +360). -1 determines this value at random.
If a spot has several pixels within required threshold, each of them will generate a sparkle. If
angle is positive, they will all be superimposed. With -1, each sparkle will have a random rotation
resulting in numerous thin spikes.

Spike density This option determines the number of sparkles on your image. It indicates the percentage
(0.0-1.0) of all possible sparkles that will be preserved.

Transparency When you increase transparency (0.0-1.0), sparkles become more transparent and the
layer beneath becomes visible. If there is no other layer, sparkle saturation decreases.

Random hue This option should change sparkle hue at random... (0.0-1.0).

Random saturation This option should change sparkle saturation at random... (0.0-1.0).

Preserve luminosity Gives to all central pixels the luminosity of the brightest pixel, resulting in increasing the whole sparkle luminosity.

Inverse Instead of selecting brightest pixels in image, Sparkle will select the darkest ones, resulting in dark sparkles.

Add border Instead of creating sparkles on brightest pixels, this option creates an image border made up of numerous sparkles.

Natural color, Foreground color, Background color You can change there the color of central pixels. This color will be added in Screen mode (Multiply if Inverse is checked). "Natural color" is the color of the pixel in the image.

17.5.6 Supernova

17.5.6.1 Overview

Figure 17.108 Applying example for the Supernova filter

(a) *Original image*   (b) *Filter "Supernova" applied*

This filter creates a big star reminding a super-nova. It works with RGB and GRAY images. Light effect decreases according to 1/r where r is the distance from star center.

17.5.6.2 Activate the filter

This filter is found in the image window menu under Filters → Light and Shadow → Supernova.

17.5.6.3   Parameter Settings

Figure 17.109 "Supernova" filter options

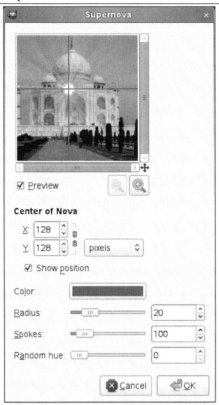

Preview If checked, parameter setting results are interactively displayed in preview. Scroll bars allow you to move around the image.

Center of Nova

> **X, Y** You can use input boxes to set horizontal (X) and vertical (Y) coordinates of SuperNova center. You can also click the SuperNova center in the *preview* box.

Tip

> To center Supernova precisely, select "percent" option in the Unit drop-down list and fix X and Y to 50%.

> **Show position** This option brings up a reticle in preview, centered on the SuperNova.

Color When you click on the color swatch, you bring up the usual color selector.

Radius This is radius of the SuperNova center (1-100). When you increase the value, you increase the number of central white pixels according to r*r (1, 4, 9...).

Spikes This is number of rays (1-1024). Each pixel in the nova center emit one pixel wide rays. All these rays are more or less superimposed resulting in this glittering effect you get when you move this slider.

Random hue Color rays at random. (0-360) value seems to be a range in HSV color circle.

17.5.7 Drop Shadow

17.5.7.1 Overview

Figure 17.110 Example for the "Drop Shadow" filter

(a) *Original image*

(b) *"Drop Shadow" applied (white background layer added manually)*

This filter adds a drop-shadow to the current selection or to the image if there's no active selection. Optional the filter resizes the image if that's necessary for displaying the shadow.

You may choose the color, position, and size of the shadow.

Please note that the filter does not add a background layer to make the shadow visible. The shadow's background is transparent. The white background in the above example has not been created by the filter, instead it has been added later to let you see the shadow.

17.5.7.2   Activate the filter

You can find this filter in the image menu menu through Filters → Light and Shadow → Drop Shadow.

17.5.7.3   Options

Figure 17.111 "Drop Shadow" filter options

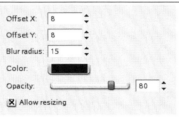

Offset X, Offset Y The layer containing the drop shadow will be moved horizontally by X pixels, vertically by Y pixels. So, X and Y offset determine where the shadow will be placed in relation to the image. High values make the imaginary source of light look like it's far away in horizontal or vertical direction, and low values will make it look closer to the image.

The offsets may be negative, leading to a shadow on the left of the selection if offset X < 0, or above the selection if offset Y < 0.

If there's no active selection, you must have Allow resizing enabled to see any effect.

Blur radius After creating the shadow, a Gaussian blur with the specified radius is applied to the shadow layer, resulting in the realistic appearance of the drop shadow. It may be necessary to enable Allow resizing, since blurring extends the shadow.

Color The shadow may have any color. Just click on the button, and select a color when the color selector pops up.

Figure 17.112 "Drop Shadow" color example

Opacity The shadow's opacity is just the opacity of the new layer containing the shadow (see Section 8.1.1). It defaults to 80%, but you may select any other value from 0 (full transparency) to 100 (full opacity) here. After applying the filter to an image you can change the opacity in the layers dialog.

Allow resizing If enabled, the filter will resize the image if that is needed to make place for the shadow. The new size depends on the size of the selection, the blur radius, and the shadow offsets.

17.5.8   Perspective

17.5.8.1   Overview

Figure 17.113 Example for the "Perspective" filter

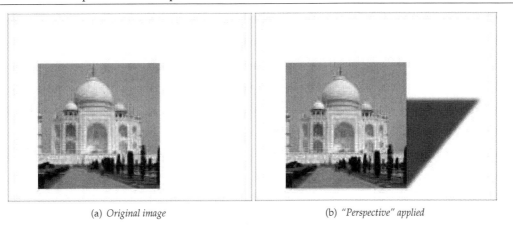

(a) *Original image*   (b) *"Perspective" applied*

This filter adds a perspective shadow to the selected region or alpha-channel as a layer below the active layer. You may select color, length and direction of the shadow as well as the distance of the horizon.

If necessary, the filter may resize the image. But it will not add a background to make the shadow visible.

17.5.8.2   Activate the filter

You can access this filter in the image window menu through Filters → Light and Shadow → Perspective.

17.5.8.3   Options

Figure 17.114 "Perspective" options

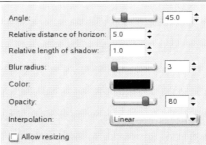

Angle   The angle determines the direction of the shadow or the imaginary source of light, respectively. Values range from 0° to 180°, where 90° represents a light source just in front of the selection or layer. For angles less than 90°, the shadow is at the right side, so the light source is on the left. For angles greater than 90°, it's the other way round. Tip: think of the slider's handle as source of light.

Figure 17.115 "Angle" example

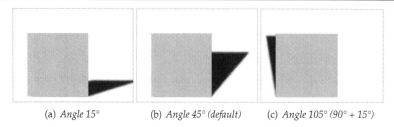

(a) Angle 15°   (b) Angle 45° (default)   (c) Angle 105° (90° + 15°)

Relative distance of horizon This option determines how far away the imaginary horizon is. The relative distance is the distance from the ground-line of the selection or layer, the "unit" of measurement is the height of the selection or layer.

Value range is from 0.1 to 24.1, where 24.1 means (nearly) "infinite". Note that the relative length of shadow must not exceed the distance of horizon.

Figure 17.116 "Distance of horizon" example

Angle = 45°. Distance = 2.4. Length = 1.8.

In the example above, the yellow area is the selection the filter is applied to. The blue line at the top represents the imaginary horizon. The angle between the selection's ground-line and the red line is 45°. The length of the red line is 1.8 times the height of the yellow selection. Extended to the horizon, the length is 2.4 times the selection's height.

Relative length of shadow With this option you can set the length of shadow with respect to the height of the selection or layer. In the above example, the red line represents the length of shadow, its length is 1.8 relative to the height of the yellow selection.

Value range is from 0.1 to 24.1, although the length of shadow must not exceed the relative distance of horizon - you can't go beyond the horizon.

Figure 17.117 "Length of Shadow" example

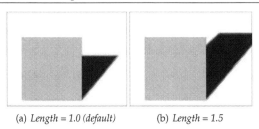

(a) Length = 1.0 (default)   (b) Length = 1.5

Blur radius After creating the shadow, a Gaussian blur with the specified radius is applied to the shadow layer, resulting in the realistic appearance of the shadow.

Figure 17.118 Blur example

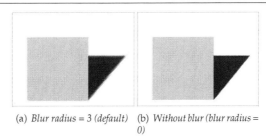

(a) *Blur radius = 3 (default)*   (b) *Without blur (blur radius = 0)*

Color Of course, the default color of the shadow is black. But a click on the button opens the color selector, where you may select any other color.

Opacity The shadow's opacity is the opacity of the new layer containing the shadow (see Section 8.1.1). It defaults to 80%, but you may select any other value from 0 (full transparency) to 100 (full opacity) here. After applying the filter to an image you can change the opacity in the layers dialog.

Interpolation This drop-down list lets you choose the method of interpolation used when the shadow layer is transformed, for example rotated by the specified angle. Using None will usually result in aliasing, using any interpolation method may change the color of the shadow in some areas. Linear is a good choice.

Allow resizing If enabled, the filter will resize the image if that is needed to make place for the shadow.

In the example below, the yellow area is the active selection, background is light blue. The white area has been added after resizing to make the shadow visible.

Figure 17.119 "Allow resizing" example

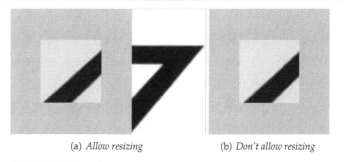

(a) *Allow resizing*   (b) *Don't allow resizing*

17.5.9 Xach-Effect

17.5.9.1 Overview

Figure 17.120 Example for the "Xach-Effect" filter

(a) *Original image*   (b) *"Xach-Effect" applied*

This filter adds a subtle translucent 3D effect to the selected region or alpha channel. This 3D effect is achieved by

1. Highlighting the selection: a new layer ("Highlight") will be created above the active layer, filled with the highlight color. Then a layer mask will be added to that layer making the unmasked pixel partially transparent.

Highlight layer with layer mask

2. Painting the selection's left and top edges with the highlight color: for that the "Highlight" layer will be extended by one pixel left and up. These small areas will be opaque.

3. Creating a drop shadow at the bottom right side of the selection.

You may vary these default settings, for example select different colors for highlight or shadow and change amount and directions of offsets.

17.5.9.2 Activate the filter

The filter is found in the image window menu under Filters → Light and Shadow → Xach-Effect.

17.5.9.3 Options

There are two groups of options, each controlling the highlight or the shadow, and a checkbox for the selection behaviour.

Figure 17.121 "Xach-Effect" options

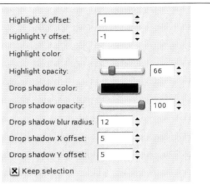

Highlight X offset, Highlight Y offset The selection's left and top edge are painted with the highlight color. The highlight offset is the size (width or height) of the respective area. If offset is less than 0 (this is the default), the left (X offset < 0) or top (Y offset < 0) area will be colored. If offset is greater than 0, the right (X offset > 0) or bottom (Y offset > 0) area will be painted.

Highlight color This is the color used to highlight the selected area. It defaults to white, but clicking on the swatch button brings up a color selector and you may select any other color.

Highlight opacity The selection will be covered by a partially transparent area filled with the highlight color. This option lets you set the level of transparency. Since a layer mask will be used, the value ranges from 0 (full transparency) to 255 (full opacity).

The highlight opacity defaults to 66, which is equivalent to 26%.

Drop shadow options These options work like the respective Drop Shadow options (without resizing). Briefly:

Drop shadow color Click on the button to open a color selector.

Drop shadow opacity The opacity (0% - 100%) of the layer containing the shadow.

Drop shadow blur radius The radius used by the Gaussian blur filter, which will be applied to the shadow.

Drop shadow X offset, Drop shadow Y offset Direction and amount, by which the shadow will be moved from the selection.

Keep selection If checked, the active selection will remain active when the filter has been applied.

17.5.10   Apply Lens

17.5.10.1   Overview

Figure 17.122 The same image, before and after applying lens effect.

(a) *Original image*   (b) *Filter "Apply lens" applied*

After applying this filter, a part of the active layer is rendered as through a spherical lens.

17.5.10.2   Activate the filter

You can find this filter in the image window menu through Filters → Light and Shadow → Apply Lens

17.5.10.3   Options

Figure 17.123 "Apply Lens" filter options

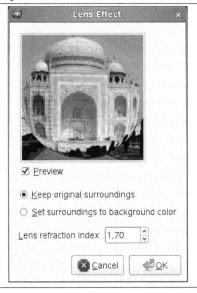

Preview If checked, parameter setting results are interactively displayed in preview. Scroll bars allow you to move around the image.

Keep original surroundings The lens seems to be put on the active layer.

Set surroundings to background color The part of the active layer outside the lens will have the background color selected in the toolbox.

Make surroundings transparent The part of the active layer outside the lens will be transparent. This option exists only if the active layer has an alpha channel.

Lens refraction index Lens will be more or less convergent (1-100).

17.5.11 Glass Tile

17.5.11.1 Overview

Figure 17.124 The same image, before and after applying glass tile effect.

(a) *Original image*   (b) *Filter "Glass Tile" applied*

After applying this filter, the active layer or selection is rendered as through a glass brick wall.

17.5.11.2 Activate the filter

You can find this filter through Filters → Light and Shadow → Glass Tile

17.5.11.3 Options

Figure 17.125 "Glass Tile" filter options

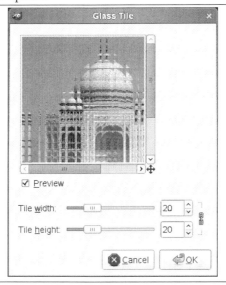

Preview If checked, parameter setting results are interactively displayed in preview. Scroll bars allow you to move around the image.

Tile width, Tile length Sets tile width and length (10-50 pixels).

By default, width and height are linked, indicated by the chain symbol next to the input boxes. If you want to set width and height separately, click on that chain symbol to unlink them.

17.6 Noise Filters

17.6.1 Introduction

Noise filters *add* noise to the active layer or to the selection. To *remove* small defects from an image, see the Despeckle and Selective Gaussian Blur filters.

17.6.2 HSV Noise

17.6.2.1 Overview

Figure 17.126 Example of applying the "HSV Noise" filter

(a) *Original image*   (b) *Filter "HSV Noise" applied*

The HSV Noise filter creates noise in the active layer or selection by using the Hue, Saturation, Value (luminosity) color model.

17.6.2.2 Activate the filter

You can find this filter through Filters → Noise → HSV Noise.

17.6.2.3 Options

Figure 17.127 "HSV Noise" filter options

Preview This preview displays interactively changes before they are applied to the image.

Holdness This slider (1 -8) controls how much the new pixel color value is allowed to be applied compared to the existing color. A low holdness will give an important hue variation. A high holdness will give a weak variation.

Hue This slider changes the color of the pixels in a random pattern. It selects an increasing available color range in the HSV color circle starting from the original pixel color.

Saturation This slider increases saturation of scattered pixels.

Value This slider increases brightness of scattered pixels.

17.6.3 Hurl

17.6.3.1 Overview

Figure 17.128 Example for the "Hurl" filter

(a) *Original image*   (b) *Filter "Hurl" applied*

You can find this filter through Filters → Noise → Hurl.

The Hurl filter changes each affected pixel to a random color, so it produces real *random noise*. All color channels, including an alpha channel (if it is present) are randomized. All possible values are assigned with the same probability. The original values are not taken into account. All or only some pixels in an active layer or selection are affected, the percentage of affected pixels is determined by the Randomization (%) option.

17.6.3.2 Options

Figure 17.129 "Hurl" options

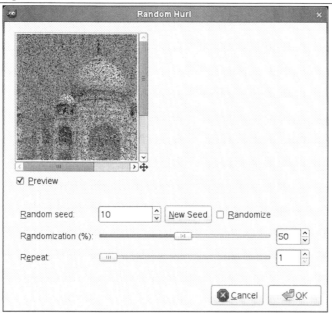

Random seed Controls randomness of hurl. If the same random seed in the same situation is used, the filter produces exactly the same results. A different random seed produces different results. Random seed can be entered manually or generated randomly by pressing New Seed button.

When the Randomize option is checked, random seed cannot be entered manually, but is randomly generated each time the filter is run. If it is not checked, the filter remembers the last random seed used.

Randomization (%) This slider represents the percentage of pixels of the active layer or selection which will be hurled. The higher value, the more pixels are hurled.

Repeat It represents the number of times the filter will be applied. In the case of the Hurl filter it is not very useful, because the same results can be obtained faster just by using a higher Randomization (%) value.

17.6.4 Pick

17.6.4.1 Overview

Figure 17.130 Example of applying the "Pick" filter

(a) *Original image*   (b) *Filter "Pick" applied*

The Pick filter replaces each affected pixel by a pixel value randomly chosen from its eight neighbours and itself (from a 3×3 square the pixel is center of). All or only some pixels in an active layer or selection are affected, the percentage of affected pixels is determined by the Randomization (%) option.

17.6.4.2 Activate the filter

You can find this filter through Filters → Noise → Pick.

17.6.4.3 Options

Figure 17.131 "Pick" filter options

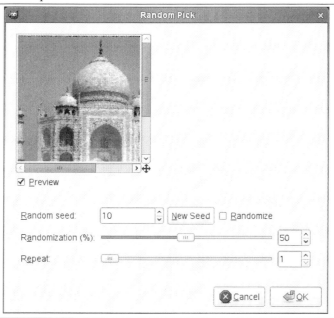

Random seed Controls randomness of picking. If the same random seed in the same situation is used, the filter produces exactly the same results. A different random seed produces different results. Random seed can be entered manually or generated randomly by pressing New Seed button.

When the Randomize option is checked, random seed cannot be entered manually, but is randomly generated each time the filter is run. If it is not checked, the filter remembers the last random seed used.

Randomization (%) This slider represents the percentage of pixels of the active layer or selection which will be picked. The higher value, the more pixels are picked.

Repeat This slider represents the number of times the filter will be applied. Higher values result in more picking, pixel values being transferred farther away.

17.6.5 RGB Noise

17.6.5.1 Overview

Figure 17.132 Example of applying the "RGB Noise" filter

(a) *Original image*   (b) *Filter "RGB Noise" applied*

The RGB Noise filter adds a normally distributed noise to a layer or a selection. It uses the RGB color model to produce the noise (noise is added to red, green and blue values of each pixel). A normal distribution means, that only slight noise is added to the most pixels in the affected area, while less pixels are affected by more extreme values. (If you apply this filter to an image filled with a solid grey color and then look at its histogram, you will see a classic bell-shaped Gaussian curve.)

The result is very naturally looking noise.

This filter does not work with indexed images.

17.6.5.2 Activate the filter

You can find this filter through Filters → Noise → RGB Noise.

17.6.5.3   Options

Figure 17.133 "RGB Noise" filter options

Preview   This preview displays interactively changes before they are applied to the image.

Correlated noise   Noise may be additive (uncorrelated) or multiplicative (correlated - also known as speckle noise). When checked, every channel value is multiplied by an normally distributed value. So the noise depends on the channel values: a greater channel value leads to more noise, while dark colors (small values) tend to remain dark.

Independent RGB   When this radio button is checked, you can move each RGB slider separately. Otherwise, sliders R, G and B will be moved all together. The same relative noise will then be added to all channels in each pixel, so the hue of pixels does not change much.

Red, Green, Blue, Alpha   These slidebars and adjacent input boxes allow to set noise level (0.00 - 1.00) in each channel. Alpha channel is only present if your layer holds such a channel. In case of a grayscale image, a Grey is shown instead of color sliders.

The value set by these sliders actually determine the standard deviation of the normal distribution of applied noise. The used standard deviation is a half of the set value (where 1 is the distance between the lowest and highest possible value in a channel).

17.6.6 Slur

17.6.6.1 Overview

Figure 17.134 Example of applying the Slur filter

(a) *Original image*   (b) *Filter "Slur" applied*

Slurring produces an effect resembling melting the image downwards; if a pixel is to be slurred, there is an 80% chance that it is replaced by the value of a pixel directly above it; otherwise, one of the two pixels to the left or right of the one above is used. All or only some pixels in an active layer or selection are affected, the percentage of affected pixels is determined by the Randomization (%) option.

17.6.6.2 Activate the filter

You can find this filter through Filters → Noise → Slur.

17.6.6.3 Options

Figure 17.135 Slur filter options

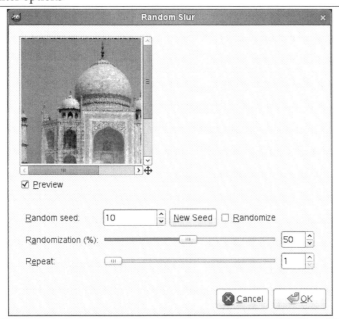

Random seed It controls randomness of slurring. If the same random seed in the same situation is used, the filter produces exactly the same results. A different random seed produces different results. Random seed can be entered manually or generated randomly by pressing New Seed button.

When the Randomize option is checked, random seed cannot be entered manually, but is randomly generated each time the filter is run. If it is not checked, the filter remembers the last random seed used.

Randomization (%) This slider represents the percentage of pixels of the active layer or selection which will be slurred. The higher value, the more pixels are slurred, but because of the way the filter works, its effect is most noticeable if this slider is set to a medium value, somewhere around 50. Experiment with it and try for yourself!

Repeat This slider represents the number of times the filter will be applied. Higher values result in more slurring, moving the color over a longer distance.

17.6.7 Spread

17.6.7.1 Overview

Figure 17.136 Example of applying the Spread filter

(a) *Original image*   (b) *Filter "Spread" applied*

The Spread filter swaps each pixel in the active layer or selection with another randomly chosen pixel by a user specified amount. It works on color transitions, not on plain color areas. No new color is introduced.

17.6.7.2 Activate the filter

You can find this filter through Filters → Noise → Spread.

17.6.7.3 Options

Figure 17.137 "Spread" filter options

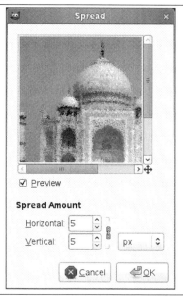

Preview This preview displays interactively changes before they are applied to the image.

Spread Amount You can set the distance that pixels will be moved along Horizontal and Vertical axis. The axis can be locked by clicking the Chain icon. You can also define the Unit to be used.

17.7 Edge-Detect Filters

17.7.1 Introduction

Edge detect filters search for borders between different colors and so can detect contours of objects. They are used to make selections and for many artistic purposes.

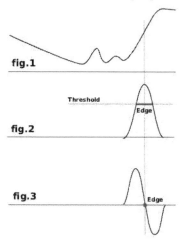

Most of them are based on gradient calculation methods and give thick border lines. Look at fig.1 which represents color intensity variations. On the left is a slow color gradient which is not a border. On the right is a quick variation which is an edge. Now, let us calculate the gradient, the variation speed, of this edge, i.e. the first derivative (fig.2). We have to decide that a border is detected when gradient is more than a threshold value (the exact border is at top of the curve, but this top varies according to borders). In most cases, threshold is under top and border is thick.

The Laplacian edge detection uses the second derivative (fig.3). The top of the curve is now at zero and clearly identified. That's why Laplace filter renders a thin border, only a pixel wide. But this derivative gives several zeros corresponding to small ripples, resulting in false edges.

Some blurring before applying edge filters is often necessary: it flattens small ripples in signal and so prevents false edges.

17.7.2   Difference of Gaussians

17.7.2.1   Overview

Figure 17.138 Applying example for the "Difference of Gaussians" filter

(a) *Original image*   (b) *Filter "Difference of Gaussians" applied*

This filter does edge detection using the so-called "Difference of Gaussians" algorithm, which works by performing two different Gaussian blurs on the image, with a different blurring radius for each, and subtracting them to yield the result. This algorithm is very widely used in artificial vision (maybe in biological vision as well!), and is pretty fast because there are very efficient methods for doing Gaussian blurs. The most important parameters are the blurring radii for the two Gaussian blurs. It is probably easiest to set them using the preview, but it may help to know that increasing the smaller radius tends to give thicker-appearing edges, and decreasing the larger radius tends to increase the "threshold" for recognizing something as an edge. In most cases you will get nicer results if Radius 2 is smaller than Radius 1, but nothing prevents you from reversing them, and in situations where you have a light figure on the dark background, reversing them may actually improve the result.

17.7.2.2   Activating the filter

You can find this filter through Filters → Edge-Detect → Difference of Gaussians.

17.7.2.3   Options

Figure 17.139 Gaussian Difference filter options

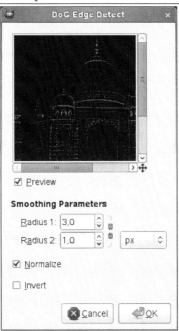

Smoothing Parameters Radius 1 and Radius 2 are the blurring radii for the two Gaussian blurs. The only constraints on them is that they cannot be equal, or else the result will be a blank image. If you want to produce something that looks like a sketch, in most cases setting "Radius 2" smaller than "Radius 1" will give better results.

Normalize Checking this box causes the brightness range in the result to be stretched as much as possible, increasing contrast. Note that in the preview, only the part of the image that is shown is taken into account, so with Normalize checked the preview is not completely accurate. (It is accurate except in terms of global contrast, though.)

Invert Checking this box inverts the result, so that you see dark edges on a white background, giving something that looks more like a drawing.

17.7.3 Edge

17.7.3.1 Overview

Figure 17.140 Applying example for the Edge filter

(a) *Original image*   (b) *After applying the filter (Sobel option)*

Figure 17.141 Applying examples for the Edge filter

(a) *After applying the filter (Prewitt compass* (b) *After applying the filter (Gradient option)* option)

Figure 17.142 Applying example for the Edge filter

 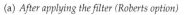 

(a) *After applying the filter (Roberts option)*   (b) *After applying the filter (Differential option)*

Figure 17.143 Applying example for the Edge filter

After applying the filter (Laplace option)

17.7.3.2   Activating the filter

You can find this filter through Filters → Edge-Detect → Edge....

17.7.3.3   Options

Figure 17.144 Edge filter options

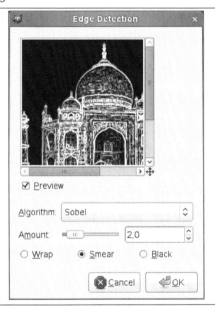

Algorithm   Edge detector offers several detection methods:

>   **Sobel**   Here, this method has no options and so is less interesting than the specific Sobel.
>
>   **Prewitt compass**   Result doesn't look different from Sobel.
>
>   **Gradient**   Edges are thinner, less contrasted and more blurred than Sobel.
>
>   **Roberts**   No evident difference from Sobel.
>
>   **Differential**   Edges less bright.
>
>   **Laplace**   Less interesting than the specific one.

Amount   A low value results in black, high-contrasted image with thin edges. A high value results in thick edges with low contrast and many colors in dark areas.

Wrap, Smear, Black Where the edge detector will get adjoining pixels for its calculations when it is working on the image boundaries. This option will only have an effect on the boundaries of the result (if any). Smear is the default and the best choice.

17.7.4 Laplace

17.7.4.1 Overview

Figure 17.145 Applying example for the Laplace filter

(a) *Original image*   (b) *Filter "Laplace" applied*

This filter detects edges in the image using Laplacian method, which produces thin, pixel wide borders.

17.7.4.2 Activating the filter

You can find this filter through Filtres → Edge-Detect → Laplace.

17.7.5 Neon

17.7.5.1 Overview

Figure 17.146 Applying example for the Neon filter

(a) *Original image*   (b) *Filter "Neon" applied*

This filter detects edges in the active layer or selection and gives them a bright neon effect.

You will find in GIMP a Script-Fu also named Neon, which works in a different manner. The Script-Fu is an easy shortcut to construct logo-like letters outlined with a configurable neon-effect. See Section 17.16.17 for details.

17.7.5.2 Activating the filter

You can find this filter through Filters → Edge-Detect → Neon....

17.7.5.3 Options

Figure 17.147 Neon filter options

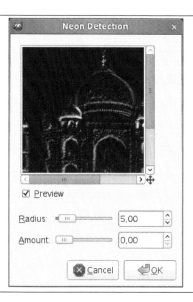

Radius This option lets you determine how wide the detected edge will be.

Amount This option lets you determine how strong the filter effect will be.

17.7.6 Sobel

17.7.6.1 Overview

Figure 17.148 Applying example of the Sobel filter

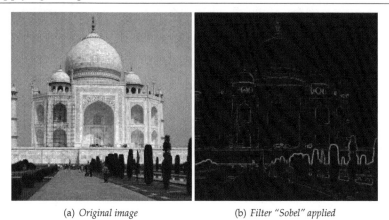

(a) *Original image*   (b) *Filter "Sobel" applied*

Sobel's filter detects horizontal and vertical edges separately on a scaled image. Color images are turned into RGB scaled images. As with the Laplace filter, the result is a transparent image with black lines and some rest of colors.

17.7.6.2 Activating the filter

You can find this filter through Filters → Edge-Detect → Sobel.

17.7.6.3 Options

Figure 17.149 Sobel filter options

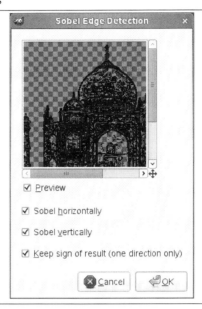

Preview If checked, changes in the image are displayed in the Preview in real time before being applied to the image.

Sobel horizontally Renders near horizontal edges.

Sobel vertically Renders near vertical edges.

Keep sign of result This option allows you to set how the filter will work if you have selected one direction for use only: a flat relief with bumps and hollows will be created.

17.8 Generic Filters

17.8.1 Introduction

Generic filters are a catch-all for filters which can't be placed elsewhere. You can find:

- The Convolution Matrix filter which lets you build custom filters.

- The Dilate filter.

- The Erode filter.

17.8.2 Convolution Matrix

17.8.2.1 Overview

Here is a mathematician's domain. Most of filters are using convolution matrix. With the Convolution Matrix filter, if the fancy takes you, you can build a custom filter.

What is a convolution matrix? It's possible to get a rough idea of it without using mathematical tools that only a few ones know. Convolution is the treatment of a matrix by another one which is called "kernel".

The Convolution Matrix filter uses a first matrix which is the Image to be treated. The image is a bi-dimensional collection of pixels in rectangular coordinates. The used kernel depends on the effect you want.

GIMP uses 5x5 or 3x3 matrices. We will consider only 3x3 matrices, they are the most used and they are enough for all effects you want. If all border values of a kernel are set to zero, then system will consider it as a 3x3 matrix.

The filter studies successively every pixel of the image. For each of them, which we will call the "initial pixel", it multiplies the value of this pixel and values of the 8 surrounding pixels by the kernel corresponding value. Then it adds the results, and the initial pixel is set to this final result value.

A simple example:

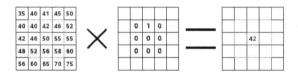

On the left is the image matrix: each pixel is marked with its value. The initial pixel has a red border. The kernel action area has a green border. In the middle is the kernel and, on the right is the convolution result.

Here is what happened: the filter read successively, from left to right and from top to bottom, all the pixels of the kernel action area. It multiplied the value of each of them by the kernel corresponding value and added results. The initial pixel has become 42: (40*0)+(42*1)+(46*0) + (46*0)+(50*0)+(55*0) + (52*0)+(56*0)+(58*0) = 42. (the filter doesn't work on the image but on a copy). As a graphical result, the initial pixel moved a pixel downwards.

17.8.2.2 Activating the filter

This filter is found in the image window menu under Filters → Generic → Convolution Matrix.

17.8.2.3   Options

Figure 17.150 "Convolution matrix" options

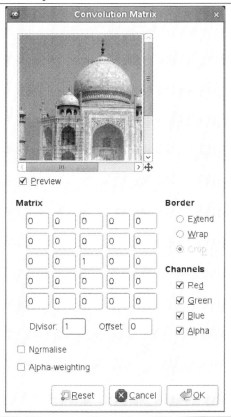

Matrix   This is the 5x5 kernel matrix: you enter wanted values directly into boxes.

> **Divisor**   The result of previous calculation will be divided by this divisor. You will hardly use 1, which lets result unchanged, and 9 or 25 according to matrix size, which gives the average of pixel values.
>
> **Offset**   This value is added to the division result. This is useful if result may be negative. This offset may be negative.

Border   When the initial pixel is on a border, a part of kernel is out of image. You have to decide what filter must do:

From left: source image, Extend border, Wrap border, Crop border

> **Extend**   This part of kernel is not taken into account.
>
> **Wrap**   This part of kernel will study pixels of the opposite border, so pixels disappearing from one side reappear on the other side.
>
> **Crop**   Pixels on borders are not modified, but they are cropped.

Channels   You can select there one or several channels the filter will work with.

Normalise If this option is checked, The Divisor takes the result value of convolution. If this result is equal to zero (it's not possible to divide by zero), then a 128 offset is applied. If it is negative (a negative color is not possible), a 255 offset is applied (inverts result).

Alpha-weighting If this option is not checked, the filter doesn't take in account transparency and this may be cause of some artefacts when blurring.

17.8.2.4 Examples

Design of kernels is based on high levels mathematics. You can find ready-made kernels on the Web. Here are a few examples:

Figure 17.151 Sharpen

Figure 17.152 Blur

Figure 17.153 Edge enhance

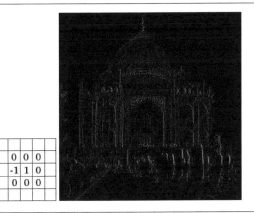

Figure 17.154 Edge detect

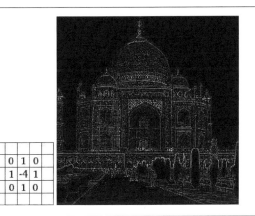

Figure 17.155 Emboss

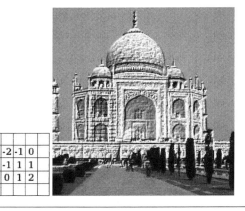

17.8.3 Dilate

17.8.3.1 Overview

Figure 17.156 Applying example for the Dilate filter

(a) *Original image*   (b) *Filter "Dilate" applied*

This filter widens and enhances dark areas of the active layer or selection.

For every image pixel, it brings the pixel Value (luminosity) into line with the lowest Value (the darkest) of the 8 neighbouring pixels (3x3 matrix). So, a dark pixel is added around dark areas. An isolated pixel on a brighter background will be changed to a big "pixel", composed of 9 pixels, and that will create some noise in the image.

In this image, the studied pixel has a red border and the studied matrix has a green border. I hope you have understood how to go on with the process and get a 3x3 pixel block: when the "I" pixel is inside the green border, the studied pixel turns to black.

A larger dark area will dilate by one pixel in all directions:

The filter was applied 3 times.

On more complex images, dark areas are widened and enhanced the same, and somewhat pixellated. Here, the filter was applied 3 times:

Of course, if background is darker than foreground, it will cover the whole image.

17.8.3.2 Activating the filter

This filter is found in the image window menu under Filters → Generic → Dilate.

17.8.3.3 Examples

Figure 17.157 Dilate text

E **E**

Figure 17.158 Dilate neon effect

17.8.4 Erode

17.8.4.1 Overview

Figure 17.159 Erode noise

(a) *Original image*   (b) *Filter "Erode noise" applied*

This filter widens and enhances bright areas of the active layer or selection.

For every image pixel, it brings the pixel Value (luminosity) into line with the upper value (the brightest) of the 8 neighbouring pixels (3x3 matrix). So, a bright pixel is added around bright areas. An isolated pixel on a brighter background will be deleted. A larger bright area will dilate by one pixel in all directions.

On complex images, bright areas are widened and enhanced the same, and somewhat pixellated.

On a solid background, this filter can delete noise:

Figure 17.160 "Erode noise" example

17.8.4.2 Activating the filter

This filter is found in the image window menu under Filters → Generic → Erode.

17.9 Combine Filters

17.9.1 Introduction

The combine filters associate two or more images into a single image.

17.9.2 Depth Merge

Depth Merge is a Combine Filter which is useful to combine two different pictures or layers. You can decide which part of every image or layer will stay visible.

17.9.2.1 Overview

Figure 17.161 Filter example

(a) *Original*   (b) *Filter applied*

Every image is associated with a map which works as a mask. Simply create this map as a grayscale gradient: when applied onto the image, dark areas of the mask will show the underlying image and bright areas will mask the image.

Note

 To work with this filter, images and maps must have the same size. All images to be selected must be present on screen.

You can also use this filter on an image with several layers. All layers will appear in the drop-down lists used to select images. These layers must have the same size.

17.9.2.2 Accessing this Filter

You can find this filter through Filters → Combine → Depth Merge

17.9.2.3 Options

Figure 17.162 "Depth Merge" filter options

Source 1:	image1.png-1/Background-2 ▼
Depth map:	map1.png-3/Background-6 ▼
Source 2:	image2.png-2/Background-4 ▼
Depth map:	map2.png-4/Background-8 ▼
Overlap:	0,000
Offset:	0,000
Scale 1:	1,000
Scale 2:	1,000

Source 1, Source 2 Defines the source images to use for the blending.

Depth map Define the picture to use as transformation maps for the sources.

Overlap Creates soft transitions between images.

Offset This option shifts the merging limit, giving more or less importance to an image against the other.

Scale 1, Scale 2 Same as above for Offset, but more sensitive and applied to each map separately. When you scale to a lower value, it will affect the map image's value, making it darker. So, black is more dominant in the merge and you will see more of the image.

17.9.2.4 Using example

Maps are grayscale gradients created with the Blend tool and modified with the Curve tool.

Figure 17.163 Source images and their maps

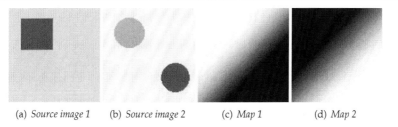

(a) *Source image 1*   (b) *Source image 2*   (c) *Map 1*   (d) *Map 2*

You can understand what's going on. Image-1 is treated by map-1: the red square is masked and the yellow square remains visible. Image-2 is treated by map-2: the red circle is masked and the green circle remains visible. In total, the green circle and the yellow square stay visible.

Figure 17.164 Results

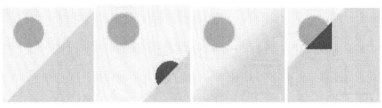

(a) No offset and no (b) Offset = *0.980 : the* (c) Overlap: *the limit* (d) Scale 1 *reduced*
overlap. *The limit be- limit, sharp, is shifted so is blurred.*   *to 0.056 : as with*
tween both images is that the image2 area is   *Offset, the limit is*
sharp and is situated in increased.   *shifted. Image-1 area is*
the middle of the mask   *increased.*
gradient.

17.9.3 Film

17.9.3.1 Overview

Figure 17.165 Applying example for the Film filter

(a) *Original image*   (b) *Filter "Film" applied*

Film filter lets you merge several pictures into a photographic film drawing.

> **Note**
>
> This filter does not invert colors, so it does not imitate negative film like the ones used to produce prints. Instead you should think of the result as an imitation of slide film or cinema film.

17.9.3.2 Accessing this Filter

You can find this filter through Filters → Combine → Film.

17.9.3.3   Options

Figure 17.166 "Film" filter options (Selection)

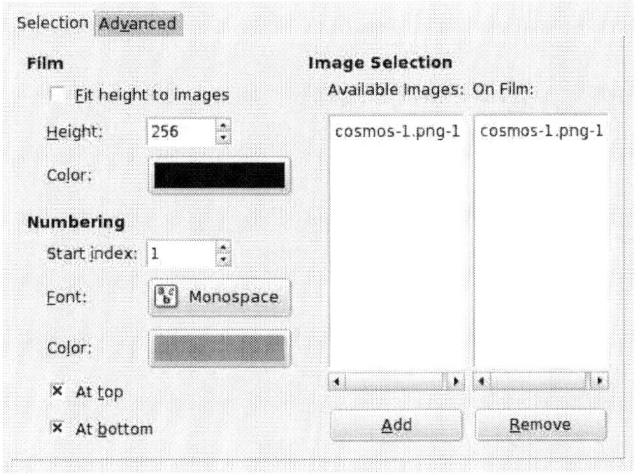

17.9.3.3.1   Selection   Film

Fit height to images Applies the height of original pictures to the resulting one.

Height This option lets you define the height of the resulting picture. If originals have different sizes, they will be scaled to this size.

Color By clicking on the color dwell you can define the color of the film (around and between pictures).

   Numbering

Start index Defines the beginning number which will be used for the images.

Font Defines the font of digits.

Color By clicking on the color dwell, you can define the font color of digits.

At top, At bottom Defines the position of the number.

   Image Selection

Available images Shows the pictures which can be used for merging. The pictures are the ones already opened in GIMP.

On film Shows the pictures chosen to be merged.

Add This button allows the user to put an available image in the "On film" section.

Remove This button allows to bring a picture from "On film " to "Available images". After that, the picture will not be used anymore in the resulting document.

Figure 17.167 "Film" filter options (Advanced)

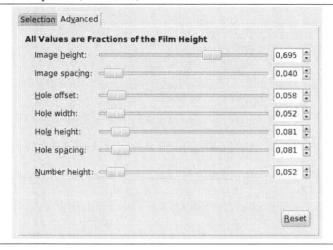

17.9.3.3.2 Advanced

Image height Defines the height of each pictures in the resulting image.

Image spacing Defines the space between the pictures as they will be inserted in the future image.

Hole offset Defines the hole position from image border.

Hole width Defines the width of the holes in the resulting image.

Hole height Defines the height of the holes in the resulting image.

Hole spacing Defines the space between holes

Number height Defines the height of the index number, proportionally to the height of the picture.

17.10 Artistic Filters

17.10.1 Introduction

Artistic filters create artistic effects like cubism, oil painting, canvas...

17.10.2 Apply Canvas

17.10.2.1 Overview

Figure 17.168 Example for the "Apply Canvas" filter

(a) *Original image*   (b) *Filter "Apply Canvas" applied*

This filter applies a canvas-like effect to the current layer or selection. It textures the image as if it were an artist's canvas.

17.10.2.2 Activate the filter

You can find this filter through Filters → Artistic → Apply Canvas....

17.10.2.3 Options

Figure 17.169 "Apply Canvas" options

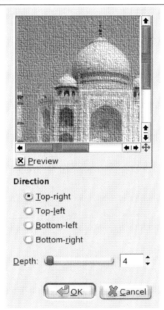

Preview Your changes are displayed in this preview before being applied to your image.

Direction Direction sets the starting direction of the canvas render. You can also consider that this option gives you the position of the light source which lightens the canvas.

Depth The Depth slider controls the apparent depth of the rendered canvas effect from 1 (very flat) to 50 (very deep).

17.10.3   Cartoon

17.10.3.1   Overview

Figure 17.170 Example for the "Cartoon" filter

(a) *Original image*   (b) *Filter "Cartoon" applied*

The Cartoon filter modifies the active layer or selection so that it looks like a cartoon drawing. Its result is similar to a black felt pen drawing subsequently shaded with color. This is achieved by darkening areas that are already distinctly darker than their neighborhood.

17.10.3.2   Activate the filter

You can find this filter in Filters → Artistic → Cartoon.

17.10.3.3   Options

Figure 17.171 "Cartoon" filter options

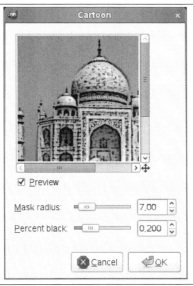

Mask radius   This parameter controls the size of areas the filter works with. Large values result in very thick black areas and much less detail in the resulting image. Small values result in more subtle pen strokes and more details preserved.

Percent black This parameter controls the amount of black color added to the image. Small values make the blend from color regions to blackened areas smoother and dark lines themselves thinner and less noticeable. Larger values make the lines thicker, darker and sharper. The maximum value makes the lines aliased. The best, most natural results are usually achieved with an intermediate value.

17.10.4 Clothify

17.10.4.1 Overview

Figure 17.172 Example of Clothify

Filter "Clothify" applied (in selection)

Clothify command is a script which adds a cloth-like texture to the selected region or alpha.

If the image is in indexed colors, this menu entry is grayed out and unavailable.

This effect is achieved through the following steps:

1. Create an image in the same size as the original image, or selection or region in alpha if it is given, then add a layer to this image filled with white and noisified strongly.

2. Reproduce a layer from the recently added layer and set the mode of the upper layer to Multiply.

3. Apply Gaussian blur in different directions, horizontally on the lower layer by the given parameter Blur X as the radius, and vertically on the upper layer with Blur Y.

4. Merge these two layers into an image and make its contrast expanded as possibly, then slightly noisify again on this working image.

5. Finally do bump map on the original image by the working image with parameters Azimuth, Elevation, and Depth.

17.10.4.2 Activate the filter

This filter is found in the image window menu under Filters → Artistic → Clothify....

17.10.4.3 Options

Figure 17.173 "Clothify" filter options

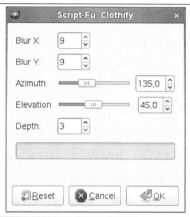

Azimuth, Elevation, and Depth come from Bump Map filter.

Blur X, Blur Y These parameters lengthen fibers of the texture, horizontally by Blur X, and vertically by Blur Y. The range of value is between 3 to 100.

Azimuth Azimuth slider controls the bearings where light comes from according to the point of the compass. Both the minimum value (0.00) and the maximum value (360.00) are the direction of three o'clock on the dial panel of an analogue clock. Increasing value goes counter-clockwise.

Elevation Elevation slider controls the height where light comes from. For the minimal value (0.50) the light comes from horizon, and for the maximum value (90.0) the light comes from zenith.

Depth Depth slider controls distance between bump height and hollow depth. Increasing value causes more rugged features. Values vary from 1 to 65.

17.10.5 Cubism

17.10.5.1 Overview

Figure 17.174 Example for the "Cubism"

(a) *Original image*   (b) *Filter "Cubism" applied*

The Cubism plug-in modifies the image so that it appears to be constructed of small squares of semi-transparent tissue paper.

Tip

 If setting possibilities of this filter are not enough for you, see GIMPressionist filter which offers more options.

17.10.5.2 Activate the filter

You can find this filter through Filters → Artistic → Cubism

17.10.5.3 Options

Figure 17.175 "Cubism" filter options

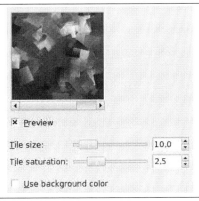

Preview Your changes are displayed in this preview before being applied to your image.

Tile size This variable determines the size, in pixels, of the squares to be used. This is, in effect, the size of the little squares of tissue paper used in generating the new image. The slider can be used, the exact pixel size can be entered into the text box, or the arrow buttons can be used.

Tile saturation This variable specifies how intense the color of the squares should be. This affects the opacity of the squares. A high value will render the squares very intensely and does not allow lower squares to show through. A lower value allows the lower squares to be more visible through the higher ones and causes more blending in the colors. If this is set to 0 and Use Background Color is not checked, the entire layer will be rendered black. If it is checked and the value here is zero, the background color will fill the entire layer.

Use background color This filter creates its tiles from all the colors of the image and paint them with a color scale which depends on the Tile Saturation. With a low Tile Saturation, this color scale lets the background color appear: default is black as you can see by setting Tile Saturation to 0. When this option is checked, the background color of the Toolbox is used. If your image has an Alpha channel, this color scale will also be transparent.

Figure 17.176 Example illustrating the action of the "Use BackGround color" option

The original image and the color area of Toolbox. BG color is blue.

Figure 17.177 The option is not checked

The option is not checked. On the left is no Alpha: background is black. On the right is Alpha: background is transparent black.

Figure 17.178 The option is checked

The option is checked. On the left, no Alpha: background is blue. On the right, with an Alpha channel, background is transparent blue.

> **Tip**
>
> If you are using this to generate background images for web pages and the like, work with a small range of colors painted randomly on a small square. Then apply the Cubism filter with the desired settings. As a last step, try Make Seamless to adjust the image so it will tile seamlessly in your background.

17.10.6 GIMPressionist

17.10.6.1 Overview

Figure 17.179 Example for the "GIMPressionist" filter

(a) *Original image*   (b) *Filter "GIMPressionist" applied*

The GIMPressionist filter is the king of Artistic filters. It can do what Cubism and Apply Canvas do and much more. It gives your image the look of a painting. All is going as if your image was painted again on a paper and with a brush you'd have chosen. It works on the active layer or selection.

17.10.6.2 Activating the filter

You can find this filter via the image menu through Filters → Artistic → GIMPressionist.

17.10.6.3   Options

Figure 17.180 GIMPressionist options

The dialog window consists of a small Preview area on the left, which is always visible, and a huge amount of GIMPressionist options organized in tabs.

17.10.6.3.1   Preview   All your setting changes will appear in the Preview without affecting the image until you click on OK. The Update button refreshes the preview window (it is not automatic, GIMPressionist has so much work to do!), and the Reset button reverts to the original image.

Figure 17.181 "Presets" tab options

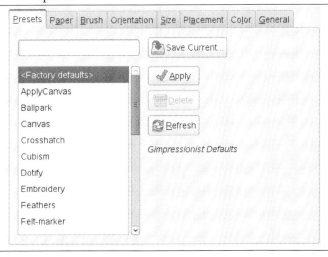

17.10.6.3.2   Presets tab   GIMPressionist has a lot of parameters. When combined, they give an astronomical number of possibilities. So, it is important, when an interesting preset has been found, to save it and also to send it to the plugin author if exceptional. Per contra, the intricacy of all these parameters makes difficult understanding and foreseeing how each one works.

Presets options

Save Current Save current parameters. You can give a name in the input box on the left and a short description in the dialog that appear.

Apply Load the parameters of the selected preset in the list.

Delete Delete the selected preset. You can delete only the presets you have created.

Refresh Update the preset list.

Figure 17.182 "Paper" tab options

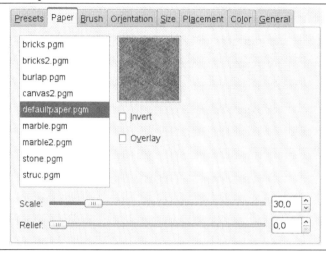

17.10.6.3.3   Paper tab   This tab concerns the texture of the canvas your image will be painted on. You have a list of textures and a Preview for the selected texture. A description is displayed on the right for every texture when selected.

Paper options

Invert Inverts the paper texture: what was a hollow turns to a bump and vice-versa.

Overlay Apply the paper as it, without embossing it. It looks like if a transparent paper has been overlayed on the image.

Scale Specifies the scale of the texture (in % of the original file): controls the graininess of the texture.

Relief Specifies the amount of embossing to apply (3-150).

Figure 17.183 "Brush" tab options

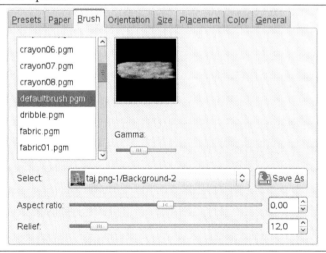

17.10.6.3.4   Brush tab   "Brush" is a general term for any material used to paint. A list of brushes is available with a Preview for the selected one.

Brush options

Gamma Changes the gamma (luminosity) of the selected brush. The gamma correction brightens or darkens midtones.

Select You can also use a brush pattern you have created by selecting its image (arrow button on the Select line). This image must be on your screen before you launch the filter to be taken in account. Of course, don't use big images.

If your image has several layers, they also will be displayed in the Select list and can be used as a brush. When selected, the layer appears in the brush preview and the normal brush is deselected.

The Save as button allows you to save the selected brush.

Aspect ratio Specifies the brush proportions, height (0 -1) and width (0 +1).

Relief Specifies the amount of paint used for each stroke. This may evoke painting with a palette knife.

Figure 17.184 "Orientation" tab options

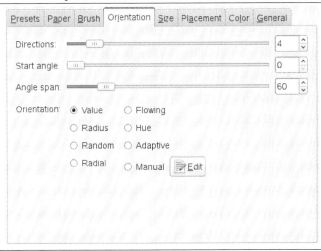

17.10.6.3.5 Orientation tab This tab allows to set the orientation of the brush strokes. A painter is not obliged to go over with the same paintbrush angle. To perform some effects, he can vary their orientation. Orientation options

Directions With this option, you can set how many times the brush will pass through a same place, with each time a different direction, resulting in a more and more thick paint.

Start angle Specifies the general direction of the strokes, the angle that the angle range will start from. Directions are often chosen to give some movement to the image.

Angle span Specifies the angle, the sector, of the stroke "fan".

Orientation Specifies the direction of the brush strokes.

> **Value** Let the value (luminosity) of the region determine the direction of the stroke.
>
> **Radius** The distance from the center of the image determines the direction of the stroke.
>
> **Random** Select a random direction for each stroke.
>
> **Radial** Let the direction from the center determine the direction of the stroke.
>
> **Flowing** Not a direction question here: the strokes follow a "flowing" pattern.
>
> **Hue** Let the hue of the region determine the direction of the stroke.
>
> **Adaptive** The brush direction that matches the original image the closest is selected.
>
> **Manual** The Edit button opens the Edit orientation Map dialog that allows you to set the directions manually.

Figure 17.185 "Size" tab options

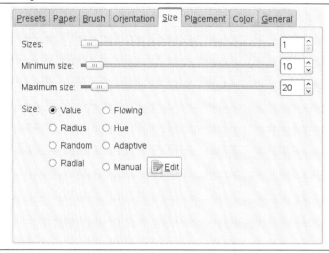

17.10.6.3.6   Size tab   This tab allows you to set the number of brush sizes that will be used to paint, the limits of variation of these sizes and the criterion used to determine them.

Size options

You can specify how many brush sizes are to be used and their sizes.

Sizes The number of brush sizes to use.

Minimum size, Maximum size The brush sizes are between these two values. The greater the size, the greater the length and width of strokes.

Size You have there options to specify how the size of strokes will be determined.

    Value Let the value (luminosity) of the region determine the size of the stroke.

    Radius The distance from the center of the image determines the size of the stroke.

    Random Select a random size for each stroke.

    Radial Let the direction from the center determine the size of the stroke.

    Flowing Not a length question here: the strokes follow a "flowing" pattern.

    Hue Let the hue of the region determine the size of the stroke.

    Adaptive The brush size that matches the original image the closest is selected.

    Manual The Edit button opens the Size Map Editor. That allows you to specify the size of strokes by yourself.

Figure 17.186 "Placement" tab options

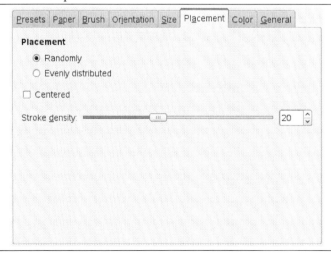

17.10.6.3.7   Placement tab   In this tab you can set how strokes will be distributed.

Placement options

Placement   In the preview of the Orientation Map Editor, all small arrows look like a flow around objects. Inside this flow, strokes may be placed in two different ways:

   Randomly   Places strokes randomly. This produces a more realistic paint.

   Evenly distributed   Strokes are evenly distributed across the image.

Stroke density   The greater the density the closer the strokes. With a low density, the paper or background may be visible in unstroke areas.

Centered   Focus brush strokes around center.

Figure 17.187 "Color" tab options

17.10.6.3.8   Color tab   In this tab, you can set what the stroke color will be.

Color options

Color   You can set the stroke color in two ways:

   Average under brush   Stroke color is computed from the average of all pixels under the brush.

   Center of brush   Samples the color from the pixel in the center of the brush.

Color noise   This slider, and its input box, allow you to introduce noise in the stroke color, that will look less homogeneous.

Figure 17.188 "General" tab options

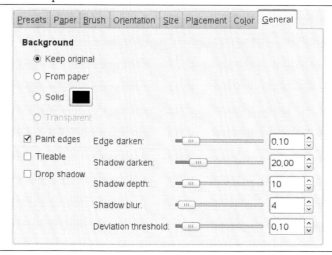

17.10.6.3.9 General tab In this tab you can set what will be the background and the relief of brush strokes.

General options

Background

>   **Keep original** The original image will be used as a background.
>
>   **From paper** Copy the texture of the selected paper as a background.
>
>   **Solid** By clicking on the color dwell you can select a solid colored background.
>
>   **Transparent** Use a transparent background. Only the painted strokes will be visible. This option is available only if your image has an alpha channel.

Paint edges If it is disabled, a thin border will not be painted around the outside border of the image.

Tileable If checked, the resulting image will be seamlessly tileable. The right side will match the left side and the top will match the bottom. This is interesting if your image will be repeatedly used in a Web background.

Drop shadow Add a shadow effect to each brush stroke.

Edge darken How much to darken the edges of each brush stroke. This increases paint relief or thickness.

Shadow darken How much to darken the brush shadow.

Shadow depth How far apart from the object the drop shadow should be.

Shadow blur How much to blur the drop shadow.

Deviation threshold A bail-out value for adaptive selections of brush size.

17.10.6.4 Orientation Map Editor

17.10.6.4.1 Overview The Orientation-map editor is an annexe of the GIMPressionist filter. You can get to it by clicking on the Edit button in the Orientation tab. With this editor, you can set the direction that brush strokes given by filter will have.

Figure 17.189 Options of the "Orientation-map Editor" dialog

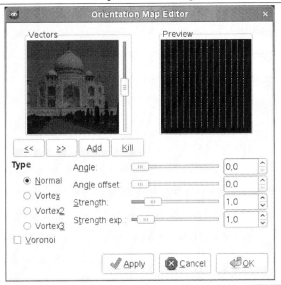

17.10.6.4.2 Options You can place one or several vectors. You can set their direction and their strength. They will act on the corresponding area of the image.

Vectors In the left windows (Vectors) you can manage your vectors. By default, a vector is at center. Vectors are red when they are active, and grey when they are not with a white point at tip.

- By clicking on the Add button, you add a vector at center of the window, whereas clicking with the mouse Middle Button puts it where you click.

- Clicking with the mouse Left Button displaces the selected vector to the clicked point.

- When clicking with the mouse Right Button, the selected vector points to where you have clicked.

- Clicking on << and >> buttons displaces focus from a vector to another.

- The Delete button allows you to delete the selected vector.

> Tip
>
> With the scroll bar on the right of the Vectors panel, you can set the image brightness. This can be very useful if the image is very dark/bright and you can't see vectors well.

Preview This Preview gives you an idea of the action of the various vectors. The slider on the right border lets you change the luminosity of this preview.

Type You have there some types to arrange the brush strokes within the selected vector domain. Describing them is difficult, but you can see the result in the Preview.

Voronoi A Voronoi's diagram consists in partitioning a plane with n master points into n polygons where each polygon has only one of these n master points and where any given other point of the polygon is closer to the master point than to any other. So each polygon limit is midway between two master point. Here is an example of a Voronoi's diagram:

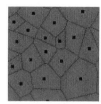

Here, when this option is checked, only the vector closest to a given point of the image influences this point.

Angle Direction of the selected vector. This slider has the same action as right-clicking (see above).

Angle offset This slider allows you to change the angle of *all* vectors.

Strength This slider acts on the influence domain of the selected vector. This influence lowers with distance. Strength is showed with the vector length.

Strength exp. This slider acts on the length of *all* vectors, and so changes the strength of all brush strokes.

17.10.6.5   Size Map Editor

17.10.6.5.1   Overview The Size-map editor is an annexe of the GIMPressionist filter. You can get to it by clicking on the Edit button in the Size tab. With this editor, you can set the size that brush strokes given by filter will have.

Figure 17.190 Size-map editor options

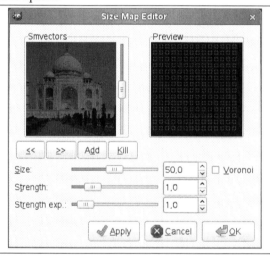

17.10.6.5.2   Options You can place one or several vectors. You can set their strength. They will act on the corresponding area of the image.

Smvectors In this window you can place your vectors. By clicking on the Add button, you add a vector at the center of the window, whereas clicking with the mouse Middle Button puts it where you click. Vectors are red when selected, and gray when they are not, with a white point at tip.

> Clicking with the mouse Left Button displaces the selected vector to the clicked point.

> Clicking on the mouse Right Button, has no evident action.

> Clicking on << and >> buttons displaces focus from a vector to another.

> The Kill button allows you to delete the selected vector.

Tip

With the scroll bar on the right of the Vectors panel, you can set the image brightness. This can be very useful if the image is very dark/bright and you can't see vectors well.

Preview This Preview gives you an idea of the action of the different vectors. The size of squares represent the size of the brushes and their strength.

Size Change the size of the brush strokes in the selected vector domain.

Strength This slider acts on the influence domain of the selected vector. This influence lowers with distance.

Strength exp. Change the exponent of the stroke.

Voronoi See Orientation Map Editor for an explanation.

17.10.7 Oilify

17.10.7.1 Overview

Figure 17.191 Example for the "Oilify" filter

(a) *Original image*   (b) *Filter "Oilify" applied*

This filter makes the image look like an oil painting. The Mask size controls the outcome: a high value gives the image less detail, as if you had used a larger brush.

Tip

The GIMPressionist filter can produce similar effects, but allows a much wider variety of options.

17.10.7.2 Activate the filter

This filter is found in the image menu through Filters → Artistic → Oilify....

17.10.7.3   Options

Figure 17.192 "Oilify" filter options

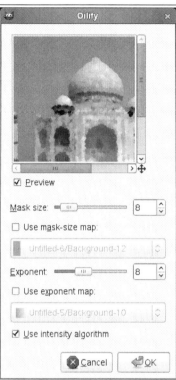

Mask size Mask size selects the size of the brush mask used to paint the oily render. Larger values here produce an oilier render.

Use mask-size map You may use a mask-size map to control Mask size partially. Mask size is reduced accordings to darkness in each pixel of the map image. You can select a map image among the current opened images of the same size as the source image.

Exponent Exponent selects density of the brush mask used to paint the oily render.

Use exponent map You may use an exponent map to control density of brush touch partially. Density is reduced accordings to darkness in each pixel of the map image. You can select a map image among the current opened images of the same size as the source image.

Use intensity algorithm "Use intensity algorithm" changes the mode of operation to help preserve detail and coloring.

17.10.8 Photocopy

17.10.8.1 Overview

Figure 17.193 Example for the "Photocopy" filter

(a) *Original image*   (b) *Filter "Photocopy" applied*

The Photocopy filter modifies the active layer or selection so that it looks like a black and white photocopy, as if toner transferred was based on the relative darkness of a particular region. This is achieved by darkening areas of the image which are measured to be darker than a neighborhood average, and setting other pixels to white.

Tip

 You may use this filter to sharpen your image. Create a copy of the active layer and use the filter on the copy. Set the Layer Mode to Multiply and adjust the opacity slider to get the best result.

17.10.8.2 Starting filter

You can find this filter from the image menu through Filters → Artistic → Photocopy.

17.10.8.3 Options

Figure 17.194 "Photocopy" filter options

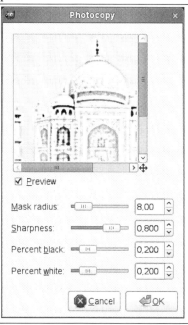

Preview Your changes are displayed in this preview before being applied to your image.

Mask radius This parameter controls the size of the pixel neighbourhood over which the average intensity is computed and then compared to each pixel in the neighborhood to decide whether or not to darken it. Large values result in very thick black areas bordering the regions of white and much less detail for black areas. Small values result in less toner overall and more details everywhere.

Sharpness With this option, you can set photocopy sharpness, from 0.0 to 1.0.

Percent black This parameter controls the amount of black color added to the image. Small values make the blend from color regions to blackened areas smoother and dark lines themselves thinner and less noticeable. Larger values make the lines thicker, darker and sharper. The maximum value makes the lines aliased. The best, most natural results are usually achieved with an intermediate value. Values vary from 0.0 to 1.0.

Percent white This parameter increases white pixels percentage.

17.10.9   Predator

17.10.9.1   Overview

Figure 17.195 Example for the "Predator" filter

(a) *Original image*   (b) *"Predator" applied*

This filter adds a "Predator" effect to the image. The predator effect makes the image/selection look something like the view the predator has in movies (kind of a thermogram and that type of thing). This will reduce the image to edges in a few basic colors on a dark background.

If there is an active selection, the filter effect will be applied to the selected region, otherwise to the alpha channel (the filter will add an alpha channel, if necessary). The filter works best on colorful RGB images.

17.10.9.2   Activate the filter

This filter is found in the image window menu under Filters → Artistic → Predator.

17.10.9.3   Options

Figure 17.196 "Predator" options

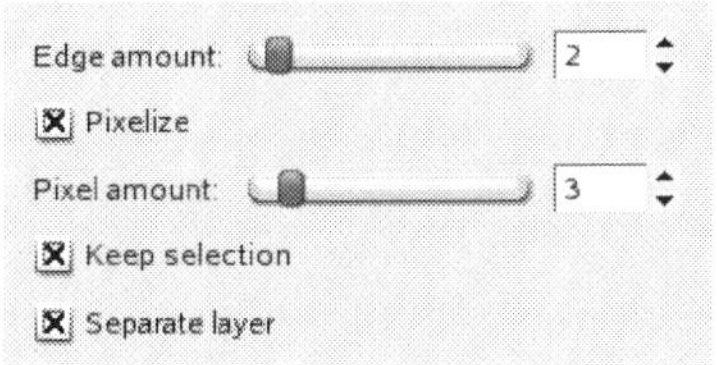

Edge amount: [====] 2
[X] Pixelize
Pixel amount: [====] 3
[X] Keep selection
[X] Separate layer

Edge amount The "predator" filter will detect edges using the Sobel edge detector. The specified "Edge amount" will be passed to the Sobel filter. A high value will result in detecting more edges.

Figure 17.197 "Edge amount" examples

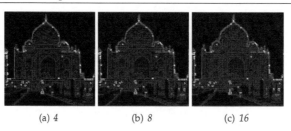

(a) 4   (b) 8   (c) 16

Pixelize If checked, the filter will simplify the image into solid-colored squares using the Pixelise filter before the real predator effect will be applied. You can select the size of these squares with the option Pixel amount, which will heavily affect the result (see examples below).

Pixel amount "Pixel amount" is the size of the color blocks the image will be simplified to if Pixelize is checked. Actually you are decreasing the resolution with this option. In the examples below, you can see directly how increasing the pixel block size leads to something like "macro pixels":

Figure 17.198 "Pixelize" examples

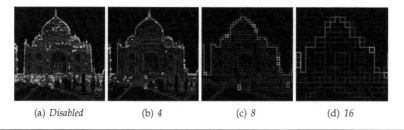

(a) Disabled   (b) 4   (c) 8   (d) 16

Keep selection If checked, the filter will be applied to the active selection. Else, it will be applied to the active layer.

Separate layer When this option is checked, a copy of the active layer will be created above the active layer and the filter will be applied to this copy, leaving the original layer untouched. If not checked, the filter will be applied to the active layer.

17.10.9.4 Filter algorithm

Since this filter delegates the essential parts to two or three other filters the algorithm is very simple:

Figure 17.199 Making the "predator" effect

(a) *Original*   (b) *Pixelize*

(c) *Min RGB*   (d) *Edge detection*

1. The original image.

2. Optionally, the filter pixelizes the image: it renders the image by using color blocks instead of pixels, thus reducing the image resolution.

3. The colors will be reduced to pure red, green, blue (and possibly gray colors), using the minimal RGB channel for every pixel.

4. Applying the Sobel edge detecting filter, the image will be reduced further on to edges, usually on a black background, with very few colors.

17.10.10   Softglow

17.10.10.1   Overview

Figure 17.200 Example for the "SoftGlow" filter

(a) *Original image*   (b) *Filter "Softglow" applied*

This filter lights the image with a soft glow. Softglow produces this effect by making bright areas of the image brighter.

17.10.10.2   Starting filter

You can find this file in the Image menu through: Filters → Artistic → Softglow.

17.10.10.3   Options

Figure 17.201 "Softglow" filter options

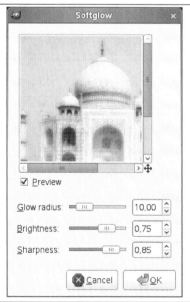

Preview Your changes are displayed in this preview before being applied to your image.

Glow radius The glow radius parameter controls the sharpness of the effect, giving a "vaseline-on-the-lens" effect.

Brightness The brightness parameter controls the degree of intensification applied to image highlights.

Sharpness The sharpness parameter controls how defined or alternatively diffuse the glow effect should be.

17.10.11   Van Gogh (LIC)

17.10.11.1   Overview

Figure 17.202 From left to right: original image, map, resulting image

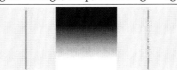

Map has three stripes: a solid black area, a vertical gradient area, a solid white area. One can see, on the resulting image, that image zones corresponding to solid areas of the map, are not blurred. Only the image zone corresponding to the gradient area of the map is blurred.

"LIC" stands for Line Integral Convolution, a mathematical method. The plug-in author uses mathematical terms to name his options... This filter is used to apply a directional blur to an image, or to create textures. It could be called "Astigmatism" as it blurs certain directions in the image.

It uses a blur map. Unlike other maps, this filter doesn't use grey levels of this blur map. *Filter takes in account only gradient direction(s).* Image pixels corresponding to solid areas of the map are ignored.

17.10.11.2   Activate the filter

You can find this filter through Filters → Artistic → Van Gogh (LIC).

17.10.11.3   Options

Figure 17.203 "Van Gogh (LIC)" filter options

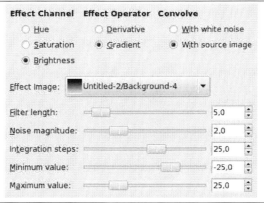

> **Tip**
>
> - To create a blur, check With Source Image. Only Filter Length slider and perhaps Integration Steps slider, are useful.
>
> - To create a texture, check With White Noise. All sliders can be useful.

Effect Channel By selecting Hue, Saturation or Brightness (=Value), filter will use this channel to treat image.

Effect Operator The "Derivative" option reverses "Gradient " direction:

Figure 17.204 Derivative option example

Using a square gradient map, Effect operator is on "Gradient" on the left, on "Derivative" on the right: what was sharp is blurred and conversely.

Convolve You can use two types of convolution. That's the first parameter you have to set:

With white noise White noise is an acoustics name. It's a noise where all frequencies have the same amplitude. Here, this option is used to create patterns.

With source image The source image will be blurred.

Effect image That's the map for blur or pattern direction. This map must have the same dimensions as the original image. It must be preferably a grayscale image. It must be present on your screen when you call filter so that you can choose it in the drop-list.

Figure 17.205 Blurring with vertical gradient map

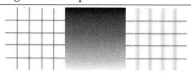

With a vertical gradient map, vertical lines are blurred.

Figure 17.206 Blurring with a square gradient map

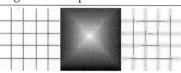

The gradient map is divided into four gradient triangles: each of them has its own gradient direction. In every area of the image corresponding to gradient triangles, only lines with the same direction as gradient are blurred.

Figure 17.207 Texture example

The "With white noise" option is checked. Others are default. With a vertical gradient map, texture "fibres" are going horizontally.

Filter length When applying blur, this option controls how important blur is. When creating a texture, it controls how rough texture is: low values result in smooth surface; high values in rough surface.

Figure 17.208 Action example of Filter Length on blur

On the left: a vertical line, one pixel wide (zoom 800%). On the right: the same line, after applying a vertical blur with a Filter Length to 3. You can see that blur width is 6 pixels, 3 pixels on both sides.

Figure 17.209 Filter Length example on texture

On the left: a texture with Filter Length=3. On the right, the same texture with Filter Length=24.

Noise magnitude This options controls the amount and size of White Noise. Low values produce finely grained surfaces. High values produce coarse-grained textures.

Figure 17.210 Action example of Noise Magnitude on texture

Noise magnitude = 4

Integration steps This options controls the influence of gradient map on texture.

Figure 17.211 Action example of Integration Steps on texture

On the left: Integration Steps = 2. On the right: Integration Steps = 4.

Minimum value, Maximum value Both values determine a range controlling texture contrast: shrunk range results in high contrast and enlarged range results in low contrast.

Figure 17.212 Action example of min/max values on texture

Minimum value = -4.0. Maximum value = 5.0.

17.10.12 Weave

17.10.12.1 Overview

Figure 17.213 Example of Weave

Filter "Weave" applied

The Weave command is a Script-Fu script which creates a new layer filled with a weave effect and adds it to the image as an overlay or bump map. The result of the image looks as if it were printed over woven ribbons of paper, thin wooden sheet, or stripped bamboo.

If the image is in indexed colors, this menu entry is grayed out and unavailable.

This filter adds a "Multiply" mode layer upon the layer where you activate this command. The weave texture is rendered in gray levels.

17.10.12.2 Activate the filter

This filter is found in the image window menu under Filters → Artistic → Weave....

17.10.12.3 Options

Figure 17.214 "Weave" filter options

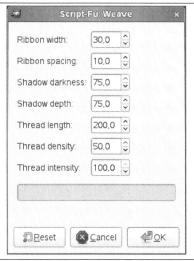

For to make coarse mesh texture, increase the ribbon spacing and/or decrease the ribbon width.

For to strain ribbons hard, decrease the shadow depth.

Ribbon width With this option you can set the tape width in pixel between 0.0 and 256.0. In default, 30.0 pixels is set.

Ribbon spacing With this option you can set the distance to the neighboring ribbon or the size of black square hole in pixel between 0.0 and 256.0. In default, 10.0 pixels is set.

Shadow darkness With this option you can set the darkness at crossings of lower ribbon in percentage. Lower value shows ribbons thinner. 75.0 percent is the default value.

Shadow depth With this option you can set the bent strength of ribbons in percentage. Higher value shows ribbons more wavy, lower value for flat surface. The actual effect is limited by the Shadow darkness. 75.0 percent is the default value.

Thread length With this option you can set the regularity of stripe texture. If this value is shorter than the summary of the ribbon width and twice of the ribbon spacing, the surface of ribbon becomes speckled. Set this value in pixel on range between 0.0 to 256.0. The default value is 200.0.

Thread density With this option you can set the density of fiber-like parallel short stripes on the surface of ribbons. To populate stripes increase this value. 50.0 percent is the default value.

Thread intensity With this option you can set the opacity of stripe texture. Lower value shows threads vague. To clear off threads set the value to 0.0 percent. The default value is 100.0 percent.

17.10.12.4 Another usage

Figure 17.215 Adding a lattice using "Weave" texture

Narrower the ribbon width, wider the ribbon spacing, and filled with the "Wood #1" pattern.

This texture can be a lattice that you can see the original image through its mesh holes. Add a new, transparent layer over the active layer for the lattice, and apply this filter. Select a black regular square in the texture layer using the Select By Color tool, then delete black squares in selection on the texture layer to be chink holes. Reverse the selection, and activate the transparent layer so that you can fill the lattice surface with a pattern, then drag and drop your favorite pattern over the image window.

17.11 Decor Filters

17.11.1 Introduction

These filters are image-dependent Script-Fu scripts. They create decorative borders, and some of them add some nice special effects to the image.

17.11.2 Add Bevel

17.11.2.1 Overview

Figure 17.216 Example for the "Add Bevel" filter

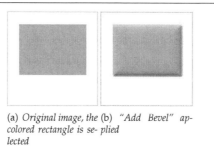

(a) *Original image, the colored rectangle is selected*
(b) *"Add Bevel" applied*

This filter adds a slight bevel to an image using a bump map (see below). If there is a selection, it is bevelled, otherwise the filter has no effect.

Figure 17.217 Another "Add Bevel" example, with bumpmap

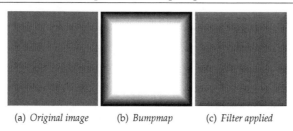

(a) *Original image*　　(b) *Bumpmap*　　(c) *Filter applied*

17.11.2.2 Activate the filter

You can find this filter in the image window menu under Filters → Decor → Add Bevel.

17.11.2.3 Options

Figure 17.218 "Add Bevel" options

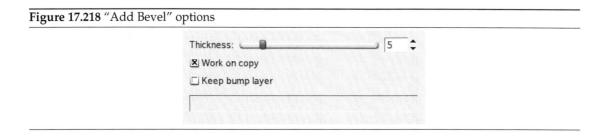

Thickness You can specify the thickness of the bevel, in pixels. Maximal thickness is 30 pixels.

Work on copy If checked, the filter creates a new window containing a copy of the image with the filter applied. The original image remains unchanged.

Keep bump layer When checked, you will keep the generated bumpmap as a new, not visible layer (below the layer dialog):

17.11.3 Add Border

17.11.3.1 Overview

Figure 17.219 Example for the "Add Border" filter

(a) *Original image*

(b) *Border added*

This filter just does what its name says: it adds a border to the image. You can specify the thickness of the border as well as the color. The four sides of the border are colored in different shades, so the image area will appear raised.

The image will be enlarged by the border size, it won't be painted over.

17.11.3.2 Activate the filter

This filter is found in the image window menu under Filters → Decor → Add Border.

17.11.3.3   Options

Figure 17.220 "Add Border" options

Border X size:	12
Border Y size:	12
Border color:	▬▬▬
Delta value on color:	25

Border X size, Border Y size Here you can select the thickness of the added border, in pixels. X size (left an right) and Y size (top and bottom) may be different. Maximum is 250 pixels.

Border color Clicking on this button brings up the color selector dialog that allows you to choose an "average" border color (see below, Delta value on color).

Delta value on color This option makes the border sides to be colored in different shades and thus makes the image to appear raised. The actual color of the respective border side is computed for every color component red, green, and blue[3] from the "average" Border color as follows (resulting values less than 0 are set to 0, values greater than 255 are set to 255):

- Top shade = Border color + Delta

- Right shade = Border color - ½ Delta

- Bottom shade = Border color - Delta

- Left shade = Border color + ½ Delta

Figure 17.221 Delta examples

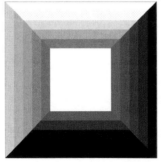

"Add Border" filter applied with Delta value 25, then with 75, 125, 175, and 225.

Example: the default color is blue (38,31,207), default delta is 25. So the shades of the borders are: top: (38,31,207) + (25,25,25) = (63,56,232), right: (38,31,207) + (-13,-13,-13) = (25,18,194), etc.

---

[3] See image types or *RGB* .

17.11.4 Coffee Stain

17.11.4.1 Overview

Figure 17.222 Example for the "Coffee Stain" filter

(a) *Original image*   (b) *"Coffee Stain" applied*

This filter adds realistic looking coffee stains to the image.

Every stain is created in a layer of its own. The stain layers are randomly moved to let the stains spread out (at the end you may see the boundary of the moved top layer). So after applying the filter you can easily edit (e.g., move, scale, remove) the coffee stains, or create additional stains using the filter again.

17.11.4.2 Activate the filter

The filter is found in the image window menu under Filters → Decor → Coffee Stain.

17.11.4.3 Options

Figure 17.223 "Coffee Stain" options

Stains The number of the coffee stains (1-10).

Darken only Since every stain is created in a layer of its own, all layers have to be merged to make the appearance of the image. If this option is checked, the relevant layer mode is set to "Darken only", otherwise it is set to "Normal".

The layer mode determines how the pixels of the layers are combined. In "Normal" mode, every coffee stain covers the pixels of the layers below. As a rule of thumb, if layer mode "Darken only" is set, coffee stains covers the corresponding pixels of the layers below them only if these pixels are lighter.

17.11.5 Fuzzy Border

17.11.5.1 Overview

Figure 17.224 Example for the "Fuzzy Border" filter

(a) *Original image*   (b) *"Fuzzy Border" applied*

This filter adds a cool fading border to an image. The border will look jagged and fuzzy, and you can specify color and thickness of the fading border. Optionally you may add a shadow to the image.

17.11.5.2 Activate the filter

You can find this filter in the image window menu through Filters → Decor → Fuzzy Border.

17.11.5.3 Options

Figure 17.225 "Fuzzy Border" options

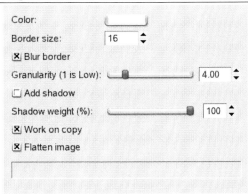

Color Clicking on this button brings up the color selector dialog that allows you to choose the border color.

Border size Here you can set the thickness of the fuzzy border, in pixels. Maximum is 300 pixels, regardless of the image width or height.

Blur border If checked, the border will be blurred. The example below shows the effect of blurring:

Figure 17.226 "Blur border" example

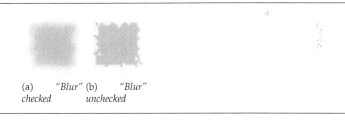

(a)   *"Blur"* (b)   *"Blur"*
checked   *unchecked*

Figure 17.227 "Blur border" zoomed (1600%)

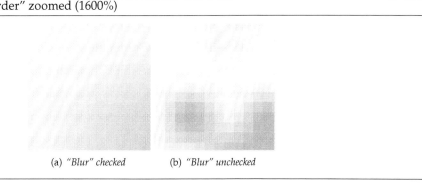

(a) *"Blur" checked*   (b) *"Blur" unchecked*

Granularity The border's granularity is almost the size of pixel blocks spread to create the effect of a jagged and fuzzy border.

Figure 17.228 Granularity example (without blurring)

(a) Granularity 1 (b) Granularity 4 (de- (c) Granularity 16
(min)   fault)   (max)

Add shadow If checked, the filter will also create a shadow at the border.

Figure 17.229 "Add shadow" example

(a) "Add shadow" (b) "Add shadow" (c) "Add shadow"
checked,   shadow with shadow weight unchecked (default)
weight 100% (default 10%.
shadow weight).

Shadow weight If Add shadow is checked, you may set the shadow opacity here. Defaults to 100% (full
opacity).

Work on copy If checked, the filter creates a new window containing a copy of the image with the filter
applied. The original image remains unchanged.

Flatten image If unchecked, the filter keeps the additional layers it used to create the border and the
shadow (if demanded). Default is to merge down all layers.

17.11.6 Old Photo

17.11.6.1 Overview

Figure 17.230 Example for the "Old Photo" filter

(a) *Original image*   (b) *"Old Photo" applied*

This filter makes an image look like an old photo: blurred, with a jagged border, toned with a brown shade, and marked with spots.

17.11.6.2 Activate the filter

The filter is found in the image window menu under Filters → Decor → Old Photo.

17.11.6.3 Options

Figure 17.231 "Old Photo" options

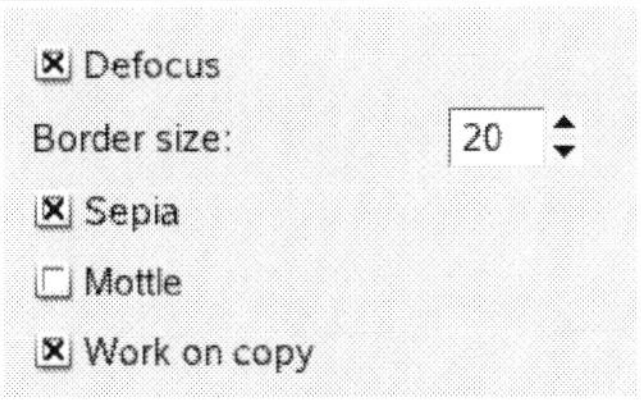

> ☒ Defocus
> Border size: 20 ⇕
> ☒ Sepia
> ☐ Mottle
> ☒ Work on copy

Defocus If checked, a Gaussian blur will be applied to the image, making it less clear.

Figure 17.232 Example for the "Defocus" option

(a) *Defocus enabled*   (b) *Defocus disabled*

Border size When you choose a border size > 0, the Fuzzy Border filter will be applied to the image, adding a white, jagged border.

Sepia If checked, the filter reproduces the effect of aging in old, traditional black-and-white photographs, toned with sepia (shades of brown).[4] To achieve this effect, the filter desaturates the image, reduces brightness and contrast, and modifies the color balance.[5]

Mottle When you check this option, the image will be marked with spots.

Figure 17.233 Example for the "Mottle" option

A plain white image mottled (without Defocus or Sepia)

Work on copy If checked, the filter creates a new window containing a copy of the image with the filter applied. The original image remains unchanged.

---

[4] See Wikipedia [WKPD-SEPIA].

[5] Compare Section 14.5.2.

17.11.7   Round Corners

17.11.7.1   Overview

Figure 17.234 Example for the "Round Corners" filter

(a) *Original image*   (b) *"Round Corners" applied*

This filter rounds the corners of an image, optionally adding a drop-shadow and a background layer.

The filter works on RGB and grayscale images that contain only one layer. It creates a copy of the image or can optionally work on the original. It uses the current background color to create a background layer.

17.11.7.2   Activate the filter

This filter is found in the image window menu under Filters → Decor → Round Corners.

17.11.7.3   Options

Figure 17.235 "Round Corners" options

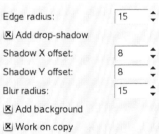

Edge radius Rounding corners is done by selecting a quarter of a circle at every corner and removing the area not covered by this selection. The "edge radius" is the radius of the constructing circle.

In the examples below, the filter was applied to a 100x100 pixels image, with varying edge radius. For radius = 50, the four quadrants just form a circle with diameter = 100, which exactly fits into the original image outline. A radius greater than 50 is possible, but look what happens...

Figure 17.236 Edge radius examples

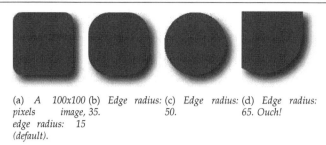

(a) A 100x100 (b) Edge radius: (c) Edge radius: (d) Edge radius:
pixels image, 35. 50. 65. Ouch!
edge radius: 15
(default).

Add drop-shadow When this option is checked, the filter will cast a shadow behind your image after rounding the image corners.

Shadow X/Y offset X and Y offset determine where the shadow will be placed in relation to the image. Offset is measured in pixels. High values make the shadow look like it's far away, and low values will make it look closer to the image.

Figure 17.237 Shadow offset examples

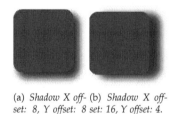

(a) Shadow X off- (b) Shadow X offset: 8, Y offset: 8 set: 16, Y offset: 4.
(default).

Note that the shadow offsets as well as the blur radius are limited to background area.

Blur radius When Add drop-shadow is checked, you may select a blur radius, which will be used by the Drop Shadow filter. The image will be enlarged in both dimensions depending on the blur radius and the shadow offsets.

Add background When you check this option (it is checked by default), the filter will add a background layer below the existing layer, filled with the current background color. The size of this new layer depends on the blur radius and the shadow offsets.

Work on copy If checked, the filter creates a new window containing a copy of the image with the filter applied. The original image remains unchanged.

17.11.8 Slide

17.11.8.1 Overview

Figure 17.238 Example for the "Slide" filter

(a) *Original image*

(b) *"Slide" applied*

This filter makes your image look like a slide, by adding a slide-film like black frame, sprocket holes, and labels.

If necessary, the image will be cropped to fit into an aspect ratio of width : height = 3:2. If image width is greater than image height, black frames will be added at the top and the bottom of the image, else the frames will be added on the left and right sides. You may select the color as well as the font of the text appearing on the frames. The current background color will be used for drawing the holes.

The script only works on RGB and grayscale images that contain one layer. Otherwise the menu entry is insensitive and grayed out.

17.11.8.2 Activate the filter

The filter is found in the image window menu under Filters → Decor → Slide.

17.11.8.3 Options

Figure 17.239 "Slide" options

Text A short label that will be displayed in the top and bottom (or the left and right) of the frame. The text must be really short.

Number Here you may enter a text for simulating consecutive numbers. Two numbers will be displayed: this number and this number with the character "A" appended.

Font Clicking on this button opens the Font dialog, where you can choose a font for the text on the frame.

Fontcolor Clicking on this button brings up a color selection dialog that allows you to choose the color of the text.

Work on copy If checked, the filter creates a new window containing a copy of the image with the filter applied. The original image remains unchanged.

17.11.9 Stencil Carve

17.11.9.1 Overview

Figure 17.240 Example for the "Stencil Carve" filter

(a) *Original image*

(b) *"Stencil Carve" applied*

This filter works with two images, source and target. The source image must be a grayscale image containing a single layer and no Alpha channel. This layer is used as selection mask and will work as stencil for the carving effect. The image to be carved (the target image) can be an RGB color or grayscale image, also with a single layer. This target image must have the same size as the source image.

17.11.9.2   Activating the filter

This filter is found in the image window menu under Filters → Decor → Stencil Carve.

> Tip
>
> If this command remains grayed out although the image is grayscale, check for an Alpha channel and delete it.

17.11.9.3   Options

Figure 17.241 "Stencil Carve" options

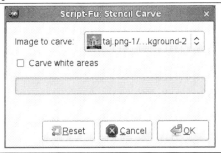

Image to carve Here you may select the target image, i.e. the image the carving effect is applied to. The drop-down list will show you a list of opened images which may be carved.

Carve white areas If checked (default), the source image is used as stencil as described above. If unchecked, the *inverted* source image is used as stencil, e.g.:

Figure 17.242 Engraving Masks

(a) *Normal mask*

(b) *Inverted mask*

In the example below, the source is a grayscale image. The target is an image with a wood pattern.

On the left, Carve white areas is enabled. The pixels of the target image corresponding to white pixels in the stencil (around the text) have been carved. The result is an embossed text.

On the right, Carve white areas is disabled. The pixels of the target image corresponding to the black pixels in the stencil (the text) have been carved. The result is a hollow text.

Figure 17.243 Example for "Carve white areas"

(a) *White areas carved*   (b) *Stencil*   (c) *Black areas carved*

Information about the many layers created by this filter can be found in [GROKKING].

17.11.10 Stencil Chrome

17.11.10.1 Overview

Figure 17.244 Example for the "Stencil Chrome" filter

(a) *Original image*   (b) *"Stencil Chrome" applied*

This filter provides a state of the art chrome effect. The source image must be an image in grayscale mode, containing a single layer without alpha channel. This layer is used as mask ("stencil") for the chrome effect.

The filter creates a new image with the chrome effect applied to the source image or, if a selection exists, to the selection of the source image (a nice background is added too).

17.11.10.2   Activating the filter

This filter is found in the image window menu under Filters → Decor → Stencil Chrome.

> **Tip**
>
> If this command remains grayed out although the image is in grayscale mode, check for an Alpha channel and delete it.

17.11.10.3   Options

Figure 17.245 "Stencil Chrome" options

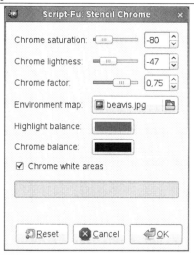

Chrome saturation, Chrome lightness Use this option to control how saturation and lightness of the "Chrome" layer are adjusted. Negative values decrease saturation and lightness respectively.

Chrome factor This factor lets you adjust offsets, feather radius, and brush size used to construct the "Chrome" and "Highlight" layer (and the "Drop Shadow" as well).

Change with caution, decreasing this value may make the chrome effect worse. The default factor 0.75 seems to be a good choice.

Environment map The environment map is an image that is added as some kind of "noise" to the source. The effect is best to see if you use a simple map with some obvious shapes:

Using a simple environment map

The environment map must be an image in grayscale mode too. Size doesn't matter, the environment map is scaled to the size of the source image.

Highlight balance This color is used to modify the color balance of the "Highlight" layer: the amount of red, green, and blue colors is increased according to the corresponding values of the specified option.

Avoid colors with red, green or blue value > 230.

Chrome balance Same as above, but modifies the color balance of the "Chrome" layer.

Chrome white areas If checked (this is the default), the source image is used as mask. If unchecked, the *inverted* source image is used.

17.11.10.4 How to create the chrome effect

The following section provides a brief and simplified description of how the script (actually this filter is a Script-Fu) creates the chrome effect.

If you apply the filter to your source images and then look at the layer dialog of the resulting image, you will see that there are two main layers which make up the chrome effect: the "Chrome" layer and the "Highlight" layer. These layers are created as follows:

1. The script constructs a somewhat simplified and blurred layer from the source image (from the inverted source image if Chrome white areas is unchecked).

   The Chrome factor controls the appearance of this layer.

2. The (scaled) environment map is blurred and merged into the above layer with 50% opacity. (Do you spot the cat in the introducing example?)

Merging the environment map

3. The brightness (value) of the layer is modified according to a spline-based intensity curve.

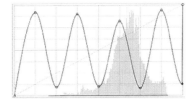

Modifying the intensity curve

4. A layer mask is added, initialized with the source image (the "Chrome Stencil"). This is the "Chrome" layer before the final step.

   The "Highlight" layer is a copy of the "Chrome" layer where the layer mask is stroked with a white brush.

Chrome and Highlight base

5. For both layers the color balance is modified (according to Highlight balance and Chrome balance), increasing the amount of red, green, and blue, with emphasis on highlights.

Additionally, saturation and lightness of the "Chrome" layer are modified (controlled by Chrome saturation and Chrome lightness).

Chrome and Highlight layer

Now add a drop shadow and a background layer and you get the Example image for the "Stencil Chrome" filter.

17.12 Map Filters

17.12.1 Introduction

Map filters use an object named *map* to modify an image: you map the image to the object. So, you can create 3D effects by mapping your image to another previously embossed image ("Bumpmap" Filter) or to a sphere ("Map Object" filter). You can also map a part of the image elsewhere into the same image ("Illusion" and "Make Seamless" filters), bend a text along a curve ("Displace" filter)...

17.12.2 Bump Map

17.12.2.1 Overview

Figure 17.246 "bump-map" example

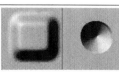

On the left, the original image that we want to emboss: a solid blue. In the middle, the bump map : a grayscale image, where black pixels will emboss backwards and white pixels will emboss forwards. On the right, the bump-mapped image. The filter adds a shadow effect.

This filter creates a 3D effect by embossing an image (the card) and then mapping it to another image. Bump height depends on pixel luminosity and you can set light direction. See Emboss for more information about embossing. You can bump map any type of image, unlike the Emboss filter.

17.12.2.2 Activate the filter

This filter is found in the image window menu under Filters → Map → Bump Map.

17.12.2.3 Options

Figure 17.247 "Bump Map" filter options

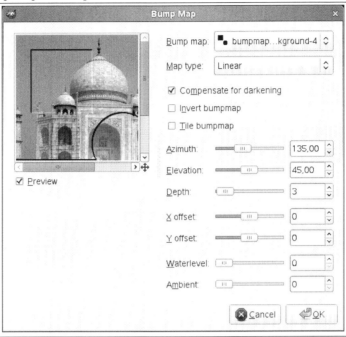

Preview If checked, parameter setting results are interactively displayed in preview. Scroll bars allow you to move around the image.

Bump map This drop-down list allows you to select the image that will be used as a map for bump-mapping. This list contains images that are present on your screen when you launch the filter. Images opened after starting filter are not present in this list.

Map type This option allows you to define the method that will be used when creating the map image:

> **Linear** Bump height is a direct function of luminosity.
>
> **Sinusoidal** Bump height is a sinusoidal function of luminosity.
>
> **Spheric** Bump height is a spheric function of luminosity.

Compensate for darkening Bump-mapping tends to darken image. You can compensate this darkening by checking this option.

Invert bumpmap Bright pixels default to bumps and dark pixels to hollows. You can invert this effect by checking this option.

Tile bumpmap If you check this option, there will be no relief break if you use your image as a pattern for a web page: patterns will be placed side by side without any visible joins.

Azimut This is about lighting according to the points of the compass (0 - 360). East (0°) is on the left. Increasing value goes counter-clockwise.

Elevation That's height from horizon (0.50°), up to zenith (90°).

Depth With this slider, you can vary bump height and hollow depth. The higher the value, the higher the difference between both. Values vary from 1 to 65.

X offset, Y offset With this slider, you can adjust the map image position compared with the image, horizontally (X) and/or vertically (Y).

Waterlevel If your image has transparent areas, they will be treated like dark areas and will appear as hollows after bump-mapping. With this slider, you can reduce hollows as if sea level was raising. This hollows will disappear when sea level value reaches 255. If the Invert bump-map option is checked, transparent areas will be treated as bright areas, and then Waterlevel slider will plane bumps down.

Ambient This slider controls the intensity of ambient light. With high values, shadows will fade and relief lessen.

17.12.3 Displace

17.12.3.1 Overview

Figure 17.248 Displacement examples

(a) *Original image*   (b) *The displacement* (c) *X displacement co-map has four grey efficient is 30. Va-stripes with values of cated pixels are black. 210, 160, 110, and 60, The image areas corre-respectively. sponding to light gray (128) were displaced 19 and 8 pixels to the left. The image areas corre-sponding to dark gray (127) were displaced 4 and 15 pixels to the right.*

This filter uses a "displace-map" to displace corresponding pixels of the image. This filter displaces the content of the specified drawable (active layer or selection) by the amounts specified in X and Y Displacement multiplied by the intensity of the corresponding pixel in the 'displace map' drawables. *Both X and Y displace maps should be gray-scale images and have the same size as the drawable .* This filter allows interesting distortion effects.

17.12.3.2 Activating the filter

You can find this filter through Filters → Map → Displace

17.12.3.3 Options

Figure 17.249 Displace filter options

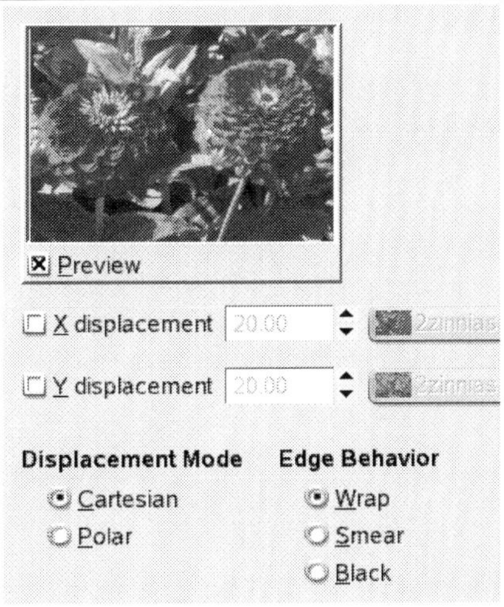

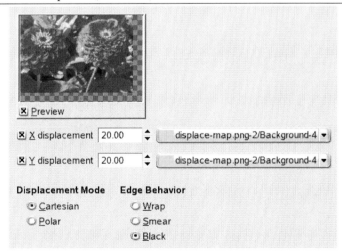

Preview Uncheck this option if your processor is slow.

Displacement Mode You can choose working in Cartesian coordinates, where pixels are displaced in X or Y direction, or working in Polar coordinates, where the image is pinched and whirled by displacing pixels in radial or tangent direction.

Please see the next sections for details about these options.

Edge Behavior These options allows you to set displacement behaviour on active layer or selection edges:

Wrap With this option, what disappears on one edge reappears on the opposite edge.

Smear With this option, pixels vacated by displacement are replaced with pixels stretched from the adjacent part of the image.

Black With this option, pixels vacated by displacement are replaced with black.

Figure 17.250 Displace filter options (Cartesian)

Displacement Mode: Cartesian

17.12.3.3.1   Cartesian Displacement Mode   In both modes, direction and amount of displacement depend on the intensity of the corresponding pixel in the displacement map.

The map, that should be a grayscale image, has 256 gray levels (0-255), the (theoretical) average value is 127.5. The filter displaces image pixels corresponding to pixels with values less than 127.5 (0 to 127) in map to one direction, corresponding to pixels with values from 128 to 255 to the opposite direction.

X displacement, Y displacement   If the respective option is activated, image pixels corresponding to pixels from 0 to 127 will be displaced to the right for X, downwards for Y, image pixels corresponding to pixels from 128 to 255 will be displaced to the left for X, upwards for Y.

What you enter in input boxes, directly or by using arrow-head buttons, is not the actual displacement. It's a coefficient used in a $displacement = (intensity x coefficient)$ formula, which gives the pixel actual displacement according to the scaled intensity [6] of the corresponding pixel in map, modulated by the coefficient you enter. Introducing intensity into formula is important: this allows progressive displacement by using a gradient map.

This value may be positive or negative. A negative displacement is reverse of a positive one. The value varies in limits equal to the double of image dimensions.

When you click on the drop-down list button, a list appears where you can select a displacement map. To be present in this list, an image must respect two conditions. First, this image must be present on your screen when you call filter. Then, this image must have the same dimensions as the original image. Most often, it will be a duplicate original image, which is transformed to grey scale and modified appropriately, with a gradient. It may be possible to use RGB images, but color luminosity is used making result prevision difficult. Map may be different in horizontal and vertical directions.

Figure 17.251 Displace filter options (Polar)

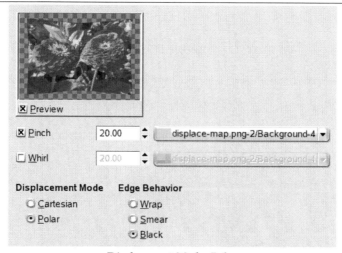

Displacement Mode: Polar

17.12.3.3.2   Polar Displacement Mode

Pinch   If this option is activated, the radial coordinates (i.e. the distance to the image's midpoint, the "pole") of the pixels will be changed. Image pixels corresponding to map pixels from 0 to 127 will be displaced outwards, image pixels corresponding to pixels from 128 to 255 will be displaced towards center.

For the values and the displacement map see above ("X/Y displacement").

The displacement is independent from the polar distance, all pixels are displaced by the same amount. So the image will not only be stretched or compressed, but also distorted:

---

[6] Scaled intensity = (intensity - 127.5) / 127.5; see Section 17.12.3.5.

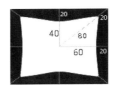

Image distortion by Pinch option

A 160x120 pixel image, plain white displacement map, and displacement coefficient 20.0: this results in a 20 pixels displacement towards center. This is a horizontal reduction in size by 25%, vertical by 33%, and diagonal by 20%, so the image will be distorted.

Whirl If this option is activated, the angular coordinates of the image pixels will be "displaced" by a map pixel dependent amount. For a plain displacement map, the image will be rotated, otherwise it will be whirled.

Image pixels corresponding to pixels from 0 to 127 in the map will be displaced counterclockwise, image pixels corresponding to pixels from 128 to 255 will be displaced clockwise.

For the values and the displacement map see above.

Note

 For a plain, non neutral map, if displace mode "Polar" is enabled, this filter works like Whirl and Pinch.

17.12.3.4 Using gradient to bend a text

Follow following steps:

1. Start with opening your image.

2. Duplicate this image. Activate this duplicate and make it gray-scaled (Image → Mode → GrayScale). Fill it with the wanted gradient. This image will be your *Displacement map*, with the dimensions of original image.

3. Activate original image. Create a *Text Layer* with your text. Set layer to image size: right-click on the layer in layer dialog and, in the pop-menu, click on "Layer to image size". Note that letters in text layer lie on a transparent background; now this filter doesn't displace transparent pixels. Only letters will be displaced.

4. Activate the text layer. Open the Displace filter window. Set parameters, particularly the displacement coefficient, according to the result in Preview. Click OK.

This method also applies to standard layers:

> **Tip**
>
> To get the wanted gradient, first draw a black to white gradient. Then use the Curves tool to modify the gradient curve.

17.12.3.5 Displacement Calculation

The following section will show you how to calculate the amount of displacement, if you are interested in these details. If you don't want to know it, you can safely omit this section.

The overview example showed the X displacement using a coefficient of 30.0: 19, 8, 4, or 15 pixels, depending on the grey level of the displacement map's color.

Why just these amounts? That's easy:

$$30.0 * \frac{I - 127.5}{127.5} = D$$

$$30.0 * \frac{210 - 127.5}{127.5} = 19$$

$$30.0 * \frac{(160 - 127.5)}{127.5} = 8$$

$$30.0 * \frac{(110 - 127.5)}{127.5} = -4$$

$$30.0 * \frac{(60 - 127.5)}{127.5} = -15$$

If you check these equations, you will notice that the values they give are not exactly the results we retained in the example (using non-integers, that's not surprising). So, were the results rounded to the nearest integer and then the pixels were displaced by a whole-numbered amount? No. Every pixel is displaced exactly by the calculated amount; a "displacement by a fractional amount" is realized by interpolation. A closer look at the example image will show it:

Figure 17.252 A closer look at the displacement example

A small area zoomed in by 800 percent.

The displacement causes small (one pixel wide) areas of intermediate colors at the edges of plain color areas. E.g., the black area (zoomed in image) is caused by a displacement of -4.12, so the intermediate color is 12% black and 88% gold.

So if you select a displacement coefficient of 30.01 instead of 30.00, you will indeed get a different image, although you won't see the difference, of course.

17.12.4 Fractal Trace

17.12.4.1 Overview

Figure 17.253 Fractal Trace

(a) *Original image*   (b) *Filter "Fractal Trace" applied*

This filter transforms the image with the Mandelbrot fractal: it maps the image to the fractal.

17.12.4.2 Activate the filter

This filter is found in the image window menu under Filters → Map → Fractal trace.

17.12.4.3 Options

Figure 17.254 "Fractal trace" filter options

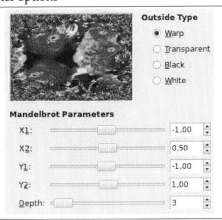

Mandelbrot parameters

X1, X2, Y1, Y2, Depth These parameters are similar to X/YMIN, X/YMAX and ITER parameters of the Fractal Explorer filter. They allow you to vary fractal spreading and detail depth.

Outside Type Mapping image to fractal may reveal empty areas. You can select to fill them with Black, White, Transparency or make what disappears on one side reappear on the opposite side with Wrap option.

17.12.5   Illusion

17.12.5.1   Overview

Figure 17.255 Illusion

(a) *Original image*   (b) *Filter "Fractal Trace" applied*

With this filter, your image (active layer or selection) looks like a kaleidoscope. This filter duplicates your image in many copies, more or less dimmed and split, and puts them around the center of the image.

17.12.5.2   Activate the filter

This filter is found in the image window menu under Filters → Map → Illusion.

17.12.5.3   Options

Figure 17.256 "Illusion" filter options

Preview If checked, parameter setting results are interactively displayed in preview. Scroll bars allow you to move around the image.

Divisions That's the number of copies you want to apply to image. This value varies from -32 to 64. Negative values invert kaleidoscope rotation.

Mode 1, Mode 2 You have two arrangement modes for copies in image:

Figure 17.257 From left to right: original image, mode 1, mode 2, with Divisions=4

17.12.6 Make Seamless

17.12.6.1 Overview

Figure 17.258 An example of Make Seamless.

(a) *Original*   (b) *Make Seamless applied*

This filter modifies the image for tiling by creating seamless edges. Such an image can be used as a pattern for a web-page. This filter has no option, and result may need correction.

17.12.6.2 Activation

You can find this filter through Filters → Map → Make Seamless

17.12.7   Map Object

17.12.7.1   Overview

Figure 17.259 The "Map Object" filter applied to a photograph

(a) *Original*   (b) *"Map Object" applied*

This filter maps a picture to an object (plane, sphere, box or cylinder).

17.12.7.2   Activate the filter

This filter is found in the image window menu under Filters → Map → Map Object.

17.12.7.3   Options

17.12.7.3.1   Preview   This preview has several possibilities:

Preview! Preview is automatic for some options but you will have to press this button to update Preview after modifying many other parameters.

When mouse pointer is on Preview and the Light tab is selected, it takes the form of a small hand to grab the *blue point* which marks light source origin and to displace it. This blue point may not be visible if light source has negative X and Y settings in the Light tab.

Zoom out, Zoom in Zoom buttons allow you to enlarge or to reduce image in Preview. Their action is limited, but may be useful in case of a large image.

Show preview wireframe Puts a grid over the preview to make displacements and rotations more easy. Works well on a plan.

Figure 17.260 "Map Object" options (General)

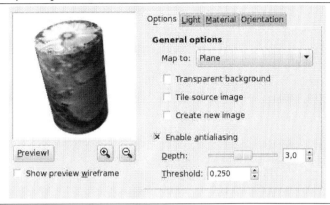

17.12.7.3.2 General Options

Map to This drop-down list allows you to select the object the image will be mapped on. It can be a *Plane*, a *Sphere*, a *Box* or a *Cylinder*.

Transparent background This option makes image transparent around the object. If not set, the background is filled with the current background color.

Tile source image When moving Plane object and displacing it with Orientation tab options, a part of the image turns empty. By checking the Tile source image, source image copies will fill this empty space in. This option seems not to work with the other objects.

> **Note**
>
> 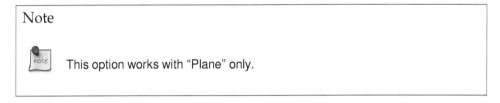   This option works with "Plane" only.

Create new image When this option is checked, a new image is created with the result of filter application, so preserving the original image.

Enable antialiasing Check this option to conceal this unpleasant aliasing effect on borders. When checked, this option lets appear two settings:

    Depth Defines antialiasing quality, to the detriment of execution speed.

    Threshold Defines antialiasing limits. Antialiasing stops when value difference between pixels becomes lower than this set value.

Figure 17.261 "Map Object" options (Light)

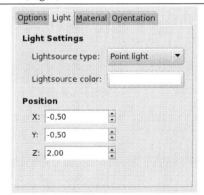

17.12.7.3.3   Light

Light Settings

> **Lightsource type** In this dropdown list, you can select among *Point light*, *Directionnal light* and *No light*.

> **Lightsource color** Press this button to open the Color Selector dialog.

Position If "Point light" is selected, you can control there light source *Position* (the blue point), according to X, Y and Z coordinates.

> If "Directional light" is selected, these X, Y and Z parameters control the "Direction vector" (effect is not evident).

Figure 17.262 "Map Object" options (Material)

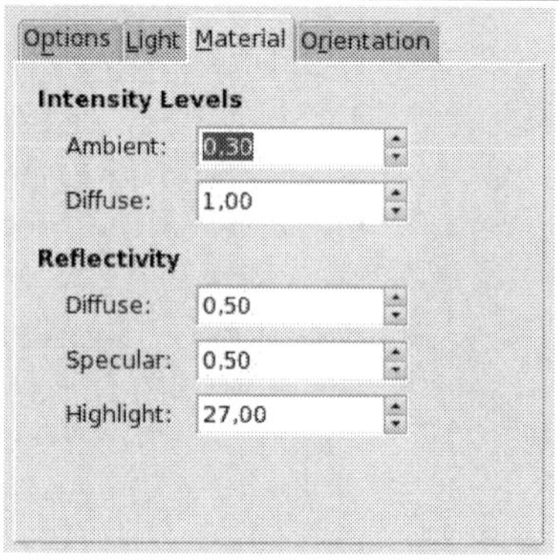

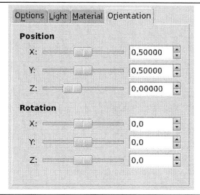

17.12.7.3.4   Material

Intensity Levels

> **Ambient** Amount of color to show where no light falls directly.

> **Diffuse** Intensity of original color when lit by a light source.

Reflectivity

> **Diffuse** Higher values make object reflect more light (looks brighter).

> **Specular** Controls how intense the highlights will be.

> **Highlight** Higher values make the highlights more focused.

Figure 17.263 "Map Object" options (Orientation)

17.12.7.3.5   Orientation

Position These three sliders and their input boxes allows you to vary object position in image, according to the X, Y, Z coordinates of the object upper left corner.

Rotation These three sliders make the object rotate around X, Y, Z axes respectively.

17.12.7.3.6   Box   This tab appears only when you select the Box object.

Figure 17.264 "Map Object" options (Box)

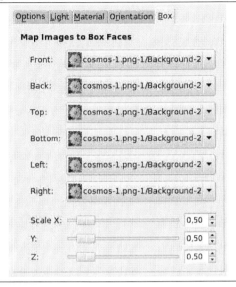

Match Images to Box Faces This function name is self explanatory: you can select an image for every face of the box. These images must be present on your screen when you call the Map Object filter.

Scale These X, Y, Z sliders allow you to change the size of every X, Y, Z dimension of the box.

17.12.7.3.7   Cylinder   This tab appears only when you select the Cylinder object.

Figure 17.265 "Map Object" options (Cylinder)

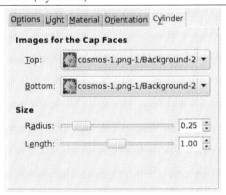

Images for the Cap Faces The name of this option is self-explanatory. Images must be present on your screen when you call the Map Object filter.

Size

   Radius This slider and its input boxes let you control the Cylinder diameter. Unfortunately, this setting works on the image mapped onto the cylinder and resamples this image to adapt it to the new cylinder size. It would be better to have the possibility of setting size cylinder before mapping so that we could map a whole image.

   Length Controls cylinder length.

17.12.8   Paper Tile

17.12.8.1   Overview

Figure 17.266 "Papertile" filter example.

(a) *Original image*   (b) *Filter "Papertile" applied*

This filter cuts the image (active layer or selection) into several pieces, with square form, and then slides them so that they, more or less, overlap or move apart. They can go out image borders a little.

17.12.8.2   Activate the filter

You can find this filter through Filters → Map → Paper Tile.

17.12.8.3   Options

Figure 17.267 "Paper Tile" filter options

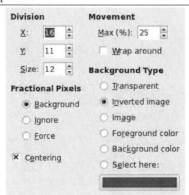

Division X, Y and Size parameters are linked, because filter starts cutting image before it displaces pieces; so, piece size and number of pieces in horizontal (X) and vertical (Y) directions must be convenient to image size.

Movement

> **Max (%)** This is the maximum displacement percentage against the side size of squares.
>
> **Wrap around** As tiles move, some can go out image borders. If this option is checked, what goes out on one side goes in on the opposite side.

Fractional Pixels Because of image cutting, original pixels can persist. There are three ways treating them:

> **Background** Remaining pixels will be replaced with the background type defined in the following section.
>
> **Ignore** Background Type option is not taken into account and remaining pixels are kept.
>
> **Force** Remaining pixels will be cut also.

Background Type You can select the background type which will be used, if the Background radio-button is checked, among six options:

> **Transparent** Background will be transparent.
>
> **Inverted image** Background colors will be inverted (255-value in every color channel).
>
> **Image** Background colors will be unchanged. The original image is the background.
>
> **Foreground color** Remaining pixels will be replaced by the Foreground color of Toolbox.
>
> **Background color** Remaining pixels will be replaced by the Background color of Toolbox.
>
> **Select here** When this radio-button is checked, clicking in the color dwell will open a Color Selector where you can select the color you want for background.

Centering If this option is checked, tiles will rather be gathered together in the center of the image.

17.12.9 Small Tiles

17.12.9.1 Overview

Figure 17.268 Example for the "Small Tiles" filter

(a) *Original image*   (b)

This filter reduces the image (active layer or selection) and displays it in many copies inside the original image.

17.12.9.2 Activate the filter

You can find this filter through Filters → Map → Small Tiles.

17.12.9.3   Options

Figure 17.269 "Small Tiles" filter options

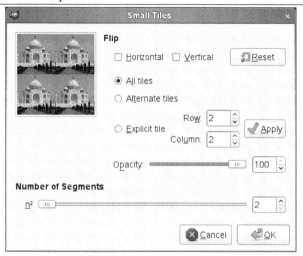

Flip You can flip tiles according to the Horizontal or/and Vertical axis by checking the corresponding option(s).

You can also decide which tiles will be flipped:

All tiles No comment.

Alternate tiles Only odd tiles will be flipped.

Explicit tile You can define a particular tile using both Row and Column input boxes. This tile will be marked with a box in Preview. Press Apply to mark this explicit tile. Repeat this procedure to mark more than one tile.

Opacity With this slider and its input box, you can set the opacity of the resulting image. This option is valid only if your image has an Alpha channel.

Number of Segments n^2 means "the image into n to the power of two tiles", where "n" is the number you set with the slider or its input box. n = 3 will make nine tiles in the image.

17.12.10   Tile

17.12.10.1   Overview

Figure 17.270 The same image, before and after applying Tile filter

(a) *Original image*   (b) *(We have reduced image size intentionally)*

This filter makes several copies of the original image, in a same or reduced size, into a bigger (new) image.

17.12.10.2 Activate the filter

You can find this filter through Filters → Map → Tile.

17.12.10.3 Options

Figure 17.271 "Tile" filter options

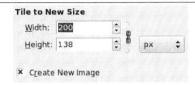

Tile to New Size

Width, Height Input boxes and their arrow-heads allow you to enter the dimensions for the new image.

Both directions are linked by default with a chain ⛓ . You can make them independent by breaking this chain. You can choose a unit else than pixel by clicking on the drop-down list button.

The new image must be bigger than the original one. Else, you will get an image sample only. Choose sizes which are multiple of original sizes if you don't want to have truncated tiles.

Create new image It's in your interest to keep this option checked to avoid modifying your original image.

17.12.11 Warp

17.12.11.1 Overview

This filter displaces pixels of active layer or selection according to the grey levels of a *Displacement map*. Pixels are displaced according to the gradient slope in the displacement map. Pixels corresponding to solid areas are not displaced; the higher the slope, the higher the displacement.

Figure 17.272 From left to right: original image, displace map, displaced image

Solid areas of displacement map lead to no displacement. Abrupt transitions give an important displacement. A linear gradient gives a regular displacement. Displacement direction is perpendicular to gradient direction (angle = 90°).

Figure 17.273 With a non-linear gradient

A non-linear gradient leads to curls.

Figure 17.274 With a complex gradient:

And a complex gradient, such as the Solid Noise filter can create, gives a swirl effect.

This filter offers the possibility of masking a part of the image to protect it against filter action.

17.12.11.2 Activating the filter

This filter is found in the image window menu under Filters → Map → Warp. This filter has no Preview.

17.12.11.3 Options

Figure 17.275 Warp filter options

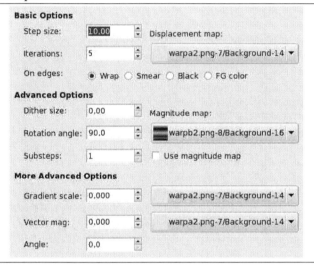

Basic Options

Step size "Step" is displacement distance for every filter iteration. A 10 value is necessary to get a one pixel displacement. This value can be negative to invert displacement direction.

Iterations The number of repetitions of effect when applying filter.

On edges Because of displacement, a part of pixels are driven over the borders of layer or selection, and, on the opposite side, pixels places are emptying. Four following options allow you to fix this issue:

Wrap What goes out on one side is going into the opposite side (this is the default).

Smear Emptying places are filled with a spreading of the neighbouring image line.

Black Emptying places are filled with black color.

Foreground color Emptying places are filled with the Foreground color of the color area in Toolbox.

Displacement map To be listed in this drop-down list, the displacement map, which should be a grayscaled image, must be *present on your screen when you call filter and must have the same size as the original image.*

Advanced Options

Dither size Once all pixels displaced, this option scatters them randomly, giving grain to the image. The higher this value (0.00-100.00), the thinner the grain.

Figure 17.276 With a 3.00 dither size:

Rotation angle This option sets displacement angle of pixels according to the slope direction of gradient. Previous examples have been created with a vertical gradient and a 90° angle: so, pixels were displaced horizontally and nothing went out of the image borders. Here is an example with a 10° angle and 6 iterations:

Figure 17.277 With a 10° angle and 6 iterations:

Displacement is made according to a 10° angle against vertical. Pixels going out the lower border on every iteration are going into through the upper border (Wrap option checked), giving a dotted line.

Substeps If you specify a value > 1, the displacement vector is computed in several substeps, giving you a finer control to the displace process.

Magnitude map In addition to displacement map, you can add a Magnitude map. This map should also be a grayscaled image, with the same size as the source image and which must be present on your screen when you call filter. This map gives more or less strength to filter on some parts of the image, according to the grey levels of this magnitude map. Image areas corresponding to white parts of this map will undergo all the strength of filter. Image areas corresponding to black parts of the map will be spared by filter. Intermediate grey levels will lessen filter action on corresponding areas of the image. Use magnitude map must be checked for that.

Figure 17.278 Magnitude Map example:

From left to right: original image, displacement map, magnitude map, after applying "Warp" filter. You can see that the black areas of magnitude map prevent filter to take action.

More Advanced Options
These extra options let you add two new maps, a gradient map and/or a vector map.

> **Note**
>
> To test these options alone, you must use a map with a solid color for all the other maps.

Gradient scale Using a gradient map, (this map should also be a grayscaled image), the displacement of pixels depends on the direction of grayscale transitions. The Gradient scale option lets you set how much the grayscale variations will influence the displacement of pixels. On every iteration, the filter works of the whole image, not only on the red object: this explains blurredness.

Figure 17.279 Gradient scale example

From left to right: original image, Gradient map, filter applied.

In the example above, "Warp" filter is applied with a gradient map (Gradient scale = 10.0). Gradient is oblique, from top left to right bottom. The part of the image corresponding to the gradient is moved obliquely, 90° rotated (Rotation angle 90° in Advanced Options).

Vector mag With this map, the displacement depends on the angle you set in the Angle text box. 0° is upwards. Angles go counter-clockwise. The *vector control map* determines by how many pixels the image will move on every iteration.

Figure 17.280 Vector mag example

From left to right: original image, displacement map, filter applied.

In the above example, "Warp" filter is applied with a Vector mag. Gradient is vertical, from top to bottom. Vector angle is 45°. The image is moved obliquely, 45° to the top left corner. The image is blurred because every iteration works on the whole image, and not only on the red bar.

Angle Angle for fixed vector map (see above).

17.13   Rendering Filters

17.13.1   Introduction

Most GIMP filters work on a layer by transforming its content, but the filters in the "Render" group are a bit different. They create patterns from scratch, in most cases obliterating anything that was previously in the layer. Some create random or noisy patterns, others regular of fractal patterns, and one (Gfig) is a general-purpose (but rather limited) vector graphics tool.

17.13.2   Difference Clouds

17.13.2.1   Overview

Figure 17.281 Example of Difference Clouds

Filter "Difference Clouds" applied

Difference Clouds command changes colors partially in cloud-like areas: The filter renders Solid Noise cloud in an automatically created new layer, and sets the layer mode to Difference, then merges this layer over the specified image.

Before merging the layer, this script opens the dialog of the Solid Noise plug-in which allows to control its effect.

If the image is in indexed colors, this menu entry is grayed out and unavailable.

17.13.2.2   Activate the filter

This filter is found in the image window menu under Filters → Render → Clouds → Difference Clouds....

17.13.2.3   Options

This script does not have its own dialog window but invokes the Solid Noise filter's dialog.

17.13.3   Fog

17.13.3.1   Overview

Figure 17.282 Example for the "Fog" filter

(a) *Original image*   (b) *"Fog" applied*

This filter adds a new layer with some clouds to the image that look like fog or smoke. The clouds are created with the Plasma texture.

17.13.3.2 Activating the filter

This filter is found in the image window menu under Filters → Render → Clouds → Fog.

17.13.3.3 Options

Figure 17.283 "Fog" options

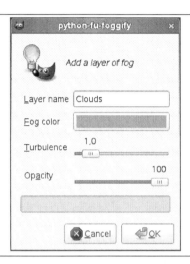

Among the few filter options, only "Turbulence" is somewhat important, because you can't change it later and have to undo and repeat the filter if the result doesn't fit your desire.

Layer name The name of the layer. You can change it later in the Layers Dialog.

Fog color Defaults to some kind of sandy brown (240, 180, 70). Click on the color button to change this if you think that is not the natural color of fog.

Turbulence This is actually the Turbulence option of the Plasma filter: it controls the complexity of the clouds, from soft (low values) to hard (high values).

Opacity The opacity of the layer. You can change it later in the Layers Dialog.

17.13.4 Plasma

17.13.4.1 Overview

Figure 17.284 Example of a rendered plasma

Filter "Plasma" applied

All of the colors produced by Plasma are completely saturated. Sometimes the strong colors may be distracting, and a more interesting surface will appear when you desaturate the image using Colors → Desaturate.

17.13.4.2   Activating the filter

This filter is found in the image window menu under Filters → Render → Clouds → Plasma.

17.13.4.3   Options

Figure 17.285 "Plasma" filter options

Preview If checked, parameter setting results are interactively displayed in preview.

Random seed This option controls the randomization element. The Randomize check-button will set the seed using the hardware clock of the computer. There is no reason to use anything else unless you want to be able to repeat the exact same pattern of randomization on a later occasion.

Turbulence This parameter controls the complexity of the plasma. High values give a hard feeling to the cloud (like an abstract oil painting or mineral grains), low values produce a softer cloud (like steam, mist or smoke). The range is 0.1 to 7.0.

17.13.5 Solid Noise

17.13.5.1 Overview

Figure 17.286 Example of turbulent solid noise

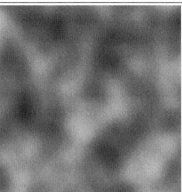

Filter "Solid noise" applied

Solid Noise is a great texture maker. Note that this noise is always gray, even if you applied it to a very colorful image (it doesn't matter what the original image looks like -- this filter completely overwrites any existing background in the layer it is applied to). This is also a good tool to create displacement maps for the Warp plug-in or for the Bump Map plug-in. With the "turbulence" setting active, the results look quite a bit like real clouds.

17.13.5.2 Activating the filter

This filter is found in the image window menu under Filters → Render → Clouds → Solid noise.

17.13.5.3 Options

Figure 17.287 "Solid Noise" filter options

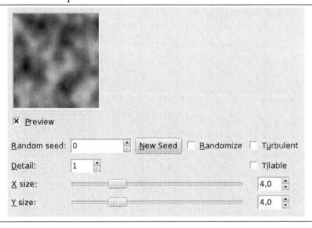

Preview If checked, parameter setting results are interactively displayed in preview.

Random seed This option controls random behaviour of the filter. If the same random seed in the same situation is used, the filter produces exactly the same results. A different random seed produces different results. Random seed can be entered manually or generated randomly by pressing New Seed button.

When the Randomize option is checked, random seed cannot be entered manually, but is randomly generated each time the filter is run. If it is not checked, the filter remembers the last random seed used.

Turbulent If you check this, you'll get very interesting effects, often something that looks much like oil on water, or clouds of smoke, or living tissue, or a Rorschach blot.

Detail This controls the amount of detail in the noise texture. Higher values give a higher level of detail, and the noise seems to be made of spray or small particles, which makes it feel hard. A low value makes it more soft and cloudy.

Tileable If you check Tileable, you'll get a noise which can be used as tiles. For example, you can use it as a background in an HTML page, and the tile edges will be joined seamlessly.

X size, Y size These control the size and proportion of the noise shapes in X (horizontal) and Y (vertical) directions (range 0.1 to 16.0).

17.13.6   Flame

17.13.6.1   Overview

Figure 17.288 Example of a rendered Flame

(b) *Filter "Flame" applied*

With the Flame filter, you can create stunning, randomly generated fractal patterns. You can't control the fractals as you can with the IFS Fractal filter, but you can steer the random generator in a certain direction, and choose from variations of a theme you like.

Warning

 Unfortunately it turned out, that this filter is not working properly for large images. Even more unfortunate is, that its developer is currently not undertaking any actions with that plug-in at all, so there seems no quick fix in sight. Although we can't give you the exact numbers, the plug-in worked in a quick test for a 1024x768 pixel image, but didn't do it for a 2500x2500 pixel image.

> **Note**
>
> This plug-in was given to GIMP by Scott Draves in 1997. He also holds the copyright for the plug-in. An descriptive page for the plug-in, provided by the author can be found in the internet [PLUGIN-FLAMES].

17.13.6.2 Activating the filter

You can find this filter through Filters → Render → Nature → Flame.

17.13.6.3 Options

Figure 17.289 "Flame" filter options

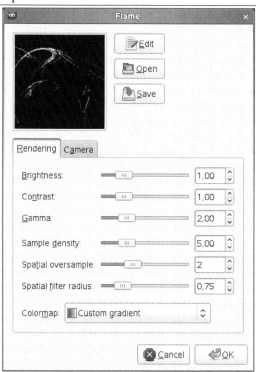

In the main window, you can set Rendering and Camera parameters. The first three parameters in the Render display are Brightness, Contrast and Gamma. The result of these options is visible in the Preview window, but it's generally better to stick to the default values, and correct the rendered image later with Image/Colors.

The other three parameters affect the rendering process and don't show in the preview window. Sample Density, which controls the resolution of the rendered pattern, is the most important of these. The Camera parameters allow you to zoom and offset the flame pattern, until you're happy with what you see in the preview window. Flame also offers the possibility to store and load your favorite patterns.

Edit Pressing this button brings up the Edit dialog:

Figure 17.290 The Edit Flame dialog

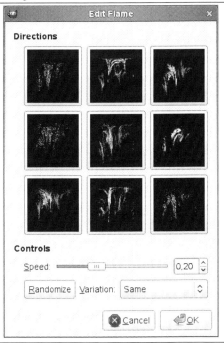

The dialog shows nine different windows. The pattern displayed in the center is the current pattern, and the eight windows surrounding it are random variations of that pattern. Clicking on the central image creates eight new variations, which can be adjusted with the Speed control. You select a variation by clicking on it, and it instantly replaces the image in the middle. To pick a certain character or theme for the variations, you can choose from nine different themes in the Variations menu. You can also use Randomize, which replaces the current pattern with a new random pattern.

Open This button brings up a file selector that allows you to open a previously saved Flame settings file.

Save This button brings up a file save dialog that allows you to save the current settings for the plug-in, so that you can recreate them later.

Rendering

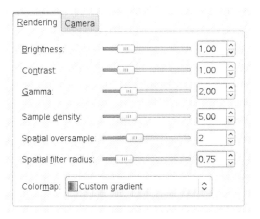

Brightness Controls the brightness of the flame object.

Contrast Controls the contrast between brighter and dimmer parts of the flame.

Gamma Sets a gamma correction for parts with intermediate brightness.

Sample density Controls the resolution of the rendered pattern. (Does not have any effect on the preview.) A high sample density results in soft and smooth rendering (like a spider's web), whereas low density rendering resembles spray or particle clouds.

Spatial oversample What does this do?

Spatial filter radius What does this do?

Colormap This menu gives you several options to set the color blend in the flame pattern:

- The current gradient as shown in the Toolbox.
- A number of preset colormaps.
- The colors from images that are presently open in GIMP.

Camera

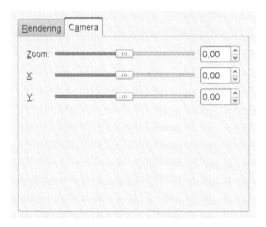

Zoom Allows you to zoom the flame in or out.

X, Y Allows you to move the flame around in the image area.

17.13.7 IFS Fractal

17.13.7.1 Overview

Figure 17.291 Applying example for the IFS Fractal filter

Filter "IFS Fractal" applied

This fractal-based plug-in is truly wonderful! With this versatile instrument, you can create amazingly naturalistic organic shapes, like leaves, flowers, branches, or even whole trees. ("IFS" stands for "Iterated Function System".)

The key to use this plug-in lies in making very small and precise movements in fractal space. The outcome is always hard to predict, and you have to be extremely gentle when you change the pattern.

If you make a component triangle too big, or if you move it too far (even ever so slightly), the preview screen will black out, or more commonly, you'll get stuck with a big shapeless particle cloud.

A word of advice: When you have found a pattern you want to work with, make only small changes, and stick to variations of that pattern. It's all too easy to lose a good thing. Contrary to what you might believe, it's really much easier to create a leaf or a tree with IFS Fractal than to make a defined geometrical pattern (where you actually know what you're doing, and end up with the pattern you had in mind).

For a brief introduction to IFS's see Foley and van Dam, et al,. *Computer Graphics, Principles and Practice*[FOLEY01].

17.13.7.2 Activating the filter

This filter is found in the image window menu under Filters → Render → Nature → IFS Fractal.

17.13.7.3 Options

Figure 17.292 "IFS Fractal" filter options

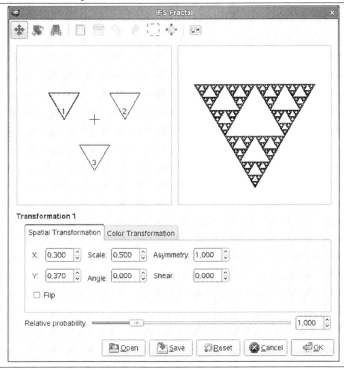

The plug-in interface consists of the compose area to the left, a preview screen to the right, and some tabs and option buttons at the bottom of the dialog. The Default setting (in the preview window) is three equilateral triangles. (This gives rise to a fractal pattern called the *Sierpinski Triangle*).

Toolbar

Click on the toolbar buttons to use the following tools, or open the context menu of the compose area.

Move, Rotate/Scale, Stretch Select the action to perform using the (mouse) pointer.

New, Delete Add or remove fractals.

Undo, Redo Standard.

Select all Link fractals and let apply actions to all fractals.

Recenter Recompute the center of the fractals. This does not have any visible effect to the resulting fractal.

Render Options

Max. memory Enables you to speed up rendering time. This is especially useful when working with a large spot radius; just remember to use even multiples of the default value: 4096, 8192, 16384, ...

Iterations Determines how many times the fractal will repeat itself. (A high value for Subdivide and Iterations is for obvious reasons a waste of process time unless your image is very large.)

Subdivide Controls the level of detail.

Spot radius Determines the density of the "brushstrokes" in the rendered image. A low spot radius is good for thin particle clouds or spray, while a high spot radius produces thick, solid color strokes much like watercolor painting. Be careful not to use too much spot radius — it takes a lot of time to render.

Spatial Transformation

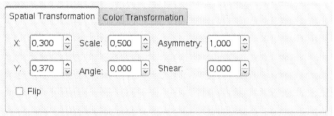

Gives you information on the active fractal, and allows you to type a value instead of changing it manually. Changing parameters with the mouse isn't very accurate, so this is a useful option when you need to be exact.

X, Y, Scale, Angle, Shear Move, scale, or shear the active fractal.

Asymmetry Stretch the active fractal.

Flip Flip the active fractal.

Color Transformation

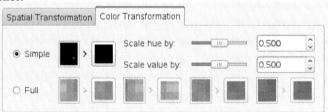

Simple Changes the color of the currently selected fractal component (default is the foreground color in the toolbox) to a color of your choice.

Full Like the Simple color transformation but this time you can manage the color transformation for each color channel and for the alpha channel (shown as a black channel).

Scale hue by, Scale value by When you have many fractals with different colors, the colors blend into each other. So even if you set "pure red" for a fractal, it might actually be quite blue in some places, while another "red " fractal might have a lot of yellow in it. Scale Hue/Value changes the color strength of the active fractal, or how influential that fractal color should be.

Other

Relative probability Determines influence or total impact of a certain fractal.

17.13.7.4 A Brief Tutorial

This is a rather complex plug-in, so to help you understand it, we'll guide you through an example where you'll create a leaf or branch.

Many forms of life, and especially plants, are built like mathematical fractals, i.e., a shape that reproduces or repeats itself indefinitely into the smallest detail. You can easily reproduce the shape of a leaf or a branch by using four (or more) fractals. Three fractals make up the tip and sides of the leaf, and the fourth represents the stem.

1. Before invoking the filter: Select File → New Image. Add a transparent layer with Layers → Layers and Channels → New Layer. Set the foreground color in the toolbox to black, and set the background to white.

2. Open IFS Fractal. Start by rotating the right and bottom triangles, so that they point upward. You'll now be able to see the outline of what's going to be the tip and sides of the leaf. (If you have problems, it may help to know that the three vertices of a triangle are not equivalent.)

Figure 17.293 Tutorial Step 2

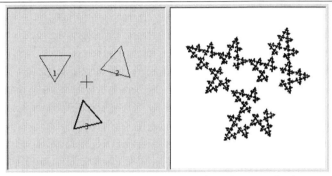

Start by rotating triangles 2 and 3, trying to keep them nearly the same size.

3. To make the leaf symmetrical, adjust the bottom triangle to point slightly to the left, and the right triangle to point slightly to the right.

4. Press New to add a component to the composition. This is going to be the stem of the leaf, so we need to make it long and thin. Press Stretch, and drag to stretch the new triangle. Don't be alarmed if this messes up the image, just use Scale to adjust the size of the overlong triangle. You'll probably also have to move and rotate the new fractal to make it look convincing.

Figure 17.294 Tutorial Step 3

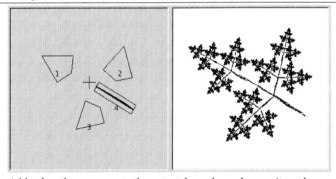

Add a fourth component, then stretch, scale, and move it as shown.

5. You still have to make it look more leaf-like. Increase the size of the top triangle, until you think it's thick and leafy enough. Adjust all fractals until you're happy with the shape. Right-click to get the pop-up menu, and choose Select all. Now all components are selected, and you can scale and rotate the entire leaf.

Figure 17.295 Tutorial Step 4

Enlarge component 1, arrange the other components appropriately, then select all, scale and rotate.

6. The final step is to adjust color. Click on the Color Transformation tab, and choose a different color for each fractal. To do this, check Simple and press the right color square. A color circle appears, where you can click or select to choose a color.

Figure 17.296 Tutorial Step 5

Assign a brownish color to component 4, and various shades of green to the other components.

7. Press OK to apply the image, and voilà, you've just made a perfect fractal leaf! Now that you've got the hang of it, you'll just have to experiment and make your own designs. All plant-imitating fractals (be they oak trees, ferns or straws) are more or less made in this fashion, which is leaves around a stem (or several stems). You just have to twist another way, stretch and turn a little or add a few more fractals to get a totally different plant.

17.13.8 Checkerboard

17.13.8.1 Overview

Figure 17.297 Example for the Checkerboard filter

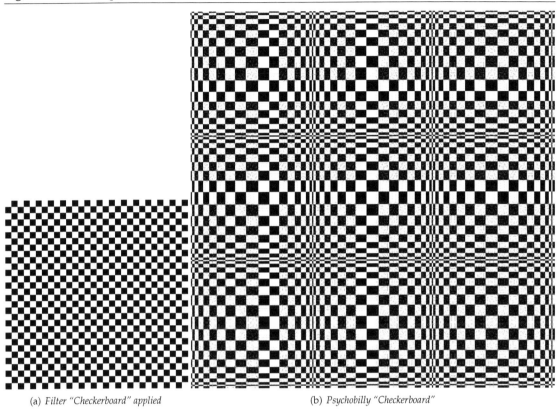

(a) Filter "Checkerboard" applied   (b) Psychobilly "Checkerboard"

This filter creates a checkerboard pattern replacing the current layer content. Colors used for pattern are current Fore- and Back ground colors of toolbox.

17.13.8.2 Starting filter

You can find this filter in the image menu through Filters → Render → Pattern → Checkerboard

17.13.8.3 Options

Figure 17.298 "Checkerboard" filter options

Size With this option, you can set checkerboard square size, in pixels, or in your chosen unit by using the drop-down list.

Psychobilly This option gives an eiderdown look to the Checkerboard.

17.13.9 CML Explorer

17.13.9.1 Overview

Figure 17.299 Example for the "CML Explorer" filter

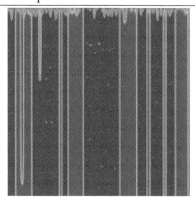

Filter "CML Explorer" applied with default options

This filter is the king of texture creating filters. It is extremely efficient but very complex. It uses a mathematical method named Cellular Automata [WKPD-CA].

17.13.9.2 Activating the filter

You can find this filter from the image menu through Filters → Render → Pattern → CML Explorer.

17.13.9.3 Options

17.13.9.3.1 General Options Filter options are distributed among Hue,Saturation, Value, Advanced, Others and Misc Ops. tabs. Some more options are available. They will be described in following section.

Preview This filter offers you a Preview where you can see the result of your settings before they are applied to the image.

New Seed, Fix Seed, Random Seed Random plays a large part in creating patterns. With these options, you can influence the way random is generated. By clicking on the New Seed button, you can force random to use a new source of random. The preview will show you the result. Fix Seed lets you keep the same seed and so to reproduce the same effect with the filter. Random Seed generates a random seed at random.

Open, Save With these both command buttons you can save pattern settings in a file, and to get them back later.

Figure 17.300 Hue tab

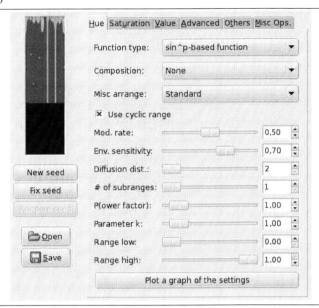

17.13.9.3.2 "CML Explorer" filter options (Hue) This filter works in the HSV color model. In this tab, you can set options for Hue.

Function type In this drop-down list, you can select the method that will be used to treat the current layer. These methods are:

Keep image's values With this option, image hue values will be kept.

Keep the first value With this option, starting color will be standard cyan.

Fill with parameter k Pattern look will depend on k that you will set later in options.

Miscellaneous f(k) See above, "Fill with k parameter".

Delta function, Delta function stepped // TODO

sin^p-based function, sin^p, stepped These options create wave-like patterns, like aurora borealis or curtain folds.

Composition Here, these options concern Hue. You can choose among several functions, and a book could be filled with results of all these functions. Please, experiment!

Misc. arrange This drop-down list offers you several other parameters. Also a book would be necessary to explain all possibilities of these parameters.

Use cyclic range // TODO

Mod. rate With this slider and the input box, you can set modification rate from 0.0 to 1.0. Low value results in a lined pattern.

Env. sensitivity Value is from 0.0 to 1.0

Diffusion dist. Diffusion distance: from 2 to 10.

# of subranges Number of sub-rangers: from 1 to 10.

(P)ower factor With this option you can influence the Function types using the p parameter. Value from 0.0 to 10.0.

Parameter k With this option you can influence the Function types using the k parameter. Value from 0.0 to 10.0.

Range low Set lower limit of hue that will be used for calculation. values vary from 0.0 to 1.0.

Range high Set the upper limit of hue that will be used for calculation. Variations are from 0.0 to 1.0.

Plot a Graph of the Settings By clicking on this large button, you can open a window that displays the graph of hue present settings.

Figure 17.301 Function graph of present settings

Figure 17.302 Saturation tab

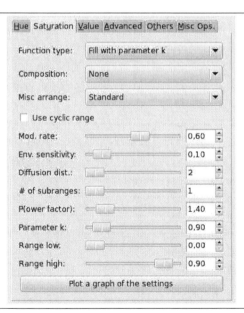

17.13.9.3.3 "CML Explorer" filter options (Saturation) In this tab, you can set how Saturation component of the HSV color model will be used in pattern calculation.

These options are similar to Hue tab options.

Figure 17.303 Value tab

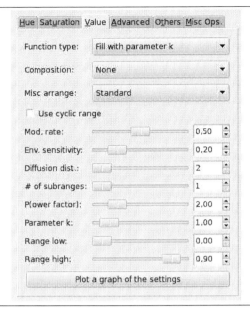

17.13.9.3.4 "CML Explorer" filter options (Value) In this tab, you can set how the Value (Luminosity) component of the HSV color model will be used in pattern calculation.

These options are similar to Hue tab options.

Figure 17.304 Advanced tab

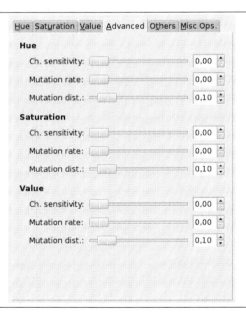

17.13.9.3.5 "CML Explorer" filter options (Advanced) These tab settings apply to the three HSV channels.

Channel sensitivity // TODO

Mutation rate // TODO

Mutation distance // TODO

Figure 17.305 Others tab

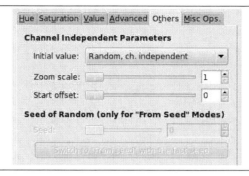

17.13.9.3.6 "CML Explorer" filter options (Others)   In this tab, you can find various parameters about image display and random intervention.

Initial value // TODO

Zoom scale // TODO

Start offset // TODO

Seed of Random // TODO

Figure 17.306 Miscellaneous options tab

17.13.9.3.7 "CML Explorer" filter options (Misc Ops.)   In this tab you can find various options about copy and loading.

Copy Settings   These options allow you to transfer information from one of the HSV channel to another one.

Selective Load Settings   With the Open button of this filter, you can load previously loaded settings. If you don't want to load all of them, you can select a source and a destination channel here.

17.13.10   Diffraction Patterns

17.13.10.1   Overview

Figure 17.307 Two examples of diffraction patterns

This filter lets you make diffraction or wave interference textures. You can change the Frequency, Contours and Sharp Edges for each of the RGB channels. You can also set Brightness, Scattering and Polarization of the texture. There is no automatic preview, so you must press the preview button to update. On a slow system, this may take a bit of time. Note that result doesn't depend on the initial image.

This is a very useful filter if you want to create intricate patterns. It's perfect for making psychedelic, batik-like textures, or for imitating patterns in stained glass (as in a church window).

It seems clear that the plugin works by simulating the physics of light striking a grating. Unfortunately, the original authors never got around to writing down the theory behind it, or explaining what the parameters mean. The best approach, then, is just to twiddle things and see what happens. Fortunately, almost anything you do seems to produce interesting results.

17.13.10.2   Activating the filter

This filter is found in the image window menu under Filters → Render → Pattern → Diffraction Patterns.

17.13.10.3   Options

Figure 17.308 "Diffraction Patterns" filter options

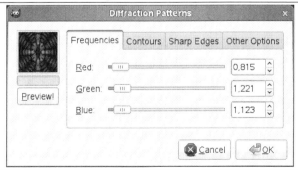

17.13.11   Grid

17.13.11.1   Overview

Figure 17.309 Applying example for the Grid filter

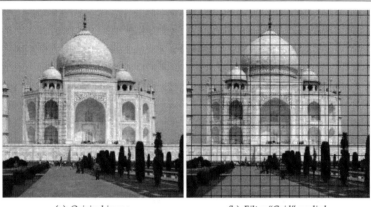

(a) *Original image*   (b) *Filter "Grid" applied*

It renders a Cartesian grid in the active layer, on top of the existing contents. The width, spacing, offsets, and colors of the grid lines can all be set by the user. By default, the lines are with the GIMP's foreground color. (Note: this plug-in was used to create demonstration images for many of the other plug-ins.)

Tip

 If you set the grid line widths to 0, then only the intersections will be drawn, as plus-marks.

17.13.11.2   Activating the filter

This filter is found in the image window menu under Filters → Render → Pattern → Grid.

17.13.11.3   Options

Figure 17.310 "Grid" filter options

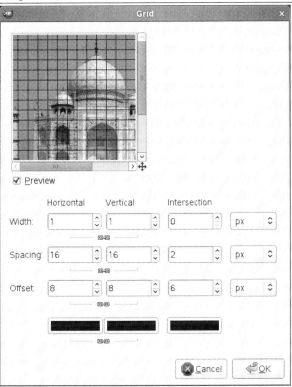

There are separate options for controlling the horizontal grid lines, vertical grid lines, and intersections. By default, the horizontal and vertical settings are locked together, so that all changes are applied symmetrically. If you want to change just one of them, click on the "chain" symbol below it to unlock them. The results of changing the Intersection parameters are rather complex.

Besides, for some options, you can select the unit of measurement thanks to a drop-down list.

Width Sets the widths of the horizontal or vertical grid lines, or of the symbols drawn at their intersections.

Spacing Sets the distance between grid lines. The Intersection parameter clears the space between the intersection point and the end of the arms of the intersection crosses.

Offset Sets the offset for grid lines with respect to the upper left corner. For intersections, sets the length of the arms of the intersection crosses.

Color Selectors These allow you to set the colors of the grid lines and intersection marks.

Figure 17.311 Intersection parameters

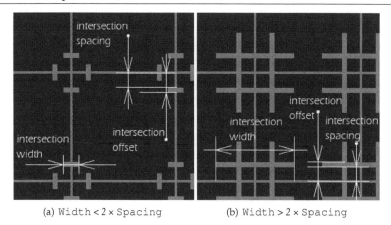

(a) Width < 2 × Spacing   (b) Width > 2 × Spacing

17.13.12   Jigsaw

17.13.12.1   Overview

Figure 17.312 Jigsaw filter example

(a) *Original image*   (b) *Filter "Jigsaw" applied*

This filter will turn your image into a jigsaw puzzle. The edges are not anti-aliased, so a little bit of smoothing often makes them look better (i. e., Gaussian blur with radius 1.0).

Tip

If you want to be able to easily select individual puzzle-piece areas, render the jig-saw pattern on a separate layer filled with solid white, and set the layer mode to Multiply. You can then select puzzle pieces using the magic wand (fuzzy select) tool on the new jigsaw layer.

17.13.12.2   Activating the filter

This filter is found in the image window menu under Filters → Render → Pattern → Jigsaw.

17.13.12.3 Options

Figure 17.313 "Jigsaw" filter options

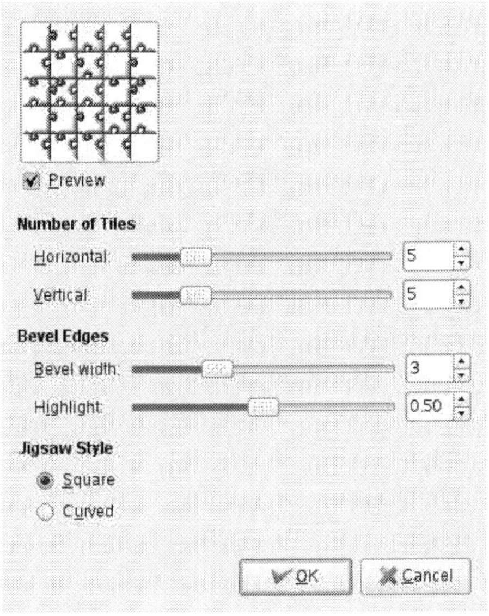

Number of Tiles How many tiles across the image is, horizontally and vertically.

Bevel Edges

Bevel width The Bevel width slider controls the slope of the edges of the puzzle pieces (a hard wooden puzzle would require a low Bevel width value, and a soft cardboard puzzle would require a higher value).

Highlight The Highlight slider controls the strength of the highlight that will appear on the edges of each piece. You may compare it to the "glossiness" of the material the puzzle is made of. Highlight width is relative to the Bevel width. As a rule of thumb, the more pieces you add to the puzzle, the lower Bevel and Highlight values you should use, and vice versa. The default values are suitable for a 500x500 pixel image.

Jigsaw Style

You can choose between two types of puzzle:

Square Then you get pieces made with straight lines.

Curved Then you get pieces made with curves.

17.13.13 Maze

17.13.13.1 Overview

Figure 17.314 An example of a rendered maze.

Filter "Maze" applied

This filter generates a random black and white maze pattern. The result completely overwrites the previous contents of the active layer. A typical example is shown below. Can you find the route from the center to the edge?

17.13.13.2 Activating the filter

This filter is found in the image window menu under Filters → Render → Pattern → Maze.

17.13.13.3 Options

Figure 17.315 "Maze" filter options

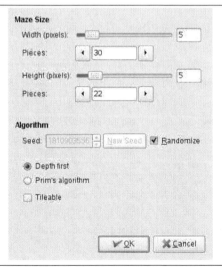

Maze Size

Width, Height These sliders control how many pathways the maze should have. The lower the values for width and height, the more paths you will get. The same happens if you increase the number of pieces in the Width and Height Pieces fields. The result won't really look like a maze unless the width and height are equal.

Algorithm

Seed You can specify a seed for the random number generator, or ask the program to generate one for you. Unless you need to later reproduce exactly the same maze, you might as well have the program do it.

Depth first, Prim's algorithm You can choose between these two algorithms for maze. Only a computer scientist can tell the difference between them.

Tileable If you want to use it in a pattern, you can make the maze tileable by checking this check-button.

17.13.14 Qbist

17.13.14.1 Overview

Figure 17.316 Applying examples for the Qbist filter

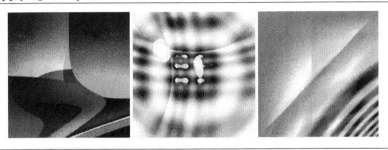

The Qbist filter generates random textures containing geometric figures and color gradients.

17.13.14.2 Activating the filter

This filter is found in the image window menu under Filters → Render → Pattern → Qbist

17.13.14.3 Options

Figure 17.317 "Qbist" filter options

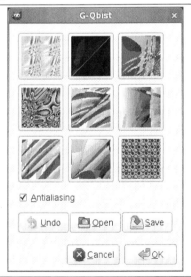

The Qbist filter generates random textures. A starting texture is displayed in the middle square, and different variations surround it. If you like one of the alternative textures, click on it. The chosen texture now turns up in the middle, and variations on that specific theme are displayed around it. When you have found the texture you want, click on it and then click OK. The texture will now appear on the currently active layer, completely replacing its previous contents.

Antialiasing If you check this, it will make edges appear smooth rather than stair-step-like.

Undo Lets you go back one step in history.

Open, Save These buttons allow you to save and reload your textures. This is quite handy because it's almost impossible to re-create a good pattern by just clicking around.

17.13.15 Sinus

17.13.15.1 Overview

Figure 17.318 Applying example for the Sinus filter

Filter "Sinus" applied

You can find this filter from the image menu through Filters → Render → Pattern → Sinus.

The Sinus filter lets you make sinusoidally based textures, which look rather like watered silk or maybe plywood. This plug-in works by using two different colors that you can define in the Colors tab. These two colors then create wave patterns based on a sine function.

You can set the X and Y scales, which determine how stretched or packed the texture will be. You can also set the Complexity of the function: a high value creates more interference or repetition in the pattern. An example is shown below.

17.13.15.2 Options

Figure 17.319 "Sinus" filter options (Settings)

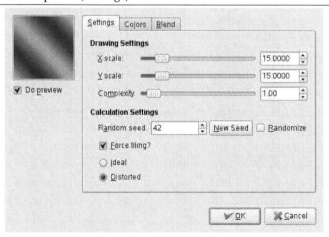

17.13.15.2.1 Settings Drawing Settings

X scale, Y scale A low X/Y value will maximize the horizontal/vertical stretch of the texture, whereas a high value will compress it.

Complexity This controls how the two colors interact with each other (the amount of interplay or repetition).

Calculation Settings

Random seed This option controls the random behaviour of the filter. If the same random seed in the same situation is used, the filter produces exactly the same results. A different random seed produces different results. Random seed can be entered manually or generated randomly by pressing the New Seed button.

When the Randomize option is checked, random seed cannot be entered manually, but is randomly generated each time the filter is run. If it is not checked, the filter remembers the last random seed used.

Force tiling? If you check this, you'll get a pattern that can be used for tiling. For example, you can use it as a background in an HTML page, and the tile edges will be joined seamlessly.

Ideal, Distorted This options give additional control of the interaction between the two colors. "Distorted" creates a more distorted interference between the two colors than "Ideal".

Figure 17.320 "Sinus" filter options (Colors)

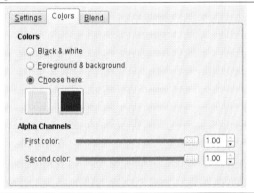

17.13.15.2.2 Colors

Colors Here, you set the two colors that make up your texture. You can use Black & white or the Foreground & background colors in the toolbox, or you can Choose a color with the color icons.

Alpha Channels This sliders allow you to assign an opacity to each of the colors. (If the layer you are working on does not have an alpha channel, they will be grayed out.)

Figure 17.321 "Sinus" filter options (Blend)

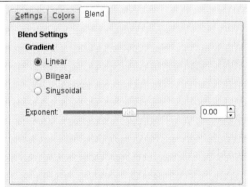

17.13.15.2.3   Blend

Gradient   You can choose between three functions to set the shapes of the waves that are produced: Linear, Bilinear and Sinusoidal.

Exponent   The Exponent controls which of the two colors is dominant, and how dominant it is. If you set the exponent to -7.5, the left color will dominate totally, and if you set it to +7.5 it will be the other way around. A zero value is neutral.

17.13.16   Circuit

17.13.16.1   Overview

Figure 17.322 Example of Circuit

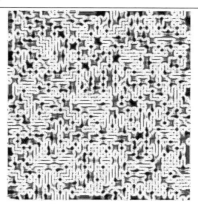

Filter "Circuit" applied.

Circuit command is a script that fills the selected region (or alpha) with traces like those on the back of an old circuit board. It looks even better when gradmapped with a suitable gradient.

> **Tip**
>
> The effect seems to work best on odd shaped selections because of some limitations in the maze codes selection handling ability.

If the image is in indexed colors, this menu entry is grayed out and unavailable.

> **Note**
>
> This filter creates a grey level image in RGB mode.
>
> The resulting image doesn't depend on the original image.

17.13.16.2   Activate the filter

This filter is found in the image window menu under Filters → Render → Circuit....

17.13.16.3 Options

Figure 17.323 "Circuit" filter options

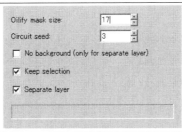

Oilify mask size With this option you can set the option value of the Oilify filter in pixels (range 3 to 50). Larger values make lines more fuzzy. 17 is the default value.

Circuit seed You can give a randomizing seed number between 1 and 3000000. The default value is 3.

No background (only for separate layer) If this option is enabled, dark pixels of the circuit are made transparent so that the underlying image is shown through these holes. This option is disabled in default settings. The Separate layer option is required.

Keep selection If an active selection exists when this script is called, you can keep the selection and its marching ants with this option. This option is enabled in default settings.

Separate layer If this option is not checked, the generated texture is drawn on the active layer. When this option is enabled (in default), this script adds a layer to draw the circuit texture is on.

17.13.16.4 Making the Circuit effect

The Circuit effect is achieved through the following steps:

1. First, draw maze with 5 pixels width pathways and walls with the "Depth First" algorithm. The pattern of maze is set by Circuit seed.

2. Oilify this maze with a brush of Oilify mask size.

3. Then apply the extract edge filter with Sobel algorithm, Smear option and Amount to 2.0, to the oilified maze image. This crowds high contrast winding curves like as a circuit map.

4. Finally, Desaturate the map with gray color in RGB mode.

17.13.17 Fractal Explorer

17.13.17.1 Overview

Figure 17.324 Example for the Fractal Explorer filter

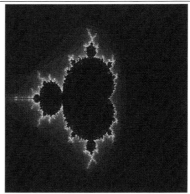

Filter "Fractal Explorer" applied

With this filter, you can create fractals and multicolored pictures verging to chaos. Unlike the IFS Fractal filter, with which you can fix the fractal structure precisely, this filter lets you perform fractals simply.

17.13.17.2   Starting filter

You can find this filter through Filters → Render → Fractal Explorer.

17.13.17.3   Options

Figure 17.325 "Fractal Explorer" filter options

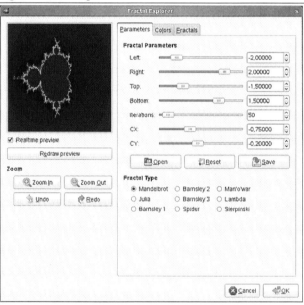

The Fractal Explorer window contains two panes: on the left there is the Preview pane with a Zoom feature, on the right you find the main options organized in tabs: Parameters, Colors, and Fractals.

17.13.17.3.1   Preview

Realtime preview   Uncheck the Realtime preview only if your computer is slow. In this case, you can update preview by clicking on the Redraw preview button.

By clicking-dragging mouse pointer on preview, you can draw a rectangle delimiting an area which will be zoomed.

Zoom   You have there some options to zoom in or zoom out. The Undo allows you to return to previous state, before zooming. The Redo allows you to reestablish the zoom you had undone, without having to re-create it with the Zoom In or Zoom Out buttons.

Figure 17.326 "Fractal Explorer" filter options (Parameters)

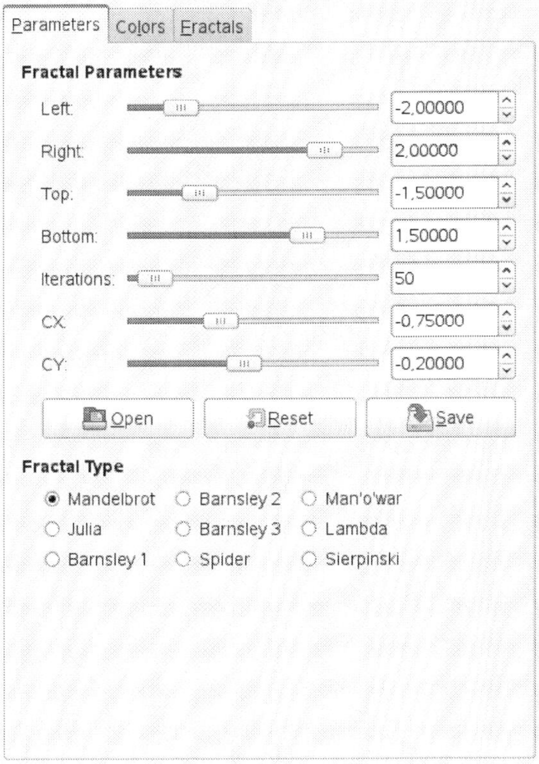

17.13.17.3.2 Parameters This tab contains some options to set fractal calculation and select fractal type.

Fractal Parameters Here, you have sliders and input boxes to set fractal spreading, repetition and aspect.

Left, Right, Top, Bottom You can set fractal spreading between a minimum and a maximum, in the horizontal and/or vertical directions. Values are from -3.0 to 3.0.

Iterations With this parameter, you can set fractal iteration, repetition and so detail. Values are from 0.0 to 1000.0

CX, CY With these parameters, you can change fractal aspect, in the horizontal (X) and/or vertical (Y) directions, except for Mandelbrot and Sierpinski types.

Open, Reset, Save With these three buttons, you can save your work with all its parameters, open a previously saved fractal, or return to the initial state before all modifications.

Fractal Type You can choose what fractal type will be, for instance Mandelbrot, Julia, Barnsley or Sierpinski.

Figure 17.327 "Fractal Explorer" filter options (Colors)

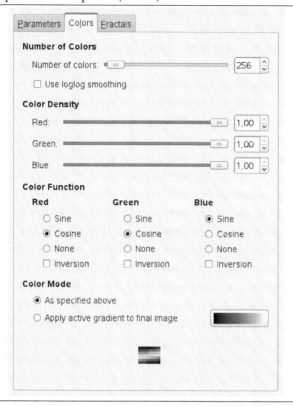

17.13.17.3.3   Colors   This tab contains options for fractal color setting.
   Number of Colors

Number of colors   This slider and its input boxes allow you to set the number of colors for the fractal, between 2 and 8192. A palette of these colors is displayed at the bottom of the tab. Actually, that's a gradient between colors in fractal: you can change colors with "Color Density" and "Color Function" options. Fractal colors don't depend on colors of the original image (you can use a white image for fractals as well).

Use loglog smoothing   If this option is checked, the band effect is smoothed.

Figure 17.328 Loglog smoothing example

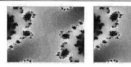

Color density

Red, Green, Blue   These three sliders and their text-boxes let you set the color intensity in the three color channels. Values vary from 0.0 to 1.0.

Color Function
For the Red, Green and Blue color channels, you can select how color will be treated:

Sine   Color variations will be modulated according to the sine function.

Cosine   Color densities will vary according to cosine function.

None   Color densities will vary linearly.

Inversion   If you check this option, function values will be inverted.

Color Mode

These options allow you to set where color values must be taken from.

As specified above Color values will be taken from the Color Density options.

Apply active gradient to final image Used colors will be that of active gradient. You should be able to select another gradient by clicking on the gradient source button.

Figure 17.329 "Fractal Explorer" filter options (Fractals)

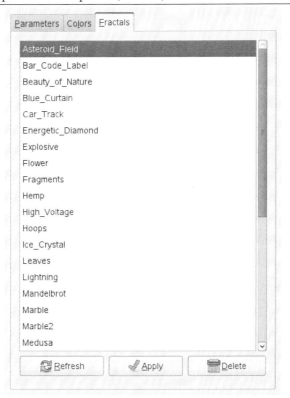

17.13.17.3.4 Fractals This tab contains a big list of fractals with their parameters, that you can use as a model: only click on the wanted one.

The Refresh allows you to update the list if you have saved your work, without needing to re-start GIMP. You can delete the selected fractal from the list by clicking on the Delete.

17.13.18   Gfig

17.13.18.1   Overview

Figure 17.330 The same image, before and after using Gfig

(a) *Original image*   (b) *Filter "Gfig" applied*

This filter is a tool: You can create geometrical figures to add them to the image. It is very complex. I hope this paper will help you.

When using this filter, elements inserted in the image will be placed in a new layer. So the image will not be modified, all modifications occurring in this layer.

17.13.18.2   Starting filter

You can find this filter through Filters → Render → Gfig

17.13.18.3   Options

Figure 17.331 "Gfig" filter options

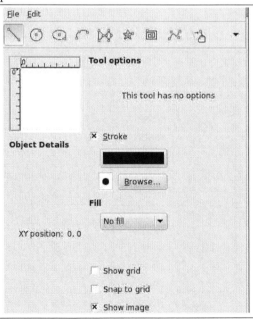

The Preview (with a horizontal and a vertical ruler) on the left of the main window actually is your working area where you are adding your figures.

You can add and modify figures using the Gfig tools (Gfig tool bar) and using the appropriate options (Gfig main window).

17.13.18.3.1 The Gfig tool bar At the top of dialog, you can find a set of icons which represents the functions of this filter. Help pop-ups are explicit.

Functions for object drawing

On the left part of tool bar, you can find some functions for object drawing. You enable them by clicking on the corresponding icon. You can create the following objects (note that *Control points* are created at the same time as object):

Create line With this tool, you can draw lines. Click on Preview to mark start point, then drag mouse pointer to the end point.

Create rectangle With this tool, you can draw rectangles. Click on Preview to mark start point, then drag mouse pointer to create the rectangle.

Create circle With this tool, you can draw circles. Click on Preview to mark center, then drag mouse pointer to the wanted radius.

Create ellipse With this tool, you can draw ellipses. Click on Preview to mark center, then drag mouse pointer to get the wanted size and form.

Create arc With this tool, you can draw circle arcs. Click on Preview to set start point. Click again to set another arc point. Without releasing mouse button, drag pointer; when you release mouse button, the arc end point is placed and an arc encompassing these three points is drawn.

Create regular polygon With this tool, you can create a regular polygon. Start with setting side number in Tool Options at the right of Preview. Then click on Preview to place center and, without releasing mouse button, drag pointer to get the wanted size and orientation.

Create star With this tool, you can create a star. Start with setting side number (spikes) in Tool Options at the right of Preview. Then click on Preview to place center and, without releasing mouse button, drag pointer to get the wanted size and orientation.

Create spiral With this tool, you can create a spiral. Start with setting spire number (sides) and spire orientation in Tool Options at the right of Preview. Then click on Preview to place center and, without releasing mouse button, drag pointer to get the wanted size.

Create bezier curve With this tool, you can create Bézier curves. Click on Preview to set start point and the other points: the curve will be created between these points. To end point creation press **Shift** key when creating last point.

Functions for object management

In the middle of tool bar, you can find tools to manage objects:

Move an object With this tool, you can move the active object. To enable an object, click on a control point created at the same time as the object.

Move a single point With this tool, you can click-and-drag one of the control points created at the same time as object. Each of these points moves the object in a different way.

Copy an object With this tool, you can duplicate an object. Click on an object control point and drag it to the wanted place.

Delete an object Click on an object control point to delete it.

Select an object With this tool, you can select an object to active it. Simply click on one of its control points.

Functions for object organisation

At the right of tool bar, you can find tools for object superimposing (you can also get them by clicking on the drop-down list button if they are not visible). You have:

Up (Raise selected object), Down (Lower selected object) With this tool, you can push the selected object one level up or down.

Top, Bottom Self explanatory.

Functions for object display

Back, Forward These functions allow you to jump from one object to another. Only this object is displayed.

Show all objects This function shows all objects again, after using both previous functions.

Note

  If your window is too small to show all icons, the tool bar provides a drop-down list which offers you the missing functions.

17.13.18.3.2   The Gfig main window

Object Details The XY position shows the position of your pointer.

Tool Options If the selected tool provides some options (like number of sides), you can change them here.

Stroke If this option is checked, the object will be drawn. Two buttons are available, to select color and brush type. Changes to color or brush apply to existing objects too.

Fill With help of this drop-down list, you can decide whether and how the object will be filled, with a color, a pattern or a gradient.

Show grid If this option is checked, a grid is applied on Preview to make object positioning easier.

Snap to grid If this option is checked, objects will align to the grid.

Show image When this option is checked, the current image is displayed in Preview (working area).

17.13.19   Lava

17.13.19.1   Overview

Figure 17.332 Example for the "Lava" filter

(a) *Original image*   (b) *"Lava" applied (on a selection)*

17.13.19.2   Activating the filter

This filter is found in the image window menu under Filters → Render → Lava.

17.13.19.3   Options

Figure 17.333 "Lava" options

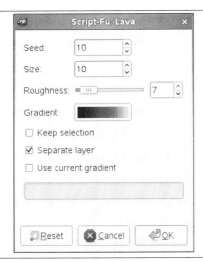

Seed TODO

Size TODO

Roughness TODO

Gradient TODO

Keep selection TODO

Separate layer TODO

Use current gradient TODO

17.13.20   Line Nova

17.13.20.1   Overview

Figure 17.334 Example for the "Line Nova" filter

(a) *Original image*   (b) *"Line Nova" applied*

The Line Nova filter fills a layer with rays emanating outward from the center of the layer using the foreground color shown in the Toolbox. The rays starts as one pixel and grew broader towards the edges of the layer.

Tip

This filter does not provide any option which allows you to set the center point of lines. If you need adjust the place of the radial lines where you want, create another transparent image and apply this filter on it, then add it on your image. Setting large size for the new nova image may help you not to break lines inside of your image.

17.13.20.2 Activating the filter

This filter is found in the image window menu under Filters → Render → Line Nova.

17.13.20.3 Options

Figure 17.335 "Line Nova" options

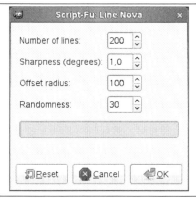

Number of lines By using this option you can set the number of lines between 40 to 1000. The default is 200.

Sharpness (degrees) This slider determines how much the rays will broaden towards the edges. The range goes from 0.0 to 10.0. If set to 0.0, nothing will be drawn. If set to 10.0, most of the area near the edges of the layer will be painted.

Figure 17.336 "Line Nova" sharpness option

From left to right: sharpness = 1; sharpness = 5; sharpness = 10

Offset radius Here you choose the distance, in pixels, from center to the starting point of the rays. If set to 0.0 the rays starts from the center. Any other value will let the starting points be on a circle at the selected distance from the center. The maximum distance is 2000 pixels. The default value is 100 pixels.

Figure 17.337 "Line Nova" offset radius option

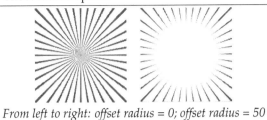

From left to right: offset radius = 0; offset radius = 50

Randomness If this slider is set to a value higher than 1, the starting point for each ray differ more or less randomly from the average starting point set as the offset radius above. With the value set to 1, all the rays will start at the circle determined by the offset radius. The maximum value is 2000. The default value is 30.

Figure 17.338 "Line Nova" randomness option

From left to right: randomness = 1; randomness = 50

17.13.21   Sphere Designer

17.13.21.1   Overview

Figure 17.339 The same image, before and after the application of "Sphere Designer" filter.

(a) *Original image*   (b) *Filter "Sphere Designer" applied*

This filter creates a three dimensional sphere with different textures. It replaces the original image.

17.13.21.2   Activating Sphere Designer

You can find this filter through Filters → Render → Sphere Designer.

17.13.21.3 Options

Figure 17.340 "Sphere Designer" filter parameters

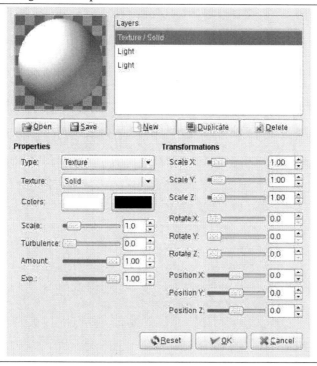

Preview All your setting changes will appear in the Preview without affecting the image until you click on OK. Note that the preview displays the whole image, even if the final result will concern a selection. Click the button *Update Preview* to see the result of the current settings.

Textures
The list of textures applied to the sphere. There textures are applied in the order listed. Each item shows the type and the name of the texture.

New Creates a new texture and adds it to the end of the list. The name and the features of this new texture are the ones which are displayed in the Texture Properties area, but you can change them by operating in this area, provided that your new texture is highlighted.

Duplicate Copies the selected texture and adds the copy to the end of the list.

Delete Deletes the selected texture from the list.

Open, Save Allows to save current settings or load previously saved settings.

Properties

Type Determines the type of action on the sphere.

> **Texture** Covers the sphere with a specific pattern.
>
> **Bumpmap** Gives some relief to the texture.
>
> **Light** Lets you set the parameters of the light shining on the sphere.

Texture Determines the pattern used by the texture type. If the texture applies to light then the light is distorted by this texture as if it was going through this texture before falling onto the sphere. If the texture applies to the texture itself, the texture is applied directly to the sphere. Several options are available.

Colors Sets the two colors to be used for a texture. By pressing the color button a color selection dialog appears.

Scale Determines the size of separate elements composing the texture. For example, for the "Checker" texture this parameter determines the size of black and white squares. Value range is from 0 to 10.

Turbulence Determines the degree of texture distortion before applying the texture to the sphere. Value range is from 0 to 10. With values of up to 1.0 you can still make out the undistorted patterns; beyond that the texture gradually turns into noise.

Amount Determines the degree of influence the texture has on the final result. Value range is from 0 to 1. With the value of 0 the texture does not affect the result.

Exponent With the Wood texture, this options gives an aspect of venetian blind, more or less open.

Transformations

Scale X, Scale Y, Scale Z Determines the degree of stretching/compression of the texture on the sphere along the three directions. The value range is from 0 to 10.

Rotate X, Rotate Y, Rotate Z Determines the amount of a turn of the texture on the sphere around the three axes. The value range is from 0 to 360.

Position X, Position Y, Position Z Determines the position of the texture relative to the sphere. When type is Light, this parameter refers to the position of the light floodlighting the sphere.

The Reset button sets all parameters to the default values.

17.13.22 Spyrogimp

17.13.22.1 Overview

Figure 17.341 Example for the "Spyrogimp" filter

(a) *Original image*   (b) *"Spyrogimp" applied*

17.13.22.2 Activating the filter

This filter is found in the image window menu under Filters → Render → Spyrogimp.

17.13.22.3   Options

Figure 17.342 "Spyrogimp" options

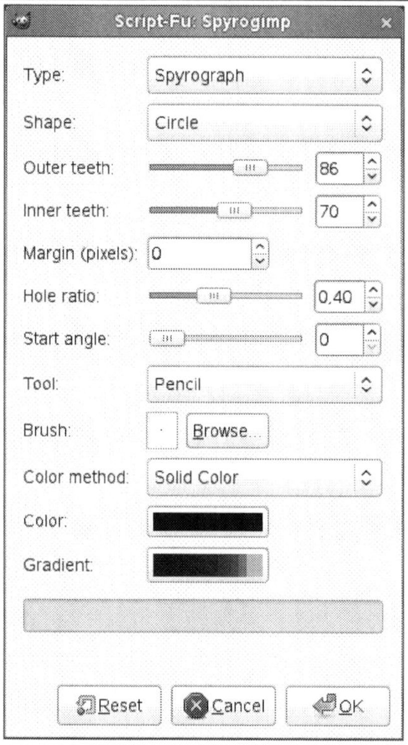

Type TODO

Shape TODO

Outer teeth TODO

Inner teeth TODO

Margin (pixels) TODO

Hole ratio TODO

Start angle TODO

Tool TODO

Brush TODO

Color method TODO

Color TODO

Gradient TODO

17.14   Web Filters

17.14.1   Introduction

Figure 17.343 The Web filters menu

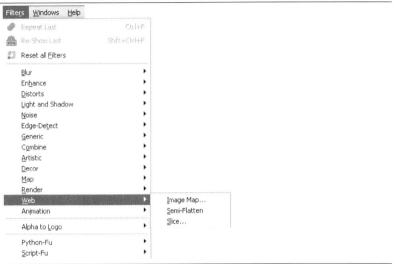

This filters are mostly used on images mentioned for web sites. The filter ImageMap is used to add clickable "hot spots" on the image. The filter Semi-Flatten is used to simulate semi-transparency in image formats without alpha channel. The Slice filter creates HTML tables of sensitive images.

17.14.2   ImageMap

In Web sensitive images are frequently used to get some effects when defined areas are enabled by the pointer. Obviously the most used effect is a dynamic link to another web page when one of the sensitive areas is clicked on. This "filter" allows you to design easily sensitive areas within an image. Web site design softwares have this as a standard function. In GIMP you can do this in a similar way.

17.14.2.1   Overview

This plug-in lets you design graphically and friendly all areas you want to delimit over your displayed image. You get the relevant part of html tags that must be merged into the right place in your page html code. You can define some actions linked to these areas too.

This is a complex tool which is not completely described here (it works about like Web page makers offering this function). However we want to describe here some of the most current handlings. If you want, you can find a more complete descriptions in Grokking the GIMP with the link [GROKKING02].

17.14.2.2   Activate the filter

From an image window, you can find this filter through Filters → Web → ImageMap
The window is a small one, but you can magnify it. The main useful areas are:

- completely on the left are vertically displayed icons, one for pointing, three for calling tools to generate various shape areas, one to edit zone properties, and finally one to erase a selected zone; you can call these functions with the Mapping menu,

- just on the right is your working area where you can draw all the shapes areas you want with the relevant tools,

- on the right is displayed an icon vertical set; its use is obvious but a help pop-up gives you some information about each function,

- finally, even on the right is a display area, as a property list of the created areas. A click on one item of the list selects automatically the corresponding shape in the working area,

17.14.2.3   Options

Figure 17.344 Imagemap filter options

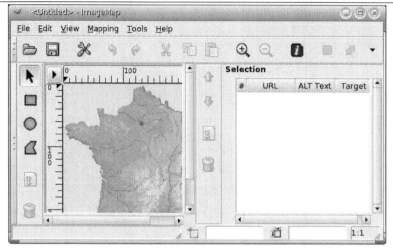

Imagemap window

17.14.2.3.1   The Menu Bar   The menu bar is similar to the image window menu bar, only a few menus or menu entries are different:

File

Save; Save As   Contrary to other filters, this plug-in doesn't make an image but a text file. So you must save your work in a text format.

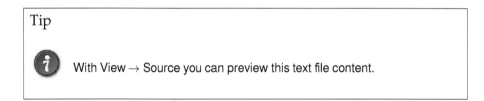

Tip

With View → Source you can preview this text file content.

Open; Open recent   In the plug-in you can open the saved text file. The areas defined in your file will be loaded and overdisplayed; if the displayed image is not the original one or not with the same size, GIMP will ask you for adapting the scale.

Edit

Edit area info

Figure 17.345 Editing an imagemap area

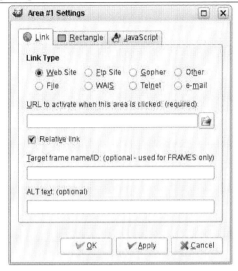

In the settings dialog you can edit the area information of a selected area. This dialog will pop up automatically whenever you create a new area.

View This menu offers you special functions:

Area list Here you can hide or show the selection area.

Source Here you see the raw data as you would save it to or read it from a file.

Color; Grayscale You can select the image mode here and work with a Grayscale display.

Mapping You will seldom use this menu, since you can more easily access selection tools by clicking on icons on the left of the working area.

Arrow The arrow here represents the Move tool. When activated tool is selected, you can select and move an area on the image.

With a polygon, you can use the arrow to move one of the red points. Right-click on a segment between two red points to open a pop-up menu that offers, with several others, the possibility to add a new point. If you right-click on a red point, you can remove it.

Rectangle; Circle; Polygon These tools let you create various shape areas: click on the image, move the pointer, and click again.

Edit Map Info

Figure 17.346 Editing the imagemap data

With this simple dialog you can enter some items, which will be written to the resulting output file; either as comments (Author, Description) or as attribute values of the HTML tags (Image name, Title, Default URL).

Tools With the "Tools" menu you can create guides and even regularly spaced rectangular areas.

Grid; Grid settings

Figure 17.347 Grid options

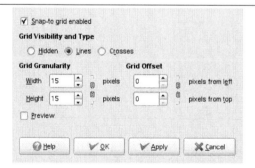

Here you can enable and disable the image grid or configure some grid properties.

Use GIMP guides; Create guides The guide lines are created at the border of the image but can be moved around by clicking on the red squares on each line something similar to the GIMP guide lines. By using the guides you are able to create active rectangles in the image.

Create guides

Figure 17.348 Guide options

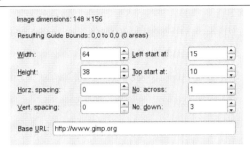

The guide options

Instead of creating geometrical shapes to select the active areas you may use an array of rectangles, each representing an active area, by clicking on the "Create guides". In the menu popping up you set the width and height of the rectangles, the space between them, the number of rows and columns, and the upper and left startpoint for the array. All measures are in pixels. If you are not satisfied with the result you may adjust each rectangle by moving the red squares as usual.

17.14.2.3.2   The Tool Bar   Most entries here are just shortcuts for some functions already described. Exceptions:

Move to Front; Send to Back   Here you can move an area entry to the bottom ("Move to Front") or top ("Send to Back") of the area list.

Figure 17.349 The Working Area

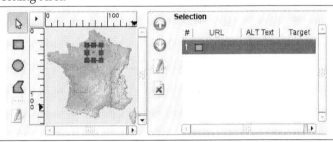

17.14.2.3.3   The Working Area   In the main area of the imagemap window, on the left side, you will find your working area where you can draw all the shapes areas you want with the relevant tools.

Beside the working area there are vertically displayed icons, one for pointing, three for calling tools to generate various shape areas, one to edit zone properties, and finally one to erase a selected zone; you can call these functions with the Mapping menu too.

Caution

   Note that the areas should not overlap.

17.14.2.3.4   The selection area   On the right is a display area, as a property list of the created areas. A click on one item of the list selects automatically the corresponding shape in the working area, then you can modify it.

Beside the display is an icon vertical set; its use is obvious but a help pop-up gives you some information about each function.

Unfortunately, the arrow symbols for moving a list entry up or down do not work here. But of course you carefully avoided to create overlapping areas, so you do not use these functions at all.

17.14.3 Semi-Flatten

17.14.3.1 Overview

The Semi-flatten filter helps those in need of a solution to anti-aliasing indexed images with transparency. The GIF indexed format supports complete transparency (0 or 255 alpha value), but not semi-transparency (1 - 254): semi-transparent pixels will be transformed to no transparency or complete transparency, ruining anti-aliasing you applied to the logo you want to put onto your Web page.

Before applying the filter, it's essential that you should know the background color of your Web page. Use the color-picker to determine the exact color which pops up as the Foreground color of the Toolbox. Invert FG/BG colors so that BG color is the same as Web background color.

Semi-flatten process will combine FG color to layer (logo) color, proportionally to corresponding alpha values, and will rebuild correct anti-aliasing. Completely transparent pixels will not take the color. Very transparent pixels will take a few color and weakly transparent will take much color.

17.14.3.2 Activate the filter

You can access this filter in the image window menu through Filters → Web → Semi-Flatten. It is available if your image holds an Alpha channel (see Section 16.7.33). Otherwise, it is greyed out.

17.14.3.3 Example

In the example below, the Toolbox Background color is pink, and the image has feathered edges on a transparent background.

Figure 17.350 Semi-Flatten example

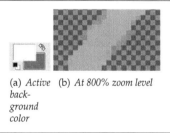

(a) *Active background color*   (b) *At 800% zoom level*

Full transparency is kept. Semi-tranparent pixels are colored with pink according to their transparency (Alpha value). This image will well merge into the pink background of the new page.

Figure 17.351 Semi-Flatten filter applied

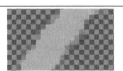

Result, in GIF format, after applying Semi-flatten filter.

17.14.4   Slice

17.14.4.1   Overview

Figure 17.352 Example for the "Slice" filter

(a) *Original image with guides*

(b) *"Slice" applied*

This filter is a simple and easy to use helper for creating sensitive images to be used in HTML files. The filter slices up the source image (like the Guillotine command does) along its horizontal and vertical guides, and produces a set of sub-images. At the same time it creates a piece of HTML code for a table saved in a text file. Every table cell contains one part of the image. The text file should then be embedded in an HTML document.

Note that this filter is really a very simple helper. A typical HTML code produced by the filter may be not much more than this:

Example 17.1 Simple "Slice" filter example output

```
<table cellpadding="0" border="0" cellspacing="0">
  <tr>
    <td><img alt="" src="slice_0_0.png"/></td>
    <td><img alt="" src="slice_0_1.png"/></td>
  </tr>
  <tr>
    <td><img alt="" src="slice_1_0.png"/></td>
    <td><img alt="" src="slice_1_1.png"/></td>
  </tr>
</table>
```

Produced HTML code; the "style" attribute has been omitted.

When there are no guides in the image, the filter will no nothing. If, however, the guides are just hidden, the filter will work.

Tip

 The ImageMap filter is a much more powerful and sophisticated tool for creating sensitive images. (But it is also much more complex...)

17.14.4.2 Activate the filter

This filter is found in the image window menu under Filters → Web → Slice.

17.14.4.3 Options

Figure 17.353 "Slice" options

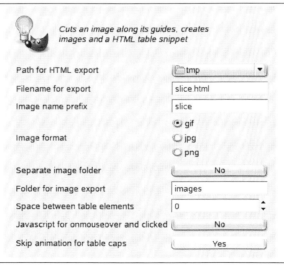

Most options are self-explanatory, but nevertheless:

Path for HTML export Where the HTML file and the image files will be saved. By default these files will be stored in the current working directory. Clicking on the button to the right opens a pull-down menu, where you can select a different location.

Filename for export The name of the HTML file. You can change the filename using the textbox.

Image name prefix The name of an image file produced by this filter is `prefix_i_k.ext`, where `prefix` is that part of the filename which you can freely select using the textbox to the right, by default: `slice`. (i and k are the numbers of the row and the column, each starting with 0; `.ext` is the filename extension depending on the selected Image format.)

This option is particularly useful when you want to create Javascript for onmouseover and clicked and need different sets of images.

Image format You can choose to create image files in the GIF, JPG, or PNG file format.

Separate image folder, Folder for image export When Separate image folder is enabled, a folder will be created where the image files will be placed. By default, the name of this destination folder is `images`, but you can change it in the Folder for image export textbox.

Example 17.2 With separate image folder

```
<table>
  <tr>
    <td><img src="images/slice_0_0.png"/></a></td>
```

Result of enabled "Separate image folder"

Space between table elements This value (0-15) will be passed as "cellspacing" attribute to the HTML table. The result is, that horizontal and vertical guides will be replaced with stripes of the specified width:

Example 17.3 Space between table elements

```
<table  cellspacing="5">
```

Corresponding HTML code snippet

Note that the image will not be enlarged by the size of these stripes. Instead, the resulting HTML image will look like you have drawn the stripes with the Eraser tool.

Javascript for onmouseover and clicked When this option is enabled, the filter will also add some JavaScript code. Like the HTML code, this code does not work as is, rather it's a good starting point for adding some dynamic functionality. The JavaScript code provides a function to handle events like "onmouseover":

Example 17.4 JavaScript code snippet

```
function exchange (image, images_array_name, event)
  {
    name = image.name;
    images = eval (images_array_name);

    switch (event)
      {
        case 0:
          image.src = images[name + "_plain"].src;
          break;
        case 1:
          image.src = images[name + "_hover"].src;
          break;
        case 2:
          image.src = images[name + "_clicked"].src;
```

```
        break;
      case 3:
        image.src = images[name + "_hover"].src;
        break;
    }
}
```

Skip animation for table caps When disabled, the filter will add a `<a href="#">` ... `</a>` hyperlink stub to every table cell. When enabled (this is the default) and there are at least two horizontal
or two vertical guides, the filter will not add a hyperlink stub to the first and last cell in a column
or row. This may be useful when you have an image with border and you don't want to make the
border sensitive.

Example 17.5 Skipped animation for table caps (simplified HTML code)

```
<table cellpadding="0" border="0" cellspacing="0">
  <tr>
    <td><img alt="" src="images/slice_0_0.png"/></td>
    <td><img alt="" src="images/slice_0_1.png"/></td>
    <td><img alt="" src="images/slice_0_2.png"/></td>
    <td><img alt="" src="images/slice_0_3.png"/></td>
  </tr>
  <tr>
    <td><img alt="" src="images/slice_1_0.png"/></td>
    <td><a href="#"><img alt="" src="images/slice_1_1.png"/></a></td>
    <td><a href="#"><img alt="" src="images/slice_1_2.png"/></a></td>
    <td><img alt="" src="images/slice_1_3.png"/></td>
  </tr>
  <tr>
    <td><img alt="" src="images/slice_2_0.png"/></td>
    <td><img alt="" src="images/slice_2_1.png"/></td>
    <td><img alt="" src="images/slice_2_2.png"/></td>
    <td><img alt="" src="images/slice_2_3.png"/></td>
  </tr>
</table>
```

Only inner cells have (empty) hyperlinks.

17.15   Animation Filters

17.15.1   Introduction

Figure 17.354 The Animation filters menu

These are animation helpers, which let you view and optimize your animations (by reducing their size). We gathered "Optimize (Difference)" and "Optimize (GIF)" filters together, because they are not much different.

17.15.2   Blend

17.15.2.1   Overview

Figure 17.355 Example for the "Blend" filter: original image

4 frames of 5 frames (white background layer omitted)

Figure 17.356 Example for the "Blend" filter: filter applied

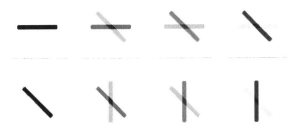

First 8 (of 16) frames

17.15.2.2 Activating the filter

This filter is found in the image window menu under Filters → Animation → Blend.

17.15.2.3 Options

Figure 17.357 "Blend" options

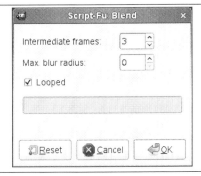

Intermediate frames TODO

Max. blur radius TODO

Looped TODO

17.15.3 Burn-In

17.15.3.1 Overview

Figure 17.358 Example for the "Burn-In" filter: original image

Opaque background layer and foreground layer with transparency

Figure 17.359 Example for the "Burn-In" filter: filter applied

Resulting image with 8 frames (depending on size and speed)

17.15.3.2 Activating the filter

This filter is found in the image window menu under Filters → Animation → Burn-In.

17.15.3.3 Options

Figure 17.360 "Burn-In" options

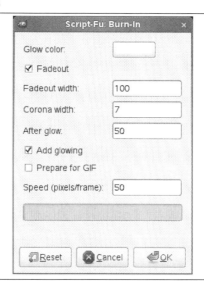

Glow color TODO

Fadeout TODO

Fadeout width TODO

Corona width TODO

After glow TODO

Add glowing TODO

Prepare for GIF TODO

Speed (pixels/frame) TODO

17.15.4 Rippling

17.15.4.1 Overview

Figure 17.361 Example for the "Rippling" filter

(a) *Original image*   (b) *A "Rippled" frame*

17.15.4.2 Activating the filter

This filter is found in the image window menu under Filters → Animation → Rippling.

17.15.4.3 Options

Figure 17.362 "Rippling" options

Rippling strength TODO

Number of frames TODO

Edge behavior TODO

17.15.5 Spinning Globe

17.15.5.1 Overview

Figure 17.363 Example for the "Spinning Globe" filter: original image

Original image

Figure 17.364 Example for the "Spinning Globe" filter: filter applied

3 (of 10) "Spinning Globe" frames (on a white background)

17.15.5.2 Activating the filter

This filter is found in the image window menu under Filters → Animation → Spinning Globe.

17.15.5.3 Options

Figure 17.365 "Spinning Globe" options

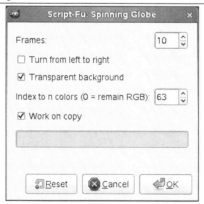

Frames TODO

Turn from left to right TODO

Transparent background TODO

Index to n colors TODO

Work on copy TODO

17.15.6 Waves

17.15.6.1 Overview

Figure 17.366 Example for the "Waves" filter

(a) *Original image*   (b) *A "Wave" frame*

17.15.6.2 Activating the filter

This filter is found in the image window menu under Filters → Animation → Waves.

17.15.6.3 Options

Figure 17.367 "Waves" options

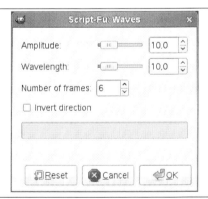

Amplitude TODO

Wavelength TODO

Number of frames TODO

Invert direction TODO

17.15.7 Optimize

17.15.7.1 Overview

An animation can contain several layers and so its size can be important. This is annoying for a Web page. The Optimize filters let you reduce this size. Many elements are shared by all layers in an animation; so they can be saved only once instead of being saved in all layers, and what has changed in each layer can be saved only.

GIMP offers two Optimize filters: Optimize (Difference) and Optimize (GIF). Their result doesn't look very different.

17.15.7.2 Activate filters

You can find these filters in the image menu:

- Filters → Animation → Optimize (Difference)

- Filters → Animation → Optimize (for GIF)

- Filters → Animation → Unoptimize

17.15.7.3 Example for the Optimize animation filters

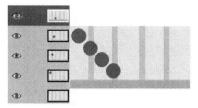

Original image

In this animation, the red ball goes downwards and past vertical bars. File size is 600 Kb.

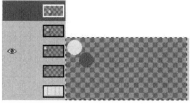

Optimize (Difference)

File size moved to 153 Kb. Layers held only the part the background which will be used to remove the trace of the red ball. The common part of layers is transparent.

Optimize (GIF)

File size moved to 154 Kb, a bit bigger in the present example, but layer size has been reduced. Layers held only a rectangular selection which includes the part of the background which will be used to remove the trace of the red ball. The common part of layers is transparent.

17.15.7.4 Unoptimize

The "Unoptimize" filter removes any optimizations on a layer-based animation. You may need this command if you want to edit the animation and it's not possible or not useful to undo any changes and start editing from the original image.

17.15.8   Playback

17.15.8.1   Overview

This plug-in lets you play an animation from a multi-layers image (that could be saved in the GIF, MNG or even XCF format), to test it.

17.15.8.2   Activate the filter

You can find this filter through Filters → Animation → Playback

17.15.8.3   Options

Figure 17.368 "Playback" filter options

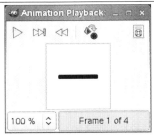

This dialog has:

Preview This preview of the animation automatically fits the frame size. The number of the displayed frame is shown below the preview.

Buttons Three buttons are available:

> **Play/Stop** Play/Stop to play or stop the animation.
>
> **Rewind** Rewind to re-launch the animation from start.
>
> **Step** Step to play the animation step by step.

17.16   Alpha to Logo Filters

17.16.1   Introduction

Figure 17.369 The Alpha to Logo filters menu

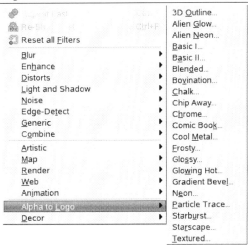

These filters correspond to the logo-generating script-fu scripts. They add all kinds of special effects to the alpha channel of the active layer (that is, to the pixels with a non-zero alpha value).

Note

The menu items and the corresponding functions are enabled only if the active layer has an alpha channel. If you see that the menu items are grayed out, try to add an alpha channel.

The filter effect will always be applied according to the alpha values. The alpha of any pixel has a value ranging from 0 (transparent) to 255 (fully opaque). It is possible to apply a filter only *partially* to some (or all) pixels by using alpha values from 1 to 254.

You will notice that this is similar to selecting pixels partially. In fact, internally these filters always create a selection from the alpha channel by transferring the alpha values to the channel which represents the selection, and then work on the selection.

How to apply an "Alpha to Logo" filter to a selection?

1. If the active layer is the background layer, make sure that an alpha channel exists, otherwise add an alpha channel.

Tip

If a layer name in the Layer Dialog is in bold, then this layer has no Alpha channel.

---

2. Invert the selection: Select → Invert.

3. Remove the (inverted) selection: Edit → Clear.

4. Apply the "Alpha to Logo" filter (the filters ignore the selection, you don't need to re-invert the selection).

17.16.2   3D Outline

17.16.2.1   Overview

Figure 17.370 Example for the "3D Outline" filter

(a) *The "3D Outline" filter*

(b) *The "3D Outline" logo*

This filter is derived from the "3D Outline" script (File → Create → Logos → 3D Outline in the image window), which creates a logo (see above) with outlined text and a drop shadow.

The filter outlines the non-transparent areas of the active layer (determined from the Alpha channel) with a pattern and adds a drop shadow. Here, we will use the *alpha* term to refer to these areas of the active layer defined by the non-transparent pixels.

The filter uses the Sobel edge detect filter to get the alpha's outline. So with a simple alpha, for example a cleared rectangle selection, you will just get the boundary. But when you use a layer mask (don't forget to Apply the Layer Mask), as in the following example, the edge detector will find more edges and thus the filter effect will be applied to these edges too.

Figure 17.371 Example based on multicolored layer mask

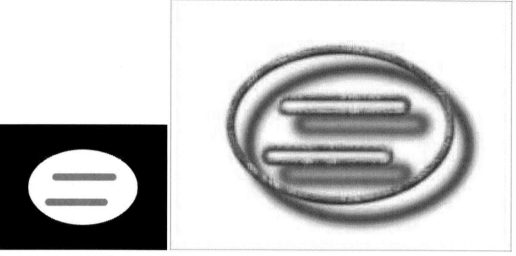

(a) *With an layer mask (alpha) like this ...*   (b) *... you will get this.*

Warning

 The image will always be resized to the active layer's size.

17.16.2.2 Activate the filter

This filter is found in the image window menu under Filters → Alpha to Logo → 3D Outline.

The filter only works if the active layer has an alpha channel. Otherwise, the menu entry is insensitive and grayed out.

17.16.2.3 Options

Figure 17.372 "3D Outline" options

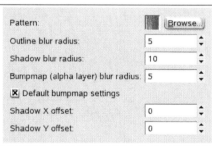

Pattern Here you can see and change the currently selected pattern. When you click on the pattern, an enlarged preview will popup. Pressing the Browse... button opens a dialog where you can select a different pattern.

Outline blur radius This radius is used to blur the alpha before the edge detector will select the area to be filled with the pattern. That's why a high value results in a wide but smeared pattern:

Figure 17.373 Outline blur radius example

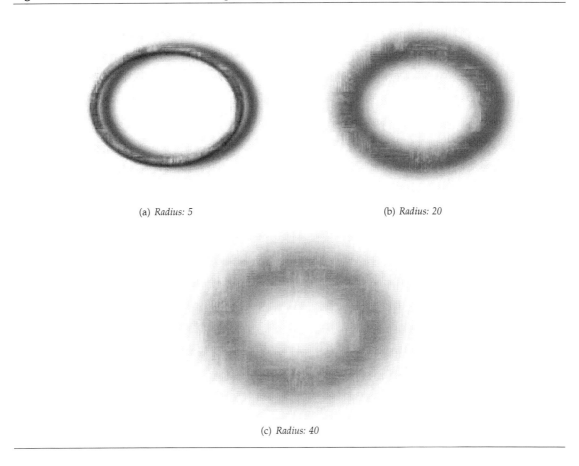

(a) *Radius: 5*   (b) *Radius: 20*

(c) *Radius: 40*

Shadow blur radius This radius is used to blur the drop shadow. A high value will smear the shadow:

Figure 17.374 Shadow blur radius example

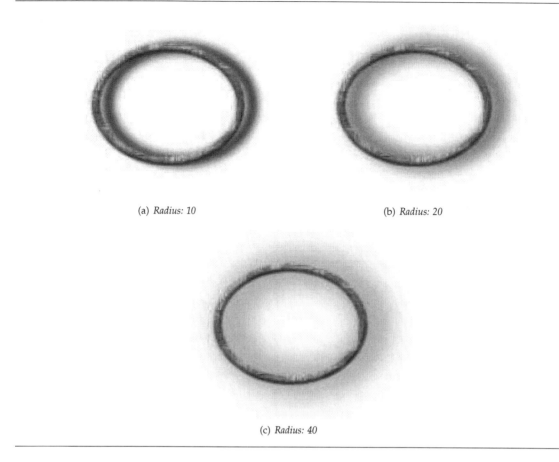

(a) *Radius: 10*   (b) *Radius: 20*

(c) *Radius: 40*

Bumpmap (alpha layer) blur radius The Bump Map used to create a 3D effect is the active layer (alpha layer) with the edge detect filter applied. Before it is used to emboss the pattern layer, another Gaussian blur will be applied with the specified radius. So a high value will reduce the 3D effect.

Default bumpmap settings If checked (this is the default) the bump map plug-in will be applied with its default options. Otherwise, the Bump Map dialog window will popup while the filter is running, and you can choose different options. Note that, when you close the window pressing the **Cancel** button, no bump map at all will be applied.

Shadow X offset; Shadow Y offset This is the amount of pixels the shadow layer will me moved to the right (X) and down (Y). Then the layer will be clipped to the image size. Note that there is no real background layer, and moving the shadow will clear its original place:

Figure 17.375 Shadow offset example

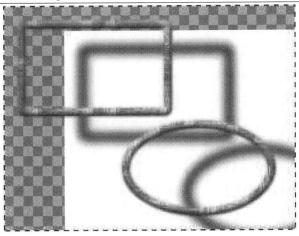

X offset: 50; Y offset: 20

17.16.3 Alien Glow

17.16.3.1 Overview

Figure 17.376 Example for the "Alien Glow" filter

(a) *The "Alien Glow" filter*

(b) *The "Alien Glow" logo*

This filter adds an eerie glow around the active layer's alpha.

The filter is derived from the "Alien Glow" script (File → Create → Logos → Alien Glow in the image window), which creates a logo with the above text effect.

Warning

 The image will always be resized to the active layer's size.

17.16.3.2 Activate the filter

You can find this filter in the image window menu under Filters → Alpha to Logo → Alien Glow.

17.16.3.3 Options

Figure 17.377 "Alien Glow" options

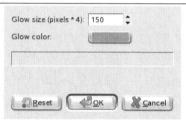

Glow size (pixels * 4) This is actually the font size option of the "Alien Glow" Script-Fu script. However, two values will be set in relation to this size: the glow will be enlarged by "Glow size" / 30, and feather radius is "Glow size" / 4. You should probably choose the height of your objects for this option (ignore "pixels * 4").

Glow color This is the color of the "eerie" glowing. Of course it defaults to green (63,252,0), but a click on the swatch button brings up the color selector where you can choose any color.

17.16.3.4 Filter details

Reproducing an eerie alien glow is easy:

- If necessary, create a selection from the alpha channel of the active layer.

- Fill the selection with the following Gradient Blend: Shape = Shaped (spherical); Gradient = FG to BG (RGB), with FG = dark gray (79,79,79), BG = black.

- Create a new layer ("Alien Glow") below. Extend the selection slightly, feather it, and fill it with the Glow color.

- Create a new background layer filled with black.

17.16.4   Alien Neon

17.16.4.1   Overview

Figure 17.378 Example for the "Alien Neon" filter

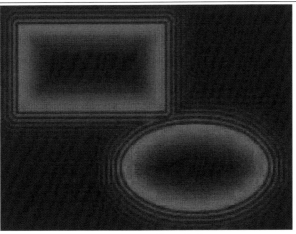

"Alien Neon" applied

Caution

   Sorry, there is no documentation for this filter as yet.

17.16.4.2   Activate the filter

This filter is found in the image window menu under Filters → Alpha to Logo → Alien Neon.

17.16.4.3   Options

Figure 17.379 "Alien Neon" options

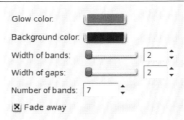

Glow color TODO

Background color TODO

Width of bands TODO

Width of gaps TODO

Number of bands TODO

Fade away TODO

17.16.5   Basic I & II

17.16.5.1   Overview

Figure 17.380 Examples for the "Basic" filters

(a) *Basic I*

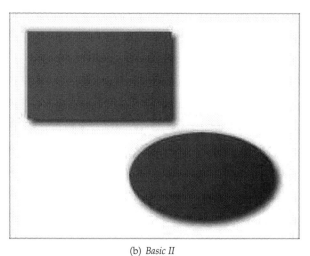

(b) *Basic II*

These filters add a gradient effect to the alpha channel of active layer as well as a drop shadow and a background layer.

The "Basic II" also adds a highlight layer.

Warning

 The image will always be resized to the active layer's size.

The filters are derived from the "Basic I" and "Basic II" logo scripts (see File → Create → Logos), which draw a text with the filter effect, e.g.

The "Basic I" logo script.

17.16.5.2   Activate the filter

You can find the filter in the image window menu under Filters → Alpha to Logo → Basic I and Filters → Alpha to Logo → Basic II.

17.16.5.3   Options

Figure 17.381 "Basic" filter options

Background color:		Background color:	
Text color:		Text color:	

(a) *"Basic I" options*   (b) *"Basic II" options*

Background color This color is used to fill the background layer created by the filter. It defaults to white. When you click on the color swatch button, a color selector pops up where you can select any other color.

Text color The name of this option refers to the text color of the logo scripts that were mentioned above. Here this color — by default blue (6,6,206) for "Basic I" and red (206,6,50) for "Basic II" — sets the basic color of the gradient effect: this is the color the alpha channel will be filled with before the gradient effect will be applied.

17.16.5.4   Filter details

You can reproduce the gradient effect manually by using the Blend tool with the following options:

- Mode: Multiply,

- Gradient: FG to BG (RGB), where FG is white and BG is black,

- Offset: 20,

- Shape: Radial,

- Dithering: checked.

17.16.6 Blended

17.16.6.1 Overview

Figure 17.382 Example for the "Blended" filter

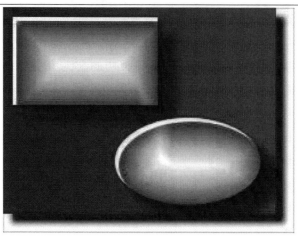

"Blended" applied

Caution

  Sorry, there is no documentation for this filter as yet.

17.16.6.2 Activate the filter

This filter is found in the image window menu under Filters → Alpha to Logo → Blended.

17.16.6.3 Options

Figure 17.383 "Blended" options

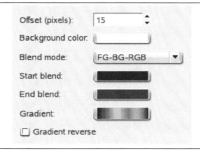

Offset (pixels) TODO

Backgroundcolor TODO

Blend mode TODO

Start blend TODO

End blend TODO

Gradient TODO

Gradient reverse TODO

17.16.7 Bovination

17.16.7.1 Overview

Figure 17.384 Example for the "Bovination" filter

"Bovination" applied

This filter adds "cow spots" to the active layer alpha channel.

 Warning

The image will always be resized to the active layer's size.

17.16.7.2 Activate the filter

You can find this filter in the image window menu under Filters → Alpha to Logo → Bovination.

17.16.7.3 Options

Figure 17.385 "Bovination" options

Spots density X, Spots density Y The horizontal (X) and vertical (Y) spots density will be used by the Solid Noise filter as X Size and Y Size options. So these values range from 1 to 16, with high values resulting in many spots in the respective dimension, low values resulting in few spots.

Figure 17.386 "Spots density" examples

(a) *Maximum X density, min-* (b) *Maximum Y density, min-*
imum Y density   *imum X density*

Background Color This is the color used to fill the "Background" layer; it defaults to white. When you click on the color button, you may choose any other color in the color selector dialog.

17.16.7.4   Filter details

The filter fills the alpha channel with Solid Noise:

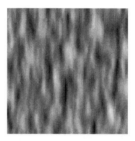

... and maximizes the Contrast:

Besides, the filter adds a Blur layer as a light gray shadow and uses this layer as a Bump Map. Finally a (by default) white "Background" layer is added below.

So the filter will end up with these layers:[7]

---

[7] If the active layer is not the top layer, it might happen that the filter messes up the layers. Then you will have to raise the active layer.

17.16.8 Chalk

17.16.8.1 Overview

Figure 17.387 Example for the "Chalk" filter

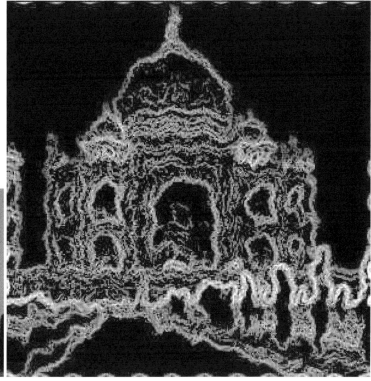

(a) *Original image*   (b) *"Chalk" applied*

This filter creates a chalk drawing effect for the active layer.

It is derived from the "Chalk" script (File → Create → Logos → Chalk in the image window), which creates a logo from a text of your choice, for instance:

The "Chalk" logo

> **Warning**
>
> The image will always be resized to the active layer's size.

17.16.8.2 Activate the filter

You can find this filter in the image window menu under Filters → Alpha to Logo → Chalk.

17.16.8.3 Options

Figure 17.388 "Chalk" option

Background color The background color is the color of the "blackboard" you are drawing on with chalk, and of course it's black. When you click on the color button, the color selector pops up and you may select any other color.

17.16.8.4 Filter details

The "Chalk" filter

1. applies a Gaussian blur to the layer, spreads the pixels, and ripples the layer horizontally and vertically,

2. extracts edges using the Sobel edge detect filter, and

> Note
>
> Sometimes the sobel edge detect produces some garbage at the image sides.

3. increases the luminosity level.

Unfortunately you cannot change the tool and filter options. But you may reproduce the process step by step using the methods listed above, varying the respective options. Then you just have to add a background layer filled with any color. That's all.

17.16.9   Chip Away

17.16.9.1   Overview

Figure 17.389 Example for the "Chip Away" filter

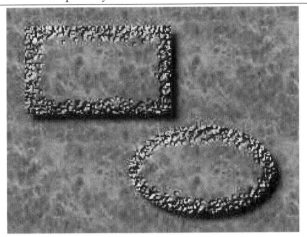

(a) *The "Chip Away" filter*

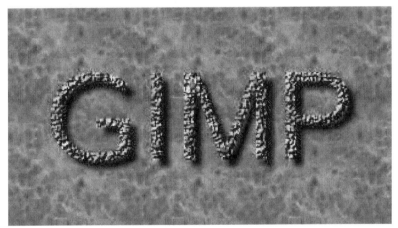

(b) *The "Chip Away" logo*

This filter adds a chipped woodcarving effect to the alpha channel of the active layer. Optionally it adds a drop shadow to the image. The content of the active layer doesn't matter, only the shape of its alpha channel does.

Warning

 The image will always be resized to the active layer's size.

The filter is derived from the "Chip Away" Script-Fu script (File → Create → Logos → Chip Away), which creates a text logo with the effect shown above.

17.16.9.2   Activate the filter

This filter is found in the image window menu under Filters → Alpha to Logo → Chip Away.

17.16.9.3 Options

Figure 17.390 "Chip Away" options

Chip amount This option lets you vary the size of chipping area. But note that "Chip amount" is not the size of this area in pixels. It is used as the maximum amount pixels are randomly spread by the Spread filter applied to the bump map. Valid range is 0-200.

Figure 17.391 "Chip amount" examples

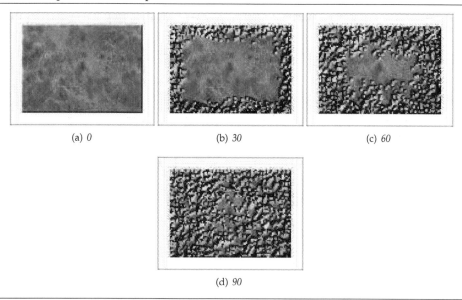

(a) *0*   (b) *30*   (c) *60*

(d) *90*

Blur amount The specified value will be passed as "Radius" option to the Gaussian blur filter, which will blur the bump layer by this amount.

Invert If checked, the bump map will be inverted and will create hollows instead of bumps, which makes the image looking carved.

Figure 17.392 "Chip Away" inverted example

Inverted, (without drop shadow)

Drop shadow If checked, a Drop shadow will be added to the image in a new layer below the active
layer.

Keep bump layer By default, the bump map used to create the chipping effect will be removed after
applying the filter. When this option is checked, the bump map will be kept as an invisible layer.

Fill BG with pattern If checked, the background layer (added by the filter) will be filled with the specified Pattern. Otherwise, it will be filled with white.

Keep background Whether or not to remove the background layer. This option is checked by default.
You can, of course, remove this layer (or toggle its visibility) later in the Layers dialog.

Pattern This option consists of a preview area, which will produce a popup preview when you click on
it and hold down the mouse button, and a Browse button. The button will popup a dialog where
you can select patterns.

The default pattern is "Burlwood". Apart from that one, the plug-in author suggests the patterns
"Dried mud", "3D Green", and "Slate":

Figure 17.393 Suggested "Chip Away" patterns

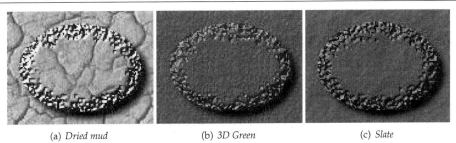

(a) *Dried mud*   (b) *3D Green*   (c) *Slate*

17.16.9.4 Filter details

To achieve a chipping effect, the filter...

1. ...creates a selection from the alpha channel in a new layer,

2. fills the selection with white,

3. spreads the pixels,

4. and applies a Gaussian blur to the layer.

5. Then it uses this layer as a Bump map, creating a 3D effect.

17.16.10 Chrome

17.16.10.1 Overview

Figure 17.394 Example for the "Chrome" filter

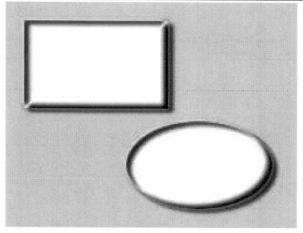

(a) *The "Chrome" filter applied*

(b) *The "Chrome" logo*

This filter is derived from the "Chrome" logo script (File → Create → Logos → Chrome), which — according to the script author — creates a "simplistic, but cool, chromed logo" (see above).

The filter adds this simple chrome effect to the alpha, that is the area of the active layer defined by the non-transparent pixels (think of it as a "selection by visibility"). The filter effect will always be applied according to the alpha values.

Apparently the effect only looks "cool" when the filter is applied to thin areas. For wide shapes you can try to increase the Offset value; see the examples below.

> **Warning**
>
> The image will always be resized to the active layer's size.

17.16.10.2 Activate the filter

This filter is found in the image window menu under Filters → Alpha to Logo → Chrome.

17.16.10.3 Options

Figure 17.395 "Chrome" options

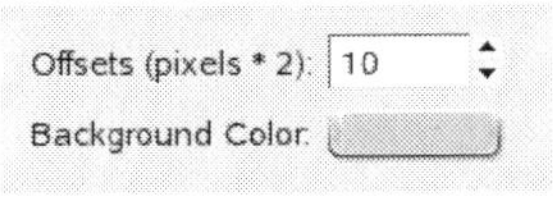

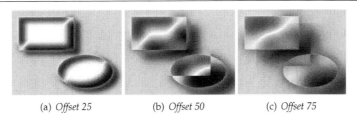

Offset (pixels * 2) This option is used when creating the chrome effect and for placing the drop shadow:

Figure 17.396 "Offset" examples

(a) *Offset 25*   (b) *Offset 50*   (c) *Offset 75*

The filter creates a drop shadow in the shape of the alpha. This shadow will be moved according to the specified offset in relation to the alpha: by 40% of the offset to the right and by 30% offset down. It will be feathered by 50% of the offset value.

The chrome effect will be achieved using some temporary layers. These layers are moved by the same amount (40% and 30% of the specified offset) and are also feathered by 50% offset. So the appearance of the alpha too is determined by the offset value.

Background Color This color is used to fill the background layer created by the filter. It defaults to light gray. When you click on the color button, a color selector pops up where you can select any other color.

17.16.11 Comic Book

17.16.11.1 Overview

Figure 17.397 Example for the "Comic Book" filter

"Comic Book" applied

Caution

 Sorry, there is no documentation for this filter as yet.

17.16.11.2 Activate the filter

This filter is found in the image window menu under Filters → Alpha to Logo → Comic Book.

17.16.11.3 Options

Figure 17.398 "Comic Book" options

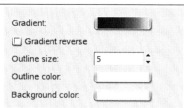

Gradient TODO

Gradient reverse TODO

Outline size TODO

Outline color TODO

Background color TODO

17.16.12   Cool Metal

17.16.12.1   Overview

Figure 17.399 Example for the "Cool Metal" filter

(a) *The "Cool Metal" filter*

(b) *The "Cool Metal" logo*

This filter creates an effect that looks like metal with a reflection in the mirrored ground, and an interesting drop shadow.

The filter is derived from the "Cool Metal" script (File → Create → Logos → Cool Metal in the image window), which creates a logo from a text as shown above.

17.16.12.2   Activate the filter

This filter is found in the image window menu under Filters → Alpha to Logo → Cool Metal.

17.16.12.3   Options

Figure 17.400 "Cool Metal" options

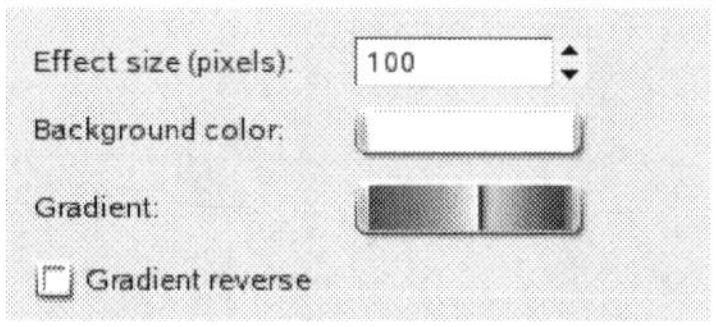

Effect size (pixels):   100
Background color:
Gradient:
☐ Gradient reverse

Effect size (pixels) This is actually the font size option of the "Cool Metal" Script-Fu script. Some internal values will be set in relation to this size, for feathering, blurring, embossing, and creating ripple patterns.

Background color The color of the background layer added by the filter. When you click in the color swatch button, the color select dialog pops up.

Gradient The default gradient to create the cool metal is "Horizon 1". Clicking in the gradient button will open a simplified gradient dialog, where you can select any other gradient.

Gradient reverse By default, the selected gradient will be applied from top to bottom. When this option is checked, the direction will be reversed.

17.16.12.4   Filter details

At least some of the filter effects should be described briefly: how the filter creates the reflection and this nice shadow, or rather, how you can reproduce these effects manually. In fact, the only trick is to know which tool to use...

Making the reflection
Assuming that the alpha has been filled with a gradient, then:

1. Create a new layer containing the area you want to mirror, for example Copy and Paste the area in a new layer.

2. To make the reflection look more natural, scale down the layer (the filter resizes to 85% of the original height). You can do this e.g. using Scale Layer command or the Scale Tool.

3. Then flip the layer vertically and move it down.

4. Now add a layer mask, fill the layer mask with a gradient (for instance white or gray to black), and, of course, apply the layer mask.

Making the shadow
Fill the alpha with black, for instance via Duplicate Layer and Alpha to Selection, then

1. shrink and slant the layer, e.g. using the Perspective tool,

2. and apply a Gaussian Blur to the layer.

17.16.13 Frosty

17.16.13.1 Overview

Figure 17.401 Example for the "Frosty" filter

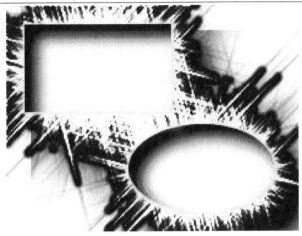

(a) *The "Frosty" filter applied*

(b) *The "Frosty" logo*

This filter is derived from the "Frosty" logo script (File → Create → Logos → Frosty in the image window), which creates a frozen logo like the example above.

The filter adds this frosty effect to the alpha, that is the area of the active layer defined by the non-transparent pixels (think of it as a "selection by visibility"). The filter effect will always be applied according to the alpha values.

Note

 Unlike the most alpha to logo filters, the "Frosty" filter will *not* resize the image to the active layer's size.

17.16.13.2 Activate the filter

This filter is found in the image window menu under Filters → Alpha to Logo → Frosty.

17.16.13.3 Options

Figure 17.402 "Frosty" options

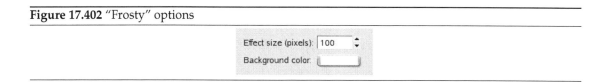

Effect size (pixels)

Figure 17.403 "Effect size" examples

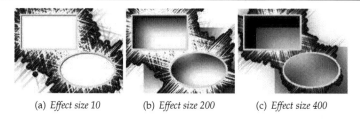

(a) *Effect size 10*   (b) *Effect size 200*   (c) *Effect size 400*

Background color This color is used to fill the background layer created by the filter. It defaults to white. When you click on the color button, a color selector pops up where you can select any other color.

17.16.14 Glossy

17.16.14.1 Overview

Figure 17.404 Example for the "Glossy" filter

(a) *The "Glossy" filter*

(b) *The "Glossy" logo*

This filter applies gradients and patterns to the alpha. A slight 3D effect will be added using a bump map, and optionally the filter adds a drop shadow.

> **Note**
>
> Here, as a language shortcut, we use *alpha* to mean the area of the active layer defined by the non-transparent pixels. You may think of it as a selection "by visibility". Applying any effect "to the alpha" just means to apply this effect to all visible pixels of the active layer.

The filter is derived from the "Glossy" script (File → Create → Logos → Glossy in the image window), which creates a logo (see above) with a glossy outlook when used with the default options, thus the name.

This filter only works if the active layer has an alpha channel. Otherwise, the menu entry is insensitive and grayed out.

> ### Warning
>
> The image will always be resized to the active layer's size.

17.16.14.2   Activate the filter

This filter is found in the image window menu under Filters → Alpha to Logo → Glossy.

17.16.14.3   Options

Figure 17.405 "Glossy" options

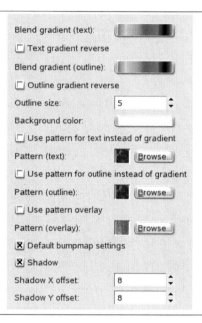

Blend gradient (text) By default, the filter will fill the alpha with a gradient blend. Clicking on the swatch button will open a simple gradient dialog, where you may select any gradient. "Text" refers to the "Glossy" logo, which creates a logo from a text, and is meaningless here.

When Text gradient reverse is checked, the alpha will be filled with a gradient blend starting at the bottom.

Pattern (text) When Use pattern for text instead of gradient is checked, the alpha will be filled with a pattern. You can open a patterns dialog to select a pattern of your choice by clicking on the Browse button. The preview area on the left will produce a popup preview of the current pattern when pressed.

Outline size This is the size of a kind of border, realised with a layer containing an enlarged copy of the alpha (details see below).

Blend gradient (outline); Pattern (outline) Just like the "text" options for the active layer, these options specify the gradient or pattern (when Use pattern for outline instead of gradient is checked) used to fill the outline area.

Use pattern overlay When checked, the original, not enlarged alpha of the outline layer will be filled with the specified pattern using the overlay mode, so that the pattern and the previous contents (pattern or gradient) will be merged.

Again, clicking on Browse button will open a patterns dialog, pressing the preview icon will produce a popup preview of the current pattern.

Default bumpmap settings This option does nothing, the filter will always apply a bump map.

Background color The color of the background layer added by the filter. When you click on the color button, a color select dialog pops up.

Shadow Optionally the filter creates a layer containing a drop shadow. The shadow layer will be moved Shadow X offset pixels to the right and Shadow Y offset pixels down. Note that this may enlarge the image, while the background layer will keep the size of the active layer.

17.16.14.4 Filter details

The numerous options may give the impression that this is a very complicate filter, but actually it is fairly simple. The interesting part is how the filter handles the active layer and the outline layer:

In the active layer, the filter creates a selection from the alpha channel and fills the selection with the specified gradient blend or pattern.

Then a new "outline" layer below the active layer will be created in a similar way: First, the active layer's alpha will be used to make a selection. But before filling the selection with a gradient or a pattern, the selection will be enlarged by Outline size pixels.

When you filled both layers with the same pattern or gradient blend, you will still see a border ("outline"), because

- a 3D effect will be applied to the outline layer using the active layer as a bump map;

- the layer mode of the active layer will be set to "Screen".

The last (optional) step is to fill the outline layer with a pattern, using the "overlay" layer mode. This will combine the pattern with the pattern or gradient used before. To learn more about the result of using the overlay mode, see the description in Section 8.2.

17.16.15 Glowing Hot

17.16.15.1 Overview

Figure 17.406 Example for the "Glowing Hot" filter

(a) *The "Glowing Hot" filter*

(b) *The "Glowing Hot" logo*

This filter adds a glowing hot metal effect to the alpha (that is to these areas of the active layer defined by the non-transparent pixels).

The filter is derived from the "Glowing Hot" script (File → Create → Logos → Glowing Hot in the image window), which creates a glowing text logo (see above).

The filter simulates a red-hot, a yellow-hot, and a white-hot area - each color representing a different metal temperature -; the alpha's outline shines through the glowing.

Warning

 The image will always be resized to the active layer's size.

17.16.15.2 Activate the filter

This filter is found in the image window menu under Filters → Alpha to Logo → Glowing Hot.

The filter only works if the active layer has an alpha channel. Otherwise, the menu entry is insensitive and grayed out.

17.16.15.3 Options

Figure 17.407 "Glowing Hot" options

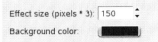

Effect size (pixels * 3) This is actually the font size option of the "Glowing Hot" logo. The value is used to calculate the size of the feathering border (cf Section 16.4.9) before the alpha is filled with red, yellow, and white. These feathered colors make the hot metal effect.

Figure 17.408 Effect size examples

(a) *Effect size 50*

(b) *Effect size 350*

Background color This is the color used to fill the "Background" layer; it defaults to black (7,0,20). Click on the button to open a color selector, if you want to choose a different color.

17.16.15.4 Filter details

To create the glowing effect (red-hot, yellow-hot, and white-hot area), the alpha is feathered and then filled with the respective color, from red to white with decreasing feather sizes and color intensities in the feathered area.

The illustration below shows the "hot metal" colors and the width of the feathering border in percent of "Effect size" (these are the values the filter actually uses).

Figure 17.409 Effect size

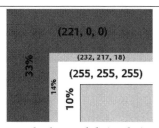

Glowing hot metal colors and their relative feather sizes

In the example images you can see how the alpha's outline shines through the glowing. This is achieved with a alpha filled with black as top layer, where the layer mode is set to overlay. Using a black overlay layer won't change pure white, but darkens light colors at the alpha's edges so that the outline appears.

17.16.16 Gradient Bevel

17.16.16.1 Overview

Figure 17.410 Example for the "Gradient Bevel" filter

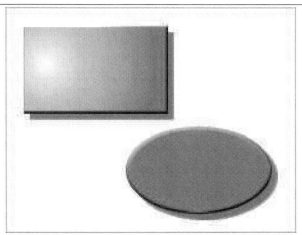

"Gradient Bevel" applied

Caution

 Sorry, there is no documentation for this filter as yet.

17.16.16.2 Activate the filter

This filter is found in the image window menu under Filters → Alpha to Logo → Gradient Bevel.

17.16.16.3 Options

Figure 17.411 "Gradient Bevel" options

Border size (pixels):	22
Bevel height (sharpness):	40
Bevel width:	2.5
Background color:	

Border size (pixels) TODO

Bevel height (sharpness) TODO

Bevel width TODO

Background color TODO

17.16.17 Neon

17.16.17.1 Overview

Figure 17.412 Example for the "Neon" filter

(a) *The "Neon" filter*

(b) *The "Neon" logo*

This filter converts the active layer's alpha into a neon-sign like object and optionally adds a shadow.

It is derived from the "Neon" Script-Fu script (File → Create → Logos → Neon), which creates a text effect that simulates neon lighting.

Warning

 The image will always be resized to the active layer's size.

17.16.17.2 Activate the filter

You can find this filter in the image window menu under Filters → Alpha to Logo → Neon.

17.16.17.3 Options

Figure 17.413 "Neon" options

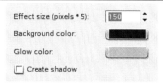

Effect size (pixels * 5) This is actually the font size option of the Neon Script-Fu script. Some internal values will be set in relation to this font size, for instance tube size, shadow offset, and blur radius. So it may be a good idea to select the height of your objects as a starting point here. ("pixels * 5" is nonsense, ignore it.)

Background color This is the color used to fill the "Background" layer; it defaults to black. When you click on the color swatch button, you can choose any other color in the color selector dialog.

Glow color This is the color of the glowing neon tubes. The default is a typical neon-like light blue (38,211,255). Again, a click on the color swatch button brings up the color selector.

Create shadow Optionally, the filter can create a drop shadow, which will have the same shape as the alpha channel. The shadow color is black, and cannot be modified. Unless you don't plan to remove the background layer, you should select a different Background color.

"Neon" with shadow

17.16.17.4 Filter details

The filter uses two layers to achieve the neon effect:

Figure 17.414 The Neon effect

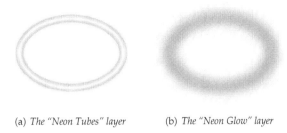

(a) The "Neon Tubes" layer   (b) The "Neon Glow" layer

The layer "Neon Tubes" is the active layer the filter is applied to. The content of this layer doesn't matter. Only the alpha channel does, especially its shape.

The "Neon Glow" layer below contains the glowing of the neon light.

Optional a "Shadow" layer is created below, containing a drop shadow in the same shape of the active layer's alpha channel. At the bottom a new "Background" layer is created filled with the Background color.

Overview of the Neon filter layers:

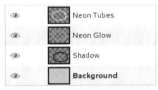

17.16.18   Particle Trace

17.16.18.1   Overview

Figure 17.415 Examples for the "Particle Trace" filter

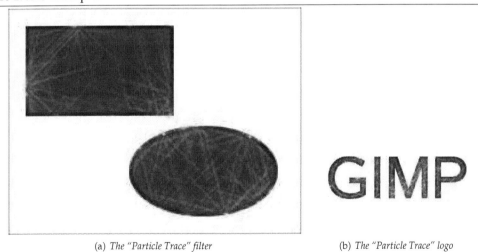

(a) The "Particle Trace" filter   (b) The "Particle Trace" logo

To get such images, open a new image with a transparent background, create selections, fill them with any color, and apply filter.

This filter adds an effect, reminding of particle traces in a bubble chamber of nuclear physics, to the active layer alpha.

> **Warning**
>
> The image will always be resized to the active layer's size.

The filter is derived from the "Particle Trace" logo script (File → Create → Logos → Particle Trace), which creates the text effect shown in the example above.

17.16.18.2 Activate the filter

You can find this filter in the image window menu under Filters → Alpha to Logo → Particle Trace.

17.16.18.3 Options

Figure 17.416 "Particle Trace" options

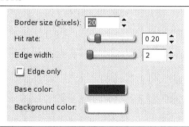

Border size (pixels) Actually this option is the text layer's border of the "Particle Trace" Script-Fu Logo (hence the misleading name). Here it determines the width of the white shadow's feathering.

Hit rate This option sets the amount of light points produced by the Noise filter and thus the amount of points converted to sparkles. The value ranges from from 0.0 to 1.0, but some values may be not useful:

Figure 17.417 "Hit rate" examples

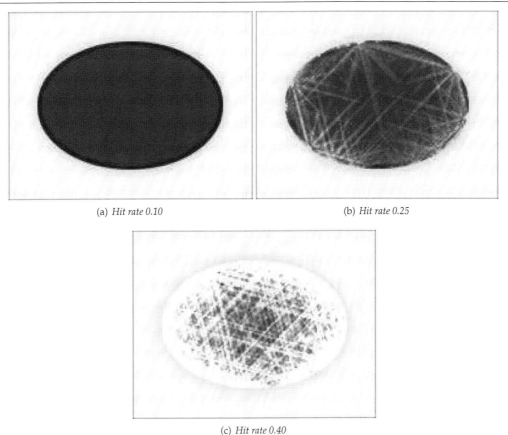

(a) *Hit rate 0.10*   (b) *Hit rate 0.25*

(c) *Hit rate 0.40*

Edge width Along the edge of the alpha, a new area will be created with radius "Edge width" (compare Section 16.4.13). This area will also be filled with the "Base color", but will be a bit darker.

Edge only If checked, the filter effect will be applied to the edge of the alpha channel only and the area of the alpha channel will be cleared.

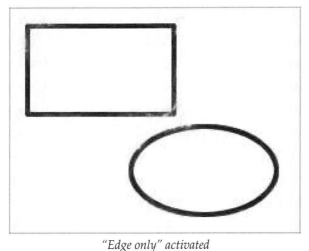

"Edge only" activated

Base color This color is used to fill the area defined by the active layer's alpha channel. It defaults to a very dark green. As usual, clicking on the color swatch button opens a color selector where you can choose any other color.

Background color This color is used to fill a new background layer. Note that above the background layer there is a white shadow layer which has opacity set to 90%, so you will see the background color only partially. If the "Edge only" option is enabled, the area of the alpha channel will be cleared and you will see the background color. Again, when you click on the color swatch button, a color selector pops up where you can select any color.

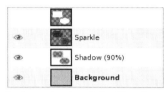

The active layer (top) and the filter layers below

17.16.18.4 Filter details

The filter adds noise to the alpha and then turns the spots into sparkles. Then it adds a feathered white shadow.

17.16.19 Textured

17.16.19.1 Overview

Figure 17.418 Example for the "Textured" filter

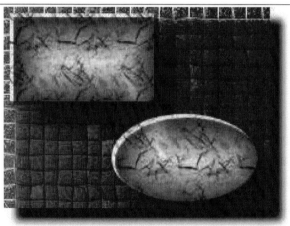

"Textured" applied

 Caution

Sorry, there is no documentation for this filter as yet.

17.16.19.2 Activate the filter

This filter is found in the image window menu under Filters → Alpha to Logo → Textured.

17.16.19.3   Options

Figure 17.419 "Textured" options

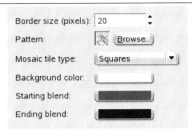

Border size (pixels) TODO

Pattern TODO

Mosaic tile type TODO

Background color TODO

Starting blend TODO

Ending blend TODO

Chapter 18

Keys and Mouse Reference

18.1 Help

Help — Key reference for Help menu

Help

F1 Help

Shift + F1 Context Help

18.2 Tools

Tools — Key reference for the Tools menu

Tools

Tools

R Rect Select

E Ellipse Select

F Free Select

Z Fuzzy Select

Shift + O Select By Color

I Scissors

B Paths

O Color Picker

M Move

Shift + C Crop and Resize

Shift + R Rotate

Shift + T Scale

Shift + S Shear

Shift + P Perspective

Shift + F Flip

T Text

Shift + B Bucket Fill

L Blend

N Pencil

P Paintbrush

Shift + E Eraser

A Airbrush

K Ink

C Clone

Shift + U Blur/Sharpen

S Smudge

Shift + D Dodge/Burn

Note

 Click on a tool icon to open its Tool Options dialog.

Context

X Swap Colors

D Default Colors

Note

 Click on the colors to change the colors.

18.3   File

File — Key reference for the File menu

File

Ctrl + N New image

Ctrl + O Open image

 Ctrl + Alt + O Open image as new layer

Ctrl + D Duplicate

Ctrl + 1 Open recent image #1

Ctrl + 2 Open recent image #2

Ctrl + 3 Open recent image #3

Ctrl + 4 Open recent image #4

Ctrl + 5 Open recent image #5

Ctrl + 6 Open recent image #6

Ctrl + 7 Open recent image #7

Ctrl + 8 Open recent image #8

Ctrl + 9 Open recent image #9

Ctrl + 0 Open recent image #10

Ctrl + S Save image

Shift + Ctrl + S Save under a new name

Ctrl + Q Quit

18.4 Dialogs

Dialogs — Key reference for Dockable Dialogs submenu

Dockable Dialogs

Ctrl + L Layers

Shift + Ctrl + B Brushes

Shift + Ctrl + P Patterns

Ctrl + G Gradients

Note
These open a new dialog window if it isn't open yet, otherwise the corresponding dialog gets focus.

Within a Dialog

Alt + F4, Ctrl + W Close the window

Tab Jump to next widget

Shift + Tab Jump to previous widget

Enter Set the new value

Space, Enter Activate current button or list

Ctrl + Alt + PgUp Ctrl + Alt + PgDn In a multi-tab dialog, switch tabs

---

> **Note**
>
> This accepts the new value you typed in a text field and returns focus to canvas.

Within a File Dialog

Shift + L Open Location

Alt + Up Up-Folder

Alt + Down Down-Folder

Alt + Home Home-Folder

Esc Close Dialog

18.5 View

View — Key reference for View menu

View

Window

F10 Main Menu

Shift + F10, right click Drop-down Menu

F11 Toggle fullscreen

Shift + Q Toggle quickmask

Ctrl + W Close document window

> **Note**
>
> Menus can also be activated by **Alt** with the letter underscored in the menu name.

Zoom

+ Zoom in

- Zoom out

1 Zoom 1:1

Ctrl + E Shrink wrap

> **Note**
>
> This fits the window to the image size.

Rulers and Guides

mouse drag Drag off a ruler to create guide

Ctrl + mouse drag Drag a sample point out of the rulers

Shift + Ctrl + R Toggle rulers

Shift + Ctrl + T Toggle guides

Note

 Drag off the horizontal or vertical ruler to create a new guideline. Drag a guideline off the image to delete it.

18.6 Edit

Edit — Key reference for Edit menu

Edit

Undo/redo

Ctrl + Z Undo

Ctrl + Y Redo

   Clipboard

Ctrl + C Copy selection

Ctrl + X Cut selection

Ctrl + V Paste clipboard

Del Erase selection

Shift + Ctrl + C Named copy selection

Shift + Ctrl + X Named cut selection

Shift + Ctrl + V Named paste clipboard

Note

 This puts a copy of the selection on the GIMP clipboard.

   Fill

Ctrl + , Fill with FG Color

Ctrl + . Fill with BG Color

Ctrl + ; Fill with Pattern

18.7 Layer

Layer — Key reference for Layer menu

Layers

PgUp, Ctrl + Tab Select the layer above

PgDn, Shift + Ctrl + Tab Select the layer below

Home Select the first layer

End Select the last layer

Ctrl + M Merge visible layers

Ctrl + H Anchor layer

18.8 Select

Select — Key reference for Select menu

Selections

Ctrl + T Toggle selections

Ctrl + A Select all

Shift + Ctrl + A Select none

Ctrl + I Invert selection

Shift + Ctrl + L Float selection

Shift + V Path to selection

18.9 Filters

Filters — Key reference for Filters menu

Filters

Ctrl + F Repeat last filter

Shift + Ctrl + F Reshow last filter

18.10 Zoom tool

Zoom tool — Key reference for the Zoom tool submenu

Zoom tool

click Zoom in

Ctrl + click Zoom out

mouse drag Zoom into the area

Part IV

Glossary

Alpha

An Alpha value indicates the transparency of a pixel. Besides its Red, Green and Blue values, a pixel has an alpha value. The smaller the alpha value of a pixel, the more visible the colors below it. A pixel with an alpha value of 0 is completely transparent. A pixel with an alpha value of 255 is fully opaque.

With some image file formats, you can only specify that a pixel is completely transparent or completely opaque. Other file formats allow a variable level of transparency.

Alpha Channel

An alpha channel of a layer is a grayscale image of the same size as the layer representing its transparency. For each pixel the gray level (a value between 0 and 255) represents the pixels's Alpha value. An alpha channel can make areas of the layer to appear partially transparent. That's why the background layer has no alpha channel by default.

The image alpha channel, which is displayed in the channels dialog, can be considered as the alpha channel of the final layer when all layers have been merged.

See also Example for Alpha channel.

Antialiasing

Antialiasing is the process of reversing an alias, that is, reducing the "jaggies". Antialiasing produces smoother curves by adjusting the boundary between the background and the pixel region that is being antialiased. Generally, pixel intensities or opacities are changed so that a smoother transition to the background is achieved. With selections, the opacity of the edge of the selection is appropriately reduced.

Bézier curve

A spline is a curve which is defined mathematically and has a set of control points. A Bézier spline is a cubic spline which has four control points, where the first and last control points (knots or anchors) are the endpoints of the curve and the inner two control points (handles) determine the direction of the curve at the endpoints.

In the non-mathematical sense, a spline is a flexible strip of wood or metal used for drawing curves. Using this type of spline for drawing curves dates back to shipbuilding, where weights were hung on splines to bend them. The outer control points of a Bézier spline are similar to the places where the splines are fastened down and the inner control points are where weights are attached to modify the curve.

Bézier splines are only one way of mathematically representing curves. They were developed in the 1960s by Pierre Bézier, who worked for Renault.

Bézier curves are used in GIMP as component parts of Paths.

The image above shows a Bézier curve. Points P0 and P3 are points on the Path, which are created by clicking with the mouse. Points P1 and P2 are handles, which are automatically created by GIMP when you stretch the line.

Bitmap

From *The Free Online Dictionary of Computing (13 Mar 01)* :

bitmap — A data file or structure which corresponds bit for bit with an image displayed on a screen, probably in the same format as it would be stored in the display's video memory or maybe as a device independent bitmap. A bitmap is characterised by the width and height of the image in pixels and the number of bits per pixel which determines the number of shades of grey or colors it can represent. A bitmap representing a colored image (a "pixmap") will usually have pixels with between one and eight bits for each of the red, green, and blue components, though other color encodings are also used. The green component sometimes has more bits than the other two to cater for the human eye's greater discrimination in this component.

BMP

BMP is an uncompressed image file format designed by Microsoft and mainly used in Windows. Colors are typically represented in 1, 4 or 8 bits, although the format also supports more. Because it is not compressed and the files are large, it is not very well suited for use in the internet.

Bump mapping

Bump mapping is a technique for displaying extremely detailed objects without increasing the geometrical complexity of the objects. It is especially used in 3-dimensional visualization programs. The trick is to put all the necessary information into a texture, with which shadowing is shown on the surface of the object.

Bump mapping is only one (very effective) way of simulating surface irregularities which are not actually contained in the geometry of the model.

Channel Mask

A channel masks is a special type of mask which determines the transparency of a selection. See *Masks* for a detailed description.

Channel

A channel refers to a certain component of an image. For instance, the components of an RGB image are the three primary colors red, green, blue, and sometimes transparency (alpha).

Every channel is a grayscale image of exactly the same size as the image and, consequently, consists of the same number of pixels. Every pixel of this grayscale image can be regarded as a container which can be filled with a value ranging from 0 to 255. The exact meaning of this value depends on the type of channel, e.g. in the RGB color model the value in the R-channel means the amount of red which is added to the color of the different pixels; in the selection channel, the value denotes how strongly the pixels are selected; and in the alpha channel the values denote how opaque the corresponding pixels are. See also Channels.

Clipboard

The Clipboard is a temporary area of memory which is used to transfer data between applications or documents. It is used when you Cut, Copy or Paste data in GIMP.

The clipboard is implemented slightly differently under different operating systems. Under Linux/XFree, GIMP uses the XFree clipboard for text and the GIMP internal image clipboard for transferring images between image documents. Under other operating systems, the clipboard may work somewhat differently. See the GIMP documentation for your operating system for further information.

The basic operations provided by the clipboard are "Cut", "Copy", and "Paste". Cut means that the item is removed from the document and copied to the clipboard. Copy leaves the item in the document and copies it to the clipboard. Paste copies the contents of the clipboard to the document. The GIMP makes an intelligent decision about what to paste depending upon the target. If the target is a canvas, the Paste operation uses the image clipboard. If the target is a text entry box, the paste operation uses the text clipboard.

CMY, CMYK

CMYK is a color model which has components for Cyan, Magenta, Yellow and Black. It is a subtractive color model, and that fact is important when an image is printed. It is complementary to the RGB color model.

The values of the individual colors vary between 0% and 100%, where 0% corresponds to an unprinted color, and 100% corresponds to a completely printed area of color. Colors are formed by mixing the three basic colors.

The last of these values, K (Black), doesn't contribute to the color, but merely serves to darken the other colors. The letter K is used for Black to prevent confusion, since B usually stands for Blue.

Figure 18.1 Subtractive color model

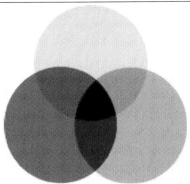

GIMP does not currently support the CMYK model. (An experimental plug-in providing rudimentary CMYK support can be found [PLUGIN-SEPARATE].)

This is the mode used in printing. These are the colors in the ink cartridges in your printer. It is the mode used in painting and in all the objects around us, where light is reflected, not emmitted. Objects absorb part of the light waves and we see only the reflected part. Note that the cones in our eyes see this reflected light in RGB mode. An object appears Red because Green and Blue have been absorbed. Since the combination of Green and Blue is Cyan, Cyan is absorbed when you add Red. Conversely, if you add Cyan, its complementary color, Red, is absorbed. This system is *subtractive*. If you add Yellow, you decrease Blue, and if you add Magenta, you decrease Green.

It would be logical to think that by mixing Cyan, Magenta and Yellow, you would subtract Red, Green and Blue, and the eye would see no light at all, that is, Black. But the question is more complex. In fact, you would see a dark brown. That is why this mode also has a Black value, and why your printer has a Black cartridge. It is less expensive that way. The printer doesn't have to mix the other three colors to create an imperfect Black, it just has to add Black.

Color depth

Color depth is simply the number of bits used to represent a color (bits per pixel : bpp). There are 3 channels for a pixel (for Red, Green and Blue). GIMP can support 8 bits per channel, referred as *eight-bit color*. So, GIMP color depth is 8 * 3 = 24, which allows 256 * 256 * 256 = 16,777,216 possible colors (8 bits allow 256 colors).

Color model

A color model is a way of describing and specifying a color. The term is often used loosely to refer to both a color space system and the color space on which it is based.

A color space is a set of colors which can be displayed or recognized by an input or output device (such as a scanner, monitor, printer, etc.). The colors of a color space are specified as values in a color space system, which is a coordinate system in which the individual colors are described by coordinate values on various axes. Because of the structure of the human eye, there are three axes in color spaces which are intended for human observers. The practical application of that is that colors are specified with three components (with a few exceptions). There are about 30 to 40 color space systems in use. Some important examples are:

- RGB
- HSV
- CMY(K)
- YUV
- YCbCr

Dithering

Dithering is a technique used in computer graphics to create the illusion of more colors when displaying an image which has a low color depth. In a dithered image, the missing colors are reproduced by a certain arrangement of pixels in the available colors. The human eye perceives this as a mixture of the individual colors.

The Gradient tool uses dithering. You may also choose to use dithering when you convert an image to Indexed format. If you are working on an image with indexed colors, some tools (such as the pattern fill tool) may also use dithering, if the correct color is not available in the colormap.

The Newsprint filter uses dithering as well. You can use the NL Filter (Non Linear filter) to remove unwanted dithering noise from your image.

Also note that although GIMP itself uses 24-bit colors, your system may not actually be able to display that many colors. If it doesn't, then the software in between GIMP and your system may also dither colors while displaying them.

See also the glossary entry on Floyd-Steinberg dithering, which is used in GIMP.

EXIF

Exchangeable image file format (official abbreviation Exif, not EXIF) is a specification for the image file format used by digital cameras. It was created by the Japan Electronic Industry Development Association (JEIDA). The specification uses the existing JPEG, TIFF Rev. 6.0, and RIFF WAVE file formats, with the addition of specific metadata tags. It is not supported in JPEG 2000 or PNG. Version 2.1 of the specification is dated June 12, 1998 and version 2.2 is dated April 2002. The Exif tag structure is taken from that of TIFF files. There is a large overlap between the tags defined in the TIFF, Exif, TIFF/EP and DCF standards [WKPD-EXIF].

Feathering

The process of Feathering makes a smooth transition between a region and the background by softly blending the edges of the region.

In GIMP, you can feather the edges of a selection. Brushes can also have feathered edges.

File Format

A file format or file type is the form in which computer data is stored. Since a file is stored by an operating system as a linear series of bytes, which cannot describe many kinds of real data in an obvious way, conventions have been developed for interpreting the information as representations of complex data. All of the conventions for a particular "kind" of file constitute a file format.

Some typical file formats for saving images are JPEG, TIFF, PNG and GIF. The best file format for saving an image depends upon how the image is intended to be used. For example, if the image is intended for the internet, file size is a very important factor, and if the image is intended to be printed, high resolution and quality have greater significance. See Format types.

Floating Selection

A floating selection (sometimes called a "floating layer") is a type of temporary layer which is similar in function to a normal layer, except that a floating selection must be anchored before you can resume working on any other layers in the image.

In early versions of GIMP, when GIMP did not use layers, floating selections were used for performing operations on a limited part of an image (you can do that more easily now with layers). Now floating selections have no practical use, but you must know what you have to do with them.

Floyd-Steinberg Dithering

Floyd-Steinberg dithering is a method of dithering which was first published in 1976 by Robert W. Floyd and Louis Steinberg. The dithering process begins in the upper left corner of the image. For each pixel, the closest available color in the palette is chosen and the difference between that color and the original color is computed in each RGB channel. Then specific fractions of these differences are dispersed among several adjacent pixels which haven't yet been visited (below and to the right of the original pixel). Because of the order of processing, the procedure can be done in a single pass over the image.

When you convert an image to Indexed mode, you can choose between two variants of Floyd-Steinberg dithering.

Gamma

Gamma or gamma correction is a non-linear operation which is used to encode and decode luminance or color values in video or still image systems. It is used in many types of imaging systems to straighten out a curved signal-to-light or intensity-to-signal response. For example, the light emitted by a CRT is not linear with regard to its input voltage, and the voltage from an electric camera is not linear with regard to the intensity (power) of the light in the scene. Gamma encoding helps to map the data into a perceptually linear domain, so that the limited signal range (the limited number of bits in each RGB signal) is better optimized perceptually.

Gamma is used as an exponent (power) in the correction equation. Gamma compression (where gamma < 1) is used to encode linear luminance or RGB values into color signals or digital file values, and gamma expansion (where gamma > 1) is the decoding process, and usually occurs where the current-to-voltage function for a CRT is non-linear.

For PC video, images are encoded with a gamma of about 0.45 and decoded with a gamma of 2.2. For Mac systems, images are typically encoded with a gamma of about 0.55 and decoded with a gamma of 1.8. The sRGB color space standard used for most cameras, PCs and printers does not use a simple exponential equation, but has a decoding gamma value near 2.2 over much of its range.

In GIMP, gamma is an option used in the brush tab of the GIMPressionist filter and in the Flame filter. The display filters also include a Gamma filter. Also see the Levels Tool, where you can use the middle slider to change the gamma value.

Gamut

In color reproduction, including computer graphics and photography, the gamut, or color gamut (pronounced / gæm t/), is a certain complete subset of colors. The most common usage refers to the subset of colors which can be accurately represented in a given circumstance, such as within a given color space or by a certain output device. Another sense, less frequently used but not less correct, refers to the complete set of colors found within an image at a given time. In this context, digitizing a photograph, converting a digitized image to a different color space, or outputting it to a given medium using a certain output device generally alters its gamut, in the sense that some of the colors in the original are lost in the process. [WKPD-GAMUT]

GIF

GIF™ stands for Graphics Interchange Format. It is a file format with good, lossless compression for images with low color depth (up to 256 different colors per image). Since GIF was developed, a new format called Portable Network Graphics (PNG) has been developed, which is better than GIF in all respects, with the exception of animations and some rarely-used features.

GIF was introduced by CompuServe in 1987. It became popular mostly because of its efficient, LZW compression. The size of the image files required clearly less disk space than other usual graphics formats of the time, such as PCX or MacPaint. Even large images could be transmitted in a reasonable time, even with slow modems. In addition, the open licensing policy of CompuServe made it possible for any programmer to implement the GIF format for his own applications free of charge, as long as the CompuServe copyright notice was attached to them.

Colors in GIF are stored in a color table which can hold up to 256 different entries, chosen from 16.7 million different color values. When the image format was introduced, this was not a much of a limitation, since only a few people had hardware which could display more colors than that. For typical drawings, cartoons, black-and-white photographs and similar uses, 256 colors are quite sufficient as a rule, even today. For more complex images, such as color photographs, however, a huge loss of quality is apparent, which is why the format is not considered to be suitable for those purposes.

One color entry in the palette can be defined to be transparent. With transparency, the GIF image can look like it is non-rectangular in shape. However, semi-transparency, as in PNG, is not possible. A pixel can only be either entirely visible or completely transparent.

The first version of GIF was 87a. In 1989, CompuServe published an expanded version, called 89a. Among other things, this made it possible to save several images in one GIF file, which is especially used for simple animation. The version number can be distinguished from the first six bytes of a GIF file. Interpreted as ASCII symbols, they are "GIF87a" or "GIF89a".

GNU

The GNU project was started in 1983 by Richard Stallman with the goal of developing a completely free operating system. It is especially well-known from the GNU General Public License (GPL) and GNU/Linux, a GNU-variant with a Linux kernel.

The name came about from the naming conventions which were in practice at MIT, where Stallman worked at the time. For programs which were similar to other programs, recursive acronyms were chosen as names. Since the new system was to be based on the widespread operating system, Unix, Stallman looked for that kind of name and came up with GNU, which stands for "GNU is not Unix". In order to avoid confusion, the name should be pronounced with the "G", not like "new". There were several reasons for making GNU Unix-compatible. For one thing, Stallman was convinced that most companies would refuse a completely new operating system, if the programs they used wouldn't run on it. In addition, the architecture of Unix made quick, easy and distributed development possible, since Unix consists of many small programs that can be developed independently of each other, for the most part. Also, many parts of a Unix system were freely available to anyone and could therefore be directly integrated into GNU, for example, the typesetting system, TeX, or the X Window System. The missing parts were newly written from the ground up.

GIMP (GNU Image Manipulation Program) is an official GNU application [WKPD-GNU].

Grayscale

Grayscale is a mode for encoding the colors of an image which contains only black, white and shades of gray.

When you create a new image, you can choose to create it in Grayscale mode (which you can colorize later, by changing it to RGB mode). You can also change an existing image to grayscale by using the Grayscale, Desaturate, Decompose, Channel Mixer, although not all formats will accept these changes. Although you can create images in Grayscale mode and convert images to it, it is not a color model, in the true sense of the word.

As explained in RGB mode, 24-bit GIMP images can have up to 256 levels of gray. If you change from Grayscale to RGB mode, your image will have an RGB structure with three color channels, but of course, it will still be gray.

Grayscale image files (8-bit) are smaller than RGB files.

Guides

Guides are lines you can temporarily display on an image while you are working on it. You can display as many guides as you would like, in either the horizontal or the vertical direction. These lines help you position a selection or a layer on the image. They do not appear when the image is printed.

For more information see Section 12.2.2.

Histogram

In digital image processing, a histogram is a graph representing the statistical frequency of the gray values or the color values in an image. The histogram of an image tells you about the occurrence of gray values or color values, as well as the contrast range and the brightness of the image. In a color image, you can create one histogram with information about all possible colors, or three histograms for the individual color channels. The latter makes the most sense, since most procedures are based on grayscale images and therefore further processing is immediately possible.

HSV

HSV is a color model which has components for Hue (the color, such as blue or red), Saturation (how strong the color is) and Value (the brightness).

The RGB mode is very well suited to computer screens, but it doesn't let us describe what we see in everyday life; a light green, a pale pink, a dazzling red, etc. The HSV model takes these characteristics into account. HSV and RGB are not completely independent of each other. You can see that with the Color Picker tool; when you change a color in one of the color models, the other one also changes. Brave souls can read *Grokking the GIMP*, which explains their interrelationship.

Brief description of the HSV components:

Hue This is the color itself, which results from the combination of primary colors. All shades (except for the gray levels) are represented in a *chromatic circle*: yellow, blue, and also purple, orange, etc. The chromatic circle (or "color wheel") values range between 0° and 360°. (The term "color" is often used instead of "Hue". The RGB colors are "primary colors".)

Saturation This value describes how pale the color is. A completely unsaturated color is a shade of gray. As the saturation increases, the color becomes a pastel shade. A completely saturated color is pure. Saturation values go from 0 to 100, from white to the purest color.

Value This value describes the luminosity, the luminous intensity. It is the amount of light emitted by a color. You can see a change of luminosity when a colored object is moved from being in the shadow to being in the sun, or when you increase the luminosity of your screen. Values go from 0 to 100. Pixel values in the three channels are also luminosities: "Value" in the HSV color model is the maximum of these elementary values in the RGB space (scaled to 0-100).

HTML notation

A hex triplet is a way of encoding a color for a computer. The "#" symbol indicates that the numbers which follow it are encoded in hexadecimal. Each color is specified in two hexadecimal digits which make up a triplet (three pairs) of hexadecimal values in the form "#rrggbb", where "rr" represents red, "gg" represents green and "bb" represents blue.

Image Hose

An image hose in GIMP is a special type of brush which consists of several images. For example, you could have a brush with footprints, which consists of two images, one for the left footprint and one for the right. While painting with this brush, a left footprint would appear first, then a right footprint, then a left one, etc. This type of brush is very powerful.

An image hose is also sometimes called an "image pipe" or "animated brush". An image hose is indicated in the Brushes dialog by a small red triangle in the lower right corner of the brush's symbol.

For information concerning creating an image hose, please see the Section 7.8 and Section 7.7.

Incremental, paint mode

Incremental mode is a paint mode where each brush stroke is drawn directly on the active layer. When it is set, each additional stroke of the brush increases the effect of the brush, up to the maximum opacity for the brush.

If incremental mode is not set, brush strokes are drawn on a canvas buffer, which is then combined with the active layer. The maximum effect of a brush is then determined by the opacity, and stroking with the brush repeatedly does not increase the effect beyond this limit.

The two images above were created using a brush with spacing set to 60 percent. The image on the left shows non-incremental painting and the image on the right shows the difference with incremental painting.

Incremental mode is a tool option that is shared by several brush tools, except those which have a "rate" control, which automatically implies an incremental effect. You can set it by checking the Incremental checkbox in the tool option dialog for the tool (Paintbrush, Pencil and Eraser).

Indexed Colors

Indexed color mode is a mode for encoding colors in an image where each pixel in the image is assigned an 8-bit color number. The color which corresponds to this number is then put in a table (the palette). Changing a color in the palette changes all the pixels which refer to this palette color. Although you can create images in *Indexed Color* mode and can transform images to it, it is, strictly speaking, not a color model.

See also the Indexed Palette section and the Convert Image to Indexed Colors command.

Interpolation

Interpolation means calculating intermediate values. When you enlarge ("digitally zoom") or otherwise transform (rotate, shear or give perspective to) a digital image, interpolation procedures are used to compute the colors of the pixels in the transformed image. GIMP offers three interpolation methods, which differ in quality and speed. In general, the better the quality, the more time the interpolation takes (see Interpolation methods).

GIMP uses interpolation when you Scale an image, Scale a layer, and when you Transform an image.

JPEG

JPEG is a file format which supports compression and works at all color depths. The image compression is adjustable, but beware: Too high a compression could severely reduce image quality, since JPEG compression is lossy.

Use JPEG to create web graphics or if you don't want your image to take up a lot of space. JPEG is a good format for photographs and for computer-generated images (CGI). It is not well suited for:

- digital line drawings (for example, screenshots or vector graphics), in which there are many neighboring pixels with the same color values, few colors and hard edges,

- Black and white images (only black and white, one bit per pixel) or

- half-toned images (newsprint).

Other formats, such as GIF, PNG or JBIG, are far better for these kinds of images.

In general, JPEG transformations are not reversible. Opening and then saving a JPEG file causes a new, lossy compression. Increasing the quality factor later will not bring back the image information which was lost.

L*a*b*

The Lab color space (also called the L*a*b* color space) is a color model developed in the beginning of the 1930s by the Commission Internationale d Eclairage (CIE). It includes all the colors that the human eye can perceive. That contains the colors of the RGB and the CMYK color spaces, among others. In Lab, a color is indicated by three values: L, a and b. Here, the L stands for the luminance component — corresponding to the gray value — and a and b represent the red-green and blue-yellow parts of the color, respectively.

In contrast to RGB or CMYK, Lab is not dependent upon the various input and output devices. For that reason, it is used as an exchange format between devices. Lab is also the internal color model of PostScript Level II.

Layer

You can think of layers as being a stack of slides which are more or less transparent. Each layer represents an aspect of the image and the image is the sum of all of these aspects. The layer at the bottom of the stack is the background layer. The layers above it are the components of the foreground.

You can view and manage the layers of the image through the Layers dialog.

Figure 18.2 Example image with layers

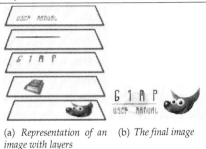

(a) *Representation of an* (b) *The final image*
image with layers

Marching Ants

Marching ants is a term which describes the dotted line which surrounds a selection. The line is animated, so it looks as if little ants are running around behind each other.

Masks

A mask is like a veil put over a layer (layer mask) or all the layers of an image (selection mask). You can remove this mask by painting with white color, and you can complete it by painting with black color. When the mask is "applied", non masked pixels will remain visible (the others will be transparent) or will be selected, according to the type of mask.

There are two types of masks:

- *Layer Mask*: Every layer can have its own mask. The layer mask represents the Alpha channel of the layer and allows you to manage its transparency. By painting on the layer mask, you can make parts of the layer opaque or transparent: painting with black makes the layer transparent, painting with white makes the layer opaque and painting with shades of gray makes the layer semi-transparent. You can use all paint tools to paint on the mask. You can also apply a filter or copy-paste. You can use the Layer mask for transition effects, volume effects, merging elements from another image, etc. See the Layer Mask section for more details.

- *Channel Mask*, also called *Selection Mask*: Channel Masks determine the transparency of a selection. By painting on a Channel Mask with white, you remove the mask and increase the selection; with black, you reduce the selection. This procedure lets you create a selection very precisely. You can also save your selections to a Channel Mask with the Save to Channel command. You can retrieve it later by using the "Channel to selection" command from the Channel menu. Channel masks are so important in GIMP that a special type has been implemented: the Quick mask. See the Selection mask section for more details.

Moiré Effect

The moiré effect (pronounce "Moa-ray") is an unintended pattern which appears when a regular pattern of grids or lines interferes with another regular pattern placed over it. This can happen, for example, when you are scanning an image with a periodic structure (such as a checkered shirt or a half-toned image), scanning a digital image, taking a digital photograph of a periodic pattern, or even when silkscreening.

If you discover the problem in time, the best solution is to move the original image a little bit in the scanner or to change the camera angle slightly.

If you cannot re-create the image file, GIMP offers some filters which may help you with the problem. For more information, see the Despeckle and NL Filter (Non-Linear) filters.

Parasite

A Parasite is additional data which may be written to an XCF file. A parasite is identified by a name, and can be thought of as an extension to the other information in an XCF file.

Parasites of an image component may be read by GIMP plug-ins. Plug-ins may also define their own parasite names, which are ignored by other plug-ins. Examples of parasites are comments, the save options for the TIFF, JPEG and PNG file formats, the gamma value the image was created with and EXIF data.

Path

A Path is a contour composed of straight lines, curves, or both. In GIMP, it is used to form the boundary of a selection, or to be *stroked* to create visible marks on an image. Unless a path is stroked, it is not visible when the image is printed and it is not saved when the image is written to a file (unless you use XCF format).

See the Paths Concepts and Using Paths sections for basic information on paths, and the Path Tool section for information on how to create and edit paths. You can manage the paths in your image with the Paths dialog.

PDB

All of the functions which GIMP and its extensions make available are registered in the Procedure Database (PDB). Developers can look up useful programming information about these functions in the PDB by using the Procedure Browser.

PDF

PDF (Portable Document Format) is a file format which was developed by Adobe to address some of the deficiencies of PostScript. Most importantly, PDF files tend to be much smaller than equivalent PostScript files. As with PostScript, GIMP's support of the PDF format is through the free Ghostscript libraries.

Pixel

A pixel is a single dot, or "picture element", of an image. A rectangular image may be composed of thousands of pixels, each representing the color of the image at a given location. The value of a pixel typically consists of several Channels, such as the Red, Green and Blue components of its color, and sometimes its Alpha (transparency).

Plugin

Optional extensions for the GIMP. Plugins are external programs that run under the control of the main GIMP application and provide specific functions on-demand. See Section 13.1 for further information.

PNG

PNG is the acronym of "Portable Network Graphic" (pronounce "ping". This recent format offers many advantages and a few drawbacks: it is not lossy and gives files more heavy than the JPEG format, but it is perfect for saving your images because you can save them several times without losing data each time (it is used for this Help). It supports True Colors (several millions of colors), indexed images (256 colors like GIF), and 256 transparency levels (while GIF supports only two levels).

PostScript

Created by Adobe, PostScript is a page description language mainly used by printers and other output devices. It's also an excellent way to distribute documents. GIMP does not support PostScript directly: it depends on a powerful free software program called Ghostscript.

The great power of PostScript is its ability to represent vector graphics—lines, curves, text, paths, etc.—in a resolution-independent way. PostScript is not very efficient, though, when it comes to representing pixel-based raster graphics. For this reason, PostScript is not a good format to use for saving images that are later going to be edited using GIMP or another graphics program.

PSD

PSD is Adobe Photoshop's native file format, and it is therefore comparable to XCF in complexity. GIMP's ability to handle PSD files is sophisticated but limited: some features of PSD files are not loaded, and only older versions of PSD are supported. Unfortunately, Adobe has now made the Photoshop Software Development Kit — which includes their file format specifications — proprietary, and only available to a limited set of developers approved by Adobe. This does not include the GIMP development team, and the lack of information makes it very difficult to maintain up-to-date support for PSD files.

Quantization

Quantization is the process of reducing the color of a pixel into one of a number of fixed values by matching the color to the nearest color in the colormap. Actual pixel values may have far more precision than the discrete levels which can be displayed by a digital display. If the display range is too small, then abrupt changes in colors (false contours, or banding) may appear where the color intensity changes from one level to another. This is especially noticeable in Indexed images, which have 256 or fewer discrete colors.

One way to reduce quantization effects is to use Dithering. The operations in GIMP which perform dithering are the Blend tool (if you have enabled the dithering option) and the Convert to Indexed command. However, they only work on RGB images and not on Indexed images.

Rendering Intent

Rendering intents are ways of dealing with colors that are out-of- *Gamut* colors present in the source space that the destination space is incapable of producing. There are four rendering intents defined by the ICC:

Perceptual This rendering intent is typically used for photographic content. It scales one gamut to fit into the other while maintaining the relative position of colors.

Relative colorimetric This rendering intent is typically used for spot colors. Colors that are not out of gamut are left unchanged. Colors outside the gamut are converted to colors with the same lightness, but different saturation, at the edge of the gamut.

Saturation This method is typically used for business graphics. The relative saturation of colors is mostly maintained, but lightning is usually changed.

Absolute colorimetric This rendering intent is most often used in proofing. It preserves the native device white point of the source image.

RGB

Figure 18.3 Additive color model

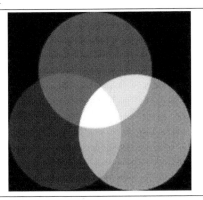

RGB is a color model which has components for Red, Green and Blue. These colors are emitted by screen elements and not reflected as they are with paint. The resulting color is a combination of the three primary RGB colors, with different degrees of lightness. If you look closely at your television screen, whose pitch is less than that of a computer screen, you can see the red, green and blue elements lit with different intensities. The RGB color model is *additive*.

GIMP uses eight bits per channel for each primary color. That means there are 256 intensities (Values) available, resulting in 256×256×256 = 16,777,216 colors.

It is not obvious why a given combination of primary colors produces a particular color. Why, for instance, does 229R+205G+229B give a shade of pink? This depends upon the human eye and brain. There is no color in nature, only a continuous spectrum of wavelengths of light. There are three kinds of cones in the retina. The same wavelength of light acting upon the three types of cones stimulates each of them differently, and the mind has learned, after several million years of evolution, how to recognize a color from these differences.

It is easy to see that no light (0R+0G+0B) produces complete darkness, black, and that full light (255R+255G+255B) produces white. Equal intensity on all color channels produces a level of gray. That is why there can only be 256 gray levels in GIMP.

Mixing two *Primary colors* in RGB mode gives a *Secondary color*, that is, a color in the CMY model. Thus combining Red and Green gives Yellow, Green and Blue give Cyan, Blue and Red give Magenta. Don't confuse secondary colors with *Complementary colors* which are directly opposite a primary color in the chromatic circle:

Figure 18.4 Colorcircle

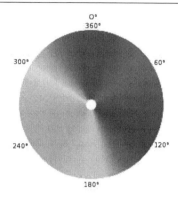

Mixing a primary color with its complementary color gives gray (a neutral color).

It is important to know what happens when you are dealing with colors in GIMP. The most important rule to remember is that decreasing the intensity of a primary color results in increasing the intensity of the complementary color (and vice versa). This is because when you decrease the value of a channel, for instance Green, you automatically increase the relative importance of the other two, here Red and Blue. The combination of these two channels gives the secondary color, Magenta, which is the complementary color of Green.

The Color Picker tool lets you find out the RGB values of a pixel and the hextriplet for the color.

Sample Merge

Sample Merged is an option you can set when you use the Bucket Fill tool, the Color Picker tool and various selection tools. It is useful when you are working on an image with several layers and the active layer is either semi-transparent or has a Layer Mode which is not set to Normal. When you check the Sample Merged option, the color which is used for the operation is the composite color of all the visible layers. When the Sample Merged option is not checked, the color used is the color of the active layer itself.

Saturation

This term refers to color purity. Imagine you add pigment to white paint. Saturation varies from 0 (white, fully toned down, fully diluted) to 100 (pure color).

Supersampling

Supersampling is a more sophisticated antialiasing technique, that is, a method of reducing jagged and stair-stepped edges along a slanted or curved line. Samples are taken at several locations *within* each pixel, not just at the center, and an average color is calculated. This is done by rendering the image at a much higher resolution than the one being displayed and then shrinking it to the desired size, using the extra pixels for calculation. The result is a smoother transition from one line of pixels to another along the edges of objects.

The quality of the result depends on the number of samples. Supersampling is often performed at a range of 2× to 16× the original size. It greatly increases the amount of time needed to draw the image and also the amount of space needed to store the image in memory.

One way to reduce the space and time requirement is to use Adaptive Supersampling. This method takes advantage of the fact that very few pixels are actually on an object boundary, so only those pixels need to be supersampled. At first, only a few samples are taken within a pixel. If the colors are very similar to each other, only those samples are used to calculate the final color. If not, more samples are used. This means that the higher number of samples is calculated only where necessary, which improves performance.

SVG

SVG stands for Scalable Vector Graphics. It is a format for two-dimensional vector graphics, both static and animated. You can export GIMP paths to SVG and you can import SVG documents into GIMP from a vector graphic software. See [WKPD-SVG] for more details.

TGA

TGA (TARGA Image File) is a file format which supports 8, 16, 24 or 32 bits per pixel and optional RLE compression. It was originally developed by the Truevision company. "TGA" stands for Truevision Graphics Adapter and "TARGA" stands for Truevision Advanced Raster Graphics Adapter.

TIFF

TIFF (Tagged Image File Format) is a file format which was developed primarily for scanned raster graphics for color separation. Six different encoding routines are supported, each with one of three different image modes: black and white, grayscale and color. Uncompressed TIFF images may be 1, 4, 8 or 24 bits per pixel. TIFF images compressed using the LZW algorithm may be 6, 8 or 24 bits per pixel. Besides Postscript format, TIFF is one of the most important formats for preliminary stages of printing. It is a high quality file format, which is perfect for images you want to import to other programs like FrameMaker or CorelDRAW.

Tile

A Tile is a part of an image which GIMP currently has open. In order to avoid having to store an entire image in memory at the same time, GIMP divides it into smaller pieces. A tile is usually a square of 64 x 64 pixels, although tiles at the edges of an image may be smaller than that.

At any time, a tile may be in main memory, in the tile cache in RAM, or on disk. Tiles which are currently being worked on are in main memory. Tiles which have been used recently are in RAM. When the tile cache in RAM is full, tiles which have been used least recently are written to disk. GIMP can retrieve the tiles from RAM or disk when they are needed.

Do not confuse these tiles with those in the Tile Filter

URI

A Uniform Resource Identifier (URI) is a string of characters that serves to identify an abstract or a physical resource. URIs are used for the identification of resources in the Internet (such as web pages, miscellaneous files, calling up web services, and for receivers of e-mail) and they are especially used in the Worldwide Web.

URL

URLs (Uniform Resource Locators) are one type of Uniform Resource Identifiers (URIs). URLs identify a resource by its primary access mechanism (commonly http or ftp) and the location of the resource in the computer network. The name of the URI scheme is therefore generally derived from the network protocol used for it. Examples of network protocols are http, ftp and mailto.

Since URLs are the first and most common kinds of URIs, the terms are often used synonymously.

Value

This term often refers to the light intensity, the luminosity of a color. It varies from 0 (black) to 100 (full light).

XCF

XCF is a file format which is special because it is GIMP's native file format: that is, it was designed specifically to store all of the data that goes to make up a GIMP image. Because of this, XCF files may be quite complicated, and there are few programs other than GIMP that can read them.

When an image is stored as an XCF file, the file encodes nearly everything there is to know about the image: the pixel data for each of the layers, the current selection, additional channels if there are any, paths if there are any, and guides. The most important thing that is *not* saved in an XCF file is the undo history.

The pixel data in an XCF file is represented in a lossless compressed form: the image byte blocks are compressed using the lossless RLE algorithm. This means that no matter how many times you load and save an image using this format, not a single pixel or other image data is lost or modified because of this format. XCF files can become very large, however GIMP allows you to compress the files themselves, using either the gzip or bzip2 compression methods, both of which are fast, efficient, and freely available. Compressing an XCF file will often shrink it by a factor of 10 or more.

The GIMP developers have made a great effort to keep the XCF file format compatible across versions. If you create a file using GIMP 2.0, it ought to be possible to open the file in GIMP 1.2.

However, some of the information in the file may not be usable: for example, GIMP 2.0 has a much more sophisticated way of handling text than GIMP 1.2, so a text layer from a GIMP 2.0 XCF file will appear as an ordinary image layer if the file is opened in GIMP 1.2.

YCbCr

YCbCr is a color model which was developed for the PAL television standard as a simple modification to the YUV color model. In the meantime, it has become the CCIR-601 standard for image and video recording. For example, it is used for JPEG pictures and MPEG videos, and therefore also on DVDs, video CDs and for most other widespread digital video standards. Note that a color model is still not a color space, since it doesn't determine which colors are actually meant by "red", "green" and "blue". For a color space, there must still be a reference to a specific absolute color value.

There are color models which do not express a color by the additive basic colors, red, green and blue (RGB), but by other properties, for example, the brightness-color model. Here, the criteria are the basic brightness of the colors (from black, through gray, to white), the colors with the largest portion (red, orange, yellow, green, blue, violet, or other pure colors that lie between them) and the saturation of the colors ("gaudy" to pale). This color model is based on the ability of the eye to recognize small differences in luminosity better than small color differences, and to recognize those better than small differences in saturation. That makes gray text written on a black background easy to read, but blue text on a red background very hard to read, even with the same basic brightness. Such color models are called brightness-color models.

The YCbCr model is a slight adaptation of such a brightness-color model. An RGB color value is divided into a basic brightness, Y, and two components, Cb and Cr, where Cb is a measurement of the deviation from gray in the blue direction, or if it is less than 0.5, in the direction of yellow. Cr is the corresponding measurement for the difference in the direction of red or turquoise. This representation uses the peculiarity of the eye of being especially sensitive to green light. That is why most of the information about the proportion of green is in the basic brightness, Y, an only the deviations for the red and blue portions need to be represented. The Y values have twice the resolution of the other two values, Cb and Cr, in most practical applications, such as on DVDs.

YUV

YUV is a color model which uses two components to represent the color information, luma (the strength of the light per area) and the chrominance, or proportion of color (chroma), where the chrominance again consists of two components. The development of the YUV color model also goes back to the development of color television (PAL), where ways were sought for transmitting the color information along with the black-and-white signal, in order to achieve backwards compatibility with old black and white televisions without having to increase the available transmission bandwidth. From the YUV color model of the analog television techiques, the YCrCb color model was developed, which is used for most kinds of digital image and video compression. Erroneously, the YUV color model is also often spoken about in those fields, although the YCbCr model is actually used. This often causes confusion.

For the calculation of the luma signals, the underlying RGB data is first adjusted with the gamma value of the output device, and an R'G'B' signal is obtained. The three individual components are added together with different weights, to form the brightness information, which also functions as the VBS signal (Video Baseband Signal, the black-and-white signal) for the old black and white televisions.

Y=R+G+B

The exact calculation is more complicated, however, since some aspects of the color perception of the human eye have to be taken into account. For example, green is perceived to be lighter than red, and this is perceived to be lighter than blue. Furthermore, in some systems gamma correction of the basic color is first performed.

The chrominance signals, and the color difference signals also, contain the color information. They are formed by the difference of blue minus luma or red minus luma.

U=B-Y

V=R-Y

From the three generated components, Y, U and V, the individual color proportions of the basic color can be calculated again later:

$Y + U = Y + (B - Y) = Y - Y + B = B$

$Y + V = Y + (R - Y) = Y - Y + R = R$

$Y - B - R = (R + G + B) - B - R = G$

Furthermore, because of the structure of the retina of the human eye, it turns out that the brightness information is perceived at a higher resolution than the color, so that many formats based on the YUV color model compress the chrominance to save bandwidth during transmission.

Part V

Bibliography

18.11 Books

[APRESS00]   Akkana Peck, *Beginning GIMP: From Novice to Professional*, Copyright © 2006 Apress Inc., Apress Inc, www.apress.com, ISBN 1-59059-587-4, http://gimpbook.com/ .

[FOLEY01]   Foley and van Dam, et al, *Computer Graphics, Principles and Practice*, Copyright © 1990 Addison Wesley, Addison Wesley, .

[GROKKING]   Carey Bunks, *Grokking the Gimp*, Copyright © 2000 New Riders Publishing, New Riders Publishing, www.newriders.com , ISBN 0-7357-0924-6, http://gimp-savvy.com/BOOK .

18.12 Online resources

[APOD]   *Astronomy Picture of the Day*, http://antwrp.gsfc.nasa.gov/apod/ .

[APOD01]   *Astronomy Picture of the Day (today)*, http://antwrp.gsfc.nasa.gov/apod/astropix.html .

[APOD02]   *Astronomy Picture of the Day - The Hubble Ultra Deep Field (2004 March 9)* , http://antwrp.gsfc.nasa.gov/apod/ap040309.html .

[APOD03]   *Astronomy Picture of the Day - M51: Cosmic Whirlpool (2002 July 10)* , http://antwrp.gsfc.nasa.gov/apod/ap020710.html .

[APOD04]   *Astronomy Picture of the Day - Saturn: Lord of the Rings (2002 February 15)* , http://antwrp.gsfc.nasa.gov/apod/ap020215.html .

[APOD05]   *Astronomy Picture of the Day - NGC 6369: The Little Ghost Nebula (2002 November 8)* , http://antwrp.gsfc.nasa.gov/apod/ap021108.html .

[APOD06]   *Astronomy Picture of the Day - Disorder in Stephan's Quintet (2000 November 13)* , http://antwrp.gsfc.nasa.gov/apod/ap001113.html .

[APOD07]   *Astronomy Picture of the Day - The Sharpest View of the Sun (2002 November 14)* , http://antwrp.gsfc.nasa.gov/apod/ap021114.html .

[ARGYLLCMS]   *Argyll Color Management System Home Page*, http://www.argyllcms.com/ .

[AdobeRGB]   *Adobe RGB (1998) ICC Profile*, http://www.adobe.com/digitalimag/adobergb.html .

[AdvanceMAME] *AdvanceMAME project*, http://advancemame.sourceforge.net/ .

[BABL]   *babl (pixel format translation library)*, http://www.gegl.org/babl .

[BACH04]   Michael Bach, *Face in blocks*, Copyright © 2004 Michael Bach, http://www.michaelbach.de/ot/fcs_mosaic/ .

[BUDIG01]   *Golden Text*, http://www.home.unix-ag.org/simon/gimp/golden.html .

[BUGZILLA]   *Bugzilla*, http://bugzilla.gnome.org .

[BUGZILLA-GIMP] *Bugzilla-GIMP*, http://bugzilla.gnome.org/browse.cgi?product=GIMP .

[CAIRO]   *Cairo*, http://www.cairographics.org .

[DARWINORTS] *Darwin Ports Package Manager for OS X*, http://darwinports.org .

[ECI]   *ECI (European Color Initiative) Profiles*, http://www.eci.org/eci/en/060_downloads.php .

[FDL-TRANSLATION] *Unofficial translation of the GNU Free Documentation License*

[FINK]   *Fink Package Manager for OS X*, http://fink.sf.net .

[FREETYPE]   *Freetype 2 home page*, http://www.freetype.org/freetype2/index.html .

[GEGL]   *GEGL (Generic Graphics Library)*, http://gegl.org .

[GEORGIEV01] Todor Georgiev, *Image Reconstruction Invariant to Relighting*, Copyright © 2005 Todor Georgiev, http://www.tgeorgiev.net/Invariant.pdf .

[GHOSTSCRIPT] *Ghostscript project page on Sourceforge.net*, http://sourceforge.net/projects/ghostscript .

[GIMP]   *GIMP - The Gnu Image Manipulation Program*, http://gimp.org .

[GIMP-DEV]   *GIMP Development*, http://developer.gimp.org .

[GIMP-DEV-PLUGIN] *GIMP Plugin Development*, http://developer.gimp.org/plug-ins.html .

[GIMP-DOCS]   *GIMP Documentation project page*, http://docs.gimp.org .

[GIMP-FONTS] *Fonts in GIMP 2.0*, http://gimp.org/unix/fonts.html .

[GIMP-NEWSYM26] *List of new symbols in GIMP 2.6*, libgimp-index-new-in-2-6.html .

[GIMP-REGISTRY] *GIMP-Plugin Registry*, http://registry.gimp.org .

[GPL]   *General Public License (GPL)*, http://www.fsf.org/licensing/licenses/gpl.html .

[GQVIEW]   *Homepage of GQview, an image browser*, http://gqview.sourceforge.net .

[GROKKING01] *Grokking the GIMP*, http://gimp-savvy.com/BOOK/index.html .

[GROKKING02] *Grokking the GIMP (9.2 Clickable Image Maps)*, http://gimp-savvy.com/BOOK/-index.html?node81.html .

[GTHUMB]   *gThumb - An Image Viewer and Browser for the GNOME Desktop*, http://gthumb.sourceforge.net .

[GUNTHER04] Gunther Dale, *Making shapes in GIMP*, Copyright © 2004 Dale (Gunther), http://gug.criticalhit.dk/tutorials/gunther1 .

[ICC]   *INTERNATIONAL COLOR CONSORTIUM*, http://www.color.org/ .

[ICCsRGB]   *ICC sRGB PROFILES*, http://www.color.org/srgbprofiles.html .

[INKSCAPE]   *Inkscape is an Open Source vector graphics editor*, http://www.inkscape.org .

[JIMMAC01]   *Alternative icon theme for GIMP 2.4*, http://jimmac.musichall.cz/zip/GIMP-Greyscale-tools-0.1.tar.bz2 .

[LPROF]   *LPROF ICC Profiler*, http://lprof.sourceforge.net/ .

[MSKB-294714] *Microsoft Knowledge Base Article 294714*, http://support.microsoft.com/kb/294714 .

[MsRGB]   *Microsoft sRVB Workspace*, http://www.microsoft.com/whdc/device/display/color/-default.mspx .

[OPENCLIPART-GRADIENT] *Open Clipart - Gradients*, http://openclipart.org/ .

[OPENICC]   *The OpenICC project*, http://freedesktop.org/wiki/OpenIcc .

[PLUGIN-EXIF] *GIMP-Plugin Exif Browser*, http://registry.gimp.org/plugin?id=4153 .

[PLUGIN-FLAMES] *GIMP-Plugin Flames*, http://draves.org/gimp/flame.html ; http://flam3.com/.

[PLUGIN-REDEYE] *A plugin to quickly remove "redeye" caused by camera flash*, http://registry.gimp.org/plugin?id=4212 .

[PLUGIN-RESYNTH] *Resynthesizer is a Gimp plug-in for texture synthesis*, http://www.logarithmic.net/-pfh/resynthesizer .

[PLUGIN-RETINEX] *A plugin providing the Retinex algorithm for GIMP*, http://www-prima.inrialpes.fr/-pelisson/MSRCR.php .

[PLUGIN-SEPARATE] *A plugin providing rudimentary CMYK support for GIMP,* http://www.blackfiveservices.co.uk/separate.shtml .

[PYTHON] *Python Programming Language,* http://www.python.org .

[SCALE2X] *Scale2x,* http://scale2x.sourceforge.net/ .

[SCRIBUS] *Scribus :: Open Source Desktop Publishing,* http://www.scribus.net/ .

[SIOX] *Simple Interactive Object Extraction,* http://www.siox.org/ .

[TUT01] Seth Burgess, *Tutorial: How to draw straight lines,* Copyright © 2002 Seth Burgess, http://www.gimp.org/tutorials/Straight_Line .

[TUT02] Carol Spears, *Tutorial: GIMPLite Quickies,* Copyright © 2004 Carol Spears, http://next.gimp.org/tutorials/Lite_Quickies/ .

[UNICODE] *Unicode,* http://www.unicode.org .

[WIKIPEDIA] Wikipedia Foundation, *Wikipedia,* Copyright © 2004 Wikipedia Foundation Inc., http://www.wikipedia.org .

[WKPD-ALPHA] *Wikipedia - Alpha channel,* http://en.wikipedia.org/wiki/Alpha_channel .

[WKPD-BEZIER] *Wikipedia - Bézier curve,* http://en.wikipedia.org/wiki/Bezier_curve .

[WKPD-BUMP] *Wikipedia - Bumpmap,* http://en.wikipedia.org/wiki/Bump_Mapping .

[WKPD-BURN] *Wikipedia - Burning,* http://en.wikipedia.org/wiki/Dodging_and_burning .

[WKPD-CA] *Wikipedia - Cellular Automata,* http://en.wikipedia.org/wiki/Cellular_Automata .

[WKPD-CMYK] *Wikipedia - CMYK,* http://en.wikipedia.org/wiki/CMYK .

[WKPD-COLORSPACE] *Wikipedia - Colorspace,* http://en.wikipedia.org/wiki/Colorspace .

[WKPD-DEFLATE] *Wikipedia - Deflate,* http://en.wikipedia.org/wiki/deflate .

[WKPD-DEINTERLACE] *Wikipedia - Deinterlace,* http://en.wikipedia.org/wiki/Deinterlace .

[WKPD-DITHERING] *Wikipedia - Dithering,* http://en.wikipedia.org/wiki/Dithering .

[WKPD-DODGE] *Wikipedia - Dodging,* http://en.wikipedia.org/wiki/Dodging_and_burning .

[WKPD-EXIF] *Wikipedia - EXIF,* http://en.wikipedia.org/wiki/EXIF .

[WKPD-FILEFORMAT] *Wikipedia - Fileformat,* http://en.wikipedia.org/wiki/Image_file_format .

[WKPD-GAMUT] *Wikipedia - Gamut,* http://en.wikipedia.org/wiki/Gamut .

[WKPD-GIF] *Wikipedia - GIF,* http://en.wikipedia.org/wiki/GIF .

[WKPD-GNU] *Wikipedia - GNU,* http://en.wikipedia.org/wiki/GNU .

[WKPD-HISTOGRAM] *Wikipedia - Histogram,* http://en.wikipedia.org/wiki/Image_histogram .

[WKPD-HSV] *Wikipedia - HSV,* http://en.wikipedia.org/wiki/HSL_and_HSV .

[WKPD-ICC] *Wikipedia - ICC Profile,* http://en.wikipedia.org/wiki/ICC_Profile .

[WKPD-INTERPOL] *Wikipedia - Interpolation,* http://en.wikipedia.org/wiki/Interpolation .

[WKPD-JPEG] *Wikipedia - JPEG,* http://en.wikipedia.org/wiki/JPEG .

[WKPD-LAB] *Wikipedia - L*a*b,* http://en.wikipedia.org/wiki/Lab_color_space .

[WKPD-LZW] *Wikipedia - LZW,* http://en.wikipedia.org/wiki/LZW .

[WKPD-MOIRE] *Wikipedia - Moire,* http://en.wikipedia.org/wiki/Moire .

[WKPD-PACKBITS] *Wikipedia - PackBits,* http://en.wikipedia.org/wiki/PackBits .

[WKPD-PNG]   *Wikipedia - PNG*, http://en.wikipedia.org/wiki/Portable_Network_Graphics .

[WKPD-RASTER] *Wikipedia - Raster Graphics*, http://en.wikipedia.org/wiki/Raster_graphics .

[WKPD-RETINA] *Wikipedia - Retina*, http://en.wikipedia.org/wiki/Retina .

[WKPD-RI]   *Wikipedia - Rendering Intent*, http://en.wikipedia.org/wiki/Rendering_intent .

[WKPD-SEPIA] *Wikipedia - Sepia*, http://en.wikipedia.org/wiki/Sepia .

[WKPD-SUBSAMPLING] *Wikipedia - Chroma subsampling*, http://en.wikipedia.org/wiki/-Chroma_Subsampling .

[WKPD-SVG]   *Wikipedia - SVG*, http://en.wikipedia.org/wiki/Scalable_Vector_Graphics .

[WKPD-URI]   *Wikipedia - URI*, http://en.wikipedia.org/wiki/Uniform_Resource_Identifier .

[WKPD-URL]   *Wikipedia - URL*, http://en.wikipedia.org/wiki/Uniform_Resource_Locator .

[WKPD-Web-colors] *Wikipedia - Web-colors*, http://en.wikipedia.org/wiki/Web_colors .

[WKPD-YCBCR] *Wikipedia - YCbCr*, http://en.wikipedia.org/wiki/YCbCr .

[WKPD-YUV]   *Wikipedia - YUV*, http://en.wikipedia.org/wiki/YUV .

[XDS]   *Direct Save Protocol (XDS)*, http://freedesktop.org/wiki/Specifications/XDS .

[XNVIEW]   *XnView*, http://perso.orange.fr/pierre.g/xnview/enhome.html .

Part VI

GIMP History

.1 The Very Beginning

According to Peter Mattis and Spencer Kimball, the original creators of GIMP, in their announcement of GIMP 0.54:

The GIMP arose from the ashes of a hideously crafted CS164 (compilers) class project. The setting: early morning. We were both weary from lack of sleep and the terrible strain of programming a compiler in LISP. The limits of our patience had long been exceeded, and yet still the dam held.

And then it happened. Common LISP messily dumped core when it could not allocate the 17 MB it needed to generate a parser for a simple grammar using yacc. An unbelieving moment passed, there was one shared look of disgust, and then our project was vapor. We had to write something... *ANYTHING* ... useful. Something in C. Something that did not rely on nested lists to represent a bitmap. Thus, the GIMP was born.

Like the phoenix, glorious, new life sprung out of the burnt remnants of LISP and yacc. Ideas went flying, decisions were made, the GIMP began to take form.

An image manipulation program was the consensus. A program that would at the very least lessen the necessity of using commercial software under "Windoze" or on the "Macintoy". A program that would provide the features missing from the other X painting and imaging tools. A program that would help maintain the long tradition of excellent and free UNIX applications.

Six months later, we've reached an early beta stage. We want to release now to start working on compatibility issues and cross-platform stability. Also, we feel now that the program is actually usable and would like to see other interested programmers developing plug-ins and various file format support.

.2 The Early Days of GIMP

Version 0.54 Version 0.54 was released in February 1996, and had a major impact as the first truly professional free image manipulation program. This was the first free program that could compete with the big commercial image manipulation programs.

Version 0.54 was a beta release, but it was so stable that you could use it for daily work. However, one of the major drawbacks of 0.54 was that the toolkit (the slidebars, menus, dialog boxes, etc.) was built on Motif, a commercial toolkit. This was a big drawback for systems like "Linux", because you had to buy Motif if you wanted to use the faster, dynamically linked GIMP. Many developers were also students running Linux, who could not afford to buy Motif.

Version 0.60 When 0.60 was released in July 1996, it had been under S and P (Spencer and Peter) development for four months. Main programming advantages were the new toolkits, GTK (GIMP Toolkit) and gdk (GIMP Drawing Kit), which eliminated the reliance on Motif. For the graphic artist, 0.60 was full of new features like: basic layers; improved painting tools (sub-pixel sampling, brush spacing); a better airbrush; paint modes; etc.

Version 0.60 was only a developer's release, and was not intended for widespread use. It served as a workbench for 0.99 and the final 1.0 version, so functions and enhancement could be tested and dropped or changed. You can look at 0.60 as the alpha version of 0.99.

Version 0.99 In February 1997, 0.99 came on the scene. Together with other developers, S and P had made several changes to GIMP and added even more features. The main difference was the new API (Application Programming Interface) and the "PDB", which made it possible to write scripts; Script-Fus (or macros) could now automate things that you would normally do by hand. GTK/gdk had also changed and was now called GTK+. In addition, 0.99 used a new form of tile-based memory handling that made it possible to load huge images into GIMP (loading a 100 MB image into GIMP is no problem). Version 0.99 also introduced a new native GIMP file format called XCF.

The new API made it really easy to write extensions and plug-ins for GIMP. Several new plug-ins and extensions emerged to make GIMP even more useful (such as SANE, which enables scanning directly into GIMP).

In the summer of 1997, GIMP had reached version 0.99.10, and S and P had to drop most of their support since they had graduated and begun jobs. However, the other developers of GIMP continued under the orchestration of Federico Mena to make GIMP ready for prime time.

GTK+ was separated from GIMP in September 1997. GTK+ had been recognized as an excellent toolkit, and other developers began using it to build their own applications.

GIMP went into feature freeze in October 1997. This meant that no new features would be added to the GIMP core libraries and program. GUM (GIMP Users Manual) version 0.5 was also released early in October 1997. The developing work continued to make GIMP stable and ready for version 1.0.

.3 The One to Change the World

Version 1.0 GIMP version 1.0 was released on June 5, 1998. Finally, GIMP was considered stable enough to warrant a worldwide announcement and professional use.

Version 1.2 GIMP version 1.2.0 was released on December 25, 2000. Compared to the version 1.0, it included mostly fixes and improvements of the user interface.

.4 Version 2.0

First, a statistic: the GIMP code base contains about 230,000 lines of C code, and most of these lines were rewritten in the evolution from 1.2 to 2.0. From the user's point of view, however, GIMP 2 is fundamentally similar to GIMP 1; the features are similar enough that GIMP 1 users won't be lost. As part of the restructuring work, the developers cleaned up the code greatly, an investment that, while not directly visible to the user, will ease maintenance and make future additions less painful. Thus, the GIMP 2 code base is significantly better organized and more maintainable than was the case for GIMP 1.2.

Basic tools The basic tools in GIMP 2 are not very different from their predecessors in GIMP 1. The "Select Regions by Color" tool is now shown in the GIMP toolbox, but was already included in GIMP 1 as a menu option in the Select menu. The Transform tool has been divided into several specialized tools: Rotation, Scale, Shearing and Perspective. Color operations are now associated with layers in the menu Layer → Colors, but this is merely a cleanup: they were already present in the Image menu (illogically, since they are layer operations). Thus no completely new tools appear in this release, but two of the tools have been totally revamped compared to the older versions: the Text tool and the Path tool. More on this below.

The user interface for tools has also changed significantly. The "Tool Options" dialog box was modified to not resize itself when a new tool is chosen. Most users felt that the window changing size when a new tool was selected was annoying. Now, by default the "Tool Options" dialog is constantly open and docked under the toolbox, where it can easily be found.

Tool options The "Tool Options" for many tools have new possibilities that weren't available in GIMP 1. Without being exhaustive, here are the most noticeable improvements.

All selection tools now have mode buttons: Replace, Add, Subtract and Intersect. In GIMP 1 the only way to change the selection mode was to use the **Ctrl** or **Shift** buttons, which could get very confusing because those buttons also had other functions. For example, pressing and holding the **Shift** key while using the Rectangle selection tool forces the rectangle to be a square. Thus, to add a square selection you would first press **Shift**, then click the mouse, then release **Shift**, then press **Shift** again, then sweep out the selection with the mouse, then release **Shift**. It can now be done more easily.

For transformation tools, buttons now control which object (layer, selection or path) is affected by the transformation. You can for example transform a rectangular selection to various quadrilateral shapes. Path transformation in particular is now easier than it was before.

"Fade out" and "Paint Using Gradient" are now available for all drawing tools. In fact, all drawing tools now have their own individual brush, gradient and pattern settings, in contrast to GIMP 1 where there was a single global setting that applied to all drawing tools. Now you can select different brushes for the Pencil and the Paint Brush, or different patterns for the Clone and Fill tools. You can change these setting by using your mouse wheel over the relevant resource button (this is most useful for quickly and easily choosing a brush).

User Interface The most visible changes in GIMP 2 concern the user interface. GIMP now uses the GTK2+ graphical toolkit in place of GTK+. One of the nice features brought by the new libraries is dockable dialogs, and tab navigation between dialogs docked in the same window — a feature present in several popular web browsers. GIMP 1 was famous for opening dialogs anywhere on your screen; GIMP 2 can be told to use fixed boxes. Dialogs now include a little tab-customization menu, which provides maximum flexibility in organizing your workspace.

The Image window has some interesting new features. These are not necessarily activated by default, but they can be checked as options in the Preferences → Interface → Image Windows menu. "Show Brush Outline", for example, allows you to see the outline of the brush when using drawing tools. In the "Appearance" sub-section, you can toggle whether a menu bar is present at the top of image windows. You can set an option to work with the new fullscreen mode. Viewing options are also available from all image windows using right click to bring up the menu, then selecting "View". The so-called "image" menu is also available by clicking on a little triangle in the top left corner of the drawing space. The setting you choose in the "Preferences" dialog is used as the default value, and options you set from an image are used only for that image. (You can also toggle fullscreen mode by using the **F11** key; the **Esc** key also exits fullscreen mode).

GIMP 2 features keyboard accelerators to ease menu access. If you find that navigating through menus using your mouse is onerous, the solution may be to use the keyboard. For example, if the menu bar is present, to create a new image just hit Alt-F-N. Without the menu bar, hit Shift-F10 to open the top-left menu, and use direction keys or **F** then **N** to create the new image. Keyboard accelerators are different from shortcuts: accelerators are useful to navigate through menus, whereas shortcuts call a specific menu item directly. For example, Ctrl-N is a shortcut, and the quickest way to open a new image.

To ease access to your most commonly used menu items, the GIMP has provided dynamic shortcuts for many years. When a menu is open, you can hover over the desired menu item and hold down your shortcut combination. This feature is still present, but is deactivated by default in the GIMP 2.0, to avoid accidental re-assigning of existing shortcuts.

The GIMP also ships with a number of sets of key-bindings for its menus. If you would like to replace the default GIMP keybindings by Photoshop bindings, for example, you can move the file `menurc` in your user data directory to `oldmenurc`, rename `ps-menurc` to `menurc` and restart GIMP.

Handling Tabs and Docks The GIMP 2.0 introduces a system of tabbed dialogs to allow you to make your workspace look the way you want it to be. Almost all dialogs can be dragged to another dialog window and dropped to make a tabbed dialog set.

Furthermore, at the bottom of each dialog, there is a dockable area: drag and drop tabs here to attach dialogs beneath the bottom tab group.

Scripting "Python-fu" is now the standard external scripting interface for GIMP 2. This means that you can now use GIMP functions in Python scripts, or conversely use Python to write GIMP plug-ins. Python is relatively easy to understand even for a beginner, especially in comparison to the Lisp-like Scheme language used for Script-Fu in GIMP 1. The Python bindings are augmented by a set of classes for common operations, so you are not forced to search through the complete GIMP Procedural Database in order to carry out basic operations. Moreover, Python has integrated development environments and a gigantic library, and runs not only on Linux but also on Microsoft Windows and Apples Mac OS X. The biggest drawback, for GIMP 2.0, is that the standard user interface offered in Python-fu does not use the complete power of the Python language. The interface is currently designed to support simple scripts, but a more sophisticated version is a goal of future development.

GIMP-Perl is no longer distributed with the standard GIMP 2 distribution, but is available as a separate package. Currently, GIMP-Perl is supported only on Unix-like operating systems. It includes both a simple scripting language, and the ability to code more polished interfaces using the Gtk2 perl module. Direct pixel manipulation is available through the use of PDL.

Script-Fu, based on "Scheme", has the same drawbacks as before: not intuitive, hard to use and lacking a real development environment. It does, however, have one major advantage compared to Python-fu: Script-Fu scripts are directly interpreted by GIMP and do not require any additional software installation. Python-fu requires that you install a package for the Python language.

The Text Tool The big problem with the standard text tool in GIMP 1 was that text could not be modified after it was rendered. If you wanted to change anything about the text, all you could do was "undo" and try again (if you were lucky enough to have sufficient undo history available, and then of course you would also undo any other work you had done in the meantime). In GIMP 1.2 there was also a "dynamic text" plug-in that allowed you to create special text layers and keep them around indefinitely, in a modifiable form, but it was buggy and awkward to use. The second generation Text tool is an enhanced combination of the old Text tool and the Dynamic Text plugin. Now all options are available in the "Tool Options" : font, font size, text color, justify, antialiasing, indent, spacing. To create a new text item, click in the image and a little editor pops up. Text appears on the image while you are editing (and carriage returns are handled properly!). A new dedicated layer is created; this layer resizes dynamically to match the text you key in. You can import plain text from a file, and you can even do things like writing from right to left in Arabic. If you select a text layer, clicking on it opens the editor, and you can then modify your text.

The Path Tool The second generation Path tool has a completely new interface. The first major difference you notice is that paths are no longer required to be closed. A path can be made up of a number of disjoint curve segments. The next major difference is that now the path tool has three different modes, Design, Edit and Move.

In Design mode, you can create a path, add nodes to an existing path and modify the shape of a curve either by dragging edges of the curve or dragging the "handles" of a node.

In Edit mode, you can add nodes in the middle of curve edges, and remove nodes or edges, as well as change the shape of the curve. You can also connect two path components.

The third mode, Move, is, as you might expect, used to move path components. If your path has several components, you can move each path component separately. To move all components at once, use the **Shift** key.

Two other path-related features are new in the GIMP 2.0. The GIMP can not only import an SVG image as a raster image, but can also keep SVG paths intact as GIMP paths. This means that the GIMP is now more able than ever to complement your favorite vector drawing tool. The other feature which has made the path tool much better is the introduction of vector-based stroking. In previous versions, stroking paths and selections was a matter of drawing a brush-stroke along the path. This mode is still available, but it is now possible to stroke a curve accurately, using the vector library libart.

Other improvements Some other improvements in brief:

- Higher-quality antialiasing in some places — most notibly in the Text tool.

- Icons and menus are skinnable. You can create your own icon set and apply it to the toolbox using the Preference → Interface menu option. A theme called "small" is included with the standard distribution.

- An image can be saved as a template and used to create new images.

- There are four new combination modes for layers that lie one on top of another within an image: "Hard Light", "Soft Light", "Grain Extract" and "Grain Merge".

- If there is an active selection, you can crop the image directly to the selection size using image menu Image → Crop.

- As well as being able to create guides, there's now a grid functionality in GIMP. It is complementary to the guides functionality and makes it easier to position objects so that they align perfectly.

- The Layers dialog is more coherent, in that there are no more hidden functions accessed only with right click on the miniature image of the layer that appears there. You can now handle layer operations directly from the image menu: Layer Mask, Transparency, Transformation and Layer Color operations are directly in the Layer submenu.

- Color display filters are now available from the image menu View → Display Filters. Using them, you can simulate different gamma values, different contrasts, or even color deficient vision, without altering your original image. This actually has been a feature of the GIMP developer versions for a long time, but it has never been stable enough to appear in a stable version of the GIMP before.

- The color selection dialog has a new CMYK mode, associated with the printer icon.

- Data stored in EXIF tags by digital cameras are now handled in read and write mode for JPEG files.

- MNG animations are now supported. The MNG file format can be considered as animated PNG. It has all the advantages of PNG over GIF, such as more colors, 256 levels of transparency, and perhaps most importantly, lack of patent encumbrance. The format is a web standard and all recent popular web browsers support it.

- The GIMP Animation package now does onion-skinning, a bluescreen feature was added as well as audio support.

- A channel mixer filter, previously available from the web as an add-on, appears in Filters → Colors.

.5 What's New in GIMP 2.2?

Here is a brief summary of some of the most important new features introduced in GIMP 2.2. There are many other smaller changes that long-time users will notice and appreciate (or complain about!). There are also important changes at the level of plug-in programming and script-fu creating that are not covered here.

Interoperability and Standards Support

- You can drag-and-drop or copy-and-paste image data from the GIMP to any application which supports image/png drops (currently Abiword and Kword at least) and image/xml+svg drops (Inkscape supports this one). So you can copy-and-paste curves into the GIMP from Inkscape, and then drag a selection into Abiword to include it inline in your document.

- Patterns can now be any supported GtkPixbuf format, including png, jpeg, xbm and others.

- GIMP can load gradients from SVG files, and palettes from ACT and RIFF files.

- Drag-and-drop support has been extended. You can now drop files and URIs onto an image window, where they will be opened in the existing image as new layers.

> Note
>
> Please note, that Drag and Drop will not work for Apple Mac OS X between GIMP and the finder. This is due to a lack of functionality on Apples X11.app

Shortcut Editor You can now edit your shortcuts in a dedicated dialog, as well as continue to use the little-known dynamic shortcuts feature (which has been there since 1.2).

Plug-in Previews We have provided a standard preview widget for plug-in authors which greatly reduces the amount of code required to support previews. David Odin has integrated this widget into all the current filters, so that now many more filters in the GIMP include a preview which updates in real time, and the various previews behave much more consistently.

Real-Time Previews of Transform Operations The transform tools (shear, scale, perspective and rotate) can now show a real-time preview of the result of the operation when the tool is in "Traditional" mode. Previously, only a transforming grid was shown.

GNOME Human Interface Guide Conformance A lot of work has been done on making the GIMP's interface simpler and more usable for newcomers. Most dialogs now follows the GNOME HIG to the best of our knowledge. In addition, dialogs have separated out or removed many "Advanced" options, and replaced them with sane defaults or hidden them in an expander.

GTK+ 2.4 Migration

- Menus use the GtkUIManager to generate menu structure dynamically from XML data files.

- A completely revamped File Chooser is used everywhere in the GIMP for opening or saving files. The best thing about it is that it lets you create a set of "bookmarks", making it possible to navigate quickly and easily to commonly used directories.

- GIMP now supports fancy ARGB cursors when they are available on the system.

Basic Vector Support Using the GFig plug-in, the GIMP now supports the basic functionality of vector layers. The GFig plug-in supports a number of vector graphics features such as gradient fills, Bezier curves and curve stroking. It is also the easiest way to create regular or irregular polygons in the GIMP. In the GIMP 2.2, you can create GFig layers, and re-edit these layers in GFig afterwards. This level of vector support is still quite primitive, however, in comparison to dedicated vector-graphics programs such as Inkscape.

Also . . . There are many other smaller user-visible features. A rapid-fire list of some of those features is below.

- It is now possible to run the GIMP in batch mode without an X server.

- We have a GIMP binary (GIMP-console) which is not linked to GTK+ at all.

- Improved interface for extended input devices

- Editable toolbox: You can now decide which tools should be shown in the Toolbox, and their order. In particular, you can add any or all of the Color Tools to the Toolbox if you wish to.

- Histogram overlays R, G and B histograms on the Value histogram, and calculates the histogram only for the contents of the selection.

- Shortcuts are now shared across all GIMP windows.

.6 What's New in GIMP 2.4?

Refreshed Look A whole new default icon theme has been created for 2.4. The icons comply with the Tango style guidelines so GIMP doesn't feel out of place on any of the supported platforms. Regardless of whether you run GIMP under Microsoft Windows, Mac OS X or Linux (GNOME, KDE or Xfce), GIMP provides a polished, consistent look.

Figure 5 New Look of the toolbox in GIMP 2.4

Additionally the icons also have enhanced usability on dark widget themes, which is a common setting among digital artists.

For artists preferring more desaturated color theme for their icons is an alternative icon theme available for download [JIMMAC01].

Scalable Brushes The tool options now include a brush size slider that affects both the parametric and bitmap brushes. This has been an oft-requested feature from both digital painters and photo editors.

Figure 6 Scalable brushes in GIMP 2.4

Unlike previous versions of GIMP, regardless of whether you're using a bitmap brush, parametric brush or even a picture tube (multiple bitmaps), you can easily set the brush size with either the tool options dock slider or an external device such as a MIDI slider or knob or a USB device like the Griffin Powermate.

Selection Tools The selection tools have been rewritten from scratch to allow resizing of existing selections. Additionally the rectangular selection tool includes a setting for creating rounded corners as this has been identified as a very common task among web designers.

Figure 7 Selection tools in GIMP 2.4

The learning curve for the tools has been flattened as the key functionality is available without obscure shortcuts that confused GIMP beginners. Most of the existing shortcuts still work, but the functionality is either available through the tool options or made obsolete due to the interactive move and resize on canvas.

While the tools have been redesigned to make them easier to understand for the newbies, all the former functionality is there. You can still constrain aspect ratios or specific sizes.

Foreground Select Tool Selecting individual objects on images is easier now with a new foreground select tool. It is done in two steps. First, you make select region of interest which contains the entire object. Then you paint over selected area with a brush, not crossing object's border. Release mouse button when you're done and look, if there are dark blue spots on your objects. If there are some, paint with a brush over them again and release to refine selection. When there are no more blue areas inside the object, press Enter and there you have a perfectly selected object.

Align Tool While GIMP has provided a grid and guideline functionality, the actual alignment of objects had to be done manually. A new tool comes at rescue ...

Changes in menus Most notable is the new top-level Color menu that accumulates most tools, plug-ins and scripts that adjust colors in RGB/Grayscale mode and color palettes in Indexed mode. So now you can reach functions like Levels or Curves much faster than before, unless you define your own keyboard shortcuts for them using the improved keyboard shortcuts manager.

In the new version of GIMP, some menu entries have changed their names and position. It was done mostly to simplify learning curve and improve user experience. After all, "HSV Noise" and "RGB Noise" sound more meaningful than "Scatter HSV" and "Scatter RGB", don't they? And status bar hints for all plug-ins and scripts are quite helpful too.

Support for file formats

- Support for Photoshop ABR brush format;
- Improved reading/writing EXIF in JPEG;
- Importing clipping paths in TIFF;
- Layer masks can be saved to PSD;

893

- 16/32 bit bitmaps and alpha-channel support in BMP;
- 24 bit and Vista icons can be opened and saved.

Fullscreen Editing The fullscreen mode has been improved to not only allow getting a full scale preview of the artwork, but also allow comfortable editing. The artist has maximum screen estate available while all functionality is quickly accessible by pressing the **Tab** key (toggles visibility of all docks) when working fullscreen.

Whether painting or touching up photos, fullscreen editing keeps all the distracting elements out of sight on a key press. It's like observing stars in a field as opposed to a light-polluted city.

Color Management and Soft-proofing GIMP now provides full support for color profiles allowing precise color modification throughout the whole "digital darkroom" process.

Figure 8 Color management in GIMP 2.4

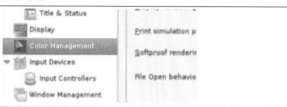

New Crop Tool Just like the selection tools, the new crop tool has been enhanced since the last release. The resize handles actually resize the crop rectangle instead of providing both resize and move functionality. The tool behaves more naturally and consistently with other GIMP tools. For details see Section 14.4.4.

To move, simply drag the rectangle clicking within the area. Resizing is possible in one or two axes at the same time dragging the handle-bars on the sides and corners. The outside area is darkened with a nice passepartout effect to better get the idea of how the final crop will look like.

Red Eye Removal While numerous red-eye workflows exist already, GIMP now features a very convenient auto-magic filter to remove red eye from your shots.

Healing Brush The healing brush is a new tool, similar in the working of the clone tool, that permits to quickly fix small defects or imperfections due to scratching or dust. In fact the tool is smart enough to being able to *understand* where and how to modify an image to cure these defects based on image color context.

Perspective Clone Here is another clone-like new tool that is able to adapt the destination geometry, instead of color as does the healing brush, based on preselected distortion settings. As the name suggests, perfect when copying images blocks with some type of prospective changes.

Lens Distortion A very common problem exposing itself especially when using cheaper lenses is barrel distortion and vignetting. Luckily GIMP provides a brand new filter to compensate for both problems. Saving photographer's pocket is our mission!

Various Other Improvements In addition to all the above, GIMP has been improved in other areas such as:

- Better status information for tools in the window status bar.
- Various speedups in composing functions and gradient drawing.
- Zoomable preview widget for plugins.

.7 What's New in GIMP 2.6?

GIMP 2.6 is an important release from a development point of view. It features changes to the user interface addressing some often received complaints, and a tentative integration of GEGL, the graph based image processing library that will eventually bring high bit-depth and non-destructive editing to GIMP.

User Interface

Toolbox Menubar removed The toolbox menubar has been removed and merged with the image window menubar. To be able to do this a window called the empty image window has been introduced. It hosts the menubar and keeps the application instance alive when no images are opened. It also acts as a drag and drop target. When opening the first image the empty image window is transformed into a normal image window, and when closing the last image, that window becomes the empty image window.

Figure 9 New Look of the image window in GIMP 2.6

Toolbox and docks are utility windows With the empty image window acting as a natural main window, the Toolbox and Docks windows are now utility windows rather than main windows. This enables window managers to do a much better job of managing the GIMP windows, including omitting the Toolbox and Docks from the taskbar and ensuring that the Toolbox and Docks always are above image windows.

Ability to scroll beyond image border The Navigation dialog now allows panning beyond the image border; so it is no longer a problem to use a brush on the edge of an image that fills the entire display window. Also, if a utility window covers the image, you can pan the image to view or edit the portion covered by the utility window.

Figure 10 Scrolling beyond border

Minor changes

- Renamed Dialogs menu to Windows.

- Keep a list of recently closed Docks and allow reopening them.

- Make opening images in already running GIMP instances work better on Windows.

- You can now enter the image zoom ratio directly in the status bar.

- Added support for using online help instead of a locally installed GIMP Help package.

- Make it possible to lock tabs in docks to prevent accidental moving.

Tools, Filters and Plug-ins

Improved Free Select Tool The freehand select tool has been enhanced to support polygonal selections. It also allows mixing free hand segments with polygonal segments, editing of existing segments, applying angle-constraints to segments, and of course the normal selection tool operations like add and subtract. Altogether this ends up making the Free Select Tool a very versatile, powerful and easy-to-use selection tool.

Figure 11 Polygonal Selection

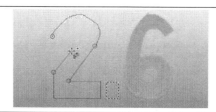

Brush Dynamics Brush dynamics uses an input dynamic such as pressure, velocity, or random, to modify brush parameters such as opacity, hardness, size, or color; every brush supports size and opacity, most support more. Velocity and random are usable with a mouse. The Ink tool, that supported velocity, has been overhauled to better handle velocity-dependent painting.

Figure 12 Brush Dynamics

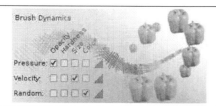

Brush dynamics have enabled a new feature in stroking paths. There is now a check box under the "paint tool" option, for emulating brush dynamics if you stroke using a paint tool. What this means is that when your stroke is painted, GIMP tells the brush that the pressure and velocity are varying along the length of the stroke. Pressure starts with no pressure, ramps up to full pressure, and then ramps down again to no pressure. Velocity starts from zero and ramps up to full speed by the end of the stroke.

Minor changes

- Added a bounding box for the Text Tool that supports automatic wrapping of text within that bounding box.

Figure 13 Text tool bounding box

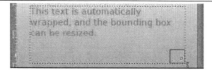

- Move handles for rectangle based tools like Crop and Rectangle Select to the outside of the rectangle when the rectangle is narrow.

Figure 14 Rectangle handles

- Added motion constraints to the Move Tool.
- Improved event smoothing for paint tools.
- Mark the center of rectangles while they are moved, and snap the center to grid and rulers.
- Enable brush scaling for the Smudge tool.
- Added ability to save presets in all color tools for color adjustments you use frequently.

- Allow to transfer settings from *Brightness-Contrast* to *Levels*, and from *Levels* to *Curves*.

- Allow changing opacity on transform tool previews.

- The Screenshot plug-in has been given the ability to capture the mouse cursor (using Xfixes).

- Display aspect ratio of the Crop and Rectangle Select Tool rectangles in the status bar.

- Desaturate has been given an on-canvas preview.

- The Flame plug-in has been extended with 22 new variations.

- Data file folders like brush folders are searched recursively for files.

- Replaced the PSD import plug-in with a rewritten version that does what the old version did plus some other things, for example reading of ICC color profiles.

- Several displays use Cairo library.

Figure 15 Comparing 2.6 display vs 2.4

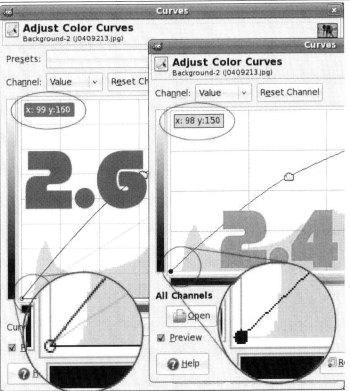

Under the Hood

GEGL Important progress towards high bit-depth and non-destructive editing in GIMP has been made. Most color operations in GIMP are now ported to the powerful graph based image processing framework GEGL [GEGL], meaning that the internal processing is done in 32bit floating point linear light RGBA. By default the legacy 8bit code paths are still used, but a curious user can turn on the use of GEGL for the color operations with Colors / Use GEGL.

In addition to porting color operations to GEGL, an experimental GEGL Operation tool has been added, found in the Tools menu. It enables applying GEGL operations to an image and it gives on-canvas previews of the results. The screenshot below shows this for a Gaussian Blur.

Figure 16 GEGL operation

Minor changes Ported many widgets to use the 2D graphics library cairo [CAIRO] for drawing. See this comparison for an example of how much better this looks.

Miscellaneous

Plug-in Development There are new things for a plug-in developer to enjoy as well. For example, procedures can now give a detailed error description in case of an error, and the error can be propagated to the user.

GIMP 2.6 also further enhances its scripting abilities. In particular there is now a much richer API for the creation and manipulation of text layers. Here is a list of new symbols in GIMP 2.6: [GIMP-NEWSYM26].

Backwards Compatibility Some old scripts could not be used with GIMP-2.4. This has been improved and 2.6 should run 2.0 and 2.2 scripts.

Known Problems

- The Utility window hint is currently only known to work well in the Linux GNOME desktop environment and on Windows starting with GIMP 2.6.1.

- Using the Text Tool is currently not an optimal experience. Making it work better is a goal for GIMP 2.8.

- If you build GIMP yourself and don't have GVfs support on your platform you need to explicitly pass `--without-gvfs` to **configure**, otherwise opening remote files will not work properly.

Part VII

Reporting Bugs and Requesting Enhancements

Sad to say, no version of GIMP has yet been absolutely perfect. Even sadder, it is likely that no version ever will be. In spite of all efforts to make everything work, a program as complicated as GIMP is bound to screw things up occasionally, or even crash.

But the fact that bugs are unavoidable does not mean that they should be passively accepted. If you find a bug in GIMP, the developers would like to know about it so they can at least try to fix it.

Suppose, then, that you have found a bug, or at least think you have: you try to do something, and the results are not what you expect. What should you do? How should you report it?

Tip

The procedure for making an *enhancement request*—that is, for asking the developers to add a missing feature—is nearly the same as the procedure for reporting a bug. The only thing you do differently is to mark the report as an "enhancement" at the appropriate stage, as described below.

In common with many other free software projects, GIMP uses a bug-reporting mechanism called *Bugzilla*. This is a very powerful web-based system, capable of managing thousands of bug reports without losing track. In fact, GIMP shares its Bugzilla database with the entire Gnome project. At the time this is being written, Gnome Bugzilla contains 148632 bug reports–no, make that 148633.

.8 Making sure it's a Bug

The first thing you should do, before reporting a bug, is to make an effort to verify that what you are seeing really *is* a bug. It is hard to give a method for doing this that applies to all situations, but reading the documentation will often be useful, and discussing the question on IRC or a mailing list may also be quite helpful. If you are seeing a *crash*, as opposed to mere misbehavior, the odds that it is a true bug are pretty high: well written software programs are not designed to crash under *any* circumstances. In any case, if you have made an conscientious effort to decide whether it is really a bug, and at the end still aren't sure, then please go ahead and report it: the worst that can happen is that you will waste a bit of time for the development team.

Note

Actually there are a few things that are known to cause GIMP to crash but have turned out to be too inconvenient to be worth fixing. One of them is asking GIMP to do something that requires vast amounts of memory, such as creating an image one million pixels on a side.

You should also make sure that you are using an up-to-date version of GIMP: reporting bugs that have already been fixed is just a waste of everybody's time. (GIMP 1 is no longer maintained, so if you use it and find bugs, either upgrade to GIMP 2 or live with them.) Particularly if you are using the development version of GIMP, make sure that you can see the bug in the latest release before filing a report.

If after due consideration you still think you have a legitimate bug report or enhancement request, the next step is to go to GIMP's bugzilla query page (http://bugzilla.gnome.org/query.cgi), and try to see whether somebody else has already reported the same thing.

There are two forms you can use for searching bugs: a simple form to "Find a Specific Bug", and an "Advanced Search".

.8.1 Find a Specific Bug

Figure 17 Bugzilla: Find a Specific Bug

Searching for bugs using the simple bug search form

Using this form, you first should select the Product "GIMP" (classified as "Other") using the drop down list. Then you just have to enter some (space separated) search terms, e.g.

```
filter crash
```

in the text box and click on Search.

.8.2 The Advanced Bug Search Form

The alternative form, the advanced query page, allows you to search the bug database in a variety of ways:

Figure 18 Bugzilla: Advanced Search

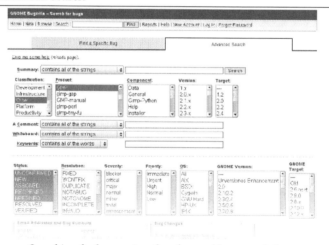

Searching for bugs using the advanced bug search form

Unfortunately this page is a bit more "complicated" to use than it really ought to be (at least, some items are hyperlinks leading to detailed help), but here is basically what you should do:

Summary Set this to "contains any of the words/strings".

In the adjoining text box, give one or more words that somebody would be likely to use in writing a one-sentence summary of a bug similar to yours. For example, if the problem is that zooming too much causes GIMP to crash, the word "zoom" would be good.

Classification Other (since GIMP is not part of the GNOME Desktop suite).

Product Set this to "GIMP" (or "GEGL", "GIMP-manual" etc., if appropriate).

Component, Version, Target Milestone Don't do anything for these.

Comment, Whiteboard, Keywords For now, leave this alone. If your search does not turn up anything, it might be worth entering your search terms in the "Comment" area here, but this often turns out to give you either great masses of stuff or nothing.

Status This field encodes the status of a bug report: whether it is still open, has been resolved, etc. You want to see all relevant bug reports, regardless of status, so you should hold down the mouse and sweep it across all entries. Leaving it alone will not work.

Resolution, Severity, Priority, OS Usually you shouldn't touch these items.

(Any other items) Don't do anything for these.

When you have set these things up, click on the "Search" button at either the top or bottom; they both do the same thing. The result is either a list of bug reports – hopefully not too long – or a message saying "Zarro boogs found". If you don't find a related bug report by doing this, it may be worth trying another search with different terms. If in spite of your best efforts, you file a bug report and it ends up being resolved as "Duplicate", don't be too upset: it has happened repeatedly to the author of this documentation, who works with GIMP Bugzilla nearly every day.

Tip

Depending on your browser configuration (i.e. whether JavaScript is enabled), you may see a link Give me some help. If you click on this link, the page will be reloaded and then moving the mouse pointer over an input widget produces a little help popup.

.9 Reporting the Bug

Okay, so you have done everything you could to make sure, and you still think it's probably a bug. You should then go ahead and file a bug report on the Bugzilla page.

Note

The first time you file a bug report, you will be asked to create a Bugzilla account. The process is easy and painless, and you probably won't even get any spam as a result.

---

1. Bugzilla: Select Classification

   Go to `http://bugzilla.gnome.org/enter_bug.cgi`, and select the classification "Other".

   If you are not logged in, you are automatically redirected to the login page. After entering your user name (login) and password, you get back to the "Select Classification" page.

2. Bugzilla: Pick Product

   Scroll down the next page until you can select the product "GIMP".

> **Tip**
>
> You can skip the above steps and go directly to `http://bugzilla.gnome.org/enter_bug.cgi?product=GIMP` (You still have to login, of course.)

3. Bugzilla: Enter Bug: GIMP

   Selecting "GIMP" as product takes you to the following bug report form, which you should fill out as follows. Note that most of the information you enter can be changed later by the developers if you get it wrong, so try to get it right but don't be obsessive about it.

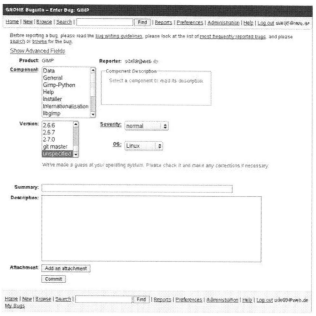

Enter Bug: GIMP

Component Set this to the part of GIMP that the bug affects. Note that you get a short "Component Description" in the text box next to the list when you select a component.

   You have to pick something here, but if you aren't sure, make a guess and don't worry about it.

Version Set this to the version of GIMP that you are using. You always find the version in the menu of the image window: Help → About.

Severity In most cases you should either leave this as "Normal" or set it to "Enhancement", if it is an enhancement request rather than a malfunction. The maintainers will adjust the severity if they think it is warranted.

OS (Operating System) Set this to your OS unless you have a very good reason for thinking that the bug applies to all operating systems.

Summary Give a one-sentence summary that is descriptive enough so that somebody searching for similar bugs would find your bug report on the basis of the words this summary contains.

Description Describe the problem. Be as specific as you can, and include all information that you think might possibly be relevant. The classic totally useless bug report is, "GIMP crashes. This program sucks". There is no hope that the developers can solve a problem if they can't tell what it is.

There are more fields which are hidden by default. (Click "Show Advanced Fields" to show them.) You can ignore them, so we won't describe these fields here.

Sometimes it is very helpful to augment a bug report with a screenshot or some other type of data. If you need to do this, click on the button Add an attachment, and follow the directions. But please don't do this unless you think the attachment is really going to be useful—and if you need to attach a screenshot, don't make it any larger than necessary. Bug reports are likely to remain on the system for years, so there is no sense in wasting memory.

When you have filled out all of these things, press the Commit button and your bug report will be submitted. It will be assigned a number, which you may want to make note of; you will, however, be emailed any time somebody makes a comment on your bug report or otherwise alters it, so you will receive reminders in any case. You can see the current state of your bug report at any time by going to `http://bugzilla.gnome.org`, entering the bug number in one of the entry boxes and pressing the Find or Quick Search button.

.10 What Happens to a Bug Report after you Submit it

At any time after it is submitted, a bug report has a "Status" that describes how it is currently being handled. Here are the possible values of *Status* and what they mean:

Unconfirmed This is the initial status of a bug report, from the time it is submitted until one of the maintainers reads it and decides whether it is really a valid bug report. Sometimes the maintainers aren't sure, and in the meantime leave the status as "Unconfirmed". In the worst cases, a bug report can stay unconfirmed for a year or longer, but this is considered a bad thing and does not happen very often.

New This means that the bug report has been read by one of the maintainers, and is considered, for the moment at least, to be valid. It does not necessarily mean that anything is going to be done about it immediately: some bug reports, especially enhancement requests, may be perfectly valid and still go for a long time before anybody is able to deal with them. Many bugs, on the other hand, are fixed within hours of being reported.

Assigned This means that a specific person has agreed to work on the bug. It does not, this world being the kind of world that it is, mean that that person will actually *do* anything in particular, so for practical purposes this status means nearly the same thing as "New".

Reopened This means that the bug report was at some point considered by the maintainers to be resolved (i.e., finished), but new information came in that caused them to change their minds: most likely, a change that was intended to fix the problem did not completely work.

Needinfo This is a status you should pay particular attention to. It means that you did not supply enough information in your bug report to enable anything to be done about it. In most cases, no further action will be taken on the bug report until you supply additional information (by adding a comment). If too much time goes by without any input from you, the bug report will eventually be resolved as "Incomplete".

Resolved This means that the maintainers believe that they have finished dealing with the bug report. If you disagree, you can re-open it, but since you cannot force anybody to work on a bug against their will, you should have a good reason for doing so. Bugs can be resolved in a variety of ways. Here are the possible values of *Resolution* and what they mean:

> **Fixed** The bug report is considered valid, and GIMP has been changed in a way that is considered to fix it.

> **Wontfix** The maintainers agree that the bug report is valid, but it would take so much effort to fix, in relation to its importance, that it is not worth the trouble.

> **Duplicate** This means that the same bug has already been reported by somebody else. If you see this resolution, you will also see a pointer to the earlier bug report, which will often give you a lot of useful information.

> **Notabug** This means that the behavior described in the bug report is intentional. It may seem like a bug to you (and there may be many people who agree with you), but the program is working the way it was intended to work, and the developers don't want to change it.

> **NotGnome** The bug report is valid, but it can't be addressed by changing GIMP. Problems in operating systems, window managers, or libraries that GIMP depends on will often be given this resolution. Sometimes the next appropriate step is to file a bug report for the software that is really at fault.

Incomplete The bug report did not contain enough information for anything to be done about it, and the reporter did not respond to requests for more information. Usually a bug report will be open for at least a month or two before it is resolved in this way.

Invalid Something is wrong with the form of the bug report: most commonly, the reporter has accidentally submitted the same bug report multiple times. (This can easily happen by mistake with some web browsers.) Bug reports that incorrectly describe how the program behaves may also be resolved as Invalid.

Note

 If you disagree with the resolution of a bug report, you are always free to add your comments to it. Any comment added to any bug report, resolved or not, causes email to be sent to the GIMP Bugzilla mailing list, so it will at least be seen by the maintainers. This does not, of course, mean that they will necessarily respond to it.

Part VIII

GNU Free Documentation License

Note that any translations of the GNU Free Documentation License are not published by the Free Software Foundation, and do not legally state the distribution terms for software that uses the GNU FDL-only the original English text of the GNU FDL does that.

The GIMP Documentation Team

Copyright (C) 2000,2001,2002 Free Software Foundation, Inc. 59 Temple Place, Suite 330, Boston, MA 02111-1307 USA. Everyone is permitted to copy and distribute verbatim copies of this license document, but changing it is not allowed.

.11 PREAMBLE

The purpose of this License is to make a manual, textbook, or other functional and useful document "free" in the sense of freedom: to assure everyone the effective freedom to copy and redistribute it, with or without modifying it, either commercially or noncommercially. Secondarily, this License preserves for the author and publisher a way to get credit for their work, while not being considered responsible for modifications made by others.

This License is a kind of "copyleft", which means that derivative works of the document must themselves be free in the same sense. It complements the GNU General Public License, which is a copyleft license designed for free software.

We have designed this License in order to use it for manuals for free software, because free software needs free documentation: a free program should come with manuals providing the same freedoms that the software does. But this License is not limited to software manuals; it can be used for any textual work, regardless of subject matter or whether it is published as a printed book. We recommend this License principally for works whose purpose is instruction or reference.

.12 APPLICABILITY AND DEFINITIONS

This License applies to any manual or other work, in any medium, that contains a notice placed by the copyright holder saying it can be distributed under the terms of this License. Such a notice grants a world-wide, royalty-free license, unlimited in duration, to use that work under the conditions stated herein. The "Document", below, refers to any such manual or work. Any member of the public is a licensee, and is addressed as "you". You accept the license if you copy, modify or distribute the work in a way requiring permission under copyright law.

A "Modified Version" of the Document means any work containing the Document or a portion of it, either copied verbatim, or with modifications and/or translated into another language.

A "Secondary Section" is a named appendix or a front-matter section of the Document that deals exclusively with the relationship of the publishers or authors of the Document to the Document's overall subject (or to related matters) and contains nothing that could fall directly within that overall subject. (Thus, if the Document is in part a textbook of mathematics, a Secondary Section may not explain any mathematics.) The relationship could be a matter of historical connection with the subject or with related matters, or of legal, commercial, philosophical, ethical or political position regarding them.

The "Invariant Sections" are certain Secondary Sections whose titles are designated, as being those of Invariant Sections, in the notice that says that the Document is released under this License. If a section does not fit the above definition of Secondary then it is not allowed to be designated as Invariant. The Document may contain zero Invariant Sections. If the Document does not identify any Invariant Sections then there are none.

The "Cover Texts" are certain short passages of text that are listed, as Front-Cover Texts or Back-Cover Texts, in the notice that says that the Document is released under this License. A Front-Cover Text may be at most 5 words, and a Back-Cover Text may be at most 25 words.

A "Transparent" copy of the Document means a machine-readable copy, represented in a format whose specification is available to the general public, that is suitable for revising the document straight-forwardly with generic text editors or (for images composed of pixels) generic paint programs or (for drawings) some widely available drawing editor, and that is suitable for input to text formatters or for automatic translation to a variety of formats suitable for input to text formatters. A copy made in an otherwise Transparent file format whose markup, or absence of markup, has been arranged to thwart or discourage subsequent modification by readers is not Transparent. An image format is not Transparent if used for any substantial amount of text. A copy that is not "Transparent" is called "Opaque".

Examples of suitable formats for Transparent copies include plain ASCII without markup, Texinfo input format, LaTeX input format, SGML or XML using a publicly available DTD, and standard-conforming simple HTML, PostScript or PDF designed for human modification. Examples of transparent image formats include PNG, XCF and JPG. Opaque formats include proprietary formats that can be read and edited only by proprietary word processors, SGML or XML for which the DTD and/or processing tools are not generally available, and the machine-generated HTML, PostScript or PDF produced by some word processors for output purposes only.

The "Title Page" means, for a printed book, the title page itself, plus such following pages as are needed to hold, legibly, the material this License requires to appear in the title page. For works in formats which do not have any title page as such, "Title Page" means the text near the most prominent appearance of the work's title, preceding the beginning of the body of the text.

A section "Entitled XYZ" means a named subunit of the Document whose title either is precisely XYZ or contains XYZ in parentheses following text that translates XYZ in another language. (Here XYZ stands for a specific section name mentioned below, such as "Acknowledgements", "Dedications", "Endorsements", or "History".) To "Preserve the Title" of such a section when you modify the Document means that it remains a section "Entitled XYZ" according to this definition.

The Document may include Warranty Disclaimers next to the notice which states that this License applies to the Document. These Warranty Disclaimers are considered to be included by reference in this License, but only as regards disclaiming warranties: any other implication that these Warranty Disclaimers may have is void and has no effect on the meaning of this License.

.13   VERBATIM COPYING

You may copy and distribute the Document in any medium, either commercially or noncommercially, provided that this License, the copyright notices, and the license notice saying this License applies to the Document are reproduced in all copies, and that you add no other conditions whatsoever to those of this License. You may not use technical measures to obstruct or control the reading or further copying of the copies you make or distribute. However, you may accept compensation in exchange for copies. If you distribute a large enough number of copies you must also follow the conditions in section 4.

You may also lend copies, under the same conditions stated above, and you may publicly display copies.

.14   COPYING IN QUANTITY

If you publish printed copies (or copies in media that commonly have printed covers) of the Document, numbering more than 100, and the Document's license notice requires Cover Texts, you must enclose the copies in covers that carry, clearly and legibly, all these Cover Texts: Front-Cover Texts on the front cover, and Back-Cover Texts on the back cover. Both covers must also clearly and legibly identify you as the publisher of these copies. The front cover must present the full title with all words of the title equally prominent and visible. You may add other material on the covers in addition. Copying with changes limited to the covers, as long as they preserve the title of the Document and satisfy these conditions, can be treated as verbatim copying in other respects.

If the required texts for either cover are too voluminous to fit legibly, you should put the first ones listed (as many as fit reasonably) on the actual cover, and continue the rest onto adjacent pages.

If you publish or distribute Opaque copies of the Document numbering more than 100, you must either include a machine-readable Transparent copy along with each Opaque copy, or state in or with each Opaque copy a computer-network location from which the general network-using public has access to download using public-standard network protocols a complete Transparent copy of the Document, free of added material. If you use the latter option, you must take reasonably prudent steps, when you begin distribution of Opaque copies in quantity, to ensure that this Transparent copy will remain thus accessible at the stated location until at least one year after the last time you distribute an Opaque copy (directly or through your agents or retailers) of that edition to the public.

It is requested, but not required, that you contact the authors of the Document well before redistributing any large number of copies, to give them a chance to provide you with an updated version of the Document.

.15 MODIFICATIONS

You may copy and distribute a Modified Version of the Document under the conditions of sections 3 and 4 above, provided that you release the Modified Version under precisely this License, with the Modified Version filling the role of the Document, thus licensing distribution and modification of the Modified Version to whoever possesses a copy of it. In addition, you must do these things in the Modified Version:

A. Use in the Title Page (and on the covers, if any) a title distinct from that of the Document, and from those of previous versions (which should, if there were any, be listed in the History section of the Document). You may use the same title as a previous version if the original publisher of that version gives permission.

B. List on the Title Page, as authors, one or more persons or entities responsible for authorship of the modifications in the Modified Version, together with at least five of the principal authors of the Document (all of its principal authors, if it has fewer than five), unless they release you from this requirement.

C. State on the Title page the name of the publisher of the Modified Version, as the publisher.

D. Preserve all the copyright notices of the Document.

E. Add an appropriate copyright notice for your modifications adjacent to the other copyright notices.

F. Include, immediately after the copyright notices, a license notice giving the public permission to use the Modified Version under the terms of this License, in the form shown in the Addendum below.

G. Preserve in that license notice the full lists of Invariant Sections and required Cover Texts given in the Document's license notice.

H. Include an unaltered copy of this License.

I. Preserve the section Entitled "History", Preserve its Title, and add to it an item stating at least the title, year, new authors, and publisher of the Modified Version as given on the Title Page. If there is no section Entitled "History" in the Document, create one stating the title, year, authors, and publisher of the Document as given on its Title Page, then add an item describing the Modified Version as stated in the previous sentence.

J. Preserve the network location, if any, given in the Document for public access to a Transparent copy of the Document, and likewise the network locations given in the Document for previous versions it was based on. These may be placed in the "History" section. You may omit a network location for a work that was published at least four years before the Document itself, or if the original publisher of the version it refers to gives permission.

K. For any section Entitled "Acknowledgements" or "Dedications", Preserve the Title of the section, and preserve in the section all the substance and tone of each of the contributor acknowledgements and/or dedications given therein.

L. Preserve all the Invariant Sections of the Document, unaltered in their text and in their titles. Section numbers or the equivalent are not considered part of the section titles.

M. Delete any section Entitled "Endorsements". Such a section may not be included in the Modified Version.

N. Do not retitle any existing section to be Entitled "Endorsements" or to conflict in title with any Invariant Section.

O. Preserve any Warranty Disclaimers.

If the Modified Version includes new front-matter sections or appendices that qualify as Secondary Sections and contain no material copied from the Document, you may at your option designate some or all of these sections as invariant. To do this, add their titles to the list of Invariant Sections in the Modified Version's license notice. These titles must be distinct from any other section titles.

You may add a section Entitled "Endorsements", provided it contains nothing but endorsements of your Modified Version by various parties-for example, statements of peer review or that the text has been approved by an organization as the authoritative definition of a standard.

You may add a passage of up to five words as a Front-Cover Text, and a passage of up to 25 words as a Back-Cover Text, to the end of the list of Cover Texts in the Modified Version. Only one passage of Front-Cover Text and one of Back-Cover Text may be added by (or through arrangements made by) any one entity. If the Document already includes a cover text for the same cover, previously added by you or by arrangement made by the same entity you are acting on behalf of, you may not add another; but you may replace the old one, on explicit permission from the previous publisher that added the old one.

The author(s) and publisher(s) of the Document do not by this License give permission to use their names for publicity for or to assert or imply endorsement of any Modified Version.

.16 COMBINING DOCUMENTS

You may combine the Document with other documents released under this License, under the terms defined in section 5 above for modified versions, provided that you include in the combination all of the Invariant Sections of all of the original documents, unmodified, and list them all as Invariant Sections of your combined work in its license notice, and that you preserve all their Warranty Disclaimers.

The combined work need only contain one copy of this License, and multiple identical Invariant Sections may be replaced with a single copy. If there are multiple Invariant Sections with the same name but different contents, make the title of each such section unique by adding at the end of it, in parentheses, the name of the original author or publisher of that section if known, or else a unique number. Make the same adjustment to the section titles in the list of Invariant Sections in the license notice of the combined work.

In the combination, you must combine any sections Entitled "History" in the various original documents, forming one section Entitled "History"; likewise combine any sections Entitled "Acknowledgements", and any sections Entitled "Dedications". You must delete all sections Entitled "Endorsements".

.17 COLLECTIONS OF DOCUMENTS

You may make a collection consisting of the Document and other documents released under this License, and replace the individual copies of this License in the various documents with a single copy that is included in the collection, provided that you follow the rules of this License for verbatim copying of each of the documents in all other respects.

You may extract a single document from such a collection, and distribute it individually under this License, provided you insert a copy of this License into the extracted document, and follow this License in all other respects regarding verbatim copying of that document.

.18 AGGREGATION WITH INDEPENDENT WORKS

A compilation of the Document or its derivatives with other separate and independent documents or works, in or on a volume of a storage or distribution medium, is called an "aggregate" if the copyright resulting from the compilation is not used to limit the legal rights of the compilation's users beyond what the individual works permit. When the Document is included in an aggregate, this License does not apply to the other works in the aggregate which are not themselves derivative works of the Document.

If the Cover Text requirement of section 4 is applicable to these copies of the Document, then if the Document is less than one half of the entire aggregate, the Document's Cover Texts may be placed on covers that bracket the Document within the aggregate, or the electronic equivalent of covers if the Document is in electronic form. Otherwise they must appear on printed covers that bracket the whole aggregate.

.19 TRANSLATION

Translation is considered a kind of modification, so you may distribute translations of the Document under the terms of section 5. Replacing Invariant Sections with translations requires special permission from their copyright holders, but you may include translations of some or all Invariant Sections in addition to the original versions of these Invariant Sections. You may include a translation of this License, and all the license notices in the Document, and any Warranty Disclaimers, provided that you also include the original English version of this License and the original versions of those notices and disclaimers. In case of a disagreement between the translation and the original version of this License or a notice or disclaimer, the original version will prevail.

If a section in the Document is Entitled "Acknowledgements", "Dedications", or "History", the requirement (section 5) to Preserve its Title (section 2) will typically require changing the actual title.

.20 TERMINATION

You may not copy, modify, sublicense, or distribute the Document except as expressly provided for under this License. Any other attempt to copy, modify, sublicense or distribute the Document is void, and will automatically terminate your rights under this License. However, parties who have received copies, or rights, from you under this License will not have their licenses terminated so long as such parties remain in full compliance.

.21 FUTURE REVISIONS OF THIS LICENSE

The Free Software Foundation may publish new, revised versions of the GNU Free Documentation License from time to time. Such new versions will be similar in spirit to the present version, but may differ in detail to address new problems or concerns. See http://www.gnu.org/copyleft/.

Each version of the License is given a distinguishing version number. If the Document specifies that a particular numbered version of this License "or any later version" applies to it, you have the option of following the terms and conditions either of that specified version or of any later version that has been published (not as a draft) by the Free Software Foundation. If the Document does not specify a version number of this License, you may choose any version ever published (not as a draft) by the Free Software Foundation.

.22 ADDENDUM: How to use this License for your documents

To use this License in a document you have written, include a copy of the License in the document and put the following copyrightand license notices just after the title page:

> Copyright (c) YEAR YOUR NAME. Permission is granted to copy, distribute and/or modify this document under the terms of the GNU Free Documentation License, Version 1.2 or any later version published by the Free Software Foundation; with no Invariant Sections, no Front-Cover Texts, and no Back-Cover Texts. A copy of the license is included in the section entitled "GNU Free Documentation License".

If you have Invariant Sections, Front-Cover Texts and Back-Cover Texts, replace the "with...Texts." line with this:

> with the Invariant Sections being LIST THEIR TITLES, with the Front-Cover Texts being LIST, and with the Back-Cover Texts being LIST.

If you have Invariant Sections without Cover Texts, or some other combination of the three, merge those two alternatives to suit the situation.

If your document contains nontrivial examples of program code, we recommend releasing these examples in parallel under your choice of free software license, such as the GNU General Public License, to permit their use in free software.

Part IX

Eeek! There is Missing Help

Sorry, but a help item is missing for the function you're looking for. You may be able to find it in the online version of the help at the GIMP docs website.

Feel free to join us and fill the gap by writing documentation for GIMP. For more information, subscribe to our Mailing list. Generally, it's a good idea to check the GIMP project page.

Found a **content error** or just something which doesn't look right? Report an error in Bugzilla and let us know.

Index

White point, 329
Wind, 633

X
Xach-Effect, 656
XCF, 871, 875
XDS, 21

Y
YCbCr, 538, 540, 542, 876
YUV, 538, 540, 542, 876

Z
Zealous Crop, 488
Zoom, 184, 346, 465

Printed in Great Britain
by Amazon